LEARNING THROUGH SOCIAL WORK STORIES-THAT-MATTER

In our increasingly tumultuous world, this book offers insight and inspiration through personal narrative. It collects the accounts of twenty-seven social workers and those in academia based in five continents, surveying a wide range of environments, communities, and systems. Each narrative serves as a testament to the profound intersections of relationships, emotions, and experiences, encapsulating stories of genuine human significance. Advocating for the cultivation of three essential intelligences – social intelligence (SQ), emotional intelligence (EQ), and experiential intelligence (XQ) – the book prompts readers to grasp the nuanced power dynamics inherent in each tale. As a prompt to critical reflection that guides readers towards self-discovery and professional identity, this collection is ideal for graduate students and researchers in social work.

PROFESSOR TONY GHAYE is a Community Activist and Positive Psychologist at UiT the Arctic University of Norway. He advocates for sustainable social change through innovative approaches rooted in kindness.

PROFESSOR RITA SØRLY specializes in Social Work at UiT the Arctic University of Norway, focusing on collaborative mental health research, and emphasizes user involvement and participatory action in Northern Norway.

LEARNING THROUGH SOCIAL WORK STORIES-THAT-MATTER

Global Perspectives

EDITED BY

TONY GHAYE

The Arctic University of Norway

RITA SØRLY

The Arctic University of Norway

CAMBRIDGE
UNIVERSITY PRESS

CAMBRIDGE
UNIVERSITY PRESS

Shaftesbury Road, Cambridge CB2 8EA, United Kingdom

One Liberty Plaza, 20th Floor, New York, NY 10006, USA

477 Williamstown Road, Port Melbourne, VIC 3207, Australia

314–321, 3rd Floor, Plot 3, Splendor Forum, Jasola District Centre, New Delhi – 110025, India

103 Penang Road, #05–06/07, Visioncrest Commercial, Singapore 238467

Cambridge University Press is part of Cambridge University Press & Assessment, a department of the University of Cambridge.

We share the University's mission to contribute to society through the pursuit of education, learning and research at the highest international levels of excellence.

www.cambridge.org
Information on this title: www.cambridge.org/9781009386227

DOI: 10.1017/9781009386180

When citing this work, please include a reference to the DOI 10.1017/9781009386180

First published 2025

A catalogue record for this publication is available from the British Library

A Cataloging-in-Publication data record for this book is available from the Library of Congress

ISBN 978-1-009-38622-7 Hardback
ISBN 978-1-009-38621-0 Paperback

Contents

Meet the Editors

In this book, Professors Tony Ghaye and Rita Sørly are collaborating as editors, collecting stories about global social work from many places. The inspiration for this project came years ago, when Tony and Rita first met, and started a dialogue about stories-that-matter, and stories that can make a difference. From this very first meeting, they both knew that they had beating hearts for stories and storytelling, and from their perspective, that is exactly what social work around the globe is about. Sharing and learning from stories.

Meet the Contributors

GLORIA ACAN (Alumni Co-ordinator, Teach for Uganda) is a twenty-six-year-old budding social worker hailing from Makerere University, formally working with Vijana Corps, a leading non-profit serving youth in Uganda. She is a Program Officer in an exciting team extending safe spaces, tools, and platforms to youth in off-grid communities across the country. In her work, Gloria explores ways to incorporate social work with a focus on working with individuals and groups for better social functioning in community. In 2023, she completed the Acumen East Africa Fellowship, an opportunity for leaders in different spheres across the region to understand leadership through self and community, and collaboratively generate solutions to the problems of poverty in the region. Holistic growth is something she pursues diligently, seeking ways to be and do better in the different parts of her life. She was also supported in that year through a leadership fellowship with USAID that supports the growth of young people in the workspace spearheading positive change in their communities through mentorship and coaching to improve the quality of our work. Gloria is enthusiastic about working with people and communities with a keen focus on children, youth, and persons with disabilities. She has volunteered with the Uganda Police and Uganda Prison Services in Lira, introducing her to the practice of social work. Gloria has also worked with urban refugee groups in adult literacy through facilitating English classes. In addition, she explored and learnt about social entrepreneurship as a tool for social change and development for the youth under United Social Ventures.

VENESIO BWAMBALE BHANGYI is Assistant Lecturer in Social Work at Kyambogo University, Uganda. He served on the board of the National Association of Social Workers of Uganda (NASWU) from 2011 to 2016. His research interests (with publications in peer-reviewed journals such as *International Social Work* and *African Journal of Social Work*, and others in edited book volumes) are in public social services, social policy, social development, environmental social work, and social work theory. He has presented papers at international, regional, and local conferences. He holds an Erasmus Mundus Master's degree in advanced development in social work (ADVANCES). He earned his BSW from Makerere University (Uganda). He is presently a Master's in Public Administration student at Uganda Management Institute.

PAULINE CAMILLERI (Senior Social Worker, Gozo, Malta), a compassionate and dedicated individual, hails from the beautiful Maltese island of Gozo. As a loving mother of two boys, she has navigated life's joys and challenges, including the heart-wrenching loss of one of her sons at the age of thirteen. Pauline's professional journey spans two decades in the mental health field. Back when she commenced her career thirty-four years ago, the social work profession was relatively unknown in the small community of Gozo. Battling against prevalent stigma on the island, she embarked on a challenging path, starting as a welfare officer and eventually operating within the mental health sector. This eventually became her passion. However, Pauline's dedication to community welfare began earlier in her career when she started off working in elderly care services. During this time, she introduced several community services around the island, laying the groundwork for her commitment to fostering a supportive and caring community. Currently serving as the President and co-founder of the Mental Health Association Gozo since 2010, Pauline has played a pivotal role in establishing collaborations with significant entities in Malta. The primary aim has been to address societal gaps and contribute to a more supportive and understanding environment. Beyond her official duties, Pauline actively engages in voluntary experiences each year, extending her impact beyond the mental health sector to various social aspects of society. Her commitment to personal and professional growth is evident in her participation in meetings, conferences, and training programmes, both abroad and locally. Approaching retirement, Pauline's aspirations remain resolute. Her enduring goal is to eliminate the stigma surrounding mental health and continue her active involvement in community and voluntary work. Upon retirement, she dreams of expanding her horizons, travelling to experience different cultures, and embracing a lifelong pursuit of learning and dreaming. In her own words, Pauline states, 'I am confident that cherishing one's dreams serves as a potent force, propelling ongoing personal growth, constant belief, and an enduring journey of personal development.' She emphasizes the importance of perpetual growth and the limitless possibilities that lie ahead. Pauline's journey reflects not only professional dedication but also a profound commitment to making a positive impact on the lives of those she serves.

MARIA DELDÉN is Lecturer in the School of Education at Dalarna University in Falun, Sweden. She has a background as an Upper Secondary School Teacher, and a doctorate in History Didactics from Umeå University (2017). Since 2014 she teaches student teachers in educational science and general didactics, as well as history didactics, and she is responsible for student placements. She also teaches in the Master's Programme in Educational Work. Her research interest is guided towards students' meaning-making in history and social science education, where the relation between teachers' curriculum stories and students' meaning-making stories is studied. Another research area is historical meaning-making through historical feature film, and in the article 'The In-between: On Arendt's Metaphor Go Visiting and Empathy-in-History in Students' Meaning Making in History Education' (2023) she elaborates the significance of historical empathy when making meaning of historiography through the film medium. She also studies narrative identity formation in life stories and film (the Swedish film *Sami Blood*). Another research area is non-formal education, and she is engaged in a collaborative project with an NGO and the University Surcolombiana, Colombia. She has published research on the pedagogical function of the metaphor in non-formal education in Colombia (2023). Together with two colleagues, Gull Törnegren and Mikael Berg, she has developed and taught a course for teachers and student teachers in studies of religion and history about how to approach Jerusalem as a centre for religious, historical, and political conflicts in education through a narrative approach. Together with these colleagues she has edited the anthology *Jerusalem – a Web of Stories* (2023) where she and the other editors have written essays together with a group of students, sharing their experiences of a study field trip to Jerusalem, where meetings with places and people – and their stories – form the core.

TONY GHAYE (Professor II at the Department of Child Welfare and Social Work, UiT The Arctic University of Norway) has an eclectic and global portfolio of professional responsibilities at the intersection of psychology, health, and education. He is the founder of a fast-growing non-governmental organization in Tanzania called UMatter, which is leading a kindness revolution there by strengthening the psychosocial well-being of youth. In addition to his professorial responsibilities at UiT, Norway, he is also a professor at Loughborough University in London in the leadership strand of the MSc. Programme. He is one of the world's first qualified Chief Physical and Mental Wellbeing Officers and in receipt of international award, in 2021, for his work in moderating and speaking at numerous global Inter-Generational Dialogues (IGDs) which addressed what a better world could look like and how to shape it. He is the president of the large charitable organization Live Healthy Initiatives in Kenya, which works to end period poverty with underprivileged populations and vulnerable groups, especially women, in the country. Tony identifies as a multidisciplinary scholar-practitioner with a passion for bringing together knowledges and practice in ways that enable a 'system' and community to move positively forward. He seeks to achieve this through enhancing mental and emotional health and well-being, applying positive psychology, appreciative inquiry, and reflective learning to create inclusive contexts where everyone has an opportunity to thrive and flourish. His expertise is in building cultures of kindness, strength-based leadership, and the psychology of mattering. Tony has written, or edited, 19 academic books and published 142 scientific papers for various audiences. He has worked in eight of the world's most innovative universities, in the UK, Norway, Sweden, Australia, and Hong Kong for example. His main attention is on the question, 'How do we improve what we do, to build a better world?

PRATIKSHA GHIMIRE is a PhD student at the University of the Sunshine Coast, Australia. Prior to commencing her PhD, she completed a Bachelor of Arts in Social work and a Master of Social Work (Qualifying) from Nepal and Australia respectively. Inspired by critical feminists such as Simone de Beauvoir, Judith Butler, and Kimberlé Crenshaw, she currently researches 'decolonizing social work with Nepali women'. She continues to write, and has published an article in the areas of social work, women, and decolonization.

KAY HAMPTON is a freelance children's author and primary school teacher in England. Kay was awarded a BEd Hons degree from the University of Greenwich, London and an M.Ed degree from the University of Worcester, England. She has taught in many primary schools in England and co-ordinated and led curriculum development in personal, social, health, and economics education. Most of her experience has been in inner-city and poorly served multicultural schools. She has also worked as a principal lecturer in the UK university sector in Teacher Education programmes in the capacity of school partnership coordinator. Kay has published academic papers and book chapters, with her main work recently being as a children's author. Her best-selling books, the 'Bungling Bert' series, have been used to develop resources in schools for the creative curriculum and to initiate discussion around social issues and personal responsibility. Each storyline focuses on particular moral, ethical, and social dilemmas for children to discuss and explore. She recently took a break from her career to take full responsibility for the care of her elderly mother who was diagnosed with Alzheimer's and vascular dementia. This has both enriched Kay's life and developed her appreciation of the importance of human connection. She has also learned much about the intricate network of health and social care services which can both support and hinder individuals and families in the care process. Living through this experience, which lasted three years, made Kay acutely aware of her own strengths but also her vulnerabilities.

SUNNIVA HESTSVEEN is currently studying for a Bachelor's degree in social work at UiT, The Arctic University of Norway, at campus Tromsø. Her main passion when it comes to social work is connections and the keys to establishing a good human connection. In her opinion a good human connection must be established to do good social work. She believes that the key element in forming these connections is to make people feel seen. And the extension of that is to make people feel that they matter, that their feelings are valid and that their behaviour is normal. She believes that when you have created such a connection, you are in a position to influence, teach, learn, and exchange wisdom that both participants are willing to listen to and grow from.

INGVILD KRISTOFFERSEN is a Bachelor student studying child protection at UiT The Arctic University of Norway, in Tromsø. In social work, she is very concerned that all people should be treated equally, with justice and respect. Her wish is for everyone to have an everyday life they enjoy, and she is genuinely interested in helping people achieve this – especially those who are in difficult or vulnerable situations. Her choice of study as a child welfare educator gives her opportunities to do health-promoting, preventive, environmentally therapeutic, and action-oriented work with children, young people, and their families. What motivates her to work as a child welfare educator is the societal mission of assisting people who need help and working for social justice and social change.

WILBERFORCE KUREVAKWESU is a social work lecturer at the Midlands State University, School of Social Work (Zimbabwe) and a PhD candidate at Stellenbosch University (South Africa). He is an Editorial Board Member of the journal *Social Work/Maatskaplike Werk*, a Managing Editor of the *Journal of Social Development in Africa*, and an Assistant Editor of the *African Journal of Social Work (AJSW).* Wilberforce has published several journal articles in refereed journals and he has more than seven years' experience in social work practice. His research interests include social work regulation, child protection, social justice, developmental social work, and mental health issues.

VÅR MATHISEN is an occupational therapist with a PhD in mental health work. She works as an associate professor at the Faculty of Health Sciences, UiT The Arctic University of Norway. Her research interests are professional work in substance abuse and mental health care, user participation as social practice, migration health, collaborative research, and not least student learning. These are topics for several articles and book chapters that she has written together with research colleagues. Among other things, her research has contributed to increased knowledge about user participation in mental health care in a Sami context. She has also contributed to a knowledge review of qualitative research on user participation at various levels within the mental health and substance abuse field in the Nordics and Sápmi. This is the first knowledge review on such a large scale in Norway, and therefore groundbreaking work. For many years, she has worked in the field of substance abuse and mental health with young people, adults, and families as an occupational therapist. Important values in her work are human rights, and strengthening individuals and their families through strength-based approaches to increase resilience and enable a better everyday life.

MÓNICA AYALA MIRA (Professor, Autonomous University of Baja California, Mexico) has a PhD in psychology, with emphasis on social psychology, from the Interinstitutional Program of the Central-West Zone of ANUIES, hosted by the University of Guanajuato; a Master's degree in psychology with a specialization in family therapy from the National Autonomous University of Mexico (UNAM); and a Bachelor's degree in organizational psychology from the Monterrey Institute of

Technology and Higher Education (ITESM). She has conducted research at the Autonomous University of Barcelona on fractalities in critical research. She has studied communication Sciences, with a speciality in political communication from UNAM. She is a member of the National Researchers System (SNII) Level 1 and holds a PRODEP profile. Her research focuses on social psychology and gender, with topics including gender and family, the construction of masculinities and femininities, gender-based violence, and gender and human mobility. Her publications include the book *Forjando igualdad* (*Forging Equality*), and she is co-coordinator of 'Diversidad metodológica en la investigación psicosocial' (Methodological Diversity in Psychosocial Research). She serves as a board member of the Mexicalense Women's Institute, as an advisor to the Committee for the Prevention and Response to Gender-Based Violence at Autonomous University of Baja California, where she is a full-time professor and researcher, and as the coordinator of the Master's in Psychology programme at the Faculty of Human Sciences at the same university. She is a member of the Ibero-American Network of Social Psychology, the Network for the Promotion of Health, Education, and Psychosocial Well-being, and the Mexican Network of Social Psychology.

HILDE MJØS (project manager of People Meet People, artist, and photographer, Arendal Municipality, Norway) is a sociologist, art educator, and project developer. For over twenty years, she has worked within the fields of art, culture, and inclusion – first, in a contemporary art gallery where she established a programme for art dissemination especially customized for children and young people. In recent years, she has focused specifically on democracy and participation in local society among newly arrived refugees and working immigrants, in the southern part of Norway, through her role as a community contact in an adult learning centre. The largest production she was involved in recently was an international costume exhibition in collaboration with the regional historical museum and the volunteer organizations in Arendal, involving historical clothes and costumes from people from all over the world presently living in Arendal. Several of the projects she has been involved in have received regional and national attention and funding. At present, she is involved in a programme for adult refugees and immigrants, using film production as a method in Norwegian language training, focusing on democracy, participation, and health-related issues. In this project, students produced films which later were used as teaching materials by fellow teachers. The project was funded by the Directorate of Integration and Diversity and developed in collaboration with researchers and media producers. Mjøs is the project manager of People Meet People, a peace-building movement bringing people with different cultural backgrounds together in public spaces through dialogue. The dialogue method has been spread to several municipalities across Norway, and to Poland, Spain, and Portugal through EU-funded projects. In October 2023, People Meet People was honoured by the Nobel Peace Centre as the dialogue voice of the month. People Meet People was deemed 'The best idea for inclusion activities' in Southern Norway.

THOMAS NDALUKA (PhD) is a senior lecturer in the Department of Sociology and Anthropology at the University of Dar es Salaam, with more than twenty years of teaching and researching. His research interests are in the sociology of religion, social policy, critical discourse analysis, and social analysis. He has developed collaboration relationships with local and international academicians and other professionals. He has worked with the government, non-governmenta; organizations, and private organizations on issues related to policies, guidelines, and strategies. He is currently the chairperson of the board of directors of UMatter – an NGO that works to empower young individuals through strength-based approaches that enhance resilience and decrease vulnerability. He is also the coordinator of the University of Dar es Salaam Society and Religion Research Centre (SORRECE) and a former Deputy Rector (Academic, Research, and Consultancy) of the Mwalimu Nyerere Memorial Academy in Dar es Salaam, Tanzania. He is the author of the book *Religious Discourse, Social Cohesion and Conflict in Tanzania: Muslim–Christian Relations in Tanzania* (2012), and co-edited the book *Religion and State Revisited in Tanzania: Reflection from 50 years of Independence* (2014). Furthermore, he has published in both international and local journals on his areas of interest.

G. NOKUKHANYA NDHLOVU (Department of Social Work/Social Development, University of Fort Hare, South Africa) has a background in social development. She holds a PhD in social work/social development from the University of Fort Hare and an MSocSci in social development from the University of Cape Town. She is currently a postdoctoral research fellow at the University of Fort Hare, South Africa. She is passionate about social justice, which has shaped her research interests to include exclusionary development, integrated and holistic people-centred development, structural violence, children's rights, and gender and African masculinities. Her desire to improve lives extends beyond academia, as she has worked extensively as a development practitioner in civil society organizations, focusing on integrated people-centred development initiatives that uplift vulnerable and marginalized communities. She also has a background in journalism, which she uses alongside her research skills to create knowledge on pertinent development issues, raise awareness, and tell high-impact stories to ensure more Africans lead better lives. Driven by a passion for connecting with diverse audiences, Ndhlovu's work spans academic and non-academic platforms, from scholarly journals to thought-provoking op-eds.

JIOJI RAVULO is Professor and Chair of Social Work and Policy Studies at the University of Sydney. His father is iTaukei (indigenous) Fijian and his late mother is Anglo Australian. He is passionate about the meaningful inclusion of indigenous perspectives and practice in Western societies and strives to demonstrate such concepts across his own social work identity. He is also an adjunct professor at the University of the South Pacific, supporting social work programmes and research across the region. His main areas of research and writing include mental health, alcohol and other drugs, young people, marginality, and decoloniality. Jioji enjoys writing across different platforms, including scholarly book chapters, journal articles, and opinion pieces for various media outlets. Outside of work, you can find him hanging out with his young son, dog, and extended family.

TRACIE ROGERS (PhD) is a lecturer in the Department of Sociology, Psychology, and Social Work and Coordinator of the Graduate Social Work programme at the University of the West Indies, Mona Campus, in Jamaica. Her research and teaching are anchored by anti-oppressive approaches that centre indigenous perspectives and decolonizing methodologies, and unapologetically amplify the voices of marginalized communities. The focus of her academic work is exploring the psychosocial vulnerabilities faced by marginalized people in the Caribbean region and Black, Indigenous, People of Colour (BIPOC) communities in the Global South context. Dr Rogers is also a research associate at the University of Johannesburg, South Africa, and a member of the Pan African Mental Health Research Network, a consortium of researchers from numerous African countries and two Caribbean states, with its secretariat at Nottingham Trent University, United Kingdom. Building South–South connections to facilitate the exchange of perspectives, experiences, and knowledge from the Global South, which counters dominant discourses and existing global power dynamics in knowledge production, is a core component of Dr Rogers's academic stance. She is also committed to building South–North collaborations, which allow researchers from developing and developed countries to share knowledge, expertise, perspectives, and insights from vastly different contexts. Dr Rogers's research explores the lived experiences of women and girls, gender-based violence prevention, stigma faced by people living with mental illness and HIV, trauma responsiveness, and epistemic violence in research. She is a qualitative researcher specializing in collaborative research frameworks, participatory action research, autoethnography, and arts-based research. Dr Rogers integrates painting, photography, and poetry in various research phases, including data collection and analysis with research participants. Dr Rogers is also the Editor of the Caribbean Journal for Social Work – the only peer-reviewed social work journal produced in the English-speaking Caribbean.

VIKAS SAWANT is a child rights activist in Mumbai, India. He completed his Master's degree in social work (MSW) and has nearly thirty years of experience of working with children and on issues related to child rights and protection. He has developed and conducted many training programmes with different groups, including government officials, police, and NGO staff. Networking and working with governmental systems are his forte. His expertise and knowledge on laws related to children led him to develop a model for the rescue and restoration of working children which was appreciated by the Gujarat High Court and then adopted by all Indian states. He has also created many other models related to the protection of children which have been adopted by governments at both state and centre level. Mr Sawant participated in the working committee of the 11th Five-Year Plan of India and has been a member of various committees of state government as a child protection expert. He is involved in creating and implementing safeguarding policies focusing on women and children for NGOs across India. Mr Sawant works closely with government systems and provides technical support and guidance to child protection systems, including the Maharashtra State Child Protection Society, Child Welfare Committees and District Child Protection Units. Mr Sawant was associated with UNICEF Maharashtra for nearly ten years. Currently he is on three state-level committees focusing on developing state policies and SOPs for the rehabilitation and reintegration of various groups of vulnerable children such as those in institutions, those without parental care, and those in conflict with the law.

RITA SØRLY is a professor and the director of the research centre Arctic Youth at the Department of Child Welfare and Social Work, UiT The Arctic University of Norway. In addition to this, Sørly also has professorial responsibilities at the University of South Eastern Norway's Department of Health, Social and Welfare Studies. Her research interests are collaborative research in mental health and substance abuse, mental health among youth, mental health care research, substance abuse research, user involvement, participatory action research, social work research, narrative theory, and methods. Professor Sørly is a community-based researcher, working to develop more user involvement and engagement in research. She believes in collaborative research, to include research participants in processes while working together. Sørly has been working to include global social work research as a developing field at UiT, together with Professor Tony Ghaye. Sørly has published many scientific articles and has been the author and editor of four scientific books. This is her second book in collaboration with Professor Tony Ghaye. Sørly has also authored two Norwegian-Northern Sami children's books, to contribute to the development of the Northern Sami language in Norway. Sørly has written several chapters in this book, some with colleagues and students from the social work field. Her wish is that you, as a reader, will find these chapters inspiring for developing your own practice, education, or research as a proud social worker, taking a part in creating stories-that-matter, and stories that can make a difference.

RAYMOND STUEN is studying for a Bachelor's degree in child protection at UIT The Arctic University of Norway in Tromsø. In his work dealing with young people with major behavioural difficulties, drug addiction, and other norm-breaking behaviour, he is concerned with being the confident adult who shows that he can tolerate the 'painful expression' that the young people show – that he stands there no matter what comes. He will be the one they can talk to when they are ready – he will be there to regulate. He is concerned with seeing the individual behind the behaviour. He is concerned with, among other things, the individual's participation in their own lives. That the young people he meets in his job can contribute to shaping their everyday life based on the prerequisites the individual young people have. Values such as respect, empathy, and understanding are central to him as a social worker. He is concerned with finding good arenas for young people, and with the young people's own values, so that through this he can give the young people an inner motivation to change. Furthermore, he is keen to be able to help and support the families around the young people he work with. This is because he sees the importance of a safe and stable home and network. And not least, he is busy being a good and safe work colleague in the demanding job of working at a treatment institution for young people.

YAMINI SUVARNA (independent consultant in research, documentation, and training, Mumbai, India) completed her PhD on provisions for children with special educational needs from Coventry University in 2000 following a Master's in social work in 1994. She has been working and researching with children and on children's issues for nearly twenty-five years now. She is passionate about research and promoting evidence-based programming. She is interested in placing evaluation reports in the public domain so that learning can emerge from shared experiences. She has developed and conducted training programmes for various groups such as children, adolescents, parents, teachers, social work professionals, as well as staff of shelter homes for female minors and women in Mumbai. She has conducted courses on qualitative and mixed methods research and presented papers at international conferences. She has been part of the E-Pathshala initiative by the UGC (India) to make quality course materials (in social work) accessible online to all students across the country. In her role of paper coordinator for Research Methods in Social Work under this project, she created a framework for the paper comprising thirty-one modules. She also developed the e-content for seven of these in accordance with the UGC guidelines. She has been associated with UNICEF (Maharashtra) from August 2015 onwards, focusing on the safety and protection of vulnerable groups of children such as those living in street situations and children of seasonal migrants. She has been on the advisory board of the Research Unit, College of Social Work, Nirmala Niketan since January 2020, and a member of the Ethics Committee, College of Social Work, Nirmala Niketan from June 2023.

FARHAT TAJ (PhD in sociology of law from the University of Oslo) is an associate professor at UiT The Arctic University of Norway, Tromsø.

Previously, she held key roles in the Education Ministry of the government of Khyber-Pakhtunkhwa, Pakistan, including Assistant Director (Colleges) and Planning Officer. She also served as an assistant professor (sociology) at Kohat University of Science and Technology (KUST), Pakistan. Her research interests include human rights, Islam, social integration, ontological security, political violence, complexity theory, international social work, and the welfare state.

GULL TÖRNEGREN, lecturer in the School of Culture and Society at Dalarna University, Falun, Sweden, has a doctorate in theology from Uppsala University (2013). Since 2002 she has taught students in ethics, human rights, studies of religions, and didactics of studies of religions. She has also taught student teachers in environmental ethics, professional ethics, social relationships, conflicts and power, and how to counteract racism in schools. She has been responsible for a five-year-long teacher and student exchange programme with the University of the Western Cape, South Africa, and the University of Stellenbosch, South Africa, with the theme 'Building a Human Rights Culture'. Her research interest is guided towards political philosophy, feminist dialogue-based ethics, formation of moral and political judgment, narrative identity formation in life stories and film (the Swedish film *Sami Blood*), and students' meaning-making through narratives in social science education. In a recent theoretically oriented article, 'Vem är du? Vem är jag? Och hur kan jag bedöma när våra vägar möts?' (2023, 'Who are you? Who am I? And how can I make judgments when our worlds meet') she has outlined a narrative approach to education of religions, aiming at enabling students to form independent judgments. Together with two colleagues, Maria Deldén and Mikael Berg, she has developed and taught a course for teachers and student teachers in studies of religion and history about how to approach Jerusalem as a centre for religious, historical, and political conflicts in education through a narrative approach. Together with these colleagues she has edited the anthology *Jerusalem – a Web of Stories* (2023) where she and the other editors wrote essays together with a group of students, sharing their experiences of a study field trip to Jerusalem, where meetings with places and people – and their stories – form the core.

JIN-YONG WANG in the Department of Social Work at the National Taipei University Taipei. His training background includes a BA degree in sociology, an MA degree in social work, and a PhD degree in social policy and social work. Before he pursued a doctoral degree at the

University of York, England, he was a licensed social work practitioner in a psychiatric hospital and a certified government civil servant responsible for homeless people, pensions, and allowances. He started his academic career in 2010. The courses he teaches mainly include group social work, group dynamics, psychiatric social work, mental health, and qualitative research methods. In addition to teaching and researching, he is also a part-time supervisor of group homes for children. Based on his social work practice in a psychiatric hospital in Taiwan and doctoral research in England, his research interests are mental health law, policy, and services, and social work practice with groups. His recent research work focuses on the issues of social inclusion for people with mental disabilities, spiritual care in social work practice, and mental health social workers' group competencies. In particular, he also explores the survival experiences of people with depression and service users' personal experiences and interpretations of mental illness. He has co-authored two books, *Mental Health Social Work* and *Social Group Work*, published in Taiwan. He loves hiking trails and playing tennis in his leisure time.

YLVA SPÅNBERGER WEITZ is an Associate Professor in Social Work at Södertörn University in Sweden. Her research and teaching mainly concern social work with children and families, as well as user perspectives and user participation in relation to child welfare services and school social work. Through her previous position as a research leader at FoU Northwest – a research and development centre linked to municipal social services around the Swedish capital of Stockholm – she has developed a close collaboration with the field of social work practice. In her research, she has worked with a broad variety of qualitative data, specializing in narrative and participatory methods. Both empirically and theoretically, her focus is on exploring how citizens experience their encounters with or perceptions of welfare institutions, how they understand and make sense of these experiences, and how they position themselves in relation to societal perceptions of and expectations of the social categories to which they belong. Her research covers, among other things, young peoples' experiences of out-of-home care and the transition to adulthood, parents' experiences of having their children placed in out-of-home care and their perspectives on support from social services, children's perceptions about social services and their views on help-seeking in the context of family adversity, school as an arena for preventive social work, and how to enhance children's access to early support through collaborative efforts between school and child welfare services. She is the co-author of a Swedish book about school social work and, in addition, has published her work in both international and national peer-reviewed journals.

RAJ YADAV (Senior Lecturer, University of the Sunshine Coast, Australia), a PhD, is from Nepal, and now makes his temporary home in Australia. His interest lies in decolonizing epistemologies and their use in advancing knowledge production in the fields of social work and development. He has worked as a lecturer and has contributed to social work curriculum development in universities in Nepal and Australia. He has published books, articles, book chapters, and magazine articles in the areas of decolonization, social work, and development.

SHEILA ZIMIC is a researcher at the Research and Development Unit for Social Services at the Association of Local Authorities, Västernorrland County, Sweden. Her work mainly focuses on systematic follow-up, digitalization, and knowledge use in social work practices. As an R&D researcher, Zimic has devoted her work to making practice-based, local knowledge accessible to practitioners, mainly through R&D reports and book chapters. She participates in several networks, at regional as well as national level, working with knowledge-based social services. She has been conducting studies about how systematic follow-up is understood by municipal officials working with monitoring and quality assurance activities in Swedish social services, and how the type of knowledge conducted through systematic follow-up is used. Zimic is doing research on 'Digitalization and Professional Development.' In one of her ongoing projects is about professionals' experiences of digital technologies in municipal home care services for the elderly.

Preface

Lived experiences are the focus of this book. We frame them as stories-that-matter drawn from across the globe and from social workers positioned in practice settings and in academia. Some storytellers have established publication track records. Others are first-time writers whom we have actively sought to encourage, and especially from the Global South. In doing so, we hope this expansive and wide-ranging collection of stories serves to strengthen social work solidarity and global connectedness. Additionally, we hope the different stories, told in different ways, will enable you to reflect on your own practices, the role of being vulnerable and open, that they will inspire, emote, and challenge the what, how, and why of your work, in your worlds. We also hope they stimulate debate, an internal one and with others, so that each one of us may more fully live our social work values out in our practices. To help with this, each story finishes by offering the reader some reflective questions to ponder and dig into.

With its emphasis on stories-that-matter, we are encouraging all social workers, students, and academics to think of themselves as knowledge creators and not simply as knowledge consumers. The implication of this is to recognize that social workers are capable of generating valid descriptions, explanations, and justifications of their own practices and of what influences their own learning in their work with others. In this way we hope the book helps readers to become the 'best version of themselves' as a social worker, student, or academic – and social work advocate. We hope the stories from the field, together with some wider perspectives, help readers to appreciate different sources of meaning, value, and action in the relational connection between social workers, significant other professionals, and those they work with and care for. We also hope they inspire to more global social work research.

Across the book, readers have the opportunity to consider the power and relevance of the following questions.

'Whose reality counts?'
'Whose knowledge is worth knowing?
'Are we doing the right thing?'
'Whose stories are being told, whose are not, and why?'

The character strengths (what makes people who they are) and performance strengths (what helps people do their work to the best of their ability) that surface in each story, are worthy of special mention. Qualities such as considerateness, kindness, helping others feel they matter, generosity of spirit, empathy, acting with a moral compass, showing compassion and respect, valuing human dignity and appreciation, to mention just a few. Additionally, the consistently thoughtful way social workers often need to live in doubt and uncertainty as they struggle to remain committed to their values while still figuring out how to get through the grind of everyday agency work and the humanly significant challenges they are addressing.

The social work stories-that-matter in this book are at once contextually rich, practical, values-led, relational, passionate, and action-based, and hence contribute to a form of social work that is political, ethical, and spiritual. Put another way, the stories reflect the thoughtful relationship between our actions and the knowledges that inform them, which contribute to making practice theory informed and research practice relevant.

Right now, there are more and different social work voices speaking up. Although some may not be identified as 'experts', they nevertheless have a voice, are open to learning from others, share their successes and challenges, and wish to co-discover how to practise-with-purpose. This book represents an honouring of lived experiences. We invite you to consider why the stories matter to you, which in turn might help to play a positive part in your continuing personal and professional growth.

Acknowledgements

We would like to thank all the contributors for sharing their stories, and for believing in the core principles of social work: social justice, human rights, collective responsibility, and respect for diversity. Together we can play our part in promoting positive social change and development, social cohesion, empowerment, and liberation of people. Thank you, storytellers, characters, listeners, and readers of these stories.

A very special thanks to Hilde Mjøs, for her beautiful photos, opening a reflective and contemplative space between every story in the first part of this book. Your close-up photos, in black and white, invite the readers to stop, breathe, think, and rethink about the stories they have just taken a part in. Your photos are telling stories of their own. Moving between the pages, new stories can be read and seen, again and again.

We are also grateful for the support from our Department of Child Care and Social Work at UiT The Arctic University of Norway, which believes in our investment, engagement, and passion for global social work.

We would also like to thank our colleagues Vanessa Jara Labarthé (Assistant Professor, University of Tarapacá, Chile), Professor Magnus Mfoafo-M'Carthy (Wilfrid Laurier University, Canada), and Professor Marie Karlsson (Uppsala University, Sweden), who participated in an early phase of this project. Thank you for your support and ideas.

We are grateful for the time you as a reader spend with the collected stories, and with the broader perspectives in Part II of the book, and we hope they will inspire you in your future studies, research, and work.

Keep sharing stories.

Tony Ghaye and Rita Sørly

Introduction

CHAPTER I

Why Are Stories of Social Work Important?

Rita Sørly

Introduction

People have told stories since the beginning of time. We understand our daily life through stories, we connect through stories, and we become the ones we are through storytelling. People create stories and organize their narratives according to culturally available stories. Over time, these narratives are accepted or rejected as evaluative versions of the past, present, and future. Some become dominant narratives, others become resistance narratives. Some are heard often, some disappear. Narratives assume moral perspectives, explaining not only what happened and what it means, but also what should have happened or what the stories were supposed to mean. Stories can be individual, they can be shared or silenced, they can be collective stories of oppression and despair, they can be stories of organizational change, or they can be everyday disruptions, telling about change or continuity. Stories can be narratives from professions or political parties. From students, or from children going to school. As human beings we are surrounded by stories, we live through stories, and we breathe stories. Social work is no exception.

The global definition of social work tells us that this a hub where stories are born, told, and resurrected in new versions every minute of the day, around the globe:

> Social work is a practice-based profession and an academic discipline that promotes social change and development, social cohesion, empowerment, and liberation of people. The principles of social justice, human rights, collective responsibility, and respect for diversity are central to social work. Based on theories in social work, other social science disciplines, humanities and indigenous knowledge, social work involves people and structures to meet challenges in life and strengthen people's lives. (FO, n.d.)

Social work is a multidisciplinary practice, fundamentally organized by humans connecting with other humans, and stories are the glue from where this discipline was born. If nobody told stories, social work would not exist. In fact, social work is stories, and stories are very often social work. Closely connected to everyday storytelling, social work is the space where we, as fellow human beings, can articulate what we find challenging and complicated in our everyday life. And not only what is hard or giving us sleepless nights, but also what works, what is giving surplus and joy of life.

In this chapter I will write about stories. The poet Muriel Rukeyser once said that the universe is not made of atoms, but of stories (1968). I believe in that. None of us can survive in a world without stories. The main theme of the chapter is storytelling, and a description of what a narrative approach can entail. Further, I will write about social work research in mental health, and stories. How we understand stories matters. As knowledge managers and fellow human beings, we have a responsibility to make it clear to those around us what we think promotes good social work in a world threatened by war, destruction, climate change, poverty, and social inequality. Perhaps it is more important today than ever. In my work, I have been, and am, concerned with storytelling, research in social work and mental health, and how these three components can be linked together, work together and not only have a meaning, but also lead to change. A change that involves more participation from those we, as social workers, think are in need of help and support. Further in the chapter, I tell a story about holding a guitar, to give an impression of how we *can* understand social work in mental health through a story. Afterwards I offer some reflections on storytelling, research, and social work as collaboration. But first, let's look at how we can understand narratives.

Storytelling: A Narrative Approach

How Do We Understand Stories?

Muriel Rukeyser is a good reference for connecting stories to social work. Rukeyser was an American poet, born in 1913, and known as one of the most pioneering women writers who expanded her poetry to include both past and present science and history. Her work was influenced by the ongoing violence and injustice in the United States at the time. Rukeyser was particularly concerned with human rights, and discrimination related to gender, class, or ethnicity. She can be understood as a writing social poet, where the distinction between life and poetry was blurred. I often wonder if we can separate life from stories. We define ourselves and the world around us through the language and the stories we tell. As people, we are the stories we tell about ourselves. The stories define who we are in time and place, and in relation to each other (Sørly, Mathisen, & Nygaard, 2021; Fævelen, Sørly, & Heggem Kojan, 2023). We organize our narratives in relation to our surrounding context, and in relation to culturally accessible narratives and plots. Stories are not born in a vacuum (Riessman, 2008). Our narratives can change over time, and they can change our understanding of the past, present, and future.

Can narratives create change? The Norwegian author and journalist Ingeborg Senneset has been open about her struggles in life, especially connected to anorexia. In a chronicle she writes a letter to herself with the title: "Dear me, with regards myself" (Senneset, 2021). She writes a letter to her younger self, about forgiveness. She writes about the anxiety she felt when she was only five years old, and how this led to challenges later in life. She writes about shame and anger, sorrow and despair. She writes to encourage her younger self, to say "It will all be good, you need to learn that independence is not the same as being alone. You need other people in your life. You need to give love place. Not everything will be perfect, but it will be good enough." I often use this text in class with bachelor students in social work. We need to know ourselves and our stories, understand and forgive ourselves, before we can go out and ask other people about their stories. Stories have a healing power for individuals. They can provide new perspectives; they can lead to dialogue and interaction. If I could hear myself, fifty years old, talking to me, sixteen years old, would I perhaps change my focus a bit, perhaps turn my course a little? Maybe I could have given my young self a better belief in myself. Stories and retellings can create new understandings. The dynamic power of narratives can lead to change.

Stories are part of everyday life, and people are storytellers. When we try to understand something that has happened to us, we do not use abstract concepts; we tell stories. All social experiences require interpretation and meaning-making (Karp & Birk, 2013). Some life events are painful and deeply problematic, and these situations require a demanding interpretative effort from those who try to make them coherent and sensible (Karp & Birk, 2013). One of life's most confusing situations is related to mental illness. When people suffer emotionally, the meaning they give to life events follows themes such as failure, regret, unworthiness, meaninglessness, and isolation (Hamkins, 2013). These themes add more pain to their suffering. Clinical narratives from psychiatry originate from interventions between the world of biomedicine and the experienced everyday life of users and professionals in mental healthcare and/or social work. Both personal and socially constructed narratives shape action and experience in mental health care. This also applies within other professional fields. A narrative approach involves the idea that we experience our lives and our identities through the stories we tell about ourselves and the world (Hamkins 2013, p.xiv).

Different Stories

Narratives are more than personal accounts, more than life stories. There are micro-stories, everyday stories, a note in your purse, a photo in your grandmother's hallway, films, photos, diaries hidden in the attic, documents from a bygone era. and a conversation between friends. The French literary theorist and philosopher Roland Barthes defines narratives to be "everything and everywhere":

> There are countless forms of narrative in the world. First of all, there is a prodigious variety of genres, each of which branches out into a variety of media, as if all substances could be relied upon to accommodate man's stories. Among the vehicles of narrative are articulated language, whether oral or written, pictures, still or moving, gestures, and an ordered mixture of all those substances; narrative is present in myth, legend, fables, tales, short stories, epics, history, tragedy, drame [suspense drama], comedy, pantomime, paintings (in Santa Ursula by Carpaccio, for instance), stained-glass windows, movies, local news, conversation. Moreover, in this infinite variety of forms, it is present at all times, in all places, in all societies; indeed narrative starts with the very history of mankind; there is not, there has never been anywhere, any people without narrative; all classes, all human groups, have their stories, and very often those stories are enjoyed by men of different and even opposite cultural backgrounds: narrative remains largely unconcerned with good or bad literature. Like life itself, it is there, international, transhistorical, transcultural. (Barthes & Duisit, 1975, p.237)

Organizations or fields of practice also use narratives. In the corridors of my Department of Child Welfare and Social Work, at the Arctic University of Norway, institutional narratives are created. According to Linde (2009, p.11), institutions try to preserve aspects of their past and use them in the present to influence the future. In this way, we share knowledge. Recollection, memories, and transmission from person to person are all important parts of creating knowledge. Making sense of the past, present, and future includes people telling stories. When individual people tell stories to their colleagues, the colleagues pick up the stories and reuse them. The collective 'we' within a field of practice can perhaps tell a collective story: 'This is what we as social workers think.' The transfer of knowledge is continuous. Quite often, collective histories become dominant narratives. Sometimes these dominant narratives are considered hegemonic, controlling stories (Linde, 2009). They are often collective representations of how we think the world is, and how we think it should be. The dominant narratives are often taken for granted, for example within a child welfare context or a psychiatric hospital ward, and represent the values of the majority (Mishler, 1995).

How Do We Tell Stories?

Dominant narratives can create social boundaries between people and categorize people as 'other' or 'different' from oneself. Child welfare workers can create dominant stories about the parents they meet throughout their working lives. Therapists working in mental health care can create institutional narratives about a certain type of young people they meet as patients. As researchers, we can have specific stories about Sami child-rearing, or what we call so-called marginalized groups in society. Identity construction, i.e., how I create you in my image, is closely linked to dominant narratives, stories, and storytelling. When using dominant narratives, we see identities as rooted in specific social processes and narrative practices (Komulainen et al., 2020). The focus in this perspective is not the narrator's ability to create a holistic narrative about the other, but rather the process of the strategies the narrator uses to assert or present certain identities in certain situations (De Fina, 2015; Komulainen et al., 2020). We may end up clinging to a dominant narrative.

There is a danger in telling one story. If you repeat the same story about a type of people, this is exactly what they become. They become a simple narrative.

Chimamanda Ngozi Adichie is a well-known Nigerian author. She has written novels such as *Purple Hibiscus*, *Half of a Yellow Sun*, *The Thing Around Your Neck*, *Americanah*, and *We Should All Be Feminists*. All critically acclaimed, strong stories from a part of the world whose art and literature many of us do not know. In one of her TED talks, "The Danger of a Single Story"(2009), the author talks about her upbringing on a university campus in eastern Nigeria. As a child she read American and English children's books, and at the age of seven she began to write herself. She made up stories and illustrated them. She wrote stories that were consistent with what she herself read. All the people in the stories were white and had blue eyes, they played in the snow, and talked a lot about how wonderful it was that the sun had finally come. “I wrote this,” says Chimamanda, “despite the fact that I lived in Nigeria and had never been outside the country. We didn’t have snow and we never talked about the weather. We didn’t have to talk about the weather.” The point of telling this is to point out how easily influenced and skinless we can be when we encounter a story. Especially as a child. Adichie had only read books where all the characters were white people, and she thought that all narratives had to have white people to be a proper narrative. They also had to be about things she couldn’t identify with. This changed when she eventually found African books. They were harder to get hold of, but she found them and discovered that she herself could take part in stories. It saved her from thinking that books can only contain a certain type of story (Sørly, 2018, 2024).

There is power in stories. How stories are told, who tells them, when they are told, and how many different stories are told. A certain narrative creates stereotypes. Stereotypes are neither true nor complete. They make a particular narrative the only possible narrative. This one narrative robs many people of dignity, it makes it harder for us to recognize ourselves in the other. A single story emphasizes our differences, instead of pointing out our similarities (Sørly, 2021, 2024). Storytelling can thus be understood as an interactive situation where identities are created and displayed (Komulainen et al., 2020) in close relation to dominant narratives. When we as researchers work with narratives, ethics is close to the work. How do we portray our study participants? For example, how did I refer to the thirty patients I interviewed in my PhD thesis? (Klausen, 2017). Did I portray them with a certain preconceived notion, unconsciously stigmatizing them in some way? Did I have a certain idea about patients in the community mental health centre, or did I actually listen to their stories? Did I perhaps understand the system, the doctors, the therapists against the background of a dominant narrative about the medical approach to mental health? Narratives carry ethical imperatives with them. How we manage narratives that come to us matters. Who tells the story is also important.

Who Is Telling the Story?

When we work with storytelling and research, positioning is an important topic. Within social work, my starting point would like to be understood as the white, privileged gaze. Who defines this understanding? What is the privileged gaze? Who has defined that this particular look is privileged?

I come from a small village in Northern Norway. No one in my family has an education from university, and some will be concerned with my position as a story about social mobility, as a class journey. If we turn the kaleidoscope, I can be a highly educated woman who is interested in researching with those who some define as having mental health challenges, or who have fallen outside the majority society. If we turn the kaleidoscope again, a different positioning will emerge. If we choose certain patterns when we tell stories, we have turned the kaleidoscope, or the perspective, to deal with certain contexts, certain ideas, certain dominant narratives. Turning the kaleidoscope in such a way that one refers to and understands particular groups of the population as different from oneself, and thus poses a kind of threat to a common conformity, is also a way of seeing the world. Perhaps we think that they are marginalized, and we need to 'give them a voice'? It can be good for our own 'mattering' to think that we give other people voices. We choose our positioning based on the context in which we operate, or research.

Collaborating on a narrative is different than giving someone a voice. But we all write from somewhere, and in my world this place is Northern Norway. I write from winter months of darkness, and I write from summer months in midnight sun. I write from an Arctic turning point, where my experiences also have their home, but I turn my gaze outwards in my research. Perhaps it is correct to say that my inner compass belongs here, this is where I define myself from. I understand the world from the north. In a meeting with another person, I have to be able to ask 'Where are you from? Where is your place? Who are you? And what experiences do you want to share with me?' And not least, I must ask with an analytical eye: 'How do you position yourself as a narrator? What is your starting point, your purpose in telling me what you are telling, and who benefits from telling the very story you are telling?' (Sørly, 2024).

To broaden my perspective from the north, I need to meet other people. Other people from the north, but also from the south, west, or east. We need global perspectives. Global perspectives give us the opportunities for new understandings, new growth. As storytellers we all matter.

Do we direct our narrative to our research colleagues, or do we direct the narrative to somebody outside our 'inner circle'? Within narrative research, we talk about who our study participants direct their narrative to; who is the 'ghostly audience' in this account? When a colleague and I collected stories from Sami people who used Norwegian mental health services, did our participants direct their stories to the majority community, or to the Sami minority community when they talked about foreign treatment contexts? About Norwegian therapists who expected them to come to the office for outpatient consultations on Thursday at 9, while they did not know where they were at that time, whether the reindeer were on the veld or something unexpected happened in the herd? (Sørly, Mathisen and Kvernmo, 2021). Or who did six refugee women direct their stories to, in another study, when they said that after arriving in Norway, their biggest fear was that the Norwegian child welfare agency would come and take their children away from them? Was it for us as researchers, for child protection, or other refugee women? (Sørly, 2024).

Who Owns the Stories We Tell?

Through qualitative research, we meet participants in our projects who work to interpret themselves and their experiences. The people we interview, observe, or in other ways interact with are concerned with meaningful work – just like us researchers. They tell about commitment, experiences, passion, desires, ideas, and dreams. We work with what is said and what is not said, within the context of the life that is lived and the context of the interview in which the stories are told. Sometimes we can become preoccupied with particular things in the conversation that took place. The silence, what is not said, can sometimes be more important than what is said (Sørly, 2021).

We learn methods to decode, rearrange, recontextualize, or abstract this raw data of experience. If we work at, for example, a university or college, we train our students in various qualitative methods. Some of us put on blinders and claim that there is only one right method, only one right way to analyse a material. Still others are more open and curious about the diversity of interpretive possibilities that are, after all, out there. As qualitative researchers, we have a responsibility to protect those who inform us, even when we return to our colleagues or students to tell our own narrative of what we think we have learned. The limits that we must impose on ourselves reflect the fact that the data we are dealing with is the very axis around which the research process revolves. It is not abstract concepts that we work with, but people's lives and stories (Sørly, 2024).

I often listen to the song "You're so Vain" by Carly Simon from 1972. "Bet you think this song is about you" is a familiar line to many. But it is also the title of a very good article by the American narrative researcher Ruthellen Josselson (2011). This article examines the dilemmas in narrative (and more generally, in qualitative) research created by the distance between the authority of the experience (the participant's understanding of his or her narrative) and the authority of the expert (the researcher's interpretation of the participant's narrative). It raises the question of who, at different levels, 'owns' the narrative (Sørly, 2021). The relationship between authority and authorship is demonstrated through a discussion around the researcher's intention and the participant's reactions to what is presented. The article highlights that the participants will not necessarily recognize themselves in the researcher's presentation of the narrative.

In 2011, Josselson and colleagues published the book *Five Ways of Doing Qualitative Analysis: Phenomenological Psychology, Grounded Theory, Discourse Analysis, Narrative Research, and Intuitive Inquiry.* In the book, key theorists within qualitative research analyse the same data material using five different approaches. The data material is the story of 'Teresa', a young opera singer who experienced a life-changing illness. By analysing the narrative within various qualitative methods, the researchers show similarities and differences, strengths and weaknesses, the researchers' roles, as well as research-related and ethical challenges in the work. In the book, 'Teresa' also gives feedback on the various methods, and which one speaks most to her own experience. This is an exciting and important topic. Especially within our professional field, where the goal, for many of us, is involvement, collaboration, and participation in research. Who owns the narratives of the participants in research projects? (Sørly, 2021, 2024). Who owns the stories we tell, and is it really our study participant's story we are telling or is it the researcher's interpretation of the story we reproduce, or is it a co-production of a common story? Our understanding will shape our approach and our research. Who owns the stories social workers hear from children, families, and their network? How we treat other people's stories are of great importance, whether we are researchers or social workers. One of the most important things we should recognize and cultivate within research and practice is diversity. People's different interpretation of their experiences and everyday life gives us a hub of narratives to relate to.

Narrative theory and method constitute a large and complex field of research, and there are many ongoing discussions about how we understand narratives. Let's take a look at social work research and stories.

Social Work Research and Stories

Research is collaboration. When I started working with research, the topic and starting point was user participation in mental health and substance abuse. I heard stories. The more stories I heard, I knew that I wanted to work with collaborative research. I wanted to study the co-creation of stories: between the researchers and the study participants, between the research field and the practice field, between the different persons taking a part in research. In other words, I think that we should write a common history when we conduct research together.

There has been a change in attitude when it comes to research within social work in mental health care. 'Users' of health and care services have been given a greater place in research projects. In several research environments, it is considered a natural and democratic right for users to participate in research that concerns them (Borg & Askheim, 2010; Borg et al., 2015; Karlsson & Borg, 2021). It has led to a change in tradition from doing research on and about people, to people being included in research with a right to get recognition and respect for first-hand experiences. 'User' can be a specific user of a service, user organizations representing an interest group, those who perform the services (the professions), and/or those who plan and organize the services (service managers and providers) (Borg et al., 2015). In my research, I collaborate with many different service users, both from the mental health and substance abuse fields, from social work and mental health practice, and with students. Through collaborative research, the necessity of breadth and diversity in knowledge development, and how research is understood and practised, is emphasized (Karlsson & Borg, 2021). Some researchers (Hancock et al., 2012) highlight ethical, moral, and therapeutic reasons, as well as reasons related to service improvement. A collaboration between experienced researchers and users with their own experience develops new understandings that will benefit services (Borg & Kristiansen, 2009). To use the kaleidoscope metaphor, we constantly see new patterns emerge. Often the motivation for working together in projects is precisely based on a desire to change practice and thus improve one's own and/or other people's lives (Karlsson & Borg, 2021).

Involving service users, or patients, in research projects also engages people to take a part in deciding which stories should be told. Often people with their own experience of services know what research should focus on. These topics are very often 'out of reach' to somebody with no experience as patients or help-seekers. It also makes the research a landscape to share. What happens if we follow this already drawn map, or if we make a map together as we walk along? What will benefit the service users the most? To be included or excluded from changing the services? Should we continue doing interviews with service users, or should we take a greater part in conversations? What will lead to change? What kind of stories do we want to create?

Are Stories Important When Working with Social Work Research?

The narrative research I work with requires co-construction between researcher and study participants. We engage in social interactions with those we collaborate with, those with whom we design a project, those with whom we conduct research, those with whom we work when we analyse, and those with whom we communicate the results. As a researcher, I help create the narratives, I am not an objective observer of what is going on, but can participate with the personal, as well as the political, in the collaboration we enter. When we use narrative in research, it opens possibilities to, with an analytical eye, take a closer look at which dominant narratives the field moves in, which structural narratives characterize the corridors of the hospital, or how to define marginalized groups within specific contexts. We can use different analytical approaches to look at large and small narratives within our field, and get closer to the turning points out of which, for example, themes such as stigmatization and alienation grow.

How Do We Understand Social Work in Mental Health? Or the Story of Holding a Guitar Upside Down

Australian First Nation singer Geoffrey Gurrumul Yunupinguv was a talented musician. I constantly listen to his music; it's amazing even though I don't understand a word of what he's singing. Gurrumul sang in several Australian First Nation languages. Sometimes he also sang in English, but that was rare. He was born blind and taught himself all the instruments he played. He was left-handed, but played the guitar right-handed and held it upside down. He did that throughout his career. In 2012, he became an honorary Doctor of Music at the University of Sydney. It is now several years since Gurrumul wandered out of time, aged forty-six. He died in hospital in Darwin, after many years of a congenital liver and kidney disease. Evil tongues say he died of alcoholism. He spent the last days of his life on the beach with other Australian First Nation people. Australian newspapers wrote about people on the beach drinking and partying, and that Gurrumul's condition was becoming more and more critical. He was in very poor shape, thin, and had not completed several vital dialysis sessions. Gurrumul's friend and musician colleague of many years, Paul Williams, found Gurrumul on the beach in a miserable condition. Williams clarified to the newspapers that he did not see Gurrumul drinking, but that he was concerned about his friend while he was living in mobile camps with other Australian First Nation people.

Locally, this lifestyle was called 'long grassing' (Sørly, 2018). Aboriginal First Nation peoples who live on the streets or are homeless (in a Western understanding of homeless), are called 'long grassers' in Australia. Compared to the rest of Australia, the number of long grassers in Darwin and the Northern Territory is much higher than elsewhere in the country. Living in the long grass will necessarily have a negative effect on health and well-being, and quality of life (Holmes & McRae-Williams, 2008). Holmes and McRae-Williams tell of the majority society's two main views on long-grassers: one romanticizes 'long grazing', and the other implies a highly discriminatory attitude. Long grassers are met with suspicion by the majority and perceived as deviants. They are irresponsible, criminal, neglect their children, drink, and use drugs. Many believe that Australian society has done enough to help Aboriginal people – now they just have to 'get their act together' (Holmes & McRae-Williams, 2008).

Williams, who worked for many years among the homeless in Northern Australia, told in 2017 about many unnecessary deaths among 'long grassers' (Fell, 2018). They didn't want to go to hospital; they knew what met them there. Williams took Gurrumul to the hospital the day after he met him. It required a lot of persuasion. Gurrumul did not want to go to the hospital – a few years earlier he had experienced lying with heavy internal bleeding for over eight hours in the emergency room. Australians were prioritized before Aboriginal First Nation peoples. Scrapes and broken bones were more important than Gurrumul's death-threatening bleeding.

Gurrumul died just days after Williams had brought him to the hospital. Williams said in an interview, soon after Gurrumul's death, that this was a disgrace to Australian society. One of the country's most high-profile and award-winning musicians died, due to a lack of adequate treatment in the hospital (Fell, 2018). On the beach where Williams found Gurrumul, he has planted a ring of trees to honour his friend's memory. The trees are still small, but they are growing bigger and bigger.

Why Write a Story about Gurrumul Yunupingu?

I write about Gurrumul and Williams because I think it is a story about the importance of relationships in our lives and in our work. Closeness, friendship, meaningful activities can be so many different things to different people, and I think the story of Gurrumul is a reminder of that. We humans can create meaning in our own ways, and that applies to all of us. Regardless of diagnoses, medications, language, culture, nationality, and challenges we face, we all need someone. We need each other, and each other's stories. I think that good relationships in our lives are essential to being able to have good health. Whether someone uses drugs, or has acute symptoms where they hear voices, or maybe needs help raising their children, regardless of all of this, we all need someone in our lives to lean on. I believe that one of the most dangerous things we humans can face is loneliness. Working with mental health is always about relationships. It's about seeing you. Seeing me. Seeing each other. Stretch out a hand. Also, when we encounter what we do not understand, and cannot relate our own experiences to.

I am writing about Gurrumul because I think it is a story about making the most wonderful and incredible things happen, when the conditions are necessarily not the best. It is about being able to act yourself, and have faith that you CAN. When Gurrumul, as a blind little boy, learns to play the guitar with his left hand, holding the guitar upside down, he does not know that he will become a world-famous musician and an honorary doctorate at the University of Sydney. He does not know that his voice will move thousands, millions, of people in the future. He does not know that he will be invited to the small village of Manndalen in Troms, Northern Norway, for an indigenous festival that he will never get to. Gurrumul had absolutely all the odds against him. He was exposed to racism, stigmatization, harassment, left out and misunderstood by the majority society, he had a handicap, had the wrong skin colour, he came from a society in poverty, characterized by drugs, missing structures, and what the majority in Australian society understood as a so-called little-developed culture with 'long grassing' and misery. But Gurrumul had his herd, and he had the music.

The story about Gurrumul is a story about how our psychosocial needs will always be contextual, and how we who work in this field must always look for the best opportunities in what we meet and face. We must have faith in the individual, in the herd, and in everything that people can achieve by their own will and strength. Even when it looks dark and difficult. Holistic health perspectives are about these things, it's about understanding the social aspects of our health as vitally important. It's about asking, 'Who are you?' It's about the fact that it's not only possible to learn to play a guitar upside down, but that you can also do it for the rest of your life, and wonderful music will be made.

Some Reflections on Storytelling, Research, and Social Work as Collaboration

I have tried to link social work to stories, and what happens between humans in dialogue. How we understand narratives and actions, how we create meaning in everyday life, depends on how we adjust our kaleidoscopes. I have interpreted the story of Gurrumul based on my perspective on social work in mental health care, and several elements that I believe are important in meeting another person. We talk a lot about recovery-oriented approaches and services in mental health care in Norway (Helsedirektoratet, 2023). Recovery as a concept and practice is about user involvement, focusing on resources and improvement of the user's or the help-seeker's premises. Recovery-oriented services can be seen in connection with work, meaningful activities, friends and family, self-determination, belonging, hope, and identity. I think Gurrumul's story is all about these themes. How we adjust our kaleidoscopes in meetings with other people is of great importance to our common health. How we listen, answer, and respond to stories is important.

In the Norwegian escalation plan for mental health that was launched this year, the following is emphasized:

> The foundations for good mental health and quality of life are laid throughout life and in many arenas: in the family, in kindergartens, schools and educational institutions, in working life, in the local environment, among friends and through participation in leisure and cultural activities. Efforts must therefore be directed towards these arenas, where the opportunities for effective prevention and mental health promotion are great. (Helse- og omsorgsdepartementet, 2023, p.19)

We see that health-promoting and preventive mental health care is, within a Norwegian perspective, closely linked to social work. The themes I have highlighted through the story of Gurrumul also weave together social work and mental health care in a beautiful tapestry. I believe that mental health care contains a great deal of social work, and vice versa. We need more mental health in the social sciences, and we need more social work in the mental health and addiction field. We need more collaboration, and a spotlight on what are *sustainable future mental health and substance abuse services.* We must collaborate on what is challenging, and I firmly believe in interdisciplinarity and collaboration between research, professions, education, and the service users who sometimes need mental health and substance abuse services.

We need stories, we need experience-based knowledge, and we need to collaborate in social work research. In this space, we must be able to invite dialogue and share stories, whether we work with mental health care, social work or are just fellow human beings in a neighborhood. We must, like Williams, go out into the field and plant trees.

Reflective Questions

1. How can we work with stories in global social work?
2. How can we include ourselves as practitioners in storytelling?
3. How can we, as social workers, safeguard the integrity of those who tell us their stories in a good and trustworthy way?
4. Being a social worker is very much like being a collector of stories. How do we learn by stories, and add them to be powerful tools in our everyday practice?

Acknowledgements

This chapter is based on my inaugural lecture as Professor of Social Work at UiT The Arctic University of Norway, 11 October 2023. The lecture is also published in another version, in a Norwegian book on narrative methods (Sørly, 2024), and for some Norwegian readers there will be an overlap with this work.

REFERENCES

Adichie, C. N. (2009). The danger of a single story. TED Talk. www.ted.com/talks/chimamanda_ngozi_adichie_the_danger_of_a_single_story?language=en (accessed 6 November 2023).

Barthes, R., & Duisit, L. (1975). An introduction to the structural analysis of narrative. *New Literary History*, *6*(2), 237–72.

Borg, M., & Askheim, O. P. (2010). Deltagerbasert forskning i psykisk helsearbeid–et bidrag til mer "brukbar" kunnskap? *Tidsskrift for psykisk helsearbeid*, *7*(2), 100–9.

Borg, M., Johnson, T. A., Bryant, W., Beresford, P., & Karlsson, B. (2015). Flerstemt forskningssamarbeid innen psykisk helse: Erfaringer fra Storbritannia og Norge. *Tidsskrift for psykisk helsearbeid*, *12*(1), 62–70.

Borg, M., & Kristiansen, K. (2009). *Medforskning – å forske sammen for kunnskap om psykisk helse*. Oslo: Universitetsforlaget.

De Fina, A. (2015). Narratives and identities. In A. De Fina & A. Georgakopoulou (eds.), *The Handbook of Narrative Analysis*, 349–368. Hobeken, NJ: John Wiley & Sons.

Fævelen, M., Sørly, R., & Heggem Kojan, B. (2023). 'Good parenting' among middle-class families: A narrative positioning analysis of Norwegian child welfare workers' stories. *European Journal of Social Work*, 27(3), 534–45.

Fell, S. J. (2018, 13 April). Geoffrey Gurrumul Yunupingu's legacy: Why his music didn't stop. *Sydney Morning Herald*, www.smh.com.au/entertainment/music/geoffrey-gurrumul-yunupingu-s-legacy-why-his-music-didn-t-stop-20180411-p4z8xd.html (accessed 6 November 2023).

FO (Norwegian Union of Social Educators and Social Workers). (n.d.). Global definisjon av sosialt arbeid. https://gammel.fo.no/nye-brosjyrer/global-defi nisjon-av-sosialt-arbeid (accessed 6 November 2023).

Hamkins, S. (2013). *The Art of Narrative Psychiatry*. Oxford University Press.

Hancock, N., Bundy, A., Tamsett, S., & McMahon, M. (2012). Participation of mental health consumers in research: Training addressed and reliability assessed. *Australian Occupational Therapy Journal, 59*(3), 218–24.

Helsedirektoratet. (2023). Kvalitativ forskning på brukermedvirkning innen psykisk helse og rus i Norden og Sápmi 2012–2022 [nettdokument]. Oslo: Helsedirektoratet (siste faglige endring 25. september 2023, lest 30. januar 2024). Available from www.helsedirektoratet.no/rapporter/kvalitativ-forskning-pa-brukermedvirkning-innen-psykisk-helse-og-rus-i-norden-og-sapmi-2012-2022.

Helse- og omsorgsdepartementet. (1997–8). St.prp. nr. 63. Om opptrappingsplan for psykisk helse 1999 – 2006 Endringer i statsbudsjettet for 1998.

(2023). Opptrappingsplanen 2022– 2032. Lastet ned 06.10.23 fra Meld. St. 23 (2022–2023) (regjeringen.no).

Holmes, C., & McRae-Williams, E. (2008). *An Investigation into the Influx of Indigenous 'Visitors' to Darwin's Long Grass from Remote NT Communities – Phase 2. Being Undesirable: Law, Health and Life in Darwin's Long Grass.* Canberra: Australian Institute of Criminology.

Josselson, R. (2011). "Bet you think this song is about you": Whose narrative is it in narrative research? *Narrative Works, 1*(1), https://journals.lib.unb.ca/index.php/NW/article/view/18472.

Karlsson, B., & Borg, M. (2021): *Samarbeidsbasert forskning: Demokratisk kunnskapsutvikling i psykisk helse- og rusarbeid.* Oslo: Gyldendal.

Karp, D. A., & Birk, L. B. (2013). Listening to voices: Patient experience and the meanings of mental illness. In C. S. Aneshensel, J. C. Phelan, and A. Bierman (eds.), *Handbook of the Sociology of Mental Health* (2nd edn). Dordrecht: Springer.

Klausen, R. K. (2017). Relational insight and user involvement in the context of Norwegian community mental health care: A narrative analysis of service users' stories. PhD thesis, UiT The Arctic University of Norway.

Komulainen, K., Siivonen, P., Kasanen, K., & Räty, H. (2020). "How to give a killer pitch?" Performances of entrepreneurial narratives as identity models in higher education. *Entrepreneurship Education and Pedagogy, 3*(3), 214–35. https://doi.org/10.1177/2515127420908039

Linde, Charlotte (2009). *Working the Past: Narrative and Institutional Memory.* Oxford University Press.

Mishler, Elliot G. (1995). Models of narrative analysis: A typology. *Journal of Narrative and Life History, 5*(2), 87–123.

Riessman, C. K. (2008). *Narrative Methods for the Human Sciences.* London: Sage.

Rukeyser, M. (1968). *The Speed of Darkness* (1st edn). New York: Random House.

Senneset, I. (2021). Kjære meg, hilsen jeg. *Aftenposten,* www.aftenposten.no/amagasinet/i/Bl98av/kjaere-meg-hilsen-jeg (accessed 10 November 2023).

Sørly, R. (2018). *En ring av trær*. Tromsø: Gateavisa Virkelig.

(2021). Jeg vedder på at du tror denne sangen handler om deg. *Tidsskrift for psykisk helsearbeid*, *18*(3), 252–4.

(2024). *Hvorfor er fortelling i forskning viktig*. In Sørly, *Narrativ metode*, 21–38. Oslo: Cappelen Damm Akademisk Forlag.

Sørly, R., Mathisen, V., & Kvernmo, S. (2021). "We belong to nature": Communicating mental health in an indigenous context. *Qualitative Social Work*, *20*(5), 1280–96.

Sørly, R., Mathisen, V., & Nygaard, V. (2021). Mental health research in an Arctic Indigenous context: The presence of silent dominant narratives. In R. Sørly, T. Ghaye, & B. Kårtveit (eds.), *Stories of Change and Sustainability in the Arctic Regions*, pp.72–87. New York: Routledge.

CHAPTER 2

Social Work for a Better World: Are We In-between Stories?

Tony Ghaye

> I believe we can change the world if we start listening to one another again. Simple, honest, human conversation. Not mediation, negotiation, problem solving, debate or public meetings. Simple, truthful conversation where each have a chance to speak, we each feel heard, and we each listen well. What would it feel like to be listening to each other . . . about what disturbs and troubles us? About what gives us energy and hope? About our yearnings, our fears, our prayers, our children?
>
> (Wheatley, 2002, p.3)

Arguably for some, this touches the heart of social work. Social work "happens" with and through conversation, verbal, pictorial, digitally, and through other mediums. In its most basic form, it's about sitting together talking about what's important to those present. Turning to each other and talking about what's relevant, meaningful, and real. The cure for despair, frustration, and anxiety is not hope. It's discovering what we want to do about something we are living through and care about.

We can do this by sharing stories. In this book and also in others (Sørly, Ghaye & Kårtveit, 2022), we name this process as one of having "conversations-that-matter." Ghaye (2022) sets out the characteristics of these kinds of conversation in detail later in that book. And of course, we need to want to tell stories-that-matter! Involved in this is an ability to harness the power of experience for personal and collective growth and progress.

Sometimes it takes courage to have these kinds of conversation and tell stories-that-matter, as few of us escape life without some broken parts. The courage to tell may be thought about not as the absence of fear, but the ability to look fear in the face and find a way to continue to walk forward positively. We stay silent for many reasons. All of us have something that frightens us, whether or not we admit it. Sometimes it's because we are frightened of each other, or fearful of the consequences of putting words to difficult emotions. One source of courage for social workers, we suggest, is to (re)appreciate that there are some who are longing to be in this kind of conversation ... again. The lonely, the marginalized, 'disturbed', stigmatized, peripheralized, those 'in recovery' and so on. They are hungry for a chance to talk, to tell their story. "Outsiders or those deemed 'other', who've been told repeatedly that they are unworthy or don't belong, often internalise negative beliefs imposed on them by others and make themselves smaller, unable to give voice to their true feelings, opinions or desires" (Novogratz, 2020, p.60).

If deep listening enables all social workers to see beyond another's words, understanding their identities can also be a potent way to empower and strengthen. If we wish to see those we work with and care for more holistically and show that we respect them, we must find an appropriate, sociocultural way to listen with our whole selves, not just with our ears. Learning through stories can help fill this need.

Novogratz suggests that the job of all of us is to:

> learn to tell stories that matter, stories that unite and inspire, reinforcing our individual and collective potential, and paint a picture of the future that we can build and inhabit together. Positive stories-that-matter are *not* stories that demean, deride, divide, ridicule, belittle, blame or shame. We must take the harder path of telling stories that hold our truths, both the ugly and the beautiful, while remaining laser-focused on the possible. Stories matter because they have consequences. (Novogratz, 2020, p. 204).

Maybe for some, conversations fuelled by storytelling require those involved to reaffirm some principles, practise some new behaviours, or dust off some old skills. Principles like acknowledging that both narrator and listener are equals in the process. This sounds plausible and even desirable, but can, of course, be difficult to achieve due, for example, to the real and perceived 'power' relations that circulate between those involved. Power inequities are everywhere (Foucault, 2000; Gaventa & Cornwall, 2015; Redman, Greenhalgh, & Adedokun, 2021).

A skill might be to ignite the process by asking a positive question. Another might be to try to stay curious about the story, as the telling of stories can be messy at times. Those involved might also need to be prepared to 'be disturbed'. By this we mean, have their thoughts, feelings, and beliefs challenged through the act of the story being told. What seems clear to us is that we need to harness and to fully appreciate the power of learning through lived experiences.

What Do You Need to Be Able to Write a Social Work Story-that-Matters?

You may feel that much of the scope of social work is focused on understanding lived experiences in the many contexts in which individuals live their lives: social, political, economic, personal, and familial for example. One consequence of this position is that, in this book, we are suggesting that social work stories-that-matter can be created at the intersection of *relationships*, *emotions*, and *experiences*. We suggest that three kinds of intelligence are therefore needed to create social work stories that embrace these three elements. As a precursor to what we are proposing, and which is evidenced throughout this book, is the need to flag up the importance of Gardner's work (2011 [1983]). He developed his theory of multiple intelligences and so challenged the idea that intelligence was simply limited to cognition (IQ). This is indeed important but, in this book, we also demonstrate three other important social work intelligences. We need social intelligence (SQ), which is not just *about* relationships but how we are *in* them (Goleman, 2006). This is fundamental, we suggest, to the social work profession. We also need emotional intelligence (EQ), and additionally an ability to critically reflect on what we've gained from our life experiences. This is often called experiential intelligence (XQ) in Kaplan's (2023) terms.

Creating a really compelling social work story needs a combination of all three intelligences (plus a bit of IQ!) because they reinforce and enrich each other. In other words, they are complementary. Throughout this book you will read stories which have elements of all three (SQ+EQ+XQ), not always in equal measure, but often striving to work in harmony. These inter-relationships are shown in Figures 1 and 2.

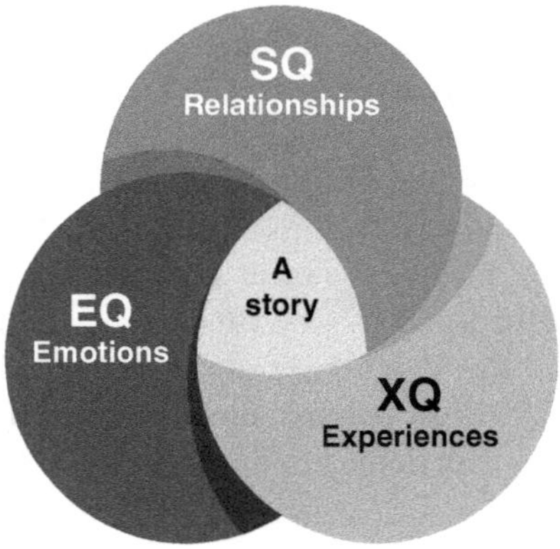

Figure 1 Three fundamental intelligences for creating social work stories-that matter

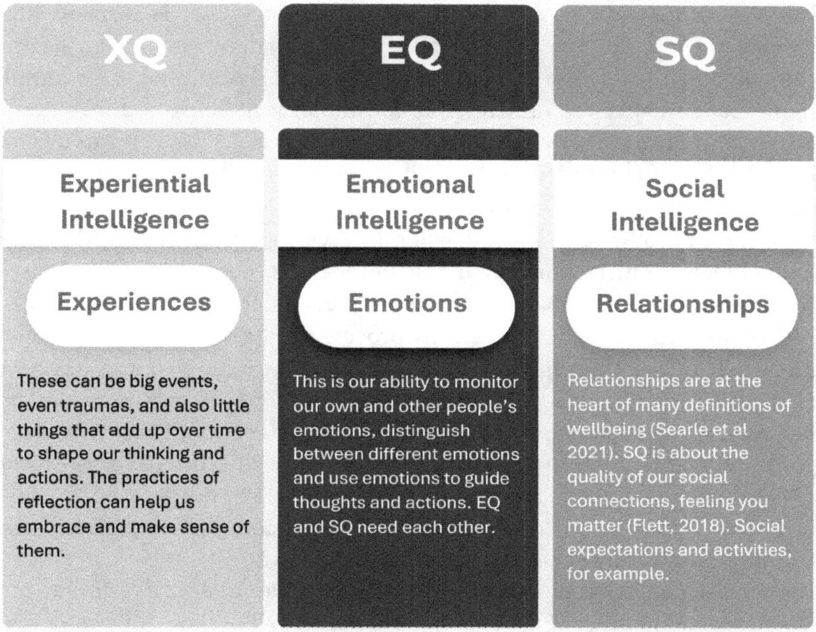

Figure 2 Fundamental intelligences elaborated

The 'What Work Do You Do Story'

This is a question Rita and I often get asked.

We have worked together for many years, and it's never 'pay or perks' which motivates us. On the contrary, it's much more about passion, people, and progress! But that's not all! So, what motivates you? Some of you may be familiar with the seminal work of Abraham Maslow (1943) and his theory of human motivation. Also, his contributions to establishing the field of humanistic psychology. This gained momentum in the late twentieth century with its focus on individuals' innate drive to self-actualize, express oneself, and achieve full potential. According to Maslow's theory, people possess higher and lower-order needs, which are arranged in a hierarchy. These needs are:

- physiological needs
- safety
- belongingness and love
- esteem
- self-actualization

(Maslow, 1943).

In other words, the first level of needs (physiological) is fundamental. Among these needs are people's need for air, water, food, sleep, health, clothes, and shelter. They are positioned at the bottom of a "pyramid" signifying that they are fundamental to human well-being and will always take priority over other needs. Once one level of need is taken care of, the focus shifts on to the next level, and so on, until self-actualization is reached at the top of Maslow's hierarchy.

According to Maslow, people will only seek the satisfaction of this need following the satisfaction of all the lower-order needs (Maslow, 1943). Maslow helps us appreciate that once we meet a need, we have to pursue a higher need to stay motivated. This process of satisfying needs is a much more useful idea than his notion of a hierarchy, as his pyramid has been well critiqued and added to (Koltko-Rivera, 2006; Kendrick et al., 2010). We are placing these ideas on the page, early in the book, because we shall go on to suggest that, in this hugely disrupted twenty-first-century world, social work might see this moment, not only as (new) needs to be satisfied, but as an opportunity to ask itself, as a profession, some critical, work-defining, and future-focused 'global' questions.

For example, most of us want to do good at work (Boccalandro, 2021). We want to be the best version of ourselves. To show up positively, hopefully, and helpfully. To help with this and as social workers, it might be useful to try to put our finger on the 'best' part of our work and even try to figure out how this can be *most* of our work. We might go further and ask, 'How far would you say that, for you, your work is about passions, people, and progress?' Is it something more and different?

Arguably, work that engenders a satisfying amount of passion, engages us with people who might benefit in some way from our character and performance strengths (Buckingham, 2007, 2011; Buckingham & Clifton, 2001; Rath & Conchie, 2008; Yeager, Fisher, & Shearon, 2011). It may give us a feeling that progress, in some way, is being made, but might still fall short and leave us with a nagging question, 'Isn't there something else?' So, what might the ultimate motivator be for you? What need/s might be fulfilled? What sense of purpose acquired? And how critical is this to your sense of identity as a social worker? How will this help you to create a personal story that you are proud of?

Whatever our jobs are, when Rita and I finish a day, shift, or programme, uplifted by the thought that we made a positive and valued difference to someone or a group, it is unquestionably a great feeling. Making a difference, of course, can be very hard work. But arguably it's time well spent. And when we see real, positive progress it can give rise to a deep, abiding sense not only of accomplishment but also of joy. We would argue that our work is values-based and that we try to live our values out in our work each day. This can be very challenging for all those who are concerned with the congruence between espoused values and values-in-action. If social work is built on notions of "justice, care, dignity, worth, equality and self-determination with the purpose of identifying and describing problematic social conditions and, in turn, taking action to contribute to social change and transformation" (Gilgun, 2023, p.1062), the challenges of congruence and also of being a living contradiction are real and ever present.

And then there is always the additional challenge of addressing the interplay between practices, policies, and structures. This inevitably involves understanding power in its many guises – hegemonic social processes, decolonialization, indigenous knowledges, institutionalized oppressions along the lines of race, genders, sexual identities, culture, and income, among others. This book has stories that illustrate many of these challenges.

Stories of Social Purpose

I am suggesting that this book reflects people working with a particular kind of purpose in mind. A social purpose! And that this relates to social good.

"Social, or eudaimonic purpose, is pursuing meaningful contributions to others or to a societal cause" (Boccalandro, 2021, p.21). Arguably, it is this social purpose that is a powerful motivator. It may also make us happier in our social work! Of course, we need to clarify what we mean by the use of the word 'meaningful' as it is construed differently by different people. What makes your social work meaningful is worth reflecting on. Also, it may be worth checking out how your personal story of working with social purpose truly contributes to the well-being of others, and yourself!

This notion of social purpose is, of course, enshrined within the 2014 global definition of social work from the International Federation of Social Work.

> Social work is a practice-based profession and an academic discipline that promotes social change and development, social cohesion, and the empowerment and liberation of people. Principles of social justice, human rights, collective responsibility and respect for diversities are central to social work. Underpinned by theories of social work, social sciences, humanities

> and indigenous knowledges, social work engages people and structures to address life challenges and enhance wellbeing. The above definition may be amplified at national and/or regional levels. (IFSW, n.d.)

One of the challenges definitions like this can pose, is that we need to find ourselves and our work, somewhere inside it. Even worse, we sometimes feel we need to 'force-fit' our practice into someone else's view of what social work 'should' be! We could describe this as the important process of alignment or congruence. For example, how far is what you do, with and for others, aligned with this global definition at the level of practice and/or principle? And if there is a close alignment, so what next? And if there are points of difference, so what and why?

Beyond a Single Social Work Story

How we narrate our past speaks to our understanding of our present and aspirations towards the future. With this in mind, if we choose to narrate the development of social work as a single story, we are in danger of creating a stereotype. In some situations, stereotyping can be useful as long as those engaged with this appreciate that a stereotype is both a generalization and therefore incomplete and lacking detail and nuances. Stereotypes can make one story become the only story. Scale this up and we soon bump into complex questions such as, 'How do "we" decolonize a hegemonic single social work story?'

Clarke (2022) argues that the genealogy of the global social work origin story, especially in the curriculum, often centres on Anglo-American ancestors and that this ancestry illustrates the development of the disciplinary boundaries of the international profession as we might know and experience it today. Furthermore, Clarke (2022) proposes that arguably the narrow ancestry often attributed to the genesis of social work reinforces coloniality in the curriculum. This narrow ancestry uplifts white Western colonial knowledge while rendering other kinds of knowledge largely invisible. There are some dangers of a single story of professional lineage. Lineage shapes how a discipline is defined, seen, understood, and whose voices matter (Zerubavel, 2012).

From your reading of some of the contents of this book, we invite you to make up your own mind about these issues and even the point made by Ioakimidis and Trimikliniotis (2020) that social work historiography has neither dealt with its troubled past of complicity with colonizing and racist ideologies, nor opened up the depths of its rich radical histories to students.

The issues of decolonized social work knowledges and practices, together with the inclusion and respect for more indigenized knowledges and their practices, are present in the book. Here we need to raise two more fundamental social work questions, namely, 'Whose reality counts?' and 'Whose knowledge is worth knowing and why?'

A more rhetorical starting question for a conversation-that-matters is a question of the kind, 'Why do we need to, and how do we decolonize the social work academy?' And for the curious, 'What are the emerging conceptualizations of social work, from voices in the Global South?'

We may not have to try too hard to find out how social work is being reframed with counter-stories, challenging the dominant and past understandings of social work (Au, 2023). There may be much to learn from addressing these questions. As Schmid (2023) suggests, they may help us deepen our appreciation of mechanisms of oppression and empowerment, acknowledge the interdependence of the local with the global, and learn about the pitfalls and potential suffering which can arise from imposing world views and practices, especially with WEIRD. origins (Henrich, Heine, & Norenzayan, 2010). This is an acronym for people from Western, Educated, Industrialized, Rich, and Democratic (WEIRD) societies. All acronyms have limitations and this is no different. For example, some change 'Western' for 'White'.

In an increasingly disrupted world, it may be opportune for social workers to reappraise the nature of their social work and thereby rethink issues of professional identity (Kurevakwesu, Chikwaiwa, & Mandau, 2023). There are a number of stories, for example from Africa and in the wider perspective of Part II of this book, which illuminate some major challenges for the social work profession on the continent of Africa and particularly with reference to a lack of recognition in professional circles and a lack of relevance and purpose in responding to the most pressing problems on that continent (Chogugudza, 2009; Kurevakwesu, 2017; Kurevakwesu, Chikwaiwa, & Mandau, 2023; Masuka, 2015; Muridzo, Mumba, & Fometu, 2021; Nhapi, 2021).

Kurevakwesu (2023) and Mugumbate (2021) eloquently argue that this is chiefly because there was a wholesale transfer of social work from the West during colonialism, and as such, social work education and practice have remained laden with Western theories, models, and intervention strategies. When a postcolonial theoretical lens is used in social work, new stories emerge. These carry the potential for alternatives to the Western Eurocentric perspectives on culture, history, and education utilized by some in the profession of social work (Baskin, 2009; Blackstock, 2009; Tamburro, 2013; Weaver, 2005).

Eco-social Stories

More contemporary, relatable, and future-focused (for some) are the stories that are emerging where social work is making more and better connections with the natural world. For example, through the theme for the Global Agenda for Social Work and Social Development 2024: "Buen vivir: Shared future for transformative change." This theme was presented at the 2024 World Conference on Social Work and Social Development in Panama in March. The conference organizers say that this resonates with the contemporary challenges and aspirations of social work around the globe. They go on to argue that:

> Our world faces multifaceted crises, ranging from violent conflicts, environmental degradation, to persisting poverty and political disparities. Against this backdrop, social work must evolve and adopt innovative, transformative approaches that are community-led and steeped in indigenous wisdom. Central to this transformative change is the principle of "Buen Vivir", emphasizing that true well-being is achievable when communities live harmoniously with nature, striving collectively for balanced development. This indigenous philosophy underscores the significance of interconnectivity, reciprocity, correspondence and complementarity in human relationships and our bond with nature. Our goal is to champion this principle, fostering an eco-social world that thrives on inclusion, respect, mutual understanding, and the upholding of human rights. (Global Agenda for Social Work and Social Development, 2024).

In this contemporary statement, the interdependence of local and global expertise, action, and support is stressed. There is also a strong participatory dimension as terms such as "co-design" and "co-building" of policies and practices are mentioned. This takes us back to how we started the Introduction to this book, when we used the phrase 'conversations-that-matter'. What seems to matter here are a social worker's relationship with, and understanding of, issues of inclusion and intergenerational respect, together with co-creating conditions for peace, balanced development, the upholding of human rights, and sustainable development. So, in addition to the point we made earlier about 'finding our place' within others' definitions of social work, this 2024 statement brings with it another challenge, namely that of relating to others and maybe generating our own eco-social stories.

Eco-social stories are relatively new kids on the block! Social work has, for some time, been wrapped up in the greening agenda, with some even saying it has been slow to react (Bhuyan, Wahab, & Park, 2019). One possible explanation for this is that this eco-social work interest may require social work to evolve from its ontological and epistemological roots as exemplified in the person-in-social-environment paradigm.

However, greater momentum and interest are producing a number of important stories. The work of Domielli (2018) reviewed many of these eco-social issues, with her edited collection emphasizing that we live in a world where there is increasing recognition that the human condition and the condition of the planet on which we depend are inextricably linked. In the preface to her book, written by Robert Glasser, we begin to appreciate that this interdependence has an impact on a social work profession which began, many years ago, with a commitment to the person-in-the-environment. He writes:

> It is clear that disaster management has to be about much more than the delivery of food, shelter and household goods, and green social work can play a major role in both disaster preparedness and post-disaster recovery. Social workers have a profound role to play in helping communities exposed to both extensive and intensive risks through the establishment of relationships with vulnerable families that help them cope with the daily challenges of life and to survive traumatic events in an intelligent and focused manner. (p.xxxii)

So how far is your practice aligned with the green social work value system?

How Far Is Social Work In-between Stories?

Over a decade ago, Longhofer and Floersch (2012) set out a case for social work being in a crisis. They stated:

> Many have argued that social work has lost its way. Some argue that this results from an increasing distance between research and practice. Others contend that social work is unique among the disciplines in its value commitments and thus cannot, or should not, aspire to be like the sciences (i.e. scientism or naturalism) in either method or theory. It might be argued that social work, like sociology, is a 'crisis science' and like sociology, social work shares a history with modernity and thus experiences the recurring crises of modernity. (p.499)

If you relate to this position in some way, what are the current crises, in your social work practices, that need to be addressed? This becomes a very significant question. There may be crises attributable to the fact that social workers address 'personal troubles'. That they are immersed in aspects of human suffering that may include child abuse and neglect, sexual assault, family violence, homelessness, mental and physical health, poverty, crime, and whatever other social ills exist. There may also be a crisis in social work education if social workers take on the tasks of understanding, serving, and trying to make things better, whatever 'better' means! We wonder what constitutes appropriate professional preparation for such work?

Although addressing crises may seem worthwhile, it does bring three things with it. First, if we only think about and address crises, how far does this mean that social work is a profession of 'repair'?

Secondly, if we focus on crises, this might tell us a lot about this or that crisis, but tells us almost nothing about success and achievement. We grow in the direction in which we ask questions. So, if our social work practices are driven by deficit-based questions like 'What's wrong?', 'Who is to blame?', 'Why are we in this mess?', 'Why don't people talk to each other?', and so on, we grow in one direction. Ask more strength or asset-based questions like, 'What's good, right, just, hopeful, joyful and loving here?', then we grow in a different direction.

Thirdly, there is a fundamental question here regarding social worker mindset. Arguably one mindset has more to do with social work focusing on what we want *less of* in our and others' lives, like stress, anxiety, depression, and so on. The other is a focus on what we want *more of* in our lives, like happiness, health, joy, pride, connection, and love. In reality, of course, we need a bit of both mindsets. Mindset issues are worth reflecting on.

Others have posited that social work has become somewhat defensive. For example:

> My experience suggests that social work has taken a defensive position in terms of our identity as a full-fledged member of the academy. We have worried ever since whether we have our own methods, methodologies, theories, values, and practices. We even argue among ourselves about whether we have lost our way from the reformist, big picture perspectives that are part of our legacy, and have become agents of social control who operate on the micro-level and ignore the hegemonic social forces that perpetuate inequalities and human suffering. (Gilgun, 2023, p.1063)

Is this your experience? Is it a self-deprecating view of social work?

What, and Whose, Knowledge Is Worth Knowing and Why?

Social work across the globe is essentially about how we look after each other. It's principal concern is people's well-being. Perhaps one of the great ironies of social work is that it tends to be treated as if it were so simple, so obvious, that anyone could do it (Beresford & Slasberg, 2023). This book demonstrates that it is far from simple.

In this book we also wish to suggest that social work is fundamentally a profession embedded in the realities of people's lives and that these can be communicated through story for example. There are many voices in the stories in this book. We wanted to give space, air, and light, for example, to "marginalised voices to soar in all their messy glory, that intimately ask us all to question what it means to be human, what it means to be hurt, and what it means to not only survive but also to thrive. We are a product of our past, but we grow upward and onward" (Leah, 2024, p.3).

We are living through a critical decade where environmental, economic, and social issues are colliding. Our constructed realities of these collisions won't change themselves. We need to act. So what actions are appropriate, socially just, ecologically viable, and positively impactful in today's VUCCAA world (volatile, uncertain, chaotic, complex, ambiguous, and accelerating)?

At this point in our Introduction to this book, another question emerges, namely, '*How will I choose to be a social worker during this decade?*'

In this book of stories (and wider perspectives) there is evidence of those trying to practise their social work with purpose and through ethical values. It is social workers' values that animate their core humanity and how this translates into action. These values, whatever they may be, compel us to take a stand on principles and for people, and to play a part in a greener, sustainable, and more socially just world. Perhaps it's timely to be even more transparent with our social work ambitions? If you interpret this book as a 'call to action', what imaginative, bold, and beneficial actions would these be? These actions are likely to require the moral imagination to ensure that our social work actions are driven, at least, by empathy, positivity, enabling people to feel they matter, human connection, and even the willingness to challenge the status quo.

Put another way, '*How far do you see your social work being in the business of building a better world?*'

Reflective Questions

1. When was the last time you had a social work conversation-that-mattered? Who was it with? What did you discuss? How did you feel? What was the outcome?
2. What do you do that gives your social work meaning and purpose?

3. What are the existing possibilities and enormous dilemmas facing social work?
4. What is the social worker's key role in an era of profound social change?
5. In what ways do you see your social work being in the business of building a better world?

REFERENCES

Au, A. (2023). Decolonization and qualitative epistemology: Toward reconciliation in the academy. *Qualitative Social Work, 22*(4), 679–99.

Baskin, C. (2009). Evolution and revolution: Healing approaches with Aboriginal adults. In R. Sinclair, M. A. Hart, & G. Bruyere (eds.), Wicihitowin: Aboriginal Social Work in Canada, pp.133–52). Winnipeg: Fernwood.

Beresford, P., & Slasberg, C. (2023). *The Future of Social Care: From Problem to Rights-Based Sustainable Solution*, Cheltenham: Edward Elgar.

Bhuyan, R., Wahab, S., & Park, Y. (2019). A Green New Deal for social work. *Affilia, 34*(3), 289–94. https://doi.org/10.1177/0886109919861700

Blackstock, C. (2009). The occasional evil of angels: Learning from the experiences of Aboriginal peoples and social work. *First Nations Child and Family Review, 4*(1), 28–37.

Boccalandro, B. (2021) *Do Good at Work: How Simple Acts of Social Purpose Drive Success and Wellbeing*, New York: Morgan James.

Buckingham, M. (2007). *Go Put Your Strengths to Work: Six Powerful Steps to Achieve Outstanding Performance*, London: Simon & Schuster.

(2011). *Standout*. Nashville, TN: One Thing Productions.

Buckingham, M., & Clifton, D. (2001). *Now, Discover Your Strengths: How to Develop Your Talents and Those of the People You Manage*. London: Simon & Schuster.

Chogugudza, C. (2009). Social work education, training and employment in Africa: The case of Zimbabwe. *Journal of African Studies, 35*(1), 1–9.

Clarke, K. (2022). Reimagining social work ancestry: Toward epistemic decolonization. *Affilia, 37*(2), 266–78.

Domielli, L. (ed.). (2018). *The Routledge Handbook of Green Social Work*, London: Routledge.

Flett, G. (2018). *The Psychology of Mattering: Understanding the Human Need to be Significant*. London: Academic Press.

Foucault, M. (2000). *Power*. New York: New Press.

Gardner, H. (2011 [1983]). *Frames of Mind: The Theory of Multiple Intelligences*. New York: Basic Books.

Gaventa, J., & Cornwall, A. (2015). Power and knowledge. In P. Reason & H. Bradbury (eds.), *The Sage Handbook of Action Research* (3rd edn). Los Angeles, CA: Sage.

Ghaye, T. (2022). Concerned Arctic peoples: Characteristics of conversations-that-matter. In R. Sørly, T. Ghaye, & B. Kårtveit (eds.), *Stories of Change and Sustainability in the Arctic Regions: The Interdependence of Local and Global.* Oxford: Routledge.

Gilgun, J. (2023). Reflections on the thoughts of Norman Denzin: His connections to the once and future social work qualitative research. *Qualitative Social Work*, *22*(6), 1061–6.

Global Agenda for Social Work and Social Development. (2024). Buen vivir: Shared future for transformative change. www.ifsw.org/wp-content/uploads/2023/10/GlobalAgenda2030-Theme2024.pdf

Goleman, D. (2006). *Social Intelligence : The New Science of Human Relationships.* London: Hutchinson.

Henrich, J., Heine, S., & Norenzayan, A. (2010). The weirdest people in the world. *Behavioral and Brain Sciences*, *33*(2–3), 61–83. https://doi.org/10.1017/S0140525X0999152X

IFSW (International Federation of Social workers). (n.d.). Global definition of social work. www.ifsw.org/what-is-social-work/global-definition-of-social-work.

Ioakimidis V., & Trimikliniotis, N. (2020). Making sense of social work's troubled past: Professional identity, collective memory and the quest for historical justice. *British Journal of Social Work*, *50*(6), 1890–908.

Kaplan, S. (2023). *Experiential Intelligence: Harness the Power of Experience for Personal and Business Breakthroughs.* Dallas, TX: Matt Holt.

Kenrick, D. T., Griskevicius, V., Neuberg, S. L., & Schaller, M. (2010). Renovating the pyramid of needs: Contemporary extensions built upon ancient foundations. *Perspectives on Psychological Science*, *5*(3), 292–314.

Koltko-Rivera, M. E. (2006). Rediscovering the later version of Maslow's hierarchy of needs: Self-transcendence and opportunities for theory, research, and unification. *Review of General Psychology*, *10*(4), 302–17.

Kurevakwesu, W. (2017). The social work profession in Zimbabwe: A critical approach on the position of social work on Zimbabwe's development. *Afro-Asian Journal of Social Sciences*, *8*(1), 1–12.

(2023). United we stand, and divided we fall: A call to action for the decolonisation of social work in Africa. *International Social Work*, *67*(5), 1–4.

Kurevakwesu, W, Chikwaiwa, B., & Mandau, M. (2023). The struggle for social work professional identity in contemporary Zimbabwe: A study on abuse of the social work title. *Qualitative Social Work*, *22*(2), 200–16.

Leah, C. (2024). What it means to be human, what it means to be hurt, and what it means to thrive. *Qualitative Social Work*, *23*(1), 3–5.

Longhofer, J., & Floersch, J. (2012). The coming crisis in social work: Some thoughts on social work and science. *Research on Social Work Practice*, *22*(5), 499–519.

Maslow, A. (1943). A theory of human motivation. *Psychological Review*, *50*(1), 370–96.

Masuka, T. (2015). Transforming social work in Zimbabwe from social control to social change. *Social Work Practitioner-Researcher, 27*(2), 204–19.

Mugumbate, J. (2021). Decolonised social work: Actions, strategies and processes. Africa Social Work Network. https://africasocialwork.net/wp-content/uploads/2021/04/decolonisedsocial-work.

Muridzo, G., Mumba, J., & Fometu, A. (2021). International Federation of Social Workers (IFSW) African Social Work Conversation Forum: Sharing social work practice stories and interventions in Africa. *African Journal of Social Work, 11*(3), 145–8.

Nhapi, T. (2021). The place of social workers in Zimbabwe's social justice endeavours. *Advances in Social Work & Welfare Education, 23*(1), 71–5.

Novogratz, J. (2020). *Manifesto for a Moral Revolution: Practices to Build a Better World*. New York: Henry Holt.

Rath, T., & Conchie, B. (2008). *Strengths-Based Leadership: Great Leaders, Teams and Why People Follow*. New York: Gallup Press.

Redman, S., Greenhalgh, T., Adedokun, L., et al. (2021). Co-production of knowledge: The future. *British Medical Journal, 372*(434). https://doi.org/10.1136/bmj.n434.

Schmid, J.. (2023). A 40 year (contextualized) social work journey. *Qualitative Social Work, 22*(3), 553–68.

Searle, B., Pykett, J., & Alfaro-Simmonds, M. A. (eds). (2021). *A Modern Guide to Wellbeing Research*. Cheltenham: Edward Elgar.

Sørly, R., Ghaye, T., & Kårtveit, B. (eds.). (2022). *Stories of Change and Sustainability in the Arctic Regions: The Interdependence of Local and Global*, Oxford: Routledge.

Tamburro, A. (2013). Including decolonization in social work education and practice, *Journal of Indigenous Social Development, 2*(1), 1–16.

Weaver, H. (2005). *Explorations in Cultural Competence: Journeys to the Four Directions*. Toronto: Nelson.

Wheatley, M. (2002). *Turning to One Another: Simple Conversations to Restore Hope to the Future*. San Francisco CA: Berrett-Kohler.

Yeager, J., Fisher, S., & Shearon, D. (2011). *Smart Strengths: Building Character, Resilience and Relationships in Youth*. New York: Kravis.

Zerubavel, E. (2012). *Ancestors and Relatives: Genealogy, Identity, and Community*. Oxford University Press.

PART I

Storying-to-Learn: How Stories-that-Matter Help Us Appreciate Social Work in Action

Do we need to introduce stories that speak for themselves? If not, here is something, briefly, of the more invisible 'back story' to Part I of the book. For some 'storytellers' here, it is their first time writing for publication. Also there are stories from relatively novice social workers (which we wanted to encourage) and from vastly different practice contexts and especially from the Global South. There are stories from hugely experienced scholars, consultants, and 'academics', either semi-detached from practice or looking into practice from outside (from universities). These different contexts generate different points of view. Reflection-on-action was the driving process in story creation.

Additionally many novice writers had to overcome their sense of modesty and feelings that they had to tell/write their story in a particular way. Many 'languages' of storytelling are used and we have encouraged this variety. A central challenge was, '*What is the most appropriate way to make your story public?*' Each story illustrates ways of being, acting, feeling, and thinking. They involved experiences, interactions, specific events, and moments of a shared life. In placing them on the page we invite you to reflect not only on how they make you feel and think about yourself and your work, but also whether they offer you a meaningful source of 'actionable knowledge'.

Of course, there are many ways to interpret a story and so we avoid detailing 'what' the stories are about and what you 'should' learn from them!! However, given the broad readership of the book, we offer you this question to think about: '*How far are there stories within stories?*' For example, what is the WHAT story? Who said what and who did what? How far would you agree that the issue/s being 'storied' are settled? Done? Finished? Complete? If not, what are the messy bits, the unresolved questions, the unfinished business? What is the FEELINGS story? What feelings are being expressed? How do you feel reading the story? Can you find any joy and pride? And, what is the IDENTITY story? In other words what does the situation being presented mean to the teller and to you? What are the issues of dignity, self-esteem, well-being, and so on?

We wonder if you are able to find CHOICES within each story? It could prove relevant and useful to reflect on the circumstances that allowed for these choices, the tensions and dilemmas that they represent for social workers, and the freedom (or otherwise) they might provide.

Tony Ghaye and Rita Sørly

CHAPTER 3

The Shortest Distance between Two People Is a Story

Tony Ghaye

Part I of this book is a collection of stories from the field. Part II is additional contributions that offer wider perspectives on the stories told. These wider perspectives 'position' the stories more generally within systems and structures. I hope the stories inspire you to do what you can, where you are, with what you have, in order to make a positive difference in the world, through the practices of social work.

Rita and I aim to illustrate throughout the book how important stories are, as they fundamentally tell of situated experiences and how these shape our relationships towards others in the communities we are part of (Klausen, Haugsgjerd, & Lorem, 2013). Of course, there are many ways to tell a story and every story has multiple threads. They are told from a particular point of view and also many stories are unfinished. In other words, they are partial stories. They may have a start and a middle but not an end. Well not right now! And the end may surprise us. For example, ask about somebody's spouse while both are in love, then ask about the same spouse post-divorce, and each time you may get one side and/or even half the story. Whatever story is created and told, through whatever medium, I always feel it has some power to reveal important elements that constitute human connection.

But we need to be a little cautious and reflective, as Gottlieb (2021) suggests:

> we are all storytellers, and if stories are the way we make sense of our lives, what happens when the stories we tell ourselves (and others) aren't accurate? What if those faulty narratives we hold in our heads and our hearts are holding us back instead of moving us forward? And what if changing those stories, updating, revising, adding missing perspectives, could alter the course of our lives? (p.vii)

In this book, 'social work practices' generally (but not always) refers to what works, for whom, when, how, and with what impact. Another way of putting this is to suggest that this book can help us reflect deeply on social work practices that may have the potential to 'give life' to others by creating an environment that supports and encourages individuals to-be and to-share aspects of themselves. Additionally, to disclose those thoughts, feelings, and actions that matter to them to significant others and especially in times of change. Part of the 'back story' to this book, I suggest, is that an appropriate social work mindset is to try to see the true and the good, the better and the possible in each practice relationship and situation. This is undeniably challenging.

You will find many kinds of practice-focused stories between the covers of this book, written in different ways and about different experiences, all of which are humanly significant in some way. We recognize and honour 'different ways of telling', which leads to variety and variation within the book. Some stories summarize experiences over a lengthy period of time, while others retell a specific episode (see below). Some are written by experienced social workers, some by more novice workers, others by allied professionals and 'carers'. Some stories are longer, some shorter. Some stories are written by social work educators and others by those embedded in the field and across many sociocultural and geopolitical contexts, including higher education. The contents of the book therefore reflect a multidisciplinary gaze, with the bottom line being that "stories are fundamental to how people understand themselves and are seen by others" (Sandberg, 2022).

As you read through the book, there are lots of experiences to appreciate and feelings to understand. Some may pull you in, others may generate a feeling of distance. Feelings of hope, belonging, recovery, connection, compassion, affirmation, alienation, and love are all in the book. There are also stories that illuminate other experiences such as guilt, fear, anguish, despair, and grief, for example. There are some stories of people struggling to take care of their frightened, lonely, marginalized, and silenced selves. Some are stories about disappointment, distress, and confusion. Others about breakthroughs, triumphs, and successes.

Rita and I hope that you, the reader, will discover how you feel when you read about social work and workers and those they care about and are responsible for, when they are trying to make a positive difference to the lives of others and when life feels purposeful or meaningless. In other words, we invite you to find your own way through the book. To be open to what each contribution can teach you about how others work through uncertainty and even chaos and how others deploy the noble human traits and social work sensitivities such as those of co-operation, caring, and generosity of spirit. More broadly, this is a book about social work in uncertain, ambiguous, chaotic, and volatile times.

What follows is our first story which, I hope, enables you get into "reflective mode" (Ghaye, 2011) and begins to help you engage with some fundamental aspects of social work. Additionally, I hope that each story, and the wider perspectives which follow in Part II, enable you to reflect on the question, '*So what do I really care about?*' Stories have the potential to do this. That is, to help us derive powerful and generative questions that we may wish to pursue with reflectivity and perhaps with actions. "They (stories) not only capture and (re)tell what has happened, they also shape the life we choose to move toward and the world we wish to create. They have this capability to help us name what we have and are living through" (Sørly, Ghaye, & Kårtveit, 2022, p.1).

There are three main characters in this first story. There is John (dad), eighty-five years, his wife Marjorie (mum), eighty-nine years, and their son Henry. Dad and mum live in a very small terraced house in an inner-city, multicultural housing estate in England. It is a low-income area which is densely populated. Benjamin, a social worker, is in this story too, as he is a close family friend and offers mum and Henry ongoing professional support and counselling after dad passes away. Benjamin and I (Tony) are professional colleagues.

Dad is recently deceased. He passes very suddenly from a massive brain haemorrhage, whilst in his beloved garden, with mum. As Dad collapses, he falls onto mum, who is very petite and frail, and fractures her femur. Dad is dead. Mum is lying on the grass, and alone in her garden, shouting for help and assistance. Nobody comes. Eventually in agony, she crawls into the house and finds her phone. She calls her son, Henry. He comes immediately and rings the emergency services. Both dad and mum are taken to a city hospital. Dad is already dead.

Some days later, as arrangements for the funeral are made, Henry, Benjamin, and I (Tony) are talking together. Henry feels he wants to express his love for his dad, and the grief he is now experiencing, by writing a short story which he subsequently called "SMILE." He contemplates reading this story at his dad's funeral. I asked for Henry's consent to place his story on the pages of this book. He said yes, gladly. I also asked Marjorie and Henry if they would like to choose two photographs to accompany the story. They did and here they are.

Figure 3 An evening in 1946 when John proposed to Marjorie (but he was late for their special dinner! But Marjorie forgave him . . . of course). They were teenage sweethearts

Figure 4 John and Marjorie fifty years later and still deeply in love

SMILE: A Story Written by Henry

Dad loved, laughed and lived. He was wise, clever and creative. Maybe too creative sometimes as he was a hugely talented tinkerer! He loved taking things apart, like watches and radios but maybe not so talented at putting them back together again!

Dad was wise. He was smart. My dad's intellect was really only matched by his humility. It didn't matter how smart he was, he respected the gifts, the intellect and the lives of others . . . and really of all the people he met. One of the many lessons I learned from him was that you should never use your own intellect to make others feel less smart than you, but as smart, or even smarter than you. And if you respected the ideas and perspectives of others, you could and would learn from anyone and everyone. I learned from my dad that whatever gifts one was given, they had to be spent lifting people up, not putting them down.

Dad was a remarkably loving, giving, devoted, dedicated, thoughtful Christian man, whose love was expressed in many kind ways. Mum always described him as a "very kind" man. His work colleagues as a "gentle man" and a gentleman.

In writing this story I've been trying to find the right words to convey just how loving and selfless dad was. It felt like in every decision and move he made, you would find mum at the heart of it all. Dad never gave us any reason to ever doubt that he loved mum and me. And he made sure that we knew it. So, as I write this story, after his passing, I am not left hungry for his love. In fact, I am living in abundance of it. For mum however, it's a very different storyline.

Dad loved reading sayings and proverbs. And he cherished a small book with lots of big messages in it, about life. The little book is called *The Rubaiyat of Omar Khayyam*. One of his favourites that he used to recite to me as a child, was one which helped me appreciate that despite what happens, life must go on, and we must step forward positively and try to embrace it. It goes like this:

> *The moving finger writes and having writ, moves on,*
> *Nor all thy piety or wit shall lure it back to cancel half a line,*
> *Nor all thy tears wash out a word of it.*

So, what did the "moving finger" write? Dad . . . these are just some of the things that come to mind.

Your passing is painful to us all and yet strangely reaffirming because you have given me the opportunity to be even more aware of the rewards of my wonderful relationship with you. I know you would want me to try to be positive, even at this time. So here is something of the positive legacy you left me.

You have left me with a burning curiosity for life, a hunger for knowledge, a passion for the outdoors, for nature, for swimming, fishing, rugby and football. You taught me to have fun flying kites, and to go and visit the troll bridge . . . on tiptoes! You were a lover of ancient history, of trains and of maps. You helped me appreciate the world around me. You were an example of a life whose riches owed little to money. Your life was an example that anything is possible, if you work hard. You taught me to take pride in what I did and to be honest in my dealings with others. You left me with a message to be the best I can be. You were a model of what a husband and dad should be. And most importantly of all, you reminded me that we should always do the very best for those we love. These are great gifts that you have given me.

So we can shed tears that dad has gone, or we can smile because he has lived.

We can close our eyes and pray that he will come back, or we can open our eyes and see all he has left.

Our hearts can be empty because we can't see him, or they can be full of the love we have shared.

We can turn our back on tomorrow and live in our yesterdays, or we can be happy for tomorrow to come because of all the yesterdays when he was with us.

We can remember him only because he is gone, or we can cherish his memory and let it live on.

Thank you dad for being the most incredible father and husband. Thank you for making me want to try to make the world a better place and for showing me a path to do so. Thank you for making sure that we have known that we were loved every day of our lives, mum and me. In this moment I am so grateful that dad showed me what to value in life. That if you put love and family at the centre of it all, you will have a life that is full and well-lived.

So, I can cry and try to close my mind to what has happened, be empty and retreat into my shell. OR I can do what dad would have wanted . . . SMILE, open my eyes, love and go on.

* * *

There is much to learn from this story. Some social work practices include appreciating and working with those experiencing grief and growth. But of course, growth through grief can be messy, long term, and painful. Social work practices can also be focused on healing and renewal, individual and collective loss, and vulnerability. Grief is a normal reaction to loss and people cope with their grief differently. Right now, Henry is coping through creating a 'document' of his feelings, through writing a short story.

> Grief can, and does, happen over any type of death or non-death loss – bereavement, disappearance, separation, divorce, loss of relationship, miscarriage, trauma, sickness, loss of health, calamity and violence . . . it is

> natural to experience grief over bereavement, but one may also experience anticipatory grief witnessing or caring for a loved one who is in a life threatening or terminal state. There is ambiguous loss and grief when a loved one is physically present but mentally and psychologically absent (such as in Alzheimer's disease or in a coma) . . . Sometimes grief can be . . . the loss of a pregnancy through miscarriage or the inability to have children, stigmatized loss (suicide or a death by drug overdose) or socially unspeakable loss, like the demise of someone with whom the mourner had a secret or socially unsanctioned relationship. (Verma & Neimeyer, 2020, pp.5–6)

For social workers, the whole experience of being with those who are grieving in one or more ways, and the impact of this on their lives, are far from simple and easy. Grief arises in life in many ways and at different times, and social workers have a very important role to play in enabling 'others' to find their way through the complex web of feelings and the painful effects of grief. Such practices, I suggest, involve not only *being available* and *being present*, together with a deep acknowledgement of what has occurred, but also a will and commitment to engage with 'others' with hope and compassion. Put another way, "If we fail to understand that we are being challenged by our (and others') difficult emotions, we are more likely to give up and less likely to connect with the future" (Gotis and Kiapoka, 2020, p.9).

In relation to this, I suggest that an important role for a social worker is to try to find some flexibility in their own, and others' stories, and to appreciate that this is a precursor to changing them in some valued way. Some of us get locked in, almost imprisoned inside a 'rigid' story which diminishes our opportunities to think about alternatives and options that might reveal new possibilities. When the narrator of the story (a social worker, a client, patient, etc.) feels they have no wriggle room, what often happens is that the narrator only provides 'evidence' that validates their story! In situations like this, a role for a social worker, I suggest, is to figure out how to move from a position of 'movement is impossible right now' to 'movement is possible and safe'. Arguably, social work is well positioned to amplify hope in times where hope is diminished.

It was this sense of hope that echoed in the words of twenty-two-year-old Amanda Gorman, American youth poet laureate, who wrote and read the inaugural poem for a new American president, Joe Biden, on 20 January 2021, when she said, "We lift our gazes not to what stands between us, but what stands before us. We close the divide because we know to put our future first, we must first put our differences aside. We lay down our arms so we can reach out our arms to one another, we seek harm to no one and harmony for all." Maybe this is part of an important rallying cry for social workers?

So, in this book you will find a variety of stories which illustrate how, through words and actions, social workers, together with allied professionals and carers, around the world, are responding to life's challenges and building resilience in themselves and with others. Taken together, these stories, I suggest, begin to weave a new fabric of hope and possibility that may inspire all social workers to speak new words that lead to new and even better actions. Rita and I make no apology for mainstreaming social worker stories. But, of course, we are acutely aware that there are many who would critique this in the same way they critique the meaningfulness, trustworthiness, and usefulness of the stories from 'service users' (Voronka & Grant, 2021). We address these issues collectively when we explore the notion of social work stories and epistemic injustices (Fricker, 2010) in Part II of the book.

Reflective Questions

1. What does the statement "The shortest distance between two people is a story" mean to you?
2. What do you think might inspire growth after loss?
3. How might you, as a social worker, amplify hope in the most complex of times?
4. What strengths do you have that promote positive human connections?

REFERENCES

Fricker, M. (2010). *Epistemic Injustice: The Power and Ethics of Knowing*. Oxford University Press.

Ghaye, T. (2011). *Teaching and Learning through Reflective Practice: A Practical Guide for Positive Action* (2nd edn). London: Routledge.

Gotis, I., & Kiapoka, A. (2020). Uncertainty, hope and utopia. *International Journal of Appreciative Inquiry*, *23*(1), 9–15.

Gottlieb, L. (2021). *Maybe You Should Talk to Someone: A Therapist, Her Therapist, and Our Lives Revealed.* Boston, MA: Houghton Mifflin Harcourt.

Klausen, R., Haugsgjerd, S., & Lorem, G. (2013). 'The lady in the coffin' – Delusions and hearing voices: A narrative performance of insight. *Qualitative Inquiry*, *19*(6), 431–40.

Sandberg, S. (2022). Narrative analysis in criminology. *Journal of Criminal Justice Education*, *33*(2), 212–29.

Sørly, R., Ghaye, T., & Kårtveit, B. (eds.). (2022). *Stories of Change and Sustainability in the Arctic Regions: The Interdependence of Local and Global.* London: Routledge.

Verma, N., & Neimeyer, R. (2020). Grief and growth: An appreciative journey. *International Journal of Appreciative Inquiry*, *22*(2), 5–10.

Voronka, J., & Grant, J. (2021). Service user storytelling in social work education: Goals, constraints, strategies, and risks. *Social Work Education*, *41*(1), 1–16.

Photo: Hilde Mjøs

CHAPTER 4

The Gift of Social Work

Blessing or Burden?

Gloria Acan

I am Gloria Acan, a third-born of four born and raised in Uganda. Until recently I worked with Vijana Corps, a non-profit in Uganda whose mission is to achieve social justice and equitable development in Uganda by extending tools, platforms, and safes spaces for the participation and innovation of young people. This work was fulfilling because of the enlightening effect of increased access to information that is relevant and timely to young people and how that causes a shift in their lives, awakening and inspiring young people that their voice matters in the pursuit of equitable development. It gives my life meaning and purpose because I am deeply entrenched in work where I can make small steps towards positive change with the work that I do; Now I work for Teach for Uganda.

I had my first encounter with the idea of social work in primary school when I was nine years of age. It sounds early I bet, so before you decide not to believe me, let me tell you about myself. I am from Lira in the northern part of Uganda, but I largely grew up closer to the city centre in Kampala where there were more opportunities for school for myself and my family due to greater access to social services in the urban areas.

As a little girl, I was very fond of my dad. He was tall with the brightest of smiles, quiet yet so full of life, I admired how he interacted with people and how he took care of us as a family. Among the many things I loved about him was what he did for a living. He would get back home with charts, talking about immunization one day, then a story on a school he visited the next day, a picture from a community he was working with, you name it. Curious as I was, for a moment I really wondered if he got paid to be a helpful person. He worked in the public service sector in our country and that meant working with all sectors of the population in different regions, in schools, with local governments and more, and that's how he made a living. It was exciting to hear which specific group he was working with at the time, from teachers, to health workers, to elderly persons, to persons living with HIV/AIDS, among others. I decided that that would be it for me too.

Reflecting on this now, I wonder if I can truly say it was my choice or maybe it was a play of Bowlby and Ainsworth's attachment theory. The theory speaks of the fact that children are born with the need to forge bonds with caregivers and such early bonds may continue to have an influence on attachments throughout life (Cherry, 2023). Either way I am glad to be on this side.

Did I Choose Social Work or Did Social Work Choose Me?

In my primary school, there was a point when we were about nine years of age when we were all asked what we wanted to do and be when we grew up. At that time I had one thing in mind. That when that time came for me to become a big girl and start working, I knew exactly what I wanted to be. I didn't have a name for it at the time so that made the journey a bit bumpy at some points. In secondary school during career days and exhibitions, I looked around searching for exactly what I watched (growing up) my dad doing.

Some of the bumps I vividly remember were endless conversations with teachers, counsellors, and the career guidance team. I think I didn't have the right words for it because surely someone should have been able to help. While at secondary school, what was challenging for me was being interested in something that no one else was familiar with. So I was worried that I would have to settle for something that did not capture my dream.

For a profession that was introduced in Uganda in the 1950s (Ministry of Planning and Development, 1965), it is unsettling to think, even with career events and guidance, social work was not a term that was commonly known. The main reasons why the profession was introduced in Uganda at that time was to extend support and help for the solving of problems to promote the well-being of individuals and communities. I believe social work was a term that was not commonly known because communities and individuals already had previous means of solving their problems and their perspectives on well-being, so it could easily feel like social work was an extension of already pre-existing frameworks and channels of local support.

On my journey to finding my place as a social worker, I almost became a development economist because of the confusion of no one being able to name exactly what I wanted to do and become; it came close enough. It came close in terms of it being a profession that seeks to better the economic, social, and fiscal conditions of countries that are developing. I think about how different my path would have been, I'll never know. In her exploration of social work education and practice in Uganda, Twikirize (2014) recommends the urgent need for in-country advanced social work training programmes, and part of that is at the forefront and entry point right after secondary and post-graduate training as well. In addition to that, for me, is the need to shine a light on social work as a profession and the value of being part of this noble profession.

What It Was Actually Like

My first course, when I went to the university to study social work, was an introduction to social work by Dr Justus Twesigye, the Dean of the School of Social Sciences at the prestigious Makerere University in Kampala. Right from the programme overview and the line-up of reading material, the excitement on my face was very evident. The main highlights of the degree programme were understanding social work, the history of it as a profession, and its entry into Uganda. Also, defining social work in its entirety and reading up on scholarly articles that spoke of the same. We also got the opportunity to share how we got into the programme and for many it seemed like it was a choice that was made for them. Like something they simply agreed to but were not particularly passionate about. Others dreaded being in the class because for some it was not their choice. For others they were simply given the course via government sponsorship. For another it was simply a good recommendation from a career counsellor. But my story was different. It was also quite unique being me then. By this I mean my experience altogether was of being overly excited in a class of people whose reasons for being there were different.

The experience of social work is what I would describe as going through the loop of self-discovery, triggered by the influx of information on understanding human psychology and how our surrounding and past experiences literally mould us into who we are. I consider that time the beginning of my healing journey. It brought a lot of things to light and it felt like I needed to do all the shadow work before I could meet any client. It was bittersweet and still feels that way sometimes. A blessing but also a burden.

I would describe my 'healing journey' in this way. With each social work class I attended, something personal was revealed. In some classes more than others, for instance the introduction to psychology was such an opener, facilitated by Dr Paul Nyende, a lecturer at the School of Psychology, Makerere University. It was those practical tools and information that I accessed that gave some structure to my healing journey and direction to what progress would look like. This is not a journey I took on my own. I was also in the company of some of my peers from class and the conversations we got to have really helped to centre us and helped us hold each other.

The Gift of Social Work, a Blessing, or a Burden?

During and after my time at the university, there's a conversation that kept recurring with my peers from school and those I got to meet in practice. It was one on the gift and burden that social work is. A gift because of all the enlightenment that comes with the wealth of knowledge that is very eclectic in nature. It is such a privilege to be able to learn and take the journey to a more knowing self and support yourself through some of life's challenges that tamper with our social functioning, and in turn extend that support to different groups and individuals.

On the other hand, the burden that comes with knowing all that you get to know so consciously, or otherwise, can feel a bit harmful. For instance, you can easily feel like there's so much to improve about yourself because of the exposure that you have to information about human psychology. There's a part of you that is either overly self-reflective or psychoanalytic in nature, constantly connecting dots in people's behaviour and your own, that makes interacting with others an opportunity to work in disguise. I use the word disguise because instead of sitting and enjoying a simple interaction, your mind can easily distract you to a place where you are asking yourself why this person behaves, thinks, and acts this way, the temptation to analyse their entire being.

For instance, social workers in Uganda are increasingly being called on to assist survivors of childhood abuse, domestic violence, violent crime, disasters, war, and terrorism (Bride, 2007). It is needless to say that the effects of such occurrences go beyond those directly affected and I have had my fair share of that. The weight of knowing someone else's story and feeling all they felt for even just a moment.

My story with regard to these issues is especially from my work in the prisons, hearing stories of men and women that were incarcerated and how one decision that they made consciously, or not, changed the trajectory of their lives. Watching how much change they experienced, and all the lessons learnt along the way, was inspiring but also saddening because regardless they would still need to serve their sentence. With some, from their stories, you could tell that they were probably innocent and because they lacked the resources and power, they could not ably defend themselves. This was my feeling anyway!

First Time in Practice, Lord Is This It?

All the dreaming, hoping, and excitement led me to my very first experience practising social work. I was attached to the Paralegal Advisory Services, a project under the Uganda Human Rights Commission that was carrying out projects in a number of prisons in Uganda. I had the privilege of selecting the location where I'd be based and among the options was my home district, Lira district where I am originally from. For many reasons, but largely because I can ably speak the local language, and while it can be considered geographically remote, it was the kind of remoteness I was familiar with. So it felt far but in the same breath I felt right at home.

I was assigned the intern role of paralegal advisor at the Uganda Prison Services Lira. Thrilled to get started interacting with inmates, I had the opportunity to listen to them and offer counsel. One of the senior social workers urged me to take it easy and not feel pressured to hear them out, if I did not want to. In their defence they meant well and were worried how deeply involved and attached to the clients I was.

Like any other conversation, ours started with greetings. There was always a humility that the inmates carried, somewhat natural but also something practised. There was a sadness that came along with it as well. I met a client one afternoon and my excited self was thrilled to hear from her. She wore a very light smile that was hiding a lot. She was also heavily pregnant. I also need to mention that my emotions were very heightened. I wondered what she had done. Her crime. Let's use Ritah as a pseudonym. Ritah was brave enough to share her story and she let me know that she was in prison because she had set her partner's hut on fire after an argument. That action was a response to her spilling the beans about her pregnancy, which he denied blatantly and that set her off and she felt like she needed an outlet, which in that case was her starting the fire at his house. She needed to punish him in some way.

We continued to talk and after all the conversation she requested to reach out to him to apologize, so he might drop the case and take her back. The situation in the prison was not good for anyone, let alone someone who was expecting a baby. It was tough. She sought my help to join her and help plead for forgiveness by physically going to him and his mother at a village a bit far from where we were. I remember just wanting to jump and do it straight after work. I thought about it when I went home that day. I was living alone and all the company I had were my thoughts. Sadly after reaching out they were not as responsive. I am not sure how her story ended. I think about her sometimes.

My experience in the prisons was just what I was hoping for. It felt like I was finally plugged in to social work and living the dream. The dream was exciting. I appreciated the connection to new people and I could feel like they did too. That slowly started to become a high for me. Seeing someone who needs support and coming through for them, working together, I knew that was where I needed to be. However, that did not last long. It started to feel like a burden, and trust me, I fought that feeling because I could not imagine the same thing that brought me fulfilment in work, was equally exhausting. I did not know what to do and that made me feel so helpless. It was a case of when the social worker needs a social worker.

The burden for me was in knowing all the people that could have benefited from my support and who needed more supporting, but I could only do so much. I stretched myself thin trying to be everything for the clients that I got to meet, because things were not easy for them at all. I refer to it as my saviour complex era. I carried the weight and responsibility of people's lives and experiences, like I was there to save them, and it almost broke me. When I got back to the university after internship, I was able to share my experiences with classmates and there I felt understood and realized that, for some, it was a very familiar experience to them also. I appreciated the beauty of community in holding each other. Some scholars have spoken about the risk to the wellness of the social worker, emphasizing the need for self-care as a tool to maintain equilibrium and bring some ease even in terms of crisis (Martin, Myers, & Brickman, 2020), and I can't agree with that enough.

Exploring New Territory

In Uganda, according to a UBOS (2018) report, 12.4 per cent of the population has some form of disability, and the population of children with disability is slightly higher at 13 per cent. The challenge with these statistics is that, in addition to the disability, 90 per cent of persons with disability are living below the poverty line. That adds another dynamic to the challenge, making it even more multifaceted.

Disability is a human rights issue and has effects likely to make persons liable to face inequalities – for instance, in access to social services like health and education, among others, in nations where there are already wide variations in access to such services. Issues of inclusion are a major challenge. This can increase their feeling of vulnerability. Inaccessible environments further create disability by creating barriers to participation and inclusion (WHO & World Bank, 2011).

A disability status report from 2019 highlights that inclusion of persons with disabilities can only be attained with empowerment and the elimination of barriers. In Uganda for instance, the coverage and inclusion of all persons with disabilities is wanting, with some disabilities not given much attention, partly due to limited knowledge about them and cultural factors that, at times, stigmatize people, leading such persons to be sidelined. This include persons with multiple disabilities, for example, deaf-blind persons, persons living with vitiligo, among others (National Council for Persons with Disabilities, 2019). In all of this, it is critical that disability be understood and addressed as an ever-changing phenomenon within a broader social development context.

During one of my internships, I was introduced to social entrepreneurship and tasked along with a small group of fellow interns to create a social venture of our own. As we narrowed down the discussion of the problem we desired to tackle, we decided to be in the education space and focus on what inclusivity looked like for persons with disabilities with a focus on children. In an attempt to understand the issue even further, we got the chance, as a team, to interact with children in special needs schools with unique stories and experiences. Conversations with their teachers helped paint a picture of what life was like for them at school but also thereafter. Some of the children had autism and attended one of the autism centres in Kampala. We visited a school with persons with dyslexia, Down syndrome, celebral palsy, children with delayed speech and challenges of that nature, among others. I think in all the visits, you could tell and see the desire from the caregivers and teachers to give these children the best experience of school life. But it was also quite clear that their caregivers and support system were limited in skill, in time, in abilities, and in knowledge. But conversely, high on motivation and devotion. I remember one of the teachers saying, "These children need time and care and attention and when they get it, you can see that they are progressing. But as teachers we are few, we cannot give each child all that time. Their friends will suffer, so sometimes we just maintain, clean after them, feed them and play with them."

Disability and the School Experience

That experience opened my eyes to the fact that the school environment is one of the most critical in a child's life, and if it is not safe and supportive, it is bound to limit a child's ability to learn, especially a child with a disability. The WHO Report on disability estimates that persons with disabilities constitute 15 per cent of the world's population or over 1 billion people (WHO & World Bank, 2011). Children with disabilities make up 5 per cent, which is equivalent to about 95 million children (UNICEF, 2014).

In Africa, an estimated 60–80 million people are living with disabilities today. This is about 10 per cent of the general African population and this number is seen to be higher in poorer regions (Disabled World, 2018). The existence of certain factors like poverty, malnutrition, HIV/AIDS, violence, and the absence of child protection, among others, also contributes to the prevalence of disability in Africa and exacerbates its impact. Based on research, the child disability prevalence in Uganda is at 13 per cent, i.e., approximately 2.5 million children live with some form of disability (UNICEF, 2014). Furthermore, in Uganda for instance, 30 per cent of all disabled people are children (under eighteen), and 42 per cent have physical disabilities (ACPF, 2011). There is hardly any documentation on the prevalence of learning disabilities in Uganda, let alone mention of specific learning disabilities like dyslexia, dyscalculia, autism, and Down syndrome.

In one of my social work classes on developmental psychology, facilitated by Dr Paul Nyende, I was introduced to the concept of learning disabilities. It was a pre-class assignment and then my lecturer walked us through what learning disabilities are and how they manifest, one hot afternoon in Mitchell Hall, Makerere University. One disability really struck me and that was dyslexia. Dyslexia is a specific learning disability that is neurobiological in origin. It is characterized by difficulties with accurate and/or fluent word recognition and by poor spelling and decoding abilities (International Dyslexia Association, n.d.).

My mind quickly sent me back to primary school and how in a class of about forty there were always students that for some reason were not able to complete assignments on time, and had difficulty reading and comprehending stories, when most of the class didn't. I wondered if maybe they had dyslexia and how different their experiences would have been. I also remember seeing this with a friend in secondary school. I could see her effort in reading and preparing for exams, but she always shared that it never added up in terms of performance and I wondered why. According to Dyslexia International, 10 per cent of any given population has dyslexia (Dyslexia International, 2014). Could my classmates have had dyslexia? I wasn't sure.

A report by Uwezo highlights the learning crisis in Uganda through a survey that was carried out in 3,347 primary schools. The English reading competence of pupils from primary three to primary seven in selected districts that are representative of the regions in Uganda was 39 per cent. A breakdown of this was also analysed for each subregion as follows: Kampala 67 per cent, South West 53.9 per cent, Central I 52 per cent, Central II 39.5 per cent, Western 38.7 per cenet, Karamoja 32.5 per cent, West Nile 28.4 per cent, Eastern 27.3 percent, East Central 25.9 per cent, and lastly Northern with 25.9 per cent (Uwezo, 2016). While such a reading crisis in the country could be attributed to the quality of teaching, availability of appropriate learning resources, and so on, it attracts attention to the possibility of dyslexia among learners, and more importantly to teachers' knowledge about dyslexia.

I am currently doing some work with primary teachers and using the knowledge I gained from my social work experiences, building on it with new learnings as well tapping into the vast experience of teachers to understand dyslexia and how to support children with the same. This is my passion project. An illustration of how I see this as an expression of my social work, is that as social workers, part of the roles that we are taught and end up practising is the role of teaching. Knowing that I am exposed to so much information by virtue of the wealth of social work knowledge, when that information can benefit someone or some people around me, I will jump on the opportunity to share it.

The gift of social work and the wealth of knowledge present an opportunity for social workers to own the role of teaching and extending information of this nature and so much more that can benefit the lives of children, young and old men, and women in society among others. I aspire to continue being part of a generation of social work professionals that are steering social change in their communities. When we understand and experience the enlightening effect that learning about ourselves and our social functioning has on us, we will pioneer spreading that to communities near and far. Social work as a professional both in the Global South and internationally has been associated with the promotion of social justice and the enjoyment of human rights, thus reducing inequalities in more ways than one (Palattiyil et.al, 2018). One of these injustices is the plight of persons with disability which is an issue of importance in the social work profession and thus deserving of more light to be shed on it to create a more socially just and fair world. I believe that as a profession that has for years been at the centre of promoting human rights and supporting people to realize their full potential, there is no better time than now for us to re-energize our collective effort and pour into tackling key issues both at a local and community level and then internationally. Now more than ever, there is a dire need to reorient and recreate what social work approaches, methods, and practices are, and their absorption and compatibility with the African context and indigenous communities (Ibrahima & Mattaini, 2019). This I think is essential. Incorporating the lived experiences of persons in local contexts as a resource and entry point for interventions and approaches is, I feel, much needed to enhance ownership and continuity of the work even after the social worker's input. This is the critical issue of social sustainability.

Reflective Questions

1. What does the term 'healing journey' mean to you?
2. In what ways do you currently feel social work is both a gift and a burden?
3. What lessons does Gloria's story teach us about who is responsible for what?
4. What is the difference for you (if any) between disability and dis Ability?

REFERENCES

ACPF (African Child Policy Forum). (2011). *Children with Disabilities in Uganda: The Hidden Reality*. Addis Ababa: African Child Policy Forum

Aissetu, B., & Mattani, M. (2017). Social work in Africa: Decolonizing methodologies and approaches. International Social Work, *62*(2), 799–813

Bride, B. (2007). Prevalence of secondary traumatic stress among social workers. *Social Work*, *52*(1), 63–70.

Cherry, K. (2023). What is attachment theory? How early emotional bonds shape our hearts. *verywellmind*, www.verywellmind.com/what-is-attachment-theory-2795337.

Disabled World. (2018, 26 November). Disability news: Africa and South Africa. www.disabled-world.com/news/africa.

Ibrahima, A. B., & Mattaini, M. A. (2019). Social work in Africa: Decolonizing methodologies and approaches. *International Social Work*, *62*(2), 799–813.

International Dyslexia Association. (n.d.). Definition of dyslexia. https://dyslexiaida.org/definition-of-dyslexia

(2014). *Examiner December 2014*. https://eida.org/examiner-december-2014

Martin, E., Myers,K., and Brickman, K.. (2020), Self-preservation in the work-place: The importance of well-being for social work practitioners and field supervisors. *Social Work*, *65*(1), 74–81.

Ministry of Planning and Community Development. (1965). Sessional Paper No.21957/58, Kampala.

National Council for Persons with Disabilities. (2019). Disability Status Report. www.ncpd.go.ug/publication/disability-status-report-2019.

Palattiyil, G., et al. (2018). Reclaiming international social work in the context of the Global Agenda for Social Work and Social Development: Some critical reflections. *International Social Work*, *62*(3), 1043–54

Twikirize, J. (2014). Social work education and practice in Uganda: A historical perspective. In H. Spitzer, J. Twikirize, & G. G. Wairire (eds.), *Professional Social Work in East Africa: Towards Social Development, Poverty Reduction and Gender Equality*, 136–48. Kampala: Fountain.

UBOS (Uganda Bureau of Statistics). (2018). *Uganda National Household Survey 2016/2017*. Kampala: UBOS.

UNICEF. (2014). *Research Study on Children Living with Disabilities Living in Uganda: Situational Analysis on the Rights of Children with Disabilities in Uganda*. http://rodra.co.za/images/countries/uganda/research/Research%20children%20with%20disabilities%20in%20Uganda.pdf.

Uwezo. (2016). *Are Our Children Learning? Uwezo Uganda 6th Learning Assessment Report 2016*. Kampala: Twaweza East Africa.

WHO & World Bank. (2011) *World Report on Disability 2011*. Geneva: World Health Organization. www.who.int/publications/i/item/9789241564182.

Photo: Hilde Mjøs

CHAPTER 5

Dreams, Reality, and Invisibility
Social Workers Unpacking Child Labour through Children's Stories in Urban and Rural Maharashtra, India

Yamini Suvarna and Vikas Sawant

Introduction

Child labour is a global issue. Despite efforts to end child labour that span nearly two decades, recent trends indicate that there has been no significant reduction in this domain since 2016. Global data compiled in 2020 puts child labour at nearly 160 million (63 million girls and 97 million boys; ILO and UNICEF, 2021). Family-based labour – in agriculture in the rural areas or in micro-enterprise in urban areas – is fast becoming a common form of work for children. Global estimates indicate that 83 per cent of working children, aged between five and eleven years, are engaged in labour within the family, in farms or family micro-enterprises (ILO and UNICEF, 2021). Poverty is both a cause and consequence of child labour. Most children who are engaged in work belong to socially and economically marginalized groups. Children who work lose out on education and the opportunity to realize their full potential. They continue to be trapped in the intergenerational cycle of poverty and economic exploitation.

Data on child labour or working children in India comes from the Government of India Census which is conducted every ten years. Data from the last Census conducted in 2011 shows that India has 4.35 million children who are engaged in work. The stories in this chapter are located in the state of Maharashtra, which has nearly 0.73 million working children, making it one of the five states that contribute close to 55 per cent of the working children population in the country; 35 per cent of the child workers in Maharashtra are from the districts of Thane, Nashik, Mumbai Suburban, Pune, and Jalgaon. The state has seen a slight decrease in the numbers of working children, from 0.76 million in 2001 to 0.73 million in 2011 (Census of India, n.d.).

The ILO UNICEF *Child Labour* report (2021) revealed that *more than a quarter of children aged five to eleven and over a third of children aged twelve to fourteen who are in child labour are out of school.* Nearly 18 million children (seven to seventeen years) in India, mostly girls (65 per cent) and in rural areas (79 per cent), are inactive, neither working nor attending school (Khan & Lyon, 2015). The likelihood of these girls being involved in domestic chores or caring for other family members is high. However, few survey tools, if any, include domestic chores and related tasks in their definition of work. The fact that these girls are excluded from the school-going children's data and the working children's data makes them invisible and leaves them open to exploitation.

India does have laws to prevent and regulate child labour. The 2016 Amendment to the Child and Adolescent Labour (Prohibition and Regulation) Act 1986 (CLPRA), prohibits a child below the age of fourteen years from being *employed or permitted to work in any occupation or process.* The only exception to this is when the child *helps his family or family enterprise, which is other than any hazardous occupations or processes set forth in the Schedule, after his/her school hours or during vacations.* It clearly states that *no such work under this clause shall affect the school education of the child* (Section 3). Rule 2Ba of the Child Labour Rules 2017 restricts the number of hours that a child (under fourteen years of age) can work to a maximum of three hours (vi) and prohibits a child from working between 7 pm and 8 am (iv). It also stresses that the work should not affect the child's attendance in school, and/or his/her ability to complete any other activity linked to education *such as homework or any extra-curricular activity assigned to him by the school* (v) nor be *detrimental to the growth, education and overall development of the child* (2Bb).

The stories here attempt to examine the different aspects of child labour and try to unpack what the lives of working children actually entail.

Putting Ourselves on the Page

We, Vikas and Yamini, have been working with children for nearly thirty years. While Vikas has been playing more of an activist role, Yamini focuses on researching and writing on issues related to children. Over the years, we have interacted with many children; their lives have touched and impacted our lives. Vikas, in particular, has worked in so many situations but one period that stands out in his memory is the ten years between 2004 and 2015 when he worked closely to rescue child workers and reunite them with their families. During this period, Vikas and his team were successful in rescuing between 60,000 and 70,000 child workers from many states across India, including Maharashtra, Delhi, Gujarat, Rajasthan, Karnataka, Uttar Pradesh, Madhya Pradesh, Andhra Pradesh.

Identifying and rescuing the children with the support of the police was only the tip of the proverbial iceberg. Reuniting them with their families and ensuring that they did not come back to work was the bigger challenge. Working closely with the different state governments, we created many programmes and schemes to help children stay in their villages and continue their education. The residential schools that were started in the state of Bihar are one such example. These schools catered to families who were unable to afford to educate their children. When provided with a viable and safe option for their children, parents were more than willing to send their children to school.

The massive raids and rescues along with the emerging challenges of reintegration and rehabilitation of the rescued children led to amendments in the Child and Adolescent Labour (Prohibition and Regulation) Act 1986. The new Child and Adolescent Labour (Prohibition and Regulation) Amendment Act 2016 reinforced the Right of Children to Free and Compulsory Education Act of 2009 by prohibiting the employment of children under the age of fourteen in any occupation or process (Raj, 2018). However, the 2016 Act came with a caveat: a child was allowed to work to help family or in-family enterprises that are non-hazardous, after school hours, or during vacations. Children were also allowed to work as artists in the audio-video entertainment industry provided such work did not affect the child's school education. This new definition of child labour put a new perspective on the entire issue of children and their work, resulting in the evolution of new approaches by civil society and non-government organizations to deal with children who work.

Our years of work with children and their families led us to believe that child labour is a serious social problem which is extremely challenging to eradicate despite the consistent efforts of government and non-government bodies. Poverty and insufficient employment opportunities for unskilled adults are two of the causal factors, as are social and cultural norms, such as caste-based discrimination and gender bias which perpetuate child labour in certain communities. Insufficient access to schools is also a contributing factor. The paucity of reliable data is yet another challenge. Data released by international organizations like the International Labour Organization rarely match that of the Indian government, in part due to differing definitions of child workers.

Despite the laws that are in place, children in India continue to work, sometimes paid, sometimes unpaid; sometimes visible, invisibly at other times and across a range of sectors such as agriculture, manufacturing, sales, domestic work, in construction, and in the entertainment industry.

Children work along with parents in the agricultural sector, sometimes in work that could be dangerous to them such as harvesting crops using sharp implements, applying chemical pesticides, grazing, and raising livestock. Those who work in small-scale industries such as textile and mat weaving work long hours with low wages. Child domestic workers are often invisible since they are employed in residences which are difficult for outsiders to access. Landlessness and insufficient employment opportunities lead many families to migrate in search of seasonal work. Children who migrate with their parents for such work often end up working with their parents. Sectors of seasonal work include brick kilns, stone quarries, agricultural labour for harvesting a variety of crops including sugarcane and cotton, as well as construction work.

While education is essential, and we have seen that children who are in schools are less likely to work full-time, it is equally important to address societal perceptions around children. Despite growing awareness regarding child participation, most adults see children as incapable of taking decisions related to their day-to-day lives. Children are viewed as extensions of their parents who are perceived as being best placed to take decisions for them. Children are rarely asked what they want or how they feel. When we interact with children, we take the time to ask them what they want, what they would like to do. Most hesitate initially but the ideas that flow and the joy that the children feel on being asked their views and having their views listened to, being respected, is always an incredible feeling. Our work has shown us that children who work are not a homogeneous group, they cannot be treated as one. As the stories in this chapter show, each child has his or her distinctive story. Solutions for children too need to be curated as per the needs and requirements of each child and are often developed by the children themselves. Through these stories, we seek to give voice to these usually invisible and voiceless children, to give you a glimpse of their lives and to help you understand the changing face of working children in Maharashtra, India.

The stories in this chapter have been harvested from our field visit diaries. Vikas and I go to different parts of Maharashtra as part of the various projects on which we have worked. We interact with children and their families during these visits and document their stories. We ask them if they are willing to share their stories, and if they are okay with these stories being presented in reports and articles. We assure them that we will not reveal their names and make sure that their identities remain hidden. Their stories are written in our diaries only after we get their oral consent and later used in the project reports. Sometimes, we meet children and families who are not directly part of the projects and programmes on which we are working. Yet, they want to be heard, they want to share their life experiences. We ask if we can write their stories down, not to be included in the project reports but to be used for teaching, learning, and maybe in print at some point in time. When they agree, we note down their stories. All the stories in this chapter are the second type of stories.

The Stories

Rani's Story: Dreaming of Being an Entrepreneur

Rani is a ten-year-old girl. She lives in a slum community in Mumbai, close to one of the many dumping grounds that dot the city. None of the houses in her community have toilets. Rani and everyone else who lives there have to use communal toilets. Drinking water also has to be bought. Rani's day starts early: usually at about 5:30 am. She helps her mother before going to school at 7 am. Though her school is close, Rani and her friends have to cross a junction – a busy main road even early in the morning. Her school ends at about 1 pm and that's when things change.

Rani's plaits fly as she hurries home from school, down the narrow 'by-lanes' of her community. Her eyes shine with excitement as she speaks: "Didi (elder sister), today I am going to make mutter Maggi (instant noodles with peas). I will sell one cup for Rs. 5 and if I sell 5 cups, I will be able to make cheese Maggi tomorrow." Rani's enthusiasm brightens the small 150 square feet room (14 square metres) she calls home. She rushes into the kitchen space, which consists of a tiled counter-top with a gas stove, a pot of water, and some utensils on it. The kitchen space is not really separate from the living space, which is converted into the sleeping area at night. Rani shares her home with her parents, three siblings, and grandmother. Rani's words trip over each other as she fills a saucepan with water and places it on the gas stove. "I started with simple Maggi," she says. "I needed money for a notebook – it cost Rs 20 and I had only Rs 10. I bought a packet of Maggi, asked the chacha (uncle) who runs the tea stall for five cups. I told him that I wanted to sell Maggi in the cups to get money for a notebook. He gave me 5 cups for free. I made Maggi and sold each cup for Rs 3. I got a profit of Rs 5 in the first day," Rani grinned as she spoke. "That was one year ago. Now, I make and sell Maggi every day. I make different types and sell at different rates. Since my cup of Maggi costs less than Rs 5, it is the same cost as a pack of wafers and more filling. Cheese or mutter Maggi costs more but I make those only once a week. If they wait for it, the children are more eager to buy it." Rani's wise words reflect her understanding of supply and demand. She has been selling Maggi noodles to her classmates for over a year. She maintains a limited stock and even takes orders if someone wants something different. Rani has big dreams, her eyes shine with confidence. She wants to study, become a teacher and make a difference. The cups of Maggi she sells help her do so. Although Rani does not come under the legal definition of a child labourer, she is one of the many working children in urban Maharashtra, but in her case she is an entrepreneur, showing skills worthy of someone with management qualifications.

Sirju's Story: A Life Where the Cane Is Not So Sweet

A deep yet sharp sound cuts through the stillness of the night. It is barely 3 am and the first alarm has sounded. Time for fourteen-year-old Sirju and other sugarcane harvesters to wake up. The tiny hutment in which Sirju and his ten-year-old brother sleep has barely enough room for Sirju to stretch.

Sirju along with his father and younger brother have come to Solapur, a district in Maharashtra. They belong to a small hamlet in another district within Maharashtra. Every year, they migrate to Solapur to harvest sugarcane. Sirju's mother usually comes with them, but this year she is unwell and has stayed back in their village.

They live in an open field, in temporary hutments made of asbestos sheets, plastic, and sugarcane sheaves. Unseasonal rainfall had resulted in waterlogging and the grounds on which the temporary hutments were erected are damp. There is no access to basic amenities such as potable water, sanitation facilities, and electricity. Most families, including Sirju's, fill water from one of two black syntax tanks provided by the sugar factory management and store it in open containers.

Sirju's workday is long – they leave at 4 am on bullock carts or tractors and head to the sugarcane fields where they cut the sugarcane till late noon, under a hot sun. It is tiring, backbreaking, non-stop work. The day's harvest is loaded onto the bullock carts, and they return to the open fields where they stay. After resting for a short while, it is time to cook dinner. Most families cook only once a day and eat the leftovers the next day.

Sirju and his family stay in an open field near the sugar factory for nearly six months. The factory management runs a school for the children who migrate seasonally with their parents. Sirju's younger brother attends this school. In the past years, Sirju also attended school. This year, however, things are different. Two of the members of the *toli* (a group of sugarcane harvesters) decided that sugarcane harvesting was not for them and left. Sirju's father, who was the link between the *toli* and the factory management, was left to plug the slack. He took on the role of one of the missing harvesters and put Sirju to work in place of the other.

The dynamics of sugarcane harvesting are complex. The sugarcane harvesters are neither direct employees of the factory nor are they contracted by the factory. The factory gives the responsibility for collecting the harvesters to a *mukaddam* (contractor). The contractor collects a *toli* of about fifteen pairs of workers. Sugarcane harvesting ideally requires two people – known as a *koyta* in Marathi. Fifteen *koytas* make up a *toli* (a troop). The details of the *toli* are sent to an employee of the sugar factory known as an agriculture officer. The agriculture officer visits the villages and verifies the composition of the *tolis*. After this visit, each of the pairs or *koyta* in the *toli* is given an advance that ranges from GBP 710/USD 907 to GBP 950/USD 1210, which is later adjusted against the quantum of sugarcane harvested. The large lump sum advance acts as a 'carrot' drawing many families into the never-ending cycle of seasonal harvesting. Most *koytas* do not manage to harvest the needed quantum of sugarcane to pay off the advance that they get. Towards the end of the season, children are drawn into the harvesting to minimize the 'carry-forward of the advance'. Although seen as a voluntary employment option, often by both the contractor and the *koytas*, the inability to 'repay the advance' with the sugarcane harvested forces them into a cycle of migration which is often intergenerational, with the children becoming part of the family workforce (for repayment of debt) and growing up to become seasonal migrants themselves.

Sirju and his family are dimly aware of this. They are also worried about Sirju's education. Year 9 is an important one, the one before the SSC exams (equivalent to O levels), and Sirju is missing out on this crucial year. Sirju's dark eyes reflect this worry – he is not sure how he will cope with his education if he misses six months of school. "I try to study at night," he says, "but usually I am too tired. I fall asleep over my book." His younger brother's eyes fill with tears, and he says with a slight tremble in his voice, "I ask the teachers to give him *dada's* (elder brother) work. They write it out for me. But he is too tired to read it most of the days."

Technically, Sirju is not a child labourer – he has no employer, he is not on anyone's payroll, he does not have a contract. The Right to Education Act provides for free and compulsory education for all children up to the age of fourteen years, till they complete Year 8. Sirju who is fourteen years and in Year 9, does not come under the purview of this act either. Like many other children from seasonal migrant families, Sirju is invisible even though he is in plain sight.

Krishna's Story of Chilli Work

Sundari is an eleven-year-old girl of medium height. Her family comprises her elder brother Krishna, younger brother Nagesh, and parents. They live in Dhadgaon, a remote village in Shahada taluka of Nandurbar district in Maharashtra, India. Krishna and his siblings are doubly disadvantaged – they are poor, landless, and belong to a nomadic tribe. Sundari's father Raja is not yet forty years old, yet looks wizened due to his hard life, while her mother Sakhubai is around thirty years old. Their lined faces and thin bodies make them look older than they are.

For many years, their occupation involved wandering through the forest, collecting *moha* flowers and extracting liquor from them. Their sustenance came from the sale of this homemade liquor. They would also collect fallen or broken branches to sell as firewood. Rarely did they cut any trees or chop branches. Being tribals, they respect and live in harmony with nature, taking only what is essential without causing any harm. "I did odd jobs, manual labour when I got a chance, it gave us money for our needs," Raja explained, "but it was never enough."

Sundari along with Krishna and Nagesh attended the village school near their tribal hamlet or *pada* as it is known locally. They did not attend regularly because they often went to forage in the forest with their parents. "I liked going to school, we all did. What the teacher said sometimes was bouncer (went over my head) but I didn't mind. It was fun, going to school, I never liked to miss school," Sundari recalled with a wistful sigh.

But things never stay the same, things always change. Raja got a job, in a chilli factory in the city of Nandurbar, 64 kilometres away from his home. The job was a seasonal one, starting in November and ending in May. The hilly terrain meant that the 64 kilometre journey took over three hours each way. "Going up and down for so long every day was not possible. So, we all went with baba for six months, to Nandurbar," Sundari narrated.

"I thought it was good, we got some money in advance, helped us eat," Raja added. "The work was very hard with long hours and the money was not always enough. But it was more than what we made by selling mora flower liquor."

The work was very difficult. The red chillies had to be dried, nearly baked under a hot sun. The red chillies were spread on sheets early in the day and had to be turned around frequently to make sure that they dried evenly. As Sundari and her siblings did not attend school in the city, Raja suggested that they help with drying the chillies. They were expected to dry 20 to 25 tons of chillies in a day. This meant that all six of the family members were engaged for nearly twelve hours every day, spreading the chillies, turning them around frequently, collecting them after about six hours, removing the stalks of the dry chillies, and repeating the entire process the next day. Many times, Sundari and her brothers felt like their bodies were on fire due to the heat of the chillies. "We missed my village, the mountains, the forests, the rivers and most of all our friends. I missed school. But what to do?" eight-year-old Nagesh stated sadly. "Aai would put oil on our bodies to make us feel better. But my heart used to hurt me."

"My brother Krishna, he was unable to breathe, his nose was burning. Aai put oil and did many more things. But the fire in his nose did not get less. Baba took him to the doctor. He gave something. Krishna felt better but then one day, he became very ill. Doctor said Krishna had chilli fever. And then in two days . . ." Sundari stops, unable to speak about her brother who passed away. Too young, too suddenly, too devastating.

"I was the reason that my son died. I wanted to die," Raja takes up the story. "I was on the way to end my life, when an elder from my village stopped me. He made me remember that I had a wife and two other children. I had to live."

Raja continues: "*The people of* our *village* were shocked to hear this. One spoke to an NGO that works in our village. *The* people from the NGO got all the people in our village together to find out how many families went for chilli work. They met the teachers, village elders and others to discuss this. Finally, the village came together to work out alternatives for *children* from families that went for chilli work. The children were allowed to stay in the school. Breakfast and dinner are provided at the school. Soap, oil, notebooks are also given. The teachers helped in this. Youth from the village were trained by the NGO and they helped look after the children. We lost Krishna, but today twelve children including Sundari and Nagesh stay in the village when we parents go for chilli work. My Krishna lives on in their smiles and their dreams."

Suraj's Story and the Tapestry of Life

Eleven-year-old Suraj was excited. He was finally going home. Although the train had picked up speed, he felt it was running slowly. Nearly fourteen to fifteen hours had passed since his train had left the city of Mumbai. Suraj looked out of the window, seeing villages and towns rushing by, moving slowly but surely towards his home state of Bihar. Looking around, Suraj saw the same excitement in the eyes of his thirteen other companions. All of them were aged between nine and twelve years. Some were jostling each other to look out of the windows. Some were talking softly to each other about seeing their parents after so long, others were trying to work out how many hours were left before they reached home. Every child was happy, joyful almost. Suraj felt that the train was saying "going home, going home" and not the usual chug chug. The sense of happiness was new to many of the children, a kind of alien yet pleasant feeling – after all, they had been surrounded by so much unhappiness and suffering over the past two years.

Suraj looked at the smiling face of the social worker seated next to him. The thirteen children were accompanied by three social workers who had been by their side for most of the time since they had been rescued. Memories of a previous train journey crowded into Suraj's mind, threatening to overwhelm him. Suraj decided to speak to the social worker about what was going on in his mind, "Sir, two years ago, we all came to Mumbai by train like this. We were very happy because we were going to see a big city like Mumbai. But for the past two years, I didn't see anything. We were working and working in a small (15 × 10 square feet) dark room. No windows, no breeze, only glaring lights and a noisy fan. We had to keep on working – 10–12 hours without a break. Even when I broke my hand, I had to work." Suraj grimaced. "How was I supposed to do embroidery with a broken hand?" he asked, the horror of those days still too close to put behind him. "Our eyes used to pain, our backs would pain, but did they listen?"

The social worker patted Suraj on his back and gave him some juice to drink. Suraj drank a few sips and continued, "In those two years, the only time we went out of that room was to go to the toilet. The public toilets where we met you and the other social workers. We were so lucky we met you and we could escape."

Suraj was one of the luckier children. Some of the children in the group had been sexually abused by the adult workers. There was no one they could complain to, no one with whom they could share their pain. The payment that the children received for the backbreaking fine embroidery work was a pittance (about GBP 4.75/USD 6 per month). "Do you think my parents received the money every month?" Suraj asked the social worker. "My employer was known to my father. He promised my father that he would send me to school but he never did. We just stayed locked in one room all the time."

The journey continued; the children were happy to move around freely even in the confines of a railway train carriage. After reaching Bihar, the children were escorted to their villages by the social workers. Two other boys were from the same village as Suraj. On reaching home, one of them, a nine-year-old boy, flew into his parents' arms, all of them crying and laughing at the same time. The other boy's parents did not know where he had gone. He had been abducted and his parents had given up hope of ever seeing their son again. As for Suraj, the ear-to-ear grin on his face and the happiness on the faces of his parents tell their own story.

Today Suraj has completed his graduation. He is a state-level Kabaddi player. Suraj spends his spare time teaching and playing with the children of his village. He is determined to not let any other child go through what he did.

Tina and Lata's Story and Dreams of Homes

"Come on Tina, hurry up. Miss is getting late." Lata pulls her friend along. Both girls are in a hurry to catch up with their teacher before she leaves. They have already changed out of their school uniforms which are now neatly packed in two separate bags. Their teacher is waiting for them near the school gate. She collects their school bags and the bags containing the uniforms. "Thank you, Miss! See you at 6:30 tomorrow morning" the girls say. The teacher smiles, nods, and leaves.

Tina and Lata slowly make their way home, planning how to spend the afternoon. They cross the busy main road and turn right to pass under the flyover that is being constructed. They walk down the underpass till they reach their homes. Home for Tina and Lata is temporary and made of asbestos sheets, with a plastic roof. It is tiny, and has just enough space for four persons to sit and have a meal. Tina and Lata are neighbours. Their shacks are next to each other, in a broader part of the underpass. All members sleep outside their homes, on the pavement. Since the flyover is under construction, no vehicular traffic is allowed here and so they are able to sleep in peace at night. "It's not too bad," says Tina. "Unless it rains," adds Lata. "Yes, when it rains it is horrible. The ground is cold and wet, our blankets get wet and everything all muddy."

After a quick lunch, Tina and Lata change into their work clothes. Their tiny homes have an even tinier space enclosed by a sheet strung as a curtain. This serves as a private space to change clothes. Tina and Lata wear old shabby salwar kameez which are probably a couple of sizes too big for them. They rub some soot to make their faces look grimy. "Our mothers say that it is safer this way," they chorus. "We can dress up and look nice in the evenings, when we are close to our houses." They collect a bag each from their mothers and make their way to the expressway. While walking, they peek in the bags to see the items they are expected to sell. These range from strings of flowers (for the hair) to small items made of beads or even packets of sticker *bindis.* Sometimes they are given fresh flowers, these sell more easily. Other times they are given bunches of pens. On Saturdays, they sell lemons strung with green chillies to ward off the evil eye. They stop near the traffic signal on the expressway and exchange greetings with other children who are already waiting there. Once the signal turns red and the vehicles stop, Tina and Lata, along with the other children, expertly weave in and out between the cars, cajoling the passengers to buy their wares. Tina and Lata are often separated by the cars, but they keep an eye on each other – standing instructions from both their mothers. A couple of hours later, having sold all their wares, Tina and Lata are ready to return as are most of the children. They give their parents most of the money they earn, keeping about 20 per cent for themselves. "We buy earrings and pretty things," says Tina. "And top up our phones when we can," Lata grins.

Tina and Lata are a growing tribe of working children who live with their families in street situations. Some, like Tina and Lata, have been enrolled in schools with the support of local NGOs. The NGO helped get them passes to the local community washrooms where Tina and Lata bathe every morning before going to school at 7 am. Tina and Lata are the lucky ones who get to go to school. Many children who live with their families on the streets of cities like Mumbai do not have any identity documents, which prevents them from accessing education and health services, as well as any other welfare schemes. They spend their time on the streets, usually without any adult supervision, which puts them at risk of abuse and exploitation. Some homes are merely two sheets of cloth slung between two lamp-poles. I asked Lata and Tina what their dreams are: "A house, with doors, windows, walls and a roof," says Tina. "With a bathroom so I can stay clean always," adds Lata. "Where we are free to be ourselves," they both add.

Ending Child Labour: What Can We as Social Workers Do?

The stories of the children in this chapter, although different, have a common thread running through them. Children like Rani and Suraj belong to the Scheduled Castes (also known as Dalits, previously known as untouchables); Sirju, Tina, and Lata to Scheduled Tribes; while Krishna and his siblings are part of the Nomadic Tribes, who as the name implies are traditionally iterant tribals moving from one place to another, sustaining themselves by foraging in the forests. All of them are from landless families, families who left their villages in search of livelihood options which were simply not available at home. Mr Gilbert F. Houngbo, ILO Director-General, in his statement at the World Day against Child Labour, pointed out that "ending discrimination" was essential as children from "marginalized groups" were more vulnerable to child labour. He added that "The antidote to poverty-driven child labour is decent work for adults, so they can support their families and send their children to school, not to work," and highlighted the fact that one of the primary causes of child labour is the lack of social justice. Appropriately enough, the theme for this year's World Day against Child Labour is "Social Justice for All, End Child Labour" (Houngbo, 2023).

This brings us to the central question: How do we as social workers promote social justice and use it to reduce child labour? To us, social justice is an integral aspect of a rights framework. Viewing the rights framework through the lens of social justice will only serve to strengthen it.

To us, access, equity, and participation (Figure 5) are central to social justice. Child rights is not merely a framework for social justice, but is also the golden thread that links and holds these central concepts together. Access focuses on ensuring that children from the marginalized and most vulnerable families avail of their rights to survival, development, participation, and protection. This can be done by promoting their access to quality services of health, nutrition, education, and by providing their parents access to opportunities for decent and viable employment. Equity ensures that priority is given to those whose rights are at greatest risk of being violated, to those who need these services most, and that special programmes and services are created for them where needed. Participation is of course a right in itself, giving marginalized groups a voice and a choice, an opportunity for self-determination and decision-making. All three are closely interlinked and true participation cannot occur if access and equity are absent.

The 2030 Agenda for Sustainable Development echoes this as it places child rights at the centre of the Sustainable Development Goals and advocates the use of a child-rights-based approach for achieving these goals. Child labour is explicitly targeted in Sustainable Development Goal 8.7:

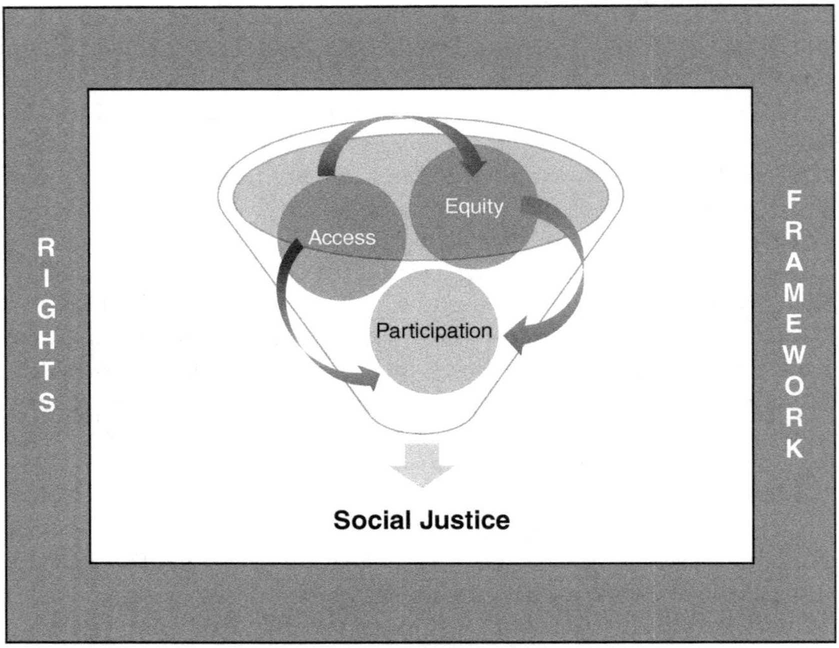

Figure 5 Social justice and a rights framework

> Take immediate and effective measures to eradicate forced labour, end modern slavery and human trafficking and secure the prohibition and elimination of the worst forms of child labour, including recruitment and use of child soldiers, and by 2025 end child labour in all its forms. (United Nations, n.d.)

The principle of 'leaving no one behind' which is fundamental to the SDGs means ensuring that no child misses out on their rights such as those to play, for recreation, to access services of education, nutrition, and health. This implies that the challenge before social workers is to ensure that all children, and especially the last mile children, have all the opportunities that they need to fulfil their true potential and develop into the person they are meant to be. One way to achieve this is through social protection. Realizing the urgency and importance of social protection in achieving the SDGs, the World Bank and International Labour Organization jointly initiated a Universal Social Protection by 2023 (USP 2030) Mission in 2016 to fulfil SDG 1.3, which is to:

> Implement nationally appropriate social protection systems and measures for all, including floors, and by 2030 achieve substantial coverage of the poor and the vulnerable. (USP 2030, n.d.)

It is important to develop social protection systems that are inclusive, well-planned, and promote the realization of fundamental rights. These not only reduce vulnerabilities of children but also relieve some of the negative effects on their physical and mental health, well-being, and development. The Office of the High Commissioner for Human Rights is of the view that inclusive social protection is integral to creating societies that are "resilient and child rights-compliant" (OHCHR, 2023). Yet, nearly three quarters of children globally have no access to social protection (ILO & UNICEF, 2022; OHCHR, 2023). Even where social protections are available, most are neither designed with children in mind nor are they meant to prevent child labour. Moreover, the quality and reach of these schemes are usually limited (ILO & UNICEF, 2022). This is also true of India, where only 24.2 per cent of children are covered by at least one social protection system and approximately 2.4 per cent of the country's GDP is spent on public social protection (ILO, 2021).

A global review of social protection schemes and policies by ILO and UNICEF (2022) reveals that although cash transfers can and do have a positive effect on reducing children's participation in economic activities (p.34), programmes with specific focus on indicators and outcomes related to children "are more effective in addressing child labour" (p.37). It pointed out that although in-kind transfers, such as midday meals in schools, help in the reduction of child labour, these are not as effective as "cash transfers of similar amounts, which allow more flexible expenditure" (p.38). Integrated social protection programmes, or "cash plus" programmes as these are known, showed mixed effects that differed based on the nature and quality of the additional intervention/programme (p.40). The report refers to three studies conducted on India's Mahatma Gandhi National Rural Employment Guarantee Act (MGNREGA) that reported increased children's participation in economic activities (p.42) and indicated that while adolescent girls take on greater household responsibilities, boys of a similar age tend to take up paid work outside the home (p.42). When the work offered through public employment programmes like the MGNREGA is related to agricultural work, the likelihood of children "substituting for adult farm work" increases (p.42).

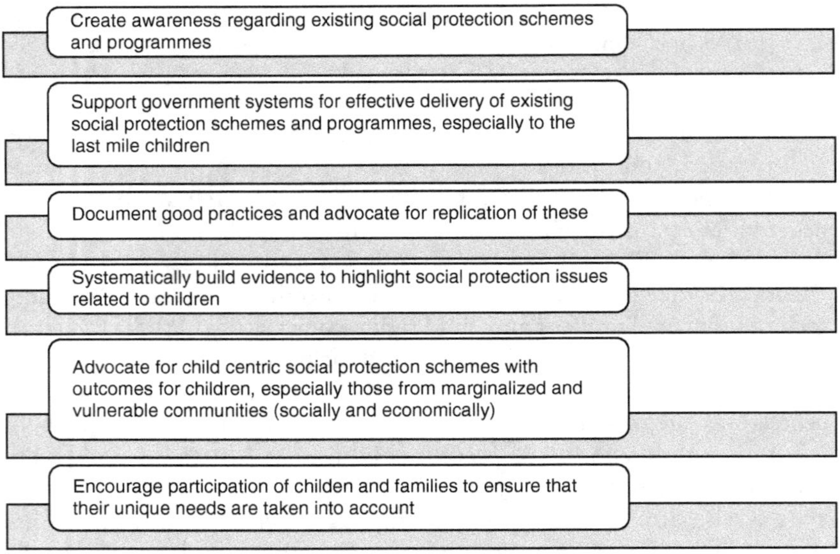

Figure 6 Action points for social workers

The complexity of the issue of child labour makes responding to it a challenge. However, our experience shows that when government systems and non-governmental organizations come together, they are able to create an ecosystem that places children at the heart of all programming. Figure 6 is a call to action for social workers.

Social protection systems, programmes, and policies cannot be static; they need to be modified and reviewed to reflect the evolving realities within which children and families live. Additionally, social protection needs to be universal and inclusive, reaching out to the most vulnerable, last mile children who face the greatest risk of child labour. Yet, at the same time, the systems need to sensitive to the needs and requirements of individual children and their families. A bouquet of social protection schemes and services which can be rearranged for specific circumstances may well be the way forward. Periodic monitoring and review of the social protection policies and programmes to ensure that they respond to and reflect ground realities (including crisis situations) are essential for improvement and upscaling. In all these processes, we as social workers play a critical role. We are best placed to act – our hearts are engaged in the field with children and families while our heads are with the policy-makers.

Reflective Questions

1. Reflect on the intersectionality of poverty and child labour as highlighted in the story. How do social and economic factors contribute to the perpetuation of child labour globally?
2. Considering the complexities of defining child labour, particularly concerning domestic chores and family-based work, how might this ambiguity impact efforts to address and eradicate child labour effectively?
3. Reflect on social constructs around children and childhood to develop actions that can give voices to children who are usually unheard and unseen. What are these constructs?
4. Think about actions that social workers can undertake to maintain a balance between promoting social protection of the most vulnerable groups of children while ensuring the agency of children and families. What would be priority actions for you?
5. Considering the diversity of experiences among working children, how can policies and interventions be tailored to meet the specific needs of individual children and their families?
6. Keeping in mind the attitude of society where a large number of people prefer to turn a blind eye to child labour, what can social workers do to evolve a society where the duty of care for children is the responsibility of every adult, regardless of whether the child is part of his/her family?
7. Reflect on the challenges faced in the reintegration and rehabilitation of rescued child workers, as discussed in the story. What strategies and initiatives could be implemented to support these children and prevent them from returning to work?

REFERENCES

Census of India. (n.d.). Census tables. https://censusindia.gov.in/census.website/data/census-tables (accessed 17 September 2023).

Child and Adolescent Labour (Prohibition and Regulation) Act 1986.

Houngbo, G. F. (2023, 12 June). To bring social justice to all we must end child labour. International Labour Organization. https://ilo.org/global/about-the-ilo/how-the-ilo-works/ilo-director-general/statements-and-speeches/WCMS_884696/lang–en/index.htm (accessed 17 September 2023).

ILO (International Labour Organization). (2021). World social protection data dashboard. www.social-protection.org/gimi/WSPDB.action?id=13 (accessed 17 September 2023).

ILO & UNICEF. (2021). *Child Labour: Global Estimates 2020, Trends and the Road Forward.* New York: International Labour Organization and UNICEF. www.ilo.org/wcmsp5/groups/public/—ed_norm/—ipec/documents/publication/wcms_797515.pdf (accessed 17 September 2023)

(2022) *The Role of Social Protection in the Elimination of Child Labour: Evidence Review and Policy Implications.* Geneva and Florence: International Labour Organization and UNICEF. www.ilo.org/wcmsp5/groups/public/—ed_norm/—ipec/documents/publication/wcms_845168.pdf (accessed 17 September 2023).

Khan, S. R., & Lyon, S. (2015). *Measuring Children's Work in South Asia: Perspectives from National Household Surveys.* Geneva: International Labour Organization. www.ilo.org/wcmsp5/groups/public/—asia/—ro-bangkok/—sro-new_delhi/documents/publication/wcms_359371.pdf (accessed 17 September 2023).

OHCHR. (2023). *Rights of the Child and Inclusive Social Protection: Report of the United Nations High Commissioner for Human Rights.* Geneva: Office of the High Commissioner for Human Rights. www.ohchr.org/en/documents/thematic-reports/ahrc5436-rights-child-and-inclusive-social-protection-report-united (accessed 17 September 2023).

Raj, K. (2018). Child labour in India with special reference to Child and Adolescent Labour (Prohibition & Regulation) Amendment Act 2016. *Editor's Desk*, 220.

United Nations. (n.d.). Goal 8: Promote sustained, inclusive and sustainable economic growth, full and productive employment and decent work for all. https://sdgs.un.org/goals/goal8 (accessed 19 September 2023).

USP 2030. (n.d.). Global Partnership for Universal Social Protection to Achieve the Sustainable Development Goals. https://usp2030.org (accessed 19 September 2023).

Photo: Hilde Mjøs

CHAPTER 6

Who Do I Want to Be as a Social Worker?

Perspectives from the Arctic Region

Rita Sørly, Raymond Stuen, Ingvild Kristoffersen, and Sunniva Hestsveen

There are many reasons to become a social worker. People often explain their choice based on childhood or family backgrounds or on experiences related to education or work. Others have been influenced by significant individuals or have come to the profession by coincidences. As someone who teaches social work to students, I often miss stories related to mattering in social work. How do the fundamental values of social work affect the student's choice of becoming a social worker? In a changing and chaotic world, with fake news, pandemic, and ongoing war, why is it important to be a social worker? Why is it important for these young people I teach? What are their hopes and dreams as a social worker, and why do they want to use their life to practise this profession?

In this chapter, three students share their stories on why they want to become a social worker. Raymond, Ingvild, and Sunniva are bachelor students in child welfare services at UiT The Arctic University of Norway. At the time of their written stories, they were in their second year, and they were preparing for a future social work practice in Norway somewhere. The stories touch the very core of their hopes and dreams, intertwined with what they understand as the values of caring about others through the practice of social work. Their stories are reminders for practitioners of being ethically conscious while meeting people who need our open hands, our ability to be present in what may be difficult, and our desire for dialogue and interaction.

In the following, I will present another story first; namely the story of how these stories from the students were born. In other words, I will present the 'teacher story', and the pedagogical reflections related to the lectures that were given when the students' stories were written. A section on mattering in social work education is presented. I write a few words about brave spaces. Thereafter, I will give the reader the possibility to read each of the students' stories and offer some reflections in relation to these.

In the end, I will present some thoughts about stories, and the capabilities of social work education-that-matters and stories-that-matter.

Rita

The Teacher Story

I had just come back to a position at the university in my hometown, after spending several years as a full-time researcher. It was April, and I had a workload waiting for me in the office. I had lectures to plan, and one of the BA topics in our social work education I was responsible for this year was "Activities and educational methods in environmental therapy work." According to the study plan, the students should gain "a broad knowledge of pedagogical theories and ways of working that can strengthen children's and young people's social skills competence and contribute to prevention and reduction of 'problematic behavior'. This included among other things, methodical use of activities to promote contact, inclusion, coping and participation." The last sentence in this section of the study plan stuck in my mind: "*The subject will also make students aware of their own resources in environmental therapeutic work*" (UiT, 2024, pp.23–6). I chewed on this last sentence. How do people become aware of their own resources? How do people, in general, know when they are using their resources in the best possible way? How did I, when I, years back, worked with children and their families in child welfare institutions, become AWARE of my own resources?

I kept reading the study plan. It said quite a lot about the expected competence and skills the students should acquire during the course. The responsibility for the transformation of all this expected knowledge weighed heavy on my shoulders. How could I be sure of my own resources as a social work scholar, teaching these students, with all their practice and experience, narratives, and stories – how could I know that my teaching would awaken something in the students, teaching them what can "contribute to children and young people's development and change"? (UiT, 2024). When do we know that we contribute to people's development and change? I tried to remember moments in my own life when people I've met had contributed to my development and change. I remembered friends, relatives, people I love and care about. I remembered stories-that-had-mattered. I remembered moments of awareness and relationships. According to Elliott, Kao, and Grant (2004), these are the two superordinate categories of mattering.

Mattering in a Social Work Education Community

Rosenberg and McCullough (1981) understand mattering as the feeling that others are depending upon you, are interested in you, are concerned with your fate, or experience you as an ego-extension. This is related to the four dimensions of attention, importance, dependence, and ego-extension (Schieman & Taylor, 2001). Mattering is having a strong sense that your actions are acknowledged and relevant in the lives of others (ibid.). Responsibilities and obligations connect us as human beings, and we are dependent upon each other. According to Schieman and Taylor (2001), the exchanges that harvest a sense of mattering reflect behavioral and affective dynamics that sustain the basic forms of social organization in work and family life. I would like to add education.

Mattering is both about feeling valued and about adding value into a community. When we as humans feel valued, we are appreciated, respected, and recognized. When we add value, we can make a difference in our community (Prilleltensky, 2020). Feeling valued includes respect for diversity, the need to belong, inclusion, and fairness. Adding value consists of empowerment, autonomy, a sense of control over our lives, mastery, self-efficacy, and self-determination (ibid., p.17.)

People have a need for community mattering, and as a social work student you want to have a sense of belonging in a social work community, so that you feel important and that you have a role to play. This includes a strong emphasis on the role of the community in reducing risk factors and promoting the development of protective resources, with community support and encouragement being one of the most important protective resources (Flett, 2018, p.265). As emphasized by Bergmark (2009), schools and educational sites are arenas for ethical practice. They are meeting places for values, and teachers are supposed to do important work together with students, encouraging them to manage their mattering in a future society. Teaching is both an ethical and moral possibility, where every lesson, every lecture, and every day can open up for new perspectives on mattering. According to Dixon and Tucker (2008) all classroom activities have an opportunity to reach every student and to promote students' academic, personal and social, and career development. If we, as teachers, focus on every student's individualized involvement during classroom guidance, we allow the opportunity for each student to have meaningful participation and to matter to the group and the lesson (ibid.). In line with Dixon and Tucker (2008), I understand the powerful experience of mattering to others as an essential aspect of healthy emotional and social development for all people, also social work students. The individual student's feeling that she or he counts, is of great importance. One of the most important work tasks for social workers, is also to make people feel they matter. So how can we bridge the gap, or build connections, between classroom and future practice when it comes to mattering?

How can we as teachers ensure that the social context in our classroom provides safety, care, and inspiration for the student's role in a learning process where mattering is a main focus? In accordance with Ambrose et al. (2010) I think that contextual factors outside the teaching situation, such as social and emotional aspects of life, can influence the learning work. The picture is further complex. The students' prior knowledge can contribute to or hinder learning. How students organize knowledge affects how they learn and use what they know. Their motivation determines, directs, and sustains what they will do to learn. Furthermore, students must acquire skills, incorporate these skills, and know when to apply them. By combining a targeted practice with targeted feedback, improvements are made in the quality of students' learning. Their current level of development interacts with the social, emotional, and intellectual climate in the classroom, and affects the entire learning situation. To become independent, students must be able to reflect on their own approaches to learning (Ambrose et al., 2010). The teaching work involves putting the student's learning processes at the centre. Over the years I have moved from the teacher-focused approach to collaborating more purposefully with the students. My experience is that increased academic security has contributed to increasing my pedagogical competence as a teacher, where I lift my gaze from subject material to be conveyed, to include those who receive it. These days I often encourage students to collaborate on material to be presented through assignments given in advance of the teaching (Herreid & Schiller, 2013), circle discussions on various topics, reflective team, research-based methods such as participant observation, mini-fieldwork, qualitative interviews, and process-oriented writing. These methods require that the students want to participate actively in the learning processes they are part of, and that they trust their fellow students and their teachers.

Back in the Classroom

I had a whole week with lectures with my second-year students in child welfare services. I felt we had been building a community of trust in the classroom this week, and I wanted the students to talk about their visions and dreams for who they wanted to be as social workers in the future. They were soon leaving school for several weeks in social work practice, and some of them were excited, other were more nervous about who and what they would be meeting out there 'in the real world'. Were they good enough? Did they know enough to meet children, families, parents, people with their challenges? How could they be of any help to anybody? I heard all these trembling expectations.

Reflection is considered to be very important in social work practice. According to Spector-Mersel (2017, p.286), "social workers are expected to routinely explore their interventions, expanding their awareness of themselves as positioned in social, cultural, and professional contexts." I wanted the students to reflect upon who they wanted to *become* as practitioners. Sometimes stories help us to understand ourselves, our place in the world, what we want to do, who we want to be perceived as by others. Quoting Baldwin (2013), as social workers we "need to understand who we are, the stories that we tell about ourselves, the stories that influence us, the identities that we are called on to perform," as this "helps us to approach others in creative . . . ways" (p.56). We had established a safe space for sharing stories in the classroom, but had we created a *brave space* for sharing stories?

Many scholars have described visions of safe space as it relates to diversity and social justice learning environments (Arao & Clemens, 2013). Holley & Steiner (2005, p. 49) describe safe space as an "environment in which students are willing and able to participate and honestly struggle with challenging issues." I agree with Rom (1998) and Arao and Clemens (2013), in their argument about the need for creating brave spaces, extending safe spaces. Bravery is needed because learning does not necessarily involve merely risk, but "the pain of giving up a former condition in favour of a new way of seeing things" (Rom, 1998, p. 399). Safe space implies that danger, risk, or harm will not happen in that space – that the space as constructed precludes the possibility of those phenomena (Cook-Sather, 2016). Arao and Clemens (2013) argue that removing risk from challenging encounters around controversial issues is impossible. Cook-Sather suggests that to claim we can create 'safe space' for social work is counterproductive, because it promises to protect and exempt people from the very difficult-ness that real learning and growth require (Cook-Sather, 2016, p.1). Furthermore, because the language of safety may "encourage entrenchment in privilege" of those who think they do not need to make themselves vulnerable, the language of safety can "contribute to the entrenchment of dominance and subordination" (Arao & Clemens, 2013, p.140).

Brave space implies that there is likely be risk, danger, or harm – threats that require bravery on the part of those who enter. But those who enter the space have the courage to face that danger and to take risks because they know they will be taken care of – that difficult experiences will be acknowledged and supported, not avoided, or eliminated (Cook-Sather, 2016, p. 1). The shift away from the concept of safety and towards an emphasis on the importance of bravery focuses our attention on the active engagement and agency required of participants in spaces intended to support learning (Arao & Clemens, 2013). In other words, using "brave" rather "safe" sets a tone for engagement and proposes a mode of engagement (Cook-Sather, 2016).

Bravery is not only a relational concept, but also the foundation of one's mattering in the community (Sørly et al., 2023). Mattering through relationship is related to importance and reliance (Carey, 2019). Mattering as a relational phenomenon contributes to an individual's self-concept (Carey, 2019; Elliott, Kao, & Grant, 2004). Our surrounding context, and dominant narratives and cultural norms, influence our self-concept. Cultural norms govern policies and everyday life. These norms accept or reject individual significance, value, or worth in relational interactions through lenses of making certain people matter, and other people not matter (Sørly et al., 2023). When I asked the students to write their stories, I asked them to create and trust in a *brave space* in the classroom. The expectations of bravery were connected to their personal stories of not only who they wanted to be as a social worker, but also *why* they wanted to become a social worker. I find this task to be closely related to how mattering relates to our self-concept. I had given the students their writing task one week before we met in the classroom, hoping for a brave space, where stories-that-matter could be performed.

The Students' Stories

All the students had written their pieces and presented them in the classroom. Some stories were short, others were longer and more informative. They were all individual pieces, different in form and style. I was moved by all the various stories. After their presentations I contacted the students and asked them whether they wanted to contribute to a book chapter on social work and stories-that-matter. Three of the students answered immediately and wanted to their stories to be shared. These were the stories of Raymond, Ingvild, and Sunniva.

Raymond

The first story presented is Raymond's story. Raymond is a man in his mid forties, who's working at a child welfare institution. He has a long working career in other professions behind him, and he decided to retrain some years ago. I find Raymond to be a very reflective and dutiful student. This is his story.

Who Do I Want to Be as a Social Worker?

1. The safe adult who listens, someone who can contribute to the good conversation. I think that by being the safe and listening adult this can contribute to the young people wanting to create a relationship with me and through that good relationship we can build a platform that can create change in the long term.

2. Someone who can weather the storm and who helps to create a safe environment. Young people who struggle in everyday life can have different 'expressions of pain', for example, inner turmoil and thoughts can be expressed through verbal threats, or that they throw things around. And then it is important that those of us who are around the young people stand there as confident adults without letting ourselves be 'tipped off the stick'. I think that the young people will feel pressured. When "Otto" wants to be paid for mowing the lawn without completing the job and he starts throwing things around and being verbally threatening, it is important for me as a social worker to be the calm and explanatory one. Such behaviour can also be thought to be a way for "Otto" to test me as an adult. Am I the one giving in or am I standing in it! Being calm and safe in such a situation will help to de-escalate the situation and show the young person that I can stand his behaviour and demeanour. The professional who can be trusted by the young people and my colleagues. By acting professionally, keeping what you promise, having a good understanding of the subject and good values. I think I am helping to create trust both among young people and colleagues.

Reflections on Raymond's Story

Raymond's story is both about who he wants to be as a social worker, and about being someone who can "weather the storm" when meeting young people, experiencing challenges. Raymond expresses what we might define as the double task of mattering, described by Prilleltensky (2020, p.16) as "the experience that you are valued and that you can add value." He knows that by being a safe adult, he will be valued by whomever he meets in his practice, and by being calm and safe in demanding situations, he is also adding values to, in this case, "Otto". The balance between these two complementary psychological experiences, is of great importance to Raymond.

Ingvild

The second story presented is Ingvild's story. She is a young woman, in her early twenties, and she was, at the time of her story, working at a child welfare institution where she met adolescents with different challenges every day. Her story starts *in medias res*, where she is in a meeting with a young boy.

My Text about Who I Want to Be as a Social Worker

The youth sits restlessly on the chair, scratches his hair and shakes his legs. His gaze is impossible to catch, and this is an uncomfortable situation for him. That car he crashed yesterday, and the other youth he hit today, are today's topic of conversation. As a social worker I will carry out a behavioural chain analysis with the young person, where we together will try to identify what influences and controls his behaviour. The goal of this the conversation is to understand why the behaviour was the way it was, and I have a big task ahead of me to communicate with the youth in the best possible way. The important thing in this situation is that I have a non-judgmental attitude. I must see the youth behind the actions, not the youth based on the actions. This is a significant difference. As a social worker, I want to be a safe person who can be trusted and who sees the youth and his resources. In addition, I want to be someone who sees the child behind actions and distinguishes between person and situation.

Children's rights in the Constitution include that they have the right to be heard, which I consider as important for this conversation. It is important to me that the young person is in an environment where he feels feel more comfortable and satisfied than in an office. I noticed as soon as he entered the door and sat down that this was the wrong place for him to be. I ask the young man if he wants to go for a ride, go for a walk or if there are other places he wants to talk about the events than inside my office. He replies that he would like to be on the shore and look at the sea while we talk, because then he doesn't feel so confined. We put on clothes, both hat and mittens, because it is a cold autumn evening with a slightly chilly wind. We go down to the shore, which is directly beyond the institution; of course he should be able to decide for himself where he wants to talk to me. Children's right to participation is a fundamental principle in the Child Welfare Act, and it is the key to a good relationship with the youth, I think.

Reflections on Ingvild's Story

Ingvild's story is also about feeling valued and adding value (Prilleltensky, 2020). She wants to meet the youth on his own terms. The office walls are too narrow, Ingvild and the young man go to the seashore. This can be understood as Ingvild's way of adding value to the situation; she is able to contribute and make a difference. In line with Prilleltensky (2020), we can understand adding value as empowerment, autonomy, a sense of control over our lives, mastery, self-efficacy, and self-determination. Ingvild contributes this in the situation with the young man.

Sunniva

The third story presented is Sunniva's story. Sunniva is in her twenties, and I imagine she is one of the students who use a lot of her time studying. She is always sitting in the front of the classroom, and she is a very eager student. She is interested in learning, and often relates her questions to social work practice.

Who Do I Want to Be as a Social Worker?

> The girl sat like a dark shadow in the corner of the sofa. She was almost invisible as she sat with her black clothes against the black leather sofa. It was almost so that you had to run away and hold her tight, for fear that the next second she would sink into the sofa, become one with it, and never get up again. This bottomless valley, where the voices had ceased to echo in the walls and the sun had cast its last rays over the landscape, was about to pass away. There were no smiles, no laughter, and no tears. No look, no movement, nothing.

Emptiness, I don't know if that word even fits.This practical story is the seed of my desire to become a social worker. And not just the title, but the identity social worker. To me, this girl is a picture of absolute darkness. That is why there is such a great contrast when a luminous figure is suddenly sent into this room. An angel in human form. A social worker.

A person who radiates goodness, care, and security for another person, only because this other person is a fellow human being. A person who is completely free from the thought of personal gain shows commitment and fearlessness on behalf of others. A person who lifts the girl off the sofa and onto a path of possibilities. A human being who uses his existence to ensure the existence of another. A social worker who uses his ability to build relationships as his superpower to empower another human being. These words are important to me precisely because of this story. Kindness, safety, commitment, fearlessness, and empowerment. I think back to this story and these words when I am stuck or need inspiration. And they apply both at work and in life because I work every day to ensure that these qualities not only characterize my professional practice, but also my identity. And when I draw up this story, I know that day after day I choose the right path. Because this girl, it was me. And this social worker was my angel. And this is what will be my foundation as a professional. My own awareness that if we could do it back then, we can do it now.

Reflections on Sunnivas' Story

The autobiographical story of Sunniva moved me, and all the students, in the classroom. Sunniva's story entails a process through which the students, our future professionals, become intimately acquainted with a part of her life story. This situates them in their various story environments, namely, the "contexts within which the work of story construction and storytelling gets done" (Holstein & Gubrium, 2009, p. xvii). We were, at this very moment when we received the story, at the core of social work that matters. Sunniva felt she was in a brave space, where her story could be told, and listened to. She was, as Raymond and Ingvild, both feeling valued and adding value to the educational community we all consisted of.

The Capabilities of Social Work Education-that-Matters and Stories-that-Matter

Social work as a practice-based profession and an academic discipline is expected to promote social change and development, social cohesion, and the empowerment and liberation of people. Principles of social justice, human rights, collective responsibility, and respect for diversities are essential to social work. Social work is meant to engage people and structures to address life challenges and enhance well-being (IFSW, n.d.).

After having done this exercise with the students, I have become more convinced that the relation to storytelling in social work is intertwined with the concept of mattering. In fact, I understand mattering per se as related to the very core practice of social work. Mattering is a fundamental human need that can be nurtured by telling stories, listening to stories, and sharing stories. What happened in the classroom while the students were sharing their stories, was a common movement towards growth. Following Prilleltensky, I understand mattering as existing both in the microcosm of relationships and stories, but also in the macrocosm of social policies (2020, p.34), just as in the core of social work. In further agreement with Schlossberg (1989), I could recognize four dimensions of mattering among the students: attention (every student felt as if someone had noticed them), importance (every student felt cared about), ego-extension (every student believed that someone would be proud of their accomplishments), and dependence (every student felt needed in the education community). As pointed out by Garte and Kronen (2020), I do believe that whether students experience themselves as mattering is directly tied to students' experiences in the classroom. In other words, we need to work with social work education-that-matters. And to be able to do that, we need to work with stories-that-matter.

Reflective Questions

1. Reflect upon the use of stories and storytelling in the classroom. What are the engagement issues in this story?
2. How can we create brave spaces for students in social work?
3. In what way can brave spaces be made transferable to social work spaces?
4. What issues of trust arise from the story?

Acknowledgements

Raymond, Ingvild, and Sunniva have read the chapter and accepted the version published. I am truly grateful for being able to share your stories. Thank you.

REFERENCES

Ambrose, S. A., Bridges, M. W., DiPietro, M., Lovett, M. C., & Norman, M. K. (2010). *How Learning Works: Seven Research-Based Principles for Smart Teaching*. San Francisco, CA: Jossey-Bass.

Arao, B., & Clemens, K. (2013). From safe spaces to brave spaces. In L. M. Landreman (ed.), *The Art of Effective Facilitation: Reflections from Social Justice Educators*, 135–150. New York: Routledge.

Baldwin, C. (2013). *Narrative Social Work: Theory and Application*. Bristol: Policy Press.

Bergmark, U. (2009). Building an ethical learning community in schools. PhD thesis, Luleå Tekniska Universitet, Sweden.

Carey, R. L. (2019). Imagining the comprehensive mattering of Black boys and young men in society and schools: Toward a new approach. *Harvard Educational Review*, *89*(3), 370–96.

Cook-Sather, A. (2016). Creating brave spaces within and through student–faculty pedagogical partnerships. *Teaching and Learning Together in Higher Education*, *1*(18), 1–5.

Dixon, A. L., & Tucker, C. (2008). Every student matters: Enhancing strengths-based school counseling through the application of mattering. *Professional School Counseling*, *12*(2), https://doi.org/10.1177/2156759X0801200 2.

Elliott, G., Kao, S., & Grant, A. M. (2004). Mattering: Empirical validation of a social-psychological concept. *Self and Identity*, *3*(4), 339–54.

Flett, G. (2018). *The Psychology of Mattering: Understanding the Human Need to be Significant*. London: Academic Press.

Garte, R., & Kronen, C. (2020). From the margins of the classroom to mattering: How community college education students develop future teacher identities. *Educational Forum*, *85*(2), 175–92).

Herreid, C. F., & Schiller, N. A. (2013). Case studies and the flipped classroom. *Journal of College Science Teaching*, *42*(5), 62–6

Holley, L. C., & Steiner, S. (2005). Safe space: Student perspectives on classroom environment. *Journal of Social Work Education*, *41*(1), 49–64.

Holstein, J. A., & Gubrium, J. F. (2009). *Analyzing Narrative Reality*. Thousand Oaks, CA: Sage.

IFSW (International Federation of Social Workers). (n.d.). Global definition of social work. www.ifsw.org/what-is-social-work/global-definition-of-social-work.

Prilleltensky, I. (2020). Mattering at the intersection of psychology, philosophy, and politics. *American Journal of Community Psychology*, *65*(1–2), 16–34.

Rom, R. B. (1998). 'Safe spaces': Reflections on an educational metaphor. *Journal of Curriculum studies*, *30*(4), 397–408.

Rosenberg, M., and McCullough, B. C. (1981). Mattering: Inferred significance and mental health among adolescents. *Research in Community and Mental Health*, *2*, 163–82.

Schieman, S., & Taylor, J. (2001). Statuses, roles, and the sense of mattering. *Sociological Perspectives*, *44*(4), 469–84.

Schlossberg, N. K. (1989). Marginality and mattering: Key issues in building community. In D. C. Roberts (ed.), *Designing Campus Activities to Foster a Sense of Community*, pp.5–15. San Francisco, CA: Jossey-Bass. https://doi.org/10.1002/ss.37119894803

Spector-Mersel, G. (2017). Life story reflection in social work education: A practical model. *Journal of Social Work Education*, 53(2), 286–99.

Sørly, R., Bartone, M., Kårtveit, B., & Normann, A. K. (2023). The Norwegian Barents Pride Festival: Reflections on bravery for LBGTQI+ activists from Russia. *Nordic Journal of Wellbeing and Sustainable Welfare Development*, 2(1), 20–33.

UiT. (2024). Fagplan, bachelor i barnevern, deltid 2020–2024, UiT Norges Arktiske Universitet. https://uit.no/utdanning/program/444428/barnevern_-_bachelor (accessed 31 January 2024).

Photo: Hilde Mjøs

CHAPTER 7

Social Work in Need of Activism

A Story about Gangs, Marginalization, and Crime in Two South African Townships

G. Nokukhanya Ndhlovu

Introduction

> He looked young, too young to be here. My guess was that he was about thirteen to fourteen years. He said he was fifteen and had joined a gang at the age of ten. He had a hardened face, a face that spoke of things, deep and dark – things he had seen and done. The first thing that he said when I asked him how long he had been in this place was "kusezintsukwana ndikhona sisi wam" ("I have been here for less than a week my sister"). He went on to tell me about his life as a gangster and what drove him to join gangs. He also shared about his drug addiction and that "iziyobisi zindenze ndalibala izinto ezininzi ezimbi" ("drugs made me forget a lot of bad things"). His mother had abandoned him, and he didn't know his father. His story was surreal – filled with a lot of disappointment, heartbreak, brokenness, guns, knives, machetes, and blood – yet here he was. Longing for a second chance in life, daring to hope, again. He was not the only one, many of them had similar stories, stories of dehumanization, marginalization, poverty, unemployment, inequality, and lack of access to basic human rights.

And this story is about them. It's a story about finding hope and identity in gangs and the social work implications that arose. It is also about my journey into the 'hidden' world of gangs, drugs, and violence. I interviewed and spent time with eighteen African[1] former youth gang members, eighteen unemployed youths between the ages of fifteen and thirty-five. They came from two South African marginalized townships – Bophelong in the Gauteng Province and Nyanga in the Western Cape Province. Townships are historically African urban residential areas characterized by high levels of poverty and underdevelopment (Ndhlovu and

[1] For this chapter, the term African is adopted from South Africa's Broad-Based Black Economic Empowerment Act 53 of 2003 (BBBEE Act) which defines black people as Africans, Coloureds, and Indians.

Tanga, 2021). The experience allowed me to explore the multifaceted and complex nature of youth gangs in both townships and the social work issues this gave rise to.

The Dehumanization and Marginalization of African Youths

> ... certain lives are not considered lives at all, they cannot be humanised: they fit no dominant frame for the human.
>
> (Butler, 2004)

Known as the city of gold, Johannesburg or Jozi is the industrial and financial capital of South Africa. However, millions of Africans living on the outskirts of the city remain marginalized and excluded from accessing fundamental human rights articulated in the country's constitution. Dilapidated houses, squatter camps, lack of sanitation and water, and dehumanization are a norm. Bophelong and Nyanga are testament of this fact. In describing townships, Manus (2011, 77) states that townships are sites "chosen by whites to dump blacks outside the limits in a similar way to dumping the city trash." The intention of the Apartheid separate development system was to dehumanize and marginalize all non-white people. Years after the democratic elections, many Africans are still dehumanized, marginalized and 'dumped outside the limits', as echoed by an informant from Bophelong:

> Bophelong has an extremely high rate of unemployment, as you saw while we were driving around there is an abnormal number of youths wandering around the streets. These are people who should be doing something productive with their lives but there is nothing to do. Secondly, this place has no sporting facilities for young people to engage in sporting activities. Thirdly, there are no facilities for youth, these young people have nothing to keep them busy ... Another thing, this place is congested, remember I showed you the shacks? You saw how congested they are, you saw how close to each other they are, so many shacks and so many people living in those small spaces. (Informant, twenty-four years' experience)

The above quote encapsulates the living conditions of the young people that I interviewed in both communities. This dehumanization is not only confined to Bophelong, but similar conditions also exist in Nyanga and in other African townships. Modise (2020) contends that while many South Africans continue to enjoy the fruits of democracy, many young people are still trapped in poverty and unemployment. African township youths are hardest hit, as many of them find themselves on the margins of exclusion with little or no access to fundamental human rights. The marginalization and dehumanization confronting them is a multifaceted and dynamic phenomenon driven by inequality – which sees many of them hindered from fully participating in community or social life (Rispel, Molomo, & Dumela, 2008). While numerous post-Apartheid interventions have been aimed at addressing and redressing Apartheid's top-down and divisive development, youths from Bophelong and Nyanga are still marginalized. As a result, many of them are embattled with various development challenges that have negatively impacted their living conditions and quality of life and left them with limited power to change the dire conditions in which they find themselves (Ndhlovu, 2020). This treatment of African youths, Africans from the township in particular, as insignificant, has driven many to the illicit economy of gangs and crime as a survival strategy and a means to communicate their frustration. Violence is a means of communication and people adopt it when other channels of communication are blocked (Galtung, 1990, 1969; Van der Merwe, 2013). African youth are resorting to violence in response to the structural violence they are faced with. To this end, Zaaroura (2016) contends that joining gangs is a desperate and last resort for African young men and women. It is indeed a survival of the fittest and for these young, marginalized men, being hardened in gangs is a survival strategy.

Youth Poverty and Unemployment

> Ausi, we need jobs ekasi. Most of us fell into crime because we just wanted to put food on the table. My sister I am not saying that what we did is right, it's wrong but at times we are pushed into these things. It's painful to go to bed hungry, it's painful to watch ingcosi zekhaya (our siblings) going to bed hungry. At times as a man you need ukuphanda (to hustle), but when there are no jobs, you are stuck. We need jobs . . .
>
> (Katleho, 29, unemployed and doing community service for mugging people)

> Ausi (sighs) it's too much, it's too much (nods head), and it's too much. There are no jobs here. The suffering in this place is too much. Look at our homes, look at those women, those are our mothers. Look at what they are forced to do because they are trying to put food on the table. Our mothers burn in the sun, get wet and blown by the wind because they spend every day trying to sell things out here. Look there, look, see the wind just blew that woman's clothes into the road, what kind of life is that?
>
> (Kamohelo, twenty-six,, unemployed and doing community service for robbery)

The above accounts show that young people in Bophelong and Nyanga find themselves ensnared in a brutally vicious cycle of gang violence as a result of structural issues like poverty, unemployment, and disadvantageous socio-economic circumstances embedded in years of political exploitation and deprivation (MacMaster, 2010). As noted in the above statements, *ekasi* youths are still plagued by unemployment, poverty, and various forms of challenge despite the country's colourful policies and strategies – an indication that South Africa has failed to meet the needs of its young people, as many of them are poor, unemployed, and uneducated (Johnson, 1977). The government through its constitution pledged to promote human rights, social justice, social change, and development without discriminating against sex, location, age, colour, or creed. The Constitution is the tool used to both heal the country from the Apartheid wounds as well as instituting a country founded on social justice, democracy, and human rights (Republic of South Africa, 1996). However, the promotion and protection of human rights articulated in the Constitution have been tainted by many pitfalls which have seen many South Africans excluded from mainstream society (Endoh, 2015) and African youths have been hardest hit – including the young men that I interviewed. The study found that in both communities, youths are confronted by hostile socioeconomic living conditions which have pushed them to a life of crime, indicating that gangs are a rebellion against socio-economic conditions (Baird, 2015).

In this work of mine, these young men have left gangs, their sources of employment, financial independence, and identity, but they still find themselves embattled with the very social issues that led them into gangs. Dziewanski's study with former gang members in Cape Town also found that even though his participants had left gangs they were still struggling with a familiar list of personal and social issues, like joblessness, racism, isolation, and hopelessness, that drove them to gangs in the first place (2021). This is the hopelessness that defines Katleho's narrative, the hopelessness echoed by other former gang members. These young boys are pushed towards gangs to survive the toxic environment (Kiewit, 2019). While other children are exploring opportunities that will add to or enhance their quality of life, opportunities that will build them up, findings show that young men from the township find themselves joining gangs as a survival strategy.

Inequality and Poor Economic Opportunities

> Bophelong suffers from poverty, most of us come from struggling families, that's why we find gangs and crime attractive. At times you

> look around you, you see untold suffering in your family. My mother wakes up very early in the morning, she comes back very late. You hardly see her because she is always at work . . . then at the end of the month you see her crying because the money is not enough. That is not life, so much hard work and so little to put on the table. So as we grow up, we want better for our brothers, we want better for our mothers. We try to look for jobs, but we are neither educated nor skilled, we don't get the jobs. We try to hustle but nothing comes up. Then you see gangs living better lives than you, what choice do you have? At least when you join a gang you know that you can't sleep on an empty stomach.
>
> (Thato, thirty-two years old, unemployed, doing community service)

> Living ekasi is rough, from the moment you open your eyes in the morning to the time you go to bed in the evening it's just suffering. At times you just don't want to get out of bed because of too many challenges. Look at white people in the suburbs, they breathe fresh air, look at their homes and shopping malls. Everything in white areas is beautiful. But come to the ekasi, our access to almost all facilities is limited. Whites have access to all good things but look at us, we live in very small houses, look at our spaces, a white man's house can be compared to all these shacks, from that shack to that shack (pointing at a long line of shacks). White people have access to resources, they own the means of survival, they own the resources, they own South Africa.
>
> (Thuto, twenty years old)

My work showed that inequalities continue to shape and define *ekasi* youths' lives – and these inequalities have impacted some of their life choices (Ndhlovu, 2020). The young men interviewed are living proof "of how someone can be rubbed raw over time by the systemic imbalances, racism and insecurity that envelop a community" (Dziewanski, 2021, p. xii). This has contributed to the youths turning to gangs and crime to empower themselves. This chapter does not in any way excuse the malevolent impact of gangs and gang violence in communities, but has an aim to acknowledge and explore the social work issues linked to gangs and gang violence.

Inequalities are still deep-rooted in the country and African youths are hardest hit as they continue to bear the brunt of the problems of living in post-Apartheid South Africa. Statistics South Africa (2021) notes that young South Africans are still socioeconomically sidelined with one in every two young people not participating in the labour market. This is reflected in the 2021 statistics, where 46.3 per cent of the fifteen to thirty-four age group were not in employment (Statistics South Africa, 2021).

Furthermore, Statistics South Africa (2020) indicates that female South African workers earn 30 per cent less than their male counterparts, and males are more likely to be employed compared to women. On the other hand, Africans earn the lowest wages in addition to being exposed to dire employment outcomes. South Africa is well known for being one of the most unequal countries in the world, with its labour market reportedly heavily racially and gender biased. This is an indication of the inequality and the poverty plaguing South African youths. Exacerbating an already dire situation are the impacts of COVID-19 and the war in Ukraine, which have further disproportionately impacted them.

African townships continue to have large numbers of youths who are unemployable and not in employment, education, or training (NEETs) (Ndhlovu, 2022). Townships have a lot of unskilled youths due to an acute shortage of skills development centres (Ndhlovu, 2020). The study identified skills development centres as drivers of youth empowerment and development, reporting that skills would help empower African youths to engage meaningfully in economic activities of society as well as enable them to be productive, as either employees or businesspeople (Ndhlovu, 2020).

The failure by the relevant role players to meet African young people at their point of need and to enhance their human capabilities has left them on the margins of development. These capabilities consist of an individual youth's capability of achieving the kind of life they consider valuable (Ndhlovu, 2020; Sen, 2005), the basic capacity to avoid ignorance, poverty, early mortality, and lead a fuller, satisfactory life, and to be able to participate in decision-making processes in their communities (Sen, 1999, 2005). Against this background, poverty and inequality are fundamental concerns in the Sustainable Development Goals (SDGs).

Dehumanization can be manifested in various ways, including through structural violence, neglect, or inhuman/poor living conditions – which can make young people more susceptible to further dehumanization. To dehumanize a person is to treat them as less than human. In the field of social work, dehumanization is linked to social inequality, actual and/or perceived poor economic conditions, and the violation of human rights (Bharti, 2012; Zlobina et al., 2023). Youth poverty, unemployment, and inequality are serious social work issues that have a profound impact on young people's lives – leading to feelings of exclusion, despair, worthlessness, powerlessness, and hopelessness (Ndhlovu, 2020). In these contexts, the role of the social worker is to promote human well-being and social justice as well as to enhance the quality of life of these young people whose humanity has been stripped away by their living circumstances. To rehumanize township people is about addressing the root conditions that limit human rights. It is also about helping them achieve their full potential. Social workers are guided by the core values of social justice which promote equal worth and dignity of all people (Yildirim, Öztürk, & Abukan, 2021). They are therefore in a unique position to understand and address the complex factors that contribute to gang violence in townships and can play a vital role in preventing and intervening in gang-related activity. This includes social change, community development, and providing relevant social services (Ife, Soldatić, and Briskman, 2022). For township people, the social worker is seen as a person dedicated to helping people who are living in poverty, unemployment, inequality, and facing other forms of social injustice. Social workers work to promote social justice by challenging inequalities, discrimination, and all the systems that perpetuate these problems (IFSW, 2018).

Living Conditions, Quality of Life, and Gang Violence: Connecting the Dots

> To deny people their human rights is to challenge their very humanity.
> (Nelson Mandela, quoted in United Nations, 2024)

Gang violence is a deeply rooted social work issue in many marginalized and disenfranchised communities across South Africa. There seems to be a shared understanding in gang violence studies that marginalization and poverty are intricately linked with gang violence – as most gangs come from disenfranchised backgrounds (Mguzulwa and Gxubane, 2019; Sefali, 2014). According to MacMaster (2010), one of the major reasons for gang violence is that the socioeconomic and structural circumstances in the affected communities have not been intentionally, forcefully, and thoroughly addressed adequately to deny gangsterism its breeding ground. In her study on youth gangs, Monareng (2016) proposes that exclusion, climbing youth unemployment, unequal distribution of resources, and a lack of access to justice and opportunities are just some of the drivers of violence and crime. My study found that despite the detrimental outcomes of gang involvement, gangs sometimes serve as a buffer for some children and young people by providing the security of a steady 'income', an identity, a home, and male role models. Since many of the young people come from broken and fatherless homes, gangs serve as a fortress and a 'sanctuary'. In the absence of socioeconomic opportunities, social networks, and other opportunities, young men join gangs where they use violence to rule, and subordinate rival gangs as a way of claiming their place as *izinja ze game* in their communities (top dogs) (Ndhlovu and Tanga, 2021). To further buttress this point, Sharkey et al. (2011) avow that gangs meet several needs that are not met at home, community, or even school. The same study highlights how gangs can meet the hierarchy of different human needs, as conjectured by Maslow's hierarchy of needs. Therefore, the authors contend that while joining gangs leads to many harmful consequences, for many youths from marginalized backgrounds being part of a gang acts as a protective factor – that protects them from falling victim to worse conditions such as continuing dehumanization and marginalization (Sharkey et al., 2011). Of the many findings on youth gang violence, what continues to stand out is the link between marginalization and youth's involvement in gangs and violence. Studies suggest that marginalization increases young people's vulnerability to and involvement in antisocial behaviour. A study of Latin American gangs by Baird (2017) concluded that violence results from conditions of exclusion – young people from deprived and poor communities are more susceptible to joining gangs or being exploited by older gangs. Baird (2017) further states that homicide statistics indicate that poor young men are also at the forefront of violence – as victims and as perpetrators. Another study on Latin American gangs by Baird (2015) also found that there is a very close link between inequality, exclusion, and violence. This is confirmed by Dziewanski (2021, p.37), who underlines: "gangs and gang-like groups are not the problem. They are symptoms of larger social dilemmas. For the youth that join them, they represent an adaptive – though admittedly aggressive – response to the division, dereliction and demoralisation afflicting African underclass."

In South Africa, despite the social work issues that underpin youth gang violence, gangs are viewed either as a law or army enforcement issue. The issue of youth and gangs in South Africa is a complicated, multifaceted, and multidimensional social work issue – yet, in the face of its complexity, the state's response is throwing gangs in prison with the hope that they will be rehabilitated. It is therefore important to understand the social work/social development issues that underpin youth gang violence.

It is vital that social workers as role players focus on enhancing young people's capabilities. Capabilities refer to what people are capable of doing and being – and producing capabilities requires material and institutional support (Nussbaum, 2006). According to Nussbaum (2006, p.23), the capability approach, which is very important in addressing inequalities, highlights that as institutional role players "you do not secure the necessary ingredients of democracy without at the same time focusing on material issues such as health care and the provision of universal primary and secondary education," and in the case of African townships, skills development centres, employment opportunities, access to basic human rights, and other socioeconomic opportunities. Nussbaum (2006) further states that if role players begin with an understanding that every citizen is entitled to a decent minimum level of capabilities, they can then work around that to think how about how nations, individuals, international organizations, NGOs, multinational corporations among others, can share the duties corresponding to the entitlements. Against this background, SDGs 1 and 10 prioritize the reduction of poverty and inequality. According to Sen (1999), development requires the removal of major sources of unfreedom, which include poverty, inequality, poor economic opportunities, systematic social deprivations, and neglect of public services, among others. The idea of unfreedom may be depicted by the lack of public facilities, social care, or educational and skills development and socioeconomic opportunities, as is often found in many South African townships where marginalized African youth bear the brunt.

There is a connection between circumstances of living, quality of life, and gang violence. Children and young people who live in communities that dehumanize them are more likely to experience stressors that can increase the risk of gang involvement. The quality of life in the townships has contributed to gang violence. Bophelong and Nyanga are poor communities with high levels of poverty, unemployment, and crime, and as research suggests, these types of environments are breeding grounds for gang problems. Gang members are often victims of their circumstances as much as they are perpetrators. These findings are supported by other studies, as noted by Pinnock (2019), who contends that the sense of powerlessness in gang-ridden communities has persisted even after Apartheid ended, as evidenced by high levels of youth unemployment. Other studies have also shown that poverty and unemployment can lead to youths perceiving benefits in gang membership. Societal factors, such as high youth unemployment, lack of support services, corrupt governments, and the belief that violence is the best way to deal with stress and conflict, contribute to violence (Van der Westhuizen & Gawulayo, 2021). Some of the community factors that can contribute to youth gang affiliation include acceptance and normalization of criminal behaviour, poverty and unemployment, and a lack of opportunities, as well as gangs that are perceived as power structures in the community (Ward, Van Der

Merwe, & Dawes, 2012). Van der Linde's (2020) study found that it is important to address the systemic factors that contribute to gang proliferation in communities. These factors include the environment, peer pressure, unemployment and poverty, and the perceived acceptance of gang culture as a way of life. Likewise, Bophelong and Nyanga are communities with limited access to resources and socioeconomic opportunities that can help dehumanized African youth stay out of gangs. Social workers working in dehumanized communities plagued with gang violence can play an important role in addressing the root causes of gang violence – this includes addressing the interconnected challenges of living conditions, quality of life, and gang violence. By working with individuals, families, and communities to improve living conditions and promote healthy lifestyles, they can prevent gang involvement. Additionally, they can also provide support to victims of gang violence and their families. This can help to reduce the risk of gang involvement and promote a more peaceful and just society.

Stripped of the Right to a Decent Childhood: The Manifestations

> Within every hopeless situation and every seemingly hopeless person lies the possibility of transformation.
>
> (Tutu & Tutu, 2014)

I met a former gang member in Nyanga who had been rubbed raw by 'life'. His mother left him with *umakhulu* (grandmother) when he was young. He doesn't remember her. He doesn't know who his father is – nobody talks about him at home. He said he was fifteen and a recovering drug addict. He joined a gang when he was ten and he started doing drugs the same year – because drugs made him forget a lot of bad things – findings consistent with that of De Wet (2016) and Van der Westhuizen and Gawulayo (2021) who expound that children as young as nine are absorbed into the gang culture on the Cape Flats in Cape Town. This argument is supported by Kiewit (2019, n.p), who elucidates that "every day, videos of running gangster gun battles are shared via social networking sites and phone apps such as WhatsApp. Shockingly, the shooters are often boys and young men." Accordingly, a majority of study participants shared that children growing up in *ekasi* (African townships) are exposed to various groups of gangs and consequently find themselves joining gangs at a very young age. As discussed above, the marginalization of youths can increase their vulnerability to exploitation as well as exposure to and involvement in gang violence. Kempen (2020) expounds on the involvement of children in gangs in the Eastern Cape, noting that older gangs expand their territories through the exploitation and recruitment of children as young as twelve to help them push drugs into schools.

This work of mine found that the involvement of young children in gangs is a deeply rooted social work issue in both these marginalized African communities – as they are exposed to and expected to commit atrocious acts of violence, including raping both men and women and murder, among others. Other consequences of gang involvement include exposure to drugs and alcohol at a very young age, dropping out of school, exposing loved ones to gang revenge acts, disconnection with family members, imprisonment, underage and inappropriate sexual behaviour, and death. In essence, they lose their childhood.

Accordingly, the fifteen-year-old boy from Nyanga told me that he was accustomed to blood. Shedding blood brought respect and recognition. For a person like him, rejected by both parents, the 'love' and recognition from older gangs meant a lot – so he was willing to do anything to get recognized.

All former gang members interviewed joined gangs when they were minors from the ages of ten to fifteen, and many of them came from families of gangs. Bandura (1977) was right when he asserted that children learn good or bad behaviour from their environment. This is a classic case of social learning. The unsanitized truth is that children learn behaviour and values from family or community members; it is therefore no surprise that many of them ended up in gangs. The social learning theory explains that behaviour is learned and modelled, and their involvement in gangs can be attributed to their environment.

Challenges for Social Workers as Activists

As already noted, the above stories unpack some of the social work issues that contribute to gang involvement and violence. These include poverty and lack of opportunity. Bophelong and Nyanga are marginalized communities with limited employment and economic opportunities, which has led to feelings of inferiority, hopelessness, and despair. In these marginalized communities, joining gangs seems like a more attractive option. Another social work issue is family disintegration and abandonment. The young men interviewed came from broken families and unstable environments, which can lead to feelings of abandonment and a need to find acceptance and support elsewhere. In gangs they found a family and a place to call home – hence joining gangs seemed like a more stable and supportive source of belonging. Lastly the gang culture and normalization of violence are some of the key social issues identified. As noted in some of the narratives, gangs often promote a culture of violence and aggression which is celebrated, encouraged, and normalized. Gang members need to be tough and aggressive in order to survive in the gang – as a result the vicious cycle of violence does not end.

It is therefore important to reiterate that young people who feel marginalized are more likely to join gangs. Gangs can provide a sense of belonging, identity, and financial support. They can also be seen as a way to achieve status and respect in communities where other opportunities are limited. Social workers need to therefore understand that the link between marginalization and gang violence is complex. There are many factors involved, such as those highlighted above. By addressing the root causes of marginalization, social workers can help to break the cycle of violence and create a more just and equitable society for all.

Some studies have, however, indicated that social work practice has often overlooked the connection between the circumstances of vulnerable groups and the role of poverty and deprivation in relation to risk (Davis & Wainwright, 2005; Jones, 1998). Another study also notes that there is evidence in literature that suggests that neither the social work profession nor its educational programmes have fulfilled their mandate to respond to or address poverty (Stoeffler, 2019). A study by Kam (2014) also highlights that although social work is widely recognized as having a dual focus on individual treatment and social justice, the profession has drifted away from the social justice orientation and has gradually abandoned the social reform objective. However, human rights and social justice are essential to the work of social workers. Social workers engage people and structures to address life challenges and enhance well-being. For the social work profession, the issue of gang violence is therefore not just a criminal issue. It is a social justice and human rights issue – which requires social workers to apply social work theories and skills to help individuals and communities address their social and economic needs and enhance their well-being.

Social work seeks to achieve two goals: helping individuals in need and making positive changes to society (Kam, 2014). For social workers working in dehumanized townships, where people who have been dehumanized now play a key role in dehumanizing others, activism becomes an important strategy. It means that the social worker has taken action to bring about significant and relevant social and even political change. As an activist, the role of the social worker is to provide hope for constructive change. In her work titled "Reflections of an activist social worker:

Challenging human rights violations," Briskman (2014) asserts that activism in the field of social work can arise from a need to respond to various human rights violations. She notes the lack of human rights advancements over the years and the negative responses by government and professionals to these violations that have infringed on the rights of the vulnerable. The author argues that social work is obligated to engage in political activism that calls for the promotion of political will to develop a humanized society. Social workers are obligated to challenge unjust principles and to affirm human rights – the principles of human rights and social justice are crucial to social work and should be upheld and respected (Briskman, 2014; IFSW, 2018). As people working on the ground, social workers are first-hand observers of poverty, subjugation, oppression, structural disadvantage, and the various abuses of human rights on the ground. They can resist and challenge these injustices and the oppression of those without social, political, and economic power (Briskman, 2014). Therefore, activists working with dehumanized communities in African townships need to be proactive, provide leadership, demonstrate vigilance, and represent the communities they serve – they must be at the forefront of issues affecting the communities (Bent-Goodley, 2015).

Marginalized people, especially youth, are often unable to participate in social change, be heard, or have their knowledge and experiences validated (Kosko et al., 2022). In these disenfranchised communities, the role of the social worker activist is to give a voice to the voiceless by creating space for the voices of the young people left out of socioeconomic and political processes. Activists create spaces for young people who feel powerless to find hope and opportunity and be part of change. Thus, planned social change and readiness to respond are key to social work activism (Bent-Goodley, 2015). Additionally, in Bophelong and Nyanga, the role of social work activist is to lobby decision-makers to act and rehumanize the communities. To this end, Bent-Goodley (2015) puts forward that the role of social work activists is to bring together interdisciplinary leaders to challenge social and economic justice issues.

This study found that like many South African townships, Bophelong and Nyanga are faced with a myriad of social, economic, and political problems, such as unemployment, poverty, inequality, a lack of educational qualifications and skills, human rights abuses, and corruption, among others. These problems are structural in nature, and they reflect the country's socioeconomic and political processes. This study also found that there is a link between these challenges and youth gangs – as many young people are drawn into the world of gangs as a means of survival.

To prevent or resolve these problems, social workers must participate in the political processes that determine the life circumstances of young people. Activism is therefore an important part in social work (Mmatli, 2008). Social workers have a broad understanding of the root causes of social problems, which allows them to advocate for solutions that address these underlying issues. Social workers can help to ensure that the voices of the most marginalized are heard and that their needs are met by participating in political processes. Activists are change agents who educate, organize, and involve the public to oppose current policies and seek positive solutions. They are also reformers who work with political and judicial structures to incorporate solutions into new laws and policies (Bent-Goodley, 2015; Briskman, 2014). In marginalized gang-plagued communities, it appears that by actively taking on the role of activists, social workers can help to ensure that the voices of vulnerable youths are represented and that their needs are prioritized. Social workers can raise awareness of the multifaceted and multidimensional issues facing marginalized groups and push for policies that will improve their lives. In South Africa, where responses to gang violence are mostly through army or police intervention, social work activists who have conducted research on gangs and listened to and documented the lived experiences of gangs, can share their research findings with communities, academics, policy-makers, and other relevant role players to dispel myths and stereotypes about gang members. Without excusing and normalizing gang violence, activists can provide information about gang violence, including the root causes, the dynamics, the impact on the gangs themselves and their communities, and the resources needed to help those involved and affected. They can also promote understanding and compassion.

Reflective Questions

1. In what way can we develop stories while working in conflict-ridden, unpredictable, and violent environments?
2. What are the human rights issues in this story?
3. What role does poverty play in relation to human rights?
4. What issues of security and safeguarding arise from this story?

REFERENCES

Baird, A. (2015). Duros and gangland girlfriends: Male identity, gang socialisation and rape in Medellín. In J. Auyero, P. Bourgois, & N. Scheper-Hughes (eds.), *Violence at the Urban Margins in the Americas*, pp.112–32. Oxford University Press.

(2017). Becoming the 'baddest': Masculine trajectories of gang violence in Medellín. *Journal of Latin American Studies*, *50*(1), 183–210. https://doi.org/10.1017/S0022216X17000761

Bandura, A. (1977). *Social Learning Theory*. Englewood Cliffs, NJ: Prentice-Hall.

Bent-Goodley, T. B. (2015). Editorial: A call for social work activism. *Social Work*, *60*(2), 101–3.

Bharti, P. (2012). *Dehumanization of Urban and Rural Poor: Applied Social Psychology*. Lap Lambert Academic Publishing.

Briskman, L. (2014). Reflections of an activist social worker: Challenging human rights violations. In C. Noble, H. Strauss, & B. Littlechild (eds.), *Global Social Work: Crossing Borders, Blurring Boundaries*, pp.301–10. Sydney University Press. https://doi.org/10.2307/j.ctv1fxm2q.25

Butler, J. (2004). *Undergoing Gender*. New York: Routledge.

Davis, A., & Wainwright, S. (2005). Combating poverty and social exclusion: Implications for social work education. *Social Work Education*, *24*(3), 259–73.

De Wet, C. (2016). The *Cape Times*'s portrayal of school violence. *South African Journal of Education*, *36*(2), 1–12. https://doi.org/10.15700/saje.v36n2a1231

Dziewanski, D. (2021). *Gang Entry and Exit in Cape Town: Getting beyond the Streets in Africa's Deadliest City*. Bingley: Emerald Publishing.

Endoh, F. T. (2015). Democratic constitutionalism in post-Apartheid South Africa: The interim Constitution revisited. *Africa Review*, *7* (1), 67–79. https://doi.org/10.1080/09744053.2014.990769

Galtung, J. (1969). Violence, peace, and peace research. *Journal of Peace Research*, *6*, 167–91.

(1990). Cultural violence. *Journal of Peace Research*, *27*, 291–305.

Ife, J., Soldatić, K., & Briskman, L. (2022). *Human Rights and Social Work*. Cambridge University Press.

IFSW (International Federation of Social Workers). (2018). Global social work statement of ethical principles. www.ifsw.org/global-social-work-statement-of-ethical-principles (accessed 2 February 2024).

Johnson, R. W. (1977). *How Long Will South Africa Survive? The Looming Crisis*. London: Hurst.

Jones, C. (1998). Social work and society. In R. Adams, L. Dominelli, & M. Payne (eds.), *Social Work: Themes, Issues and Critical Debates*, pp.33–40. Basingstoke: Macmillan.

Kam, P. K. (2014). Back to the 'social' of social work: Reviving the social work profession's contribution to the promotion of social justice. *International Social Work*, *57*(6), 723–40. https://doi.org/10.1177/0020872812447118

Kempen, A. (2020). Community safety tips – gangs: Recruitment often starts with children – being forewarned is being forearmed. *Servamus Community-based Safety and Security Magazine*, *113*(2), 56–9.

Kiewit, L. (2019, 19 July). Boys join gangs to survive in toxic environment. *Mail & Guardian*, https://mg.co.za/article/2019-07-19-00-boys-join-gangs-to-survive-in-toxic-environment.

Kosko, S. J., Dastin, A., Merrill, M., & Sheth, R. (2022) Marginalised youth activism: Peer-engaged research and epistemic justice. *Journal of Human Development and Capabilities*, *23*(1), 136–56.

MacMaster, L. (2010). In search of a family: The challenge of gangsterism to faith communities on the Cape Flats. PhD thesis, University of Stellenbosch.

Manus, V. B. (2011). *Emerging Traditions: Toward a Postcolonial Stylistics of Black South African Fiction in English*. Lanham, MD: Lexington Books.

Mguzulwa, S., & Gxubane, T. (2019). The impact of youth gang violence on the educational attainment of male high school learners in Khayelitsha. *Social Work*, *55*(3), 267–83.

Mmatli, T. (2008). Political activism as a social work strategy in Africa. *International Social Work*, *51*(3), 297–310. https://doi.org/10.1177/0020872807083913

Modise, K. (2020, 16 June). SA's young people still face unemployment and poverty. *iAfrica*, https://iafrica.com/sas-young-people-still-face-unemployment-and-poverty.

Monareng, C. (2016). Making the number positive: Addressing youth needs that gangs fulfil. *Safer Spaces*, www.saferspaces.org.za/blog/entry/making-the-number-positive-addressing-youth-needs-that-gangs-fulfil.

Ndhlovu, G. N. (2020). Youth and gang violence in South Africa: An intended or unintended outcome of institutional systems. PhD thesis, University of Fort Hare.

(2022, 1 March). Idle and frustrated: Young South Africans speak about the need for recreational facilities. *The Conversation*, https://theconversation.com/idle-and-frustrated-young-south-africans-speak-about-the-need-for-recreational-facilities-176921.

Ndhlovu, G. N., & Tanga, P. (2021, 12 October). Study paints a grim picture of what young gangsters think about violence and manhood. *The Conversation*, https://theconversation.com/study-paints-a-grim-picture-of-what-young-gangsters-think-about-violence-and-manhood-168861.

Nussbaum, M. (2006). Human Rights and Human Capabilities. Oxford University Press.

Pinnock, D. (2019, 10 August). Cape Town's bloody gang violence is inextricably bound up in its history. *Mail & Guardian*, https://mg.co.za/article/2019-08-10-00-cape-towns-bloody-gang-violence-is-inextricably-bound-up-in-its-history.

Republic of South Africa. (1996). *Constitution of the Republic of South Africa*. Pretoria: Government Printers.

Rispel, L., Molomo, B., & Dumela, S. (2008). *South African Case Study on Social Exclusion*. Cape Town: Human Sciences Research Council.

Sefali, P. (2014, 27 May). Young, high and dangerous: Youth gangs and violence in Khayelitsha. *GroundUp*, https://groundup.org.za/article/young-high-and-dangerous-youth-gangs-and-violence-khayelitsha_1823.

Sen, A. (1999). *Development as Freedom*. Oxford University Press.
(2005). Human rights and capabilities. *Journal of Human Development and Capabilities*, *6*(2), 151–66.
Sharkey, J. D., Shekhtmeyster, Z., Chavez-Lopez, L., Norris, E. & Sass, L. (2011). The protective influence of gangs: Can schools compensate? *Aggression and Violent Behavior*, *16*(1), 45–54. https://doi.org/10.1016/j.avb.2010.11.001
Statistics South Africa. (2020). How unequal is South Africa? www.statssa.gov.za/?p=12930
(2021). Youth still find it difficult to secure jobs in South Africa. www.statssa.gov.za/?p=14415
Stoeffler, S. W. (2019). Social work and poverty: A critical examination of intersecting theories. *Social Development Issues*, *41*(2), 21–32.
Tutu, D., & Tutu, M. (2014). *The Book of Forgiving: The Fourfold Path for Healing Ourselves and Our World*. London: William Collins.
United Nations. (2024). Building on the legacy of Nelson Mandela. www.un.org/en/exhibits/page/building-legacy-nelson-mandela
Van der Linde, D. (2020). The criminalisation of gang activity in South Africa: Reassessing the rationale. *South African Crime Quarterly*, 69, 35–44. https://dx.doi.org/10.17159/2413-3108/2020/i69a6464
Van der Merwe, H. (2013). *Violence as a Form of Communication: Making Sense of Violence in South Africa*. Cape Town: Centre for the Study of Violence and Reconciliation.
Van der Westhuizen, M., & Gawulayo, S. (2021). Youths in gangs on the Cape Flats: If not in gangs, then what? *Social Work*, *57*(1), 118–32.
Ward, C. L., Van der Merwe, A., & Dawes, A. (2012). *Youth Violence: Sources and Solutions in South Africa*. Cape Town: UCT Press.
Yildirim, F., Öztürk, H., & Abukan, B. (2021). Examination of social workers' attitudes towards sustainable development and environment in the focus of the COVID-19 pandemic. *International Journal of Sustainability in Higher Education*, *22*(7), 1592–608.
Zaaroura, M. (2016, 7 June). Youth turn to violence and gangs as local governments struggle with security. *Safer Spaces*, www.saferspaces.org.za/blog/entry/youth-turn-to-violence-and-gangs-as-local-governments-struggle
Zlobina, A., Bettinsoli, M. L., Miranda, M. P., & Formanowicz, M. (2023). Back to basics: Human rights violations and dehumanization. *Current Opinion in Behavioral Sciences*, *51*, 101263. https://doi.org/10.1016/j.cobeha.2023.101263

Photo: Hilde Mjøs

CHAPTER 8

On My Toes

Reflections from a Research Project about Birth Parents of Children in Foster Care in Sweden

Ylva Spånberger Weitz

I stepped off the commuter train at Tranbärsbacken, a suburb of a Swedish city, and opened my maps app to type in Eva's address. We had spoken briefly on the phone before and made plans to meet at her house for an interview. At the time, I was working on a research project where we interviewed birth parents of children in foster care, asking about their experiences of finding themselves in this situation and about their wishes for support from the child welfare services regarding this. I was in my thirties, and I was a mother of three myself. My oldest were seven and ten and my youngest was still just a baby. I had received Eva's contact information from a social worker at the local child welfare unit and I knew that she had at least one child placed in foster care. Other than that, I didn't know much about her or about any other circumstances in her life. I followed the suggested route and arrived at a townhouse area where I oriented myself to the right address. I had found Eva's house. From inside I could hear the sound of children playing and a television humming in the background. I rang the doorbell.

I made this similar journey many times and met and talked to many other parents like Eva. I rang the doorbell of apartments and houses in different suburbs. I listened to parents' different stories about how their children had been taken away from them. All contacts between these parents and me were arranged through the child welfare services. If a parent agreed to talk to me I was provided only with their name and phone number. Thus, before ringing the doorbell I usually knew nothing about the person I was about to meet other than them being a parent of a child in foster care.

What is it like to lose the trust and ability to care for your child on a day-to-day basis? What is it like to be deemed unfit as a parent? Before conducting these interviews, I for sure could not imagine, or at least I could not relate. The first few times before a new interview, I expected to meet someone who was somehow different from me. I expected to be able to grasp, just by spending time with them, why they could not take care of their children. Sometimes that was also the case. Sometimes I felt that I could make sense of the situation and comprehend why the parent had been assessed unable to provide good enough everyday care. But far from every time. Sometimes when I listened to these parents' stories about losing their child, I felt that this could just as easily have happened to me. Their stories were as full of incomprehension and grief as mine would have been if I had gone through the same thing.

The Weight of Having One's Parental Ability Called into Question

At the time of conducting these interviews, my family and I had recently moved to a new townhouse. We were adjusting to our newest family member and to the larger home we had now moved into. Our everyday life was a bit of a challenge. On the other side of a thin wall lived a middle-aged woman. One day in the kitchen, my youngest child was banging happily on pots and pans on the kitchen floor beside me, and the woman called on me from her balcony door. She was appalled by the noise we made, not just today but ever since we moved in – loud screams and banging on things from the youngest, loud steps on the stairs and slamming the doors from the older ones. She expressed that she had noticed our ignorance and our indulgence towards our children, which was apparent at this specific moment by the fact that I would just keep letting the child bang on casseroles while doing my own things on the side. I don't remember exactly what I was doing, maybe preparing lunch, maybe reading the newspaper. The point she made, though, was that I was keeping on with whatever I was doing instead of interfering with the loud (but cheerful) pot banging. And this was just the last straw, she made that clear to me. This was just another day of continuous and uninterrupted noise-making stemming from our side of the wall, just another example of our neglectful parental behaviour. She had never seen anything like this, she said.

Our neighbour's complaints continued over the following months and nothing I would say could appease her. I argued that small children try out their voices and the effects of their actions (such as throwing wooden blocks on the floor) and that they ought to be able to express their frustration when trying and failing to learn new things (such as trying to get to a ball out of reach when learning to crawl). I explained that our older children sometimes get anxious when finding themselves alone on the upper floor of our townhouse, and therefor run down the stairs. I also explained that sometimes they're just eager to reach the next floor and so they forget about the noise that their running will cause, but that we talked to them about trying to walk carefully so as not to create disturbing noises. She claimed that our children needed more discipline. She suggested that we establish punishment routines for when they run loudly on the stairs. She suggested there was a lot to learn about the art of disciplining children from TV psychologists and Super Nanny shows. I counterargued by virtue of my position as a researcher on child–family relations and as a trained social worker. It did not impress her.

Meanwhile, I continued interviewing parents who had had their children removed, parents who couldn't for the world understand what had happened, who told stories about how their lives had turned upside down when this or that person had filed a complaint against them to the child welfare services. Many of them were lost in trying to understand how things had ended up like this, trying to understand why they had been deemed unfit to care for their children. They were grasping at straws to understand. Was it because the headmaster of their school had noticed a pair of torn trousers (mind you, not from home but from playing on the school ground)? Was it because of yesterday's pizza boxes on the living room table when this specific person came to visit? They had no clue, and they lived their nightmare.

Some of the parents told stories about how their children were suddenly taken away from them without warning, how one day they received a message from the child welfare services telling them not to pick their children up from school because they had been moved to a foster home. Eva, for example, told me how she had left her child at preschool one morning not knowing that she wouldn't be allowed to see him again for eight weeks. She told me about her mental breakdown when being informed about this by two social workers, about her despair when she was not even allowed the opportunity to say goodbye. Another woman I interviewed, Gabi, told a similar story. She described this experience as falling down a hole, of not being able to hear anything, of wondering if what was happening was real.

Other parents told stories about how anything they did would be misinterpreted and turned against them. Some parents told me how they had been strictly informed not to show any sad feelings in front of their children, but after trying to adjust to these instructions they were instead accused of being too cold and emotionless towards them. Jake, a father who was failing to get any clear answers on why his children were removed and what he needed to do for them to be able to move back, described his experiences of this process as Kafkaesque.[1]

As a fellow parent, I could relate to the feelings and experiences described by these parents, and I began to be able to imagine myself in their situation. When repeatedly confronted by my neighbour, I felt their distress as if it could become my own. What would happen if my neighbour made a complaint about us? Would my life turn upside down just like theirs? At this point, I became extra sensitive not only to my neighbour's complaints but also to occasional comments in passing from school or preschool staff about anything from the appropriate clothing for current weather conditions to the best way to manage my child's troublesome behaviour. In fact, I was overly worried about what anyone who interacted with me, or my children, would make of my parenting.

I was on my toes! Things I did: Hushing my kids (so much hushing!). Warning my kids about the angry neighbour (watch out doing that or the neighbour will get cross with us!). Putting up reminder notes on the stairs to walk carefully, and on the door to close it softly. (She suggested notes like "Don't slam the door!" I modified her suggestions and instead wrote, "Let's walk gently out of the door. Welcome back!" Small acts of resistance while at the same time appeasing her). I was ashamed for being scolded, and in turn, I think I shamed my kids. I didn't want to do that, but feelings of shame tend to spread. She banged the walls. I hushed my kids.

Other things I did: I became obsessed about keeping my children clean and tidy. One morning we were on our way to school. We were in a hurry. After leaving the house, I noticed a ketchup stain on my child's t-shirt. "Oh no, you've got a stain there" I said with a stressed-out voice. As if having a stain on their clothes was that bad. Being last-minute off to school, we were already stressed out and my reaction did not improve the situation. Another time we had a meeting with the school nurse. Again, I noticed a stain on the clothes of my child. "Oh my," I said out loudly. "I see you've got a stain there. We should have changed that t-shirt." I was

[1] Feeling extremely unpleasant, frightening, and confusing, and similar to situations described in the novels of Franz Kafka (1883–1924, a well-known author from Czechia, Europe).

smiling leniently (seemingly addressing my child, but who was I fooling? This was clearly a performative act aimed towards the school nurse). The nurse answered something in agreement, referring to some mistake of her own in the same area of failing to keep her children clean.

What was the output for my children from all of this? What feelings did situations like this (of which there were many) evoke in them? “Mum, why is it so bad if I have stains on my clothes?” they asked sometimes, in frustration. What would be a good answer to a question like that? So that I don’t have to be ashamed of you? So that other grownups don’t take me for a neglectful mother? Of course, I couldn’t give an answer like that. What answer could I possibly give? My child didn’t care about the stains. Nor did their peers. Nor did I ever care much about these things before. There is really no logic to the importance of stain-free clothes on the bodies of playing-aged children other than the symbolic value of these stains in the eyes of other adults.

Worries over cleanliness and tidiness were recurrent themes also in my interviews with the parents in the research project. Some of them thought that their failure to keep both their children and their house tidy enough (in the view of others) was a central cause for the removal of their children. Gabi told a story about how a visitor to their home had notified the child welfare services about the apartment being in a mess with unmade beds, empty pizza boxes, and a newly discarded diaper folded up on the table. Lily and Mark told a story about how the school headmaster made remarks about their children having torn clothes (which according to them were never torn when they left their home but got torn at the school playground). Patrick and Irene told a story about how the child welfare services, when paying them a visit, became suspicious about the smell of detergent, implying they had cleaned their home too thoroughly as if covering something up. Common to all these events was that the parents all referred to them as significant for why their children were eventually removed from them.

The parents’ understanding that failures in housekeeping or childcare activities were crucial to their children ending up in foster care could easily be dismissed as proof of their failure to understand the actual reasons behind this outcome. Even though I never knew anything about the assessments made by child welfare services in these cases, I am confident that of course there must have been more to it than occasional events of untidiness. Still, are the parents’ interpretations about the impacts of these events really that far-fetched? Even if these events were not the solitary reason, or even a primary one, for taking their children into care, might it still have played some part in the child welfare services' assessment of their parental ability?

Ideals of Good Parenthood and the Stigma of Parental Failure

A memory comes to mind from my own days as a social worker at a child welfare unit. During a coffee break, there was talk about this parent who hadn't cleared the living room table of breadcrumbs when the child welfare services made a scheduled home visit. I so clearly remember the puzzled reactions among my colleagues about these unremoved breadcrumbs, of how this parent had left them there even though they knew that we (the child welfare services) were coming. There was an expression of astonishment and estrangement about this, as if the presence of these breadcrumbs were really a sign of not being able to take proper care of themselves and their children. A sign of otherness, of dealing with a person who was not quite the same as us. I said nothing during this conversation but was quietly ashamed; I've never been very good at keeping my home clean and tidy.

At this point in life, I had no children of my own, but this and similar incidents still made me feel inferior and a bit overwhelmed. Was this what would be expected of me when I became a parent (or rather, a mother)? I've been a mother now for twenty years and I know for a fact that, yes, this is expected. I also know that I'm not living up to these expectations. Ever since I became a parent, I've always had these conflicting feelings about tidiness. On the one hand, rebelliously wanting to ignore the expectations (so what if our kitchen curtains are totally dusty or our children have stains and scratches on their clothes). On the other hand, struggling with feelings of shame for these signs of untidiness. Cleaning and covering up when expecting visitors, checking the clothes and the hairstyles of my children and struggling with how much to correct them. Trying to keep them from bearing my shame while at the same time preventing them from ending up in the marginalized position of untidiness. All these underlying feelings of parental inferiority were brought into play when confronted by my neighbour and this, in turn, intensified my sense of relatedness with the parents I interviewed.

At one point during the time of conducting these interviews, I came to talk about the norm of tidiness with a fellow academic and social worker. We reflected on the symbolic meaning of keeping both your house and your children clean and tidy, and on how a failure to do so may (or may not!) define how others perceive you and your parental abilities. She told me about a foster home that she had come across during her career as a social worker. The parents in this home were middle-class, academics, skilled in communicating with welfare professionals. They were also a bit untidy and careless. But for them that was no big deal. They were seen as a bit eccentric, sure, but charming and lovable. A good home. I suspect that this is how my family and I are looked upon as well. As opposed to parents within the system of child welfare services where a similar carelessness may rather be interpreted as just another sign of parental neglect. Despite my worries, I was relieved to have good communication with the school staff. I was fluent in the language and cultural codes of the welfare society, and I believed (when reflecting on it more closely) that although my children were sometimes difficult to control and although they did not always show up in clean and appropriately sized clothes, school staff were still confident enough about my parental skills.

A while after having completed the interviews I visited some of the foster care units that had helped mediate contact between me and the parents, to present findings from the research project to them. On one such occasion, a social worker recounted an anecdote about a parent who, the social worker had learnt, was hiding the fact that her children were in foster care. What was striking to me was that although the social workers clearly expressed sympathy for this parent, they showed no sign of real comprehension of why the parent wanted to hide their situation from the world.

I wondered if they had never reflected on how they themselves would have handled the same situation. How did they think it would have felt for them? Would they not have experienced this situation as shameful? The social workers did not seem to make that connection. Lipsky (2010) writes about how the working conditions of street-level bureaucrats (such as social workers) can contribute to an alienation from their clients: when processing clients through the system, street-level bureaucrats need to turn them into categories built on bureaucratically relevant attributes, which effectively hinders their professional ambition to recognize them as whole persons.

Is this what was at stake here? An institutionalized othering of clients stemming from the internal logic of street-level bureaucracy, a sense that they (the clients, the parents of children in foster care) are not like us, that we as social workers are not the kind of people whose children may be taken away? And perhaps due to our life circumstances, it is difficult to imagine a scenario where they as social workers, or I as a social work researcher, would end up in a situation where our children were to be placed in foster care. But even if that scenario is unimaginable for us, even if they or you or I, we who are social workers and researchers and well-established in society, even if we are mostly not people who risk having our children taken into care, even so, as human beings we are no different from those who do live through this experience. It should still be possible for us to understand that losing a child is as traumatic and shameful for anyone who experiences it, as it would be for you or for me. If there is one thing I have learnt through my encounters with these parents, through my relatedness to them as a parent, it is this.

What is it like to lose the trust and ability to care for your child on a day-to-day basis? What is it like to be deemed unfit as a parent? Research suggests that having your children placed in foster care may be a deeply stigmatizing experience characterized by both grief and guilt (see Schofield et al., 2011). Even though this specific experience only applies to a few, I do believe that most parents can relate to the shame and stigma associated with feelings of not being a good enough parent. Goffman (1963) describes a stigma as an attribute that is deeply discrediting within a given social context. Stigma thus relates to norms and ideals about what it means to lead a normal and eligible life, and it strongly connects to ideals of good parenting, ideals which are to some extent always unattainable. Perhaps the shame related to feelings of parental failure – and with that, the fear of being stigmatized as result of these failures – is an inherent part of being a parent. If most parents are aware of this stigma, would this also make it possible for us, as social workers and fellow parents, to relate to one of the most stigmatizing parental experiences of all, that of losing the trust to care for your child?

My children are older now. Many years have passed. I rarely think back on my encounters with the parents I interviewed anymore, nor do I worry about neighbours calling the child welfare services with an anonymous complaint. Still, echoes from these experiences remain within me, embodied in my parental reactions: moments of worrying about too loud steps on the stairs or neglected toothpaste stains on the cheekbone of my youngest child or me losing my temper amid everyday turmoil. Small signs that, under some circumstances, might be interpreted by others as just another sign of parental neglect. But for now, those are not my circumstances. My moments of worrying pass and fade.

Foster Care and Parenting Ideals in Sweden: Contextualizing the Narrative

In Sweden, foster care rarely leads to adoption or to the termination of parental rights for the birth parents. Instead, the common practice is that of long-term foster care where foster parents, birth parents, and child welfare services create a co-parenting partnership, often referred to as three-part parenting, around the child (Skoog, Khoo, and Nygren, 2015). Hence, all the parents I interviewed were still legal guardians to their children in care although some of them had experienced having their children removed recently while others had lived apart from their children for many years. Furthermore, some had their children placed in care on a voluntary basis (although often as result of strong persuasion from child welfare services) while others had their children placed under coercive legislation.

When looking back on my experiences from interviewing these parents, and from being confronted by my neighbour about my own parenting abilities, I'm struck by the power of parenthood ideals that both I and the interviewed parents related to when trying to understand (and, in part, defend) our position as parents. In Sweden, parenting ideals are situated in a modern Western context and closely related to the moral discourse of "intensive mothering" (Hays, 1996), which in a Swedish context may be rephrased in the similar concept of 'involved parenting' due to an ideal that both mothers and fathers take active (and preferably equal) part in parenting activities (Forsberg, 2009). Within these moral discourses, good parenting is expected to be (among other things) responsible, labour-intensive, child-centred, emotionally engaging, physically and emotionally present, and a lifelong commitment. Furthermore, ideals of motherhood in a Western context are also closely intertwined with being a co-resident parent and the provider of everyday care, an ideal that in a sense turns non-residential motherhood into a contradiction (see Kielty, 2008).

In our narrative analysis of my interviews with birth parents, a colleague and I showed how the parents dealt with these parenting ideals by downplaying the significance of the everyday care that was performed by foster parents and emphasizing the significance of a lifelong emotional engagement which they argued formed a basis for their own unique bonds with their children (Spånberger Weitz & Karlsson, 2021). In a similar way, I too seem to deal with these ideals by negotiating which aspects of parenthood are to be considered more significant than others; in recounting the arguments with my neighbour, I emphasize my approach as a perceptive and reasoning parent as a counterbalance to her suggestion that our children need more discipline; in reflections about my relatedness to the parents I interviewed, I downplay the importance of keeping my children (and my home) clean and tidy in favour (again) of being perceptive to the views of my children. Looking at it from a distance, it becomes clear to me that the discursive ideals of intensive mothering or involved parenthood are at play also in these negotiations. It also leads me to reflect on the overwhelmingness of these ideals. Perhaps negotiating which aspects of these ideals can be downplayed, and which should be emphasized, is in fact a perfectly reasonable approach to being a parent.

Reflective Questions

1. What parenting ideals and what moral discourses on parenthood have you encountered in the contexts of your life?
2. In your experience, what are differences between parenting ideals across different groups of parents, for example depending on gender, class, or culture?
3. In your view, how can knowledge about parenting ideals and moral discourses on parenthood be useful in social work with children and families?

REFERENCES

Forsberg, L. (2009). *Involved Parenthood: Everyday Lives of Swedish Middle-Class Families*. PhD thesis, Linköping University.

Goffman, E. (1963). *Stigma: Notes on the Management of Spoiled Identity*. Englewood Cliffs, NJ: Prentice-Hall.

Hays, S. (1996). *The Cultural Contradictions of Motherhood*. New Haven, CT: Yale University Press.

Kielty, S. (2008). Non-resident motherhood: Managing a threatened identity. *Child & Family Social Work*, *13*(1), 32–40.

Lipsky, M. (2010). *Street-Level Bureaucracy. Dilemmas of the Individual in Public Services*. New York: Russell Sage Foundation.

Schofield, G., Moldestad, B., Höjer, I., Ward, E., Skilbred, D., Young, J., & Havik, T. (2011). Managing loss and a threatened identity: Experiences of parents of children growing up in foster care, the perspectives of their social workers and implications for practice. *British Journal of Social Work*, *41*(1), 74–92.

Skoog, V., Khoo, E., & Nygren, L. (2015) Disconnection and dislocation: Relationships and belonging in unstable foster and institutional care. *British Journal of Social Work*, *45*(6), 1888–904.

Spånberger Weitz, Y., & Karlsson, M. (2021) Professional or authentic motherhood? Negotiations on the identity of the birth mother in the context of foster care. *Qualitative Social Work*, *23*(3), 703–17.

Photo: Hilde Mjøs

CHAPTER 9

A Story of Love, Family, and Mental Health

Jin-Yong Wang

After my father's death, I experienced complex feelings towards him and was later depressed from time to time for around three years. During that period of mourning time, I felt not only sad but also angry, regretful, lonely, and hopeless. Maybe my condition is like "complicated grief" (Mason & Tofthagen, 2019), but why me? All my brothers and sisters seem to live well without similar conditions. I realized later that it may relate to my ambivalent feelings towards my father, who was a good enough father and a lousy husband in my mind. As a mental health social worker and researcher, I know it feels like depression, but I never think I need to see a psychiatrist. So, rather than asking for a psychiatrist's prescription for an antidepressant, I have tried various ways to figure out what is going on in my mind and learned how to stop dwelling on negative thoughts and emotions, such as by participating in dream appreciation groups and hiking in the forest. Although challenging, I am well enough now after five years of struggling. Most importantly, no matter how unwilling I used to be, I now realize that accepting all my feelings towards my father is imperative and healthy for me.

This is a story about my personal life and professional career, which are intertwined and associated with my family. It is a continuous recovery journey through alternative healing and professional training from my adverse childhood experiences. After years of social work practice, teaching, and researching, I have gradually understood what mental health means and how important and relevant it is to people's every aspect of life. As a personal narrative, I will tell my story and retrospect my experiences from my childhood to my current professional job. As a social worker, I have also met and worked with some people with mental health issues. Their struggles and difficulties have also taught me what mental health means to them and how they take care of it uniquely. Now let me tell you what my family looks like in my eyes.

Low-Income Family with Lots of Children

I was born in the early 1970s when Taiwan transformed from an agricultural country to an industrial one. My parents had five children, and almost every family had many children then. As the youngest of my siblings, my eldest sister was ten years older than me. When I went to elementary school, three of my elder siblings had already finished school, not because they did not like to study, but because they were expected to earn our family's living for my parents. My earliest black-and-white photo was taken with my second brother when I was about six, and he was around the second grade in elementary school. I held a bowl in the picture, and my brother raised his right hand to pose respectfully. We stood in front of our old house, enclosed by wattle-and-daub walls and a thatch roof, with dusty ground inside. Once, the roof leaked all day and night, caused by a heavy typhoon in summertime. I stood on the muddy, slightly sticky ground with my bare feet, feeling relaxed and fresh throughout my ankles. My family was poor, but I was happy!

My parents did not finish elementary school because of the air attacks during their childhood in the 1940s when Taiwan was occupied and governed by the Japanese. According to my mother, she had been a little worker helping my grandparents with farming and cooking for quite a few years in her childhood. Later, when she was a teenager, she went to Dadaocheng and DiHua Street, Taipei's central business district at that time, to be hired by one of her relatives. There, she met my father, a porter travelling through Taiwan for goods transportation. After they got married, they left Taipei and settled in my paternal grandparents' house in Central Taiwan, where agriculture was the primary source of family income. I did not know what my father and mother did to earn our living, but I know my father would sometimes carry a unique electric toolkit to catch frogs, eels, or even snakes at night. In the 1970s, the natural environment was not polluted, and fish were swimming in the stream. I remember those starry evenings when I watched my father prepare the toolkit and battery after dinner. When he was ready to go, he would turn on the headlight on his forehead, with a long electric stick held in his right hand and a fully charged battery and bucket bag behind his back. The following day, when I woke up, with luck a bucket full of crowded creatures was in it. The snakes, if there were any, that were valuable in the market would be kept alone in a long, white clothes bag hung on a tree branch. A vivid memory of my father is that he once took me on a bike to the market and sold all the captured animals. Then, we happily bought meats and vegetables. On the way home, my father's back seemed so huge that I have never forgotten it until now.

It seemed to me like a worry-free childhood before my school age. However, in my early memory, my father's binge drinking had already become a big issue, often compounded by notorious frightening behaviours such as shouting, self-talking, and even violence towards my mother. Once, when he got drunk, he even asked my junior high school teacher to lend him money. Nonetheless, he could earn wages as a construction worker when in a good condition. Also, when he mentioned my second elder brother and me to his friends, he was very proud of my brother and me, who had won several awards for excellent grades at school. All of these memories induced my ambivalent feelings towards my father. In one way, he was a loving giant in my mind, giving me unforgettable paternal love and joy; in another way, however, he was hated by my mother and siblings due to his drunken behaviour, particularly the domestic violence towards my mother. For a long time, I felt ashamed not only because of delaying payment of tuition fees but also because of my parents' unsolvable conflicts. For years, I have witnessed my parents arguing, and even violence, during their almost-broken marriage. It was a frightening, confusing, and annoying family environment throughout my childhood and teenage years.

Of course, as research suggests, witnessing domestic violence significantly impacts children (Forke et al., 2019). For instance, such family experiences had pushed me away from my family, both psychologically and physically. When I passed the official exam for civil servants in the early 2000s, I felt like escaping from my family as far as possible. As a result, even though my mother was in a late stage of terminal cancer and asked me to stay with her in Taipei, I still chose to be a social worker in a public psychiatric hospital in eastern Taiwan, which was very far away from her. I rejected her cruelly without hesitation but felt that this was what I could do for myself then. I was probably a selfish old child experiencing the rebellious stage at thirty-three and escaping my worry about my mother's death, wishing she could have lived longer under my brother's care. Sadly, she passed away in the next year of my employment. I am not sure if my father felt sad during my mother's funeral, but I know he must have been even lonelier than before. He lived alone for another fifteen years after my mother died.

No matter how miserable my family used to be, my siblings and I have never been defeated. Partly, this may be due to our resilience, but mainly it was owing to people's benevolent attitude towards us. Many family relatives, neighbours, and even schoolteachers were kind to us when my family was in trouble and needed money to live and pay tuition fees, etc. Gradually, my family's finances have improved, and the muse of social work has come into my mind, inspiring me to be a giver for others. You could say that my family is the birthplace and aspiration of my social work soul. Having suffered bitterly in my life made me compassionate to others' suffering, particularly to those kids who are in poverty. Now, I have come up with a new perspective on my parents and family. So, in the following section, I will transfer the scenario to my professional career to describe what I have learned from the people I have encountered in my professional career.

Volunteer as a Book Reader

Like many other social work students, I started to learn how to work with clients by volunteering at the beginning of my social work education. I had a chance to be a book reader and a brother-like companion for preschool kids in a poor community. When kids gathered around me to listen to and enjoy my book stories, it was also a big reward for me. In my childhood, I had no chance to be in a book-reading audience or attend any storytelling activities. Before entering elementary school, I spent most of my time playing outdoors. Since my parents did not finish elementary school, they were nearly illiterate and never read books before me. So, when I read books to the young kids around me, it felt like my inner child was listening to the story simultaneously. At the moment of book-reading, I felt accomplished to give joy to young kids and pleased to comfort my inner child. The volunteering experience offered a great chance to transform myself from a receiver to a giver.

Group Therapy

My healing journey went further when I studied in a graduate school of social work. As a graduate student, social group work was one of my most unforgettable classes. The lecturer is the leader and one of the advanced therapists of a family organization, where I applied for my social work placement later. Based upon her psychodrama training and clinical practice wisdom over many years, she would direct psychodrama in the class, and we MA students played various roles according to the protagonist's scenes. In the beginning, I did not even dare to be the auxiliary ego, not to mention the protagonist, and I was often only part of the audience group. Even so, I found it so compelling and rewarding to learn the fundamentals of psychodrama. Moreover, participating in the protagonist's story and finally enacting the role of the protagonist's father gave me the motivation and courage to approach my own family's dynamics and relationships later when I decided to apply for social work placement. It was one of the critical capstones in my professional training that paved the way to delve into my family's dynamics and relationships.

Social Work Placement and Play Therapy

Based on my growing-up experience, children are my priority for social work placement. I entered a family counselling organization to learn how to work with families, including observing and assessing family dynamics and implementing psychodynamic and behavioural skills of interpersonal intervention for parents and their children. Various activities are designed to facilitate children's interaction, and social workers will intervene when there are arguments or quarrels. During my social work placement, I learned how family interactions shape children's personalities and behaviours in everyday life. It opened a window for me to appreciate how family significantly impacts every aspect of children and the dynamic relationships between various family members, such as parental, marital, and sibling ones.

As a social work trainee, my placement in the family organization was a fruitful result. Moreover, after witnessing the power of social workers' intervention with families, I accepted sand tray therapy after my placement in the organization. During the sessions, I was helped to tell my therapist what had happened to me and my family through the representative idols I selected and put in the sandbox. While in the therapy room, it seemed natural to find myself in tears under the therapist's guidance. It shows that I needed to release my strong emotions towards my family. Meanwhile, I usually felt anxious and vulnerable in the middle of every session, then tired and relieved. I could not have come so far on my professional road without those therapy sessions. As the concept of wounded healers indicates, therapists must heal themselves before they can be a healer for others (Ryan, 2020). In short, although there are still many other issues in my life, I have learned to appreciate my family dynamics and the art of psychotherapy through direct involvement in therapy sessions.

A Social Worker in a Psychiatric Hospital

From 2002 to 2005, I was a social worker in a public psychiatric specialist hospital, well-known in Taiwan for its long-term care services. Located in a remote town in eastern Taiwan, the hospital was initially established as an asylum in the 1960s to accommodate poor people with serious mental illness. When I worked there, various local health administrations transferred patients who had long waited to be admitted to the hospital. It is free hospital care for mainly targeted patients, so we social workers had to ensure the legal procedures and all required documents for admission were ready. Even so, I found that patients were not psychologically prepared for it after realizing it was a hospital for the rest of their lives. For family caregivers who have travelled to many hospitals to treat the mental illness of their loved ones, it acts like a terminal stop where they can finally hand in their care responsibility to professionals and live their own lives. For patients, however, this is rarely an expected happy ending. Often, when I entered the hospital ward, several inmates approached me and asked me when they could be discharged and go home. I could not tell them what I knew; they would probably stay in the hospital for the rest of their lives. Instead, I would encourage them to take good care of themselves, and I promised to do my best to ring their family and pass on their information or concerns.

"Sorry, I have been unable to go to the hospital to visit my brother recently; I need to take care of my baby at home." "I am busy now. Can you make a phone call again later?" These are the typical answers I received from the families when I rang them for my patients. Some family caregivers told me how they had cared for their sons or daughters and felt frustrated, exhausted, and hopeless. Besides, some family caregivers rejected any more contact with their family members due to their violence towards them during a psychotic episode. As the literature mentions, family caregivers are likely to be attacked or threatened by their ill family members (Labrum et al., 2021). After hearing many stories about family caregivers' distress and difficulties, how can I blame them for abandoning their family members or ignoring their mails and phone calls?

While disappointed, many inmates still queued in line every weekend to use the public phone when no mobiles were available in the hospital. Some would argue with their families on the phone; others would beg their families to visit them. After hearing these family communications many times, I wondered whether hospital care was the best solution for people with mental illness. As mentioned above, many families have already become so exhausted after caring for their ill loved ones for years that their decision to adopt long-term care is understandable. However, what about the patients who do not want to stay in the hospital for the rest of their lives? The hospital is designed as an alternative 'home' for the patients, but I am not quite sure how many inmates feel a home-like atmosphere in the hospital. In particular, after knowing some patients can take care of themselves and help staff quite well, I was astonished and disappointed that among 2,000 patients, less than 10 of them were discharged during my three years in the hospital.

A Gatekeeper of Social Assistance Resources

In 2005, after I resigned from my social work job in the hospital, I had a new position in the Department of Social Welfare, T. City Government. One of my duties was to look for homeless people after work hours in the evening. As the city mayor's policy was to keep the streets 'tidy', social workers were expected to care for people looking like the homeless or lying on the sidewalks. As a social worker with this duty, I would approach homeless people and ask if they needed any help. Meanwhile, police officers would go with me and check their IDs so they could contact their families if they had the contact information. When homeless people needed medical services, I would call an ambulance and accompany them to the hospital. In T. City, free lunch boxes would be offered daily at the service stop, and homeless people would queue for food every day. If homeless people needed to shower and find shelter or warm clothes in the cold wintertime, they could also go to the service stop. Based on my work experience, this was the service that I knew homeless people could receive at that time.

One day, a sixty-something homeless man came to the Department's Office for Financial Assistance. In T. City, citizens could come to the Department of Social Welfare and ask for a subsidy, and they would be served or consulted by the staff on the ground floor. However, appearing in the Department on the fourth floor was unusual for homeless people. In my impression, homeless people would not be so assertive. Moreover, it never occurred to me that a homeless man would appear on the fourth floor, where the staff's office is, and ask for money. That is why I was stunned by the man's appearance.

"There is a man who needs your help," said my colleague when I was sitting in front of my desk doing my job. Although he looked slightly untidy, he knew what he wanted apparently: "I need money to buy food," he said. "You can go to the service stop for free food. Lunch box will be offered at lunchtime," I replied. He did not say anything for a moment but stood still. "I want to go home, and I need money to buy a train ticket," he said to me instead. "I cannot give you any money. If you need money for transportation, you can go to the police station," I rejected his demand. He was not going to give up quickly, and I did not want to compromise easily. I thought, "Lying! This is just another way of begging, and he was so audacious to do it!" I returned to my desk even though the man was still standing at the office gate. After I sat on my chair, my manager told me he came for money occasionally. "Give him some money and let him go," said my manager. "No! He should not ask us for money. If he needs help, he should go to the service stop," I explained to my manager. "But if you don't give him some money, he won't leave," my manager emphasized. I insisted on my position without any hesitation. Finally, the man left after my manager took out his wallet and gave the man some money.

I was unhappy and angry, even though my manager solved my problem. "This is ridiculous!" I thought. According to my judgement, the man was a liar. He just overused the public resources shamelessly. As a gatekeeper of social assistance resources, I had no mercy for liars, even if he was homeless and may have had unspoken difficulties. The man was not like those I had met on the street or in the pedestrian underpass. I was angry and impatient with the homeless man who openly asked for money. Of course, he contradicted my image of vulnerable clients; he even 'manipulated' me or my manager to give him money. However, maybe I was overreacting. Maybe my strong feelings about the 'assertive' homeless man were associated with my father. In other words, I had unconsciously related the man to my father, who was similar in age and behaviour, so it was my countertransference towards the homeless man. My ambivalent feelings towards my father had been a serious, embarrassing, and challenging issue for a long time. It was an emotional complex that constantly bothered me until my father passed away in 2018.

Adverse Childhood Experiences

The homeless man incident reminded me of my adverse childhood experiences (ACE). ACE research has drawn considerable attention in recent years (Schiraldi, 2021). It reveals that people with more adverse childhood experiences have a higher probability of developing physical and mental health problems. This was pretty convincing after I counted my score according to the ACE scale. My parents had argued with each other many times since my childhood. In addition, domestic violence, alcohol abuse, suicide attempts, and my parents' separation were the adverse events I can recall in my childhood. If it happened now, I would probably be protected or even taken away by a child protection social worker. However, in

Taiwan, the laws and services concerning child protection and domestic violence were not passed and created until the 1990s (Chen, 2010; Yu, 1999). As I was born in 1970, it was impossible for any social worker to come to rescue me and my family. I still remember that police officers arrived at my house and left without any fundamental effect of stopping my family's violence.

As witnesses to my parents' conflict, sometimes my brother and I were forced to take a stand. With my mother standing aside, my drunken father would ask us whom we would like to live with. He seemed to imply that if they got divorced, we had to choose one of them. For me, it felt like a judge's question about the custody arrangement, but it was a question proposed by my drunken father, who probably had no idea what he was talking about. At the moment of my father's questioning, I had no idea what to say but felt scared and vulnerable. I cannot recall how often my father had asked us such a question, but it would end whenever my father suddenly fell asleep.

Offender and Victim of Domestic Violence

Regarding marriage in Taiwan, the relationship typically extends beyond the couple. For instance, when a crisis happens in marriage, traditionally the husband's and wife's family members would get involved and try to solve the problems for the couple. As far as I can remember, my mother's siblings visited us once or twice when my father's violence seriously injured my mother. My uncles must have considered the necessity of divorce and suggested it to my mother, although divorce was not the final result of their marriage. Ultimately, they lived separately for the rest of their lives until they passed away. Why did my mother not want to divorce my father? Once, my mother told me that even though my father had beaten and abused her for many years, she did not choose to divorce my father because of me and my siblings. In her mind, she tried to keep my family intact no matter how seriously she had suffered in her marriage.

For many years, I thought my mother was the only victim of domestic violence in my family and alcohol abuse was the culprit for my father's domestic violence. However, after some years of social work practice and establishing my own family, I have come up with an alternative perspective. According to the literature on intimate partner violence, sometimes there are no definite roles of offender and victim; instead, two respondents might be involved in overlapping roles (Tillyer & Wright, 2014).

Therefore, the so-called offenders are not always the only ones who should be blamed and punished. This is my viewpoint on the incidence of domestic violence. For children witnessing domestic violence like me, the value of learning to appreciate their parents' conflict and violence is enormous. Although I still cannot figure out what went wrong with my parents' marriage, I am grateful for what they have done for me as parents, and I do not blame either of them for what happened in their marriage. I still remember when I was a little kid, my parents took me to a zoo, and we all looked happy in the black-and-white photograph. It will always be an unforgettable and cherished memory with my parents.

Resilience

Regarding resilience, a Taiwanese saying aptly expresses a similar meaning: "Good bamboo shoots grow from bad bamboo." In my case, my family was viewed by our neighbours as 'bad bamboo' because they had witnessed my father's binge drinking and incidents of domestic violence. However, my brother and I always earned excellent school grades and never did anything wrong from childhood on. When we grew up and had good jobs, old neighbours were amazed by our achievements and appraised us highly. In their eyes, we were the classic case of "Good bamboo shoots grow from bad bamboo." I have a PhD and am a university faculty member, but my parents did not even finish elementary school. They were born in the 1930s, the Japanese colonial period, when people were barely able to live their lives. Later, the Second World War extended to Taiwan, and it was extremely tough for families to raise children, not to mention that there was no public education for Taiwanese children in the 1940s. In short, my family's endurance has kept us bravely facing and tackling all kinds of disadvantages and suffering.

Social Work Educator

After finishing my PhD program in England, I returned to Taiwan and soon found a faculty job at a university in 2010. Since then, I have become a social work educator and a researcher. Although I could not do social work practice anymore, I have transferred my attention to my students, who are like my clients in some ways. The following section focuses on what happened to my students and how I responded to their needs and difficulties. These experiences reveal my concerns about the mental health issues future social workers may have.

Self-Harm for Love

Occasionally, I would receive an email observing that a student of mine cut herself. As a mentor, I would then meet the student, express my concerns, and try to understand what bothered the student. The common reasons why students harm themselves are associated with interpersonal issues, such as conflicts in peer relationships and romantic breakups. In addition to counselling, some students also seek medication at a psychiatric clinic. According to what I know at my university, over the past decade, more and more college students cut themselves to relieve their feelings of loss, anxiety, or depression. With social media, nowadays, students seem to feel more pressure from interpersonal issues. One student used to tell me how she felt sad and lost when her friends had lots of fun things to share on Instagram. For this generation, it is an era to show off personal life. They are good at posting short messages and gorgeous photographs, but whether they can talk to each other socially and negotiate with each other sincerely is a concern to me.

Among the students in a self-harm crisis, I was apprehensive about a female student who continued to cut her wrists and legs for quite a long time. I first met her when she got drunk on campus, and her classmates helped her rest in a classroom. "Help me, teacher!" she said to me in a drunk tone. Since then, I have seen and interviewed her in my office for over two years. Although she visited my office many times, she rarely opened her mind to tell me much about her suffering. On the contrary, she often kept silent for quite a while or sometimes would mention her trivial matters. I patiently waited for her and hoped she could share her distress with me, but it did not happen. Not surprisingly, her condition did not improve to any significant degree during the period of our interviews. She also accepted counselling arranged by the university staff, but she participated in a way similar to what I saw in my office.

After she graduated, she proposed to continue our interviews by emailing each other. I agreed to email her but told her I could not reply to her email very promptly. Later, she revealed many of her sufferings and childhood adversities in the emails; until then, I could barely guess what might have happened to her. She was stable for some months, but unfortunately, it was not always the case. After graduation, she suffered a severe injury and was admitted into an acute psychiatric ward more than once. From her emails, I learned that she was diagnosed with borderline personality, which seems reasonable after considering her relationship with me and other counsellors. I did not think the diagnosis or medication would help her too much. Instead, psychotherapy or meaningful relationships with friends and family could help her overcome her distress in the long run.

A Psychotic Episode

According to what I have seen on campus, students need help when they experience a romantic breakup. Once upon a time, several students sent me messages regarding their worries about a male student who posted photos of a knife on his Instagram, fearing he might hurt himself after a girl rejected his love confession. They thought something was wrong with him and that he might be in a manic state. I contacted the student and asked if he could come to see me. He showed up at my office, looked calm, and promised he would not harm himself or anyone else. However, after he returned to his room, he had an outbreak of religious delusion. For example, he believed he had some magic power and needed to rescue a girl he admired. Later, police officers came to help his parents take him home, but he jumped out of his parents' car and ran away without any contact information. That evening, I spent hours searching for him. I was slightly scared when I saw the missing student wandering on a dark street. His eyes revealed his suspicion when he saw me approaching him. As a psychiatric social worker, I knew my words might provoke unpleasant feelings or even unexpected reactions like running away again. So I was cautious about slowing my car and asking him if he was all right. Finally, I was able to accompany him to the emergency room.

When the doctor saw him to check his condition, he appeared calm and answered questions logically. Because he did not want to stay in the hospital, the doctor put him in the observation room for rest without prescribing any medication and planned to discharge him later. While he remained alone, his mother and I chatted outside the room. Less than an hour later, he suddenly ran out of his room and stripped naked, trying to leave the emergency room by fiercely hitting the gate with his body. Several medical staff immediately caught him and tied him on the bed. Then the doctor injected him to sedate him and arranged his admission to the psychiatric ward. He stayed in the hospital ward for about two weeks and was discharged to go home. As far as I know, he has not had any other psychotic outbreak since then.

Final Words

Some research findings have reported that a certain proportion of helping professionals, such as social workers and psychologists, have a traumatic life history (Mercer et al., 2023). My students above and myself are among this population. My traumatic childhood influenced my identity as a father and a husband, and it took me a while to cultivate the confidence to establish my own family. Now, I can stop looking for a male role model and learn to appreciate what my father has done for me as a father. If there is any lesson to be learned from my story, I hope that social workers with childhood adversity will find the courage to retrospect their life story and learn to take good care of themselves.

Reflective Questions

1. What can social work educators do to help students with mental health issues?
2. What kinds of resources are needed to help social workers recover from childhood adversity?
3. What are the human rights issues in this story?

REFERENCES

Chen, S.-F. (2010). The present and future of domestic violence prevention in Taiwan from the view of victims' protection and offenders' treatment. *Asian Journal of Domestic Violence and Sexual Offense*, *6*(1), 187–210.

Forke, C. M., Catallozzi, M., Localio, A. R., Grisso, J. A., Wiebe, D. J., & Fein, J. A. (2019). Intergenerational effects of witnessing domestic violence: Health of the witnesses and their children. *Preventive Medicine Reports*, *15*, 100942.

Labrum, T., Zingman, M. A., Nossel, I., & Dixon, L. (2021). Violence by persons with serious mental illness toward family caregivers and other relatives: A review. *Harvard Review of Psychiatry*, *29*(1), 10–19.

Mason, T. M., & Tofthagen, C. S. (2019). Complicated grief of immediate family caregivers: A concept analysis. *Advances in Nursing Science*, *42*(3), 255–65.

Mercer, L., Cookson, A., Simpson-Adkins, G., & van Vuuren, J. (2023). Prevalence of adverse childhood experiences and associations with personal and professional factors in health and social care workers: A systematic review. *Psychological Trauma: Theory, Research, Practice, and Policy*, *15*(S2), S231–45.

Ryan, S. (2020). The wounded healer: Personal experiences of mental health difficulties and trauma and their influence on the professional practice of clinical psychologists and other therapy professionals. PhD thesis, Staffordshire University.

Schiraldi, G. R. (2021). *The Adverse Childhood Experiences Recovery Workbook: Heal the Hidden Wounds from Childhood Affecting Your Adult Mental and Physical Health*. Oakland, CA: New Harbinger.

Tillyer, M. S., & Wright, E. M. (2014). Intimate partner violence and the victim–offender overlap. *Journal of Research in Crime and Delinquency*, *51*(1), 29–55.

Yu, H.-Y. A. (1999). Modulation of the child protection movement in Taiwan. *NTU Social Work Review*, *1*, 149–79.

Photo: Hilde Mjøs

CHAPTER 10

Pieces of Walnut

Kay Hampton

"Is my dad coming home tonight?"

I turned and looked at the sadness in the face beside me. This was the third time she had asked me the question today and I still had no answer that would comfort her.

She held his photo in her hands and her tears wet her face.

"Why doesn't he see me now?"

Another question impossible to answer truthfully.

We were driving through familiar streets again. It was dark. This was the hardest time of the day, especially in winter. I could distract her for a while and make her believe that we were going somewhere, rather than nowhere.

I reached out and took her hand in mine. It was easier for me to look ahead at the road than to see the anguish in her eyes.

How could I tell her that her father would never be coming home, never see her again, pick her up, make her laugh? He was her world and she must never believe that he had abandoned her.

"If I had a magic wand, I would wave it and your dad would be back with us right now," I heard myself saying. It was the only answer that had ever helped to settle her, but it still didn't give her any reason.

"We have each other now. I will look after you. I'll be here for you."

Her hand squeezed mine and she fell silent. This was the usual pattern. She would cry, search for answers, hear none, accept reassurance, fall silent.

There was nothing more that I could say or do. The drive would continue to places linked to her dad, where she would find some comfort for a while, and then we would return home. She would get out of the car, look in bewilderment at the front door, and have to be encouraged back inside the house.

She didn't want to be here, she wanted to be in her own home, with her own family and especially her dad.

I knew it would be pointless to try and take off her coat. She would clutch it to her tightly because that meant she wasn't staying. Her shoes too: they would stay on her feet ready for when she could go home again. I would wait patiently until she accepted that we were staying.

If I timed things right, it would be almost bed time. Some television viewing and a drink would help her to forget her sadness for a while and then, hopefully, climb the stairs to her bedroom.

Sitting on the side of her pretty, pink bed, she still clutched the photo tight. I combed her thick, shiny hair until she relaxed enough to allow me to put the photo next to her bed, beside her teddy bears.

Then followed the encouragement to go to the toilet, to wash her hands and clean her teeth before I helped her undress for bed. Each step needed to be handled so sensitively and at any point her mood could change. As to what the night would bring, I never knew.

I tucked her in, kissed her goodnight, told her that I would leave the door open and the light on outside. I reassured her that I was there, that I would still be there in the morning too and I would not leave her.

But inside my stomach was tight again and a mixed feeling of relief and dread swept over me. How long could I keep this going? I felt out of my depth so often now that each day was becoming a struggle.

Like walking on eggshells, there were occasions when I said the wrong thing, or I gave the wrong look, and she would get so upset. Sometimes she shouted, screamed, cried out in frustration and I would search for any way to calm her down and stop myself from feeling despair. A gentle hug, a softer voice, combing her hair. But there were no guarantees, no template that said 'this will work today'.

My own mind cast back to childhood and the happy years that I had spent in this very house. A beautiful, period property with a large garden, full of all the flowers that my grandfather and mum had planted. My dad mowed the lawns and cut the hedges because mum wouldn't trust him to do anything else!

There were four of us children – one boy and three girls.

Mum was the busy type, always on the go, always there for us. She was sociable, outgoing, fun to be with, and had lots of friends. She baked cakes for charity events and opened the garden for coffee mornings.

My dad worked hard and was the opposite in character: a gentle, quiet, thoughtful man. They say opposites attract, which must have been the case with mum and dad. It didn't make life easy at times though!

Dad died suddenly when he was just fifty years old. Mum never married again. Her life centred on us, her dogs, and the church.

My grandfather became more central to our lives and was very dear to mum and to me. We shared the same interests and the same sense of humour. He spent much of his time with us, working in the garden, then cycling back home to be with my grandma. He lived to be ninety-two years old, spending the last few years of his life with mum in this house. She saw him through to the very end, accepting his blindness and his deafness, giving him all the love that he deserved.

No one could ever take her father's place.

And now I picked up the black and white photo of that man. The photo that this sleeping charge of mine had clutched so tightly in the car. A man in his prime, kind-looking, a gentle heart.

The photo had been taken eighty-four years ago.

I looked at the teddy bears beside the bed.

"Best nan" said the words on the love heart that one held. Beside that bear, another one with the words, "I love you mum."

Both belonged to the one person in my life who had always been there for me: the beautiful, caring, independent spirit that was my mum. But now she had been taken away from me, bit by bit, until a helpless and vulnerable 'child' remained.

Dementia is a cruel thief.

I can date the moment her life was turned upside down precisely, because that was also the date that my life was turned upside down. It wasn't when her dementia was diagnosed but when a stroke followed two years later, which accelerated her condition, caused aphasia, and left her dependent on others.

Those 'others' would be her family and, because we were a close-knit and large family, I assumed that the caring would be shared, with each of us four children playing our part. She had nine grandchildren too, four of whom were now young, independent women. They thought the world of her.

It all started so well, with an extended family meeting, mum included, where we discussed her needs and a way to move forward. I would be the principal carer as I had the most flexibility with my job and my living circumstances. A rota of the others could then be drawn up to fit around their roles and responsibilities.

I felt reassured and comforted. My family were set on the same path as me: caring for the person who had cared for us over so many decades. It would present its challenges, for sure, but it would be a shared experience and that made the prospect far less daunting for me.

And so my journey of discovery began. A journey that would take me down unknown paths, with so many twists and turns that I would often lose my way and stumble along. It would draw on all my strengths, but also reveal my vulnerabilities. I would learn so much about myself, my family, my mum, her friends, the complex world of care and all it entailed.

It highlighted to me that there are times in our lives when we are forced to make choices and yet we don't really think we have a choice (Hobson's choice). It can happen in those situations where we really care so deeply about someone, or something, that we are prepared to make difficult choices and live with the consequences.

That was how my story developed over the next three years. For most of the decisions that were made in relation to mum's care, I had expected the same degree of unity and shared decision-making which had shaped our initial meeting but, sadly, that did not happen.

It soon became apparent to me that my siblings were not going to shoulder much of the responsibility. I lost the support of my sister-in-law after she had spent just one afternoon with mum and decided that caring for her would be too traumatic. My brother tried his best but he felt overwhelmed with the changes in mum's behaviour. The grandchildren expressed their desire to help but only one granddaughter was able to fulfil her promise.

I compared it to the reality check that a young parent can experience with the birth of a newborn baby. The network of support may be there but the weight of the responsibility falls heavily on one pair of shoulders. Walking away is not regarded as an option when you know that you must provide the care and the love for one who is totally dependent on you.

If I had been given a crystal ball at the start, I would have disbelieved it. So much of what I thought would happen, did not happen.

So what drove my decision-making and my choices?

Everything revolved around valuing mum. I knew her history, her character, her needs and wants, her fears and her vulnerabilities. She didn't have to explain things to me or get me to understand her. She trusted me and loved me.

I wanted mum to feel appreciated and I wanted her to keep her dignity. It was all too easy to just see an 'old person'. This had been brought home to me when she had been admitted to hospital following her stroke. Of all the things which isolated mum from others it was her loss of hearing and this, together with the after-effects of the stroke, meant that it was critical she had her hearing aids.

Each time I went to the hospital to visit her, she had none in her ears. When I asked where they were, a search began. Maybe in a drawer, or in the bed, or on the side, or under a pillow? Sometimes she only had one available and so the second would need to be found.

Once I had an ear infection that left me very deaf for several days. I had never appreciated just how debilitating it was to see people's lips moving and hear a murmur but to have no idea what they were saying. I couldn't imagine having to live with it daily.

Knowing that hearing aids release people from this isolating world, meant that I became very upset and frustrated at the lack of attention given to such a simple action as putting them in for her. If staff were required to wear ear plugs on just one shift, to experience that level of disability, it might highlight and emphasize the need for simple actions that ensure a person's mental well-being is not neglected. Then the physical recovery might be swifter and less traumatic.

When a person has no way of communicating clearly, then the impact on them can be devastating. I have heard stories of patients not having their glasses so that they are unable to see, or not having their teeth so that they are unable to speak.

This revolves around an individual's sensitivity: the carer, the nurse, the social worker, the friend, the relative. It's not about a policy. It is about preserving dignity and giving respect. It is also a basic human right, especially in establishments that are focused on restoring health.

In so many other aspects of mum's care, I found that dignity played the greatest part. Perhaps this was because I knew mum before she became reliant on carers, when dignity was so important to her. My goal was to treat her as I knew she wanted to be treated. That did not mean following a simple tick-list but, unlike strangers, I was able to picture mum in any given situation and imagine how she would have behaved, what she would have needed, or liked.

"But she's not mum anymore," was a comment made by my sister on several occasions.

It was true that some of mum's behaviours were so bizarre and unsettling that she would have been horrified at what she now did, but that wasn't how I saw her. To me she may have been a different version of the mum we knew before dementia took a hold, but it was impossible to know how she was truly seeing the world. I had to believe that there were times when she understood what was happening around her, when her humour appeared or she found words to express herself.

"I am useless," she would say on occasions. She needed to know that this was not true, that there was still a place and a purpose for her. Maintaining her dignity was key to that.

In those moments, she left the child behind her and appeared to know that she was an adult and that her history was depicted in all the photo books and albums that she looked through every day. Then she would look into my eyes and I would see mum again.

Perhaps the fear of strangers not knowing the 'real' person drove me to resist outside intervention for too long? Handing mum over to others was not on my agenda, especially given the fact that we were a large family. But the stress gradually crept over me as weeks turned into months and then years. Feelings of sadness and disappointment with my family consumed me.

Mum was no longer there for us, as she had been all our lives. We needed to be there for her. Was that a duty, or a reasonable expectation, or an act of love? To me it was all three. To others her years of unconditional support seemed to be forgotten. She appeared to be an 'inconvenience', someone who now 'disrupted' daily life, plans, and leisure time. Despite the fact that I had willingly offered to care for her for the majority of each month, I sensed huge resistance.

I vividly recall the sickness that I felt in my stomach and the impact that these months, then years, had on my own health. It dawned on me that mum being placed in a care home was, by far, the preferred option for others. Why? Because this took away all responsibility from family members. They would convince themselves that mum was in the 'right' place, with 'professional' carers and that I could get on with my life, hence allowing them to get on, guilt free, with their own lives.

The huge flaw in their argument was that I would 'get on with my life'. Not so. This would never be an option for me because mum was at the centre of my thinking now. I would rather be the one who helped mum wash and dress each morning, who prepared her meals, shared her love of the garden, walked with her, talked and tried to understand her world. If that meant seeing sadness in her eyes, hopelessness and frustration too, then so be it. At least I had the time, love, and empathy to manage those aspects in the least traumatic way for her. The one-to-one care that I gave mum would be gone if she went elsewhere and this, for me, was the difference between a care home setting and a 'being at home' setting.

It struck me how culturally different we are in how we see the care of elderly members in our society. Removing someone from their own home to a care home conveniently removes personal responsibility for their welfare. I cannot count the times that I was told that mum would 'adjust' once she was there. How a person with dementia adjusts is a mystery to me. It is so different to a physical impairment where the person is able to understand what is happening and, hopefully, have a say in what care they receive and where they receive it.

With advanced dementia like mum's, the short-term memory is so impaired that only very distant past events and places, familiar routines, objects and people, can trigger any sort of recognition. A person with dementia awakening each morning does not recollect what happened during that night, the previous evening, or day. Arguably the only 'adjustment' is made on the part of family members, who have elected to place that person in a care home.

I commend and admire those cultures where the elderly are respected and rewarded for the love and devotion that they have given their families over the years. I applaud the extended family who share the responsibility and ensure that the pressures are more evenly distributed. Do strong cultural values and beliefs override any economic factors where decisions are made? If there is an option to pay for care, or receive free care, is it far easier to let strangers be responsible?

As a 'lone' carer, searching for support, I was told several times, by well-meaning friends, that mum's situation 'would only get worse' and that I needed to 'take care of myself'. This was in some way meant to be in recognition of how hard my role was, and how much harder it would become, but it gave me no solutions. I saw it as totally counterproductive, especially when my overriding need was to stay positive and resilient.

I was not ignorant of the stages of dementia, in the same way as a carer for someone with cancer need not be ignorant. What I needed as things 'got worse' was the kind of support which certain cultures mutually give family members. This was not forthcoming and the cultural acceptance here of displacing the elderly to institutions sadly became very apparent to me.

Accepting my family's withdrawal from mum's care took me a long time. I felt betrayed and alone. The only sibling who supported me whenever she possibly could lived 300 miles away with her young family. Friends rarely appeared, even those from mum's beloved church. Introducing strangers to mum's home and life was an unknown and fearful path for me to tread. I had no idea how I would relinquish control and trust others to take care of her. If I was to have meaningful respite time, then carers would need to be staying for a weekend, not just a few hours.

Mum's bizarre behaviours concerned me the most. How would strangers deal with them? It had taken me, as her daughter, a long time to come to terms with them. I did not want anyone to misunderstand her actions and chastise her for them.

One behaviour, in particular, had horrified me when she first did it. Mum took herself to the toilet whenever she needed to go, but there were occasions when she would put her hand inside her trousers, then her knickers and take out small lumps of faeces. I was so shocked when it first happened that I hurriedly gave her a tissue and begged her not to do it again. I told her that it was dirty, that she would get germs, that she must wash her hands.

Each time it happened mum looked bewildered at my reaction. This astonished me as she had been one of the most fastidious of people, never even wanting to discuss bodily functions, let alone deal with them. The horror on my face and the urgency I showed clearly confused her. She would secretly do it and then try to hide it from me. This made me think that she knew I would be upset and angry, but she couldn't help doing it nevertheless.

Then one day she did exactly the same thing but openly showed it to me in her hand and said, "Oh, pieces of walnut."

Everything changed from that point on for me. This was as confusing to her as it was to me, but for completely different reasons. There was nothing dirty, or smelly, or forbidden as far as mum was concerned. What she saw in her hand was not what I saw in it. She had no idea how or why the "pieces of walnut" were in her knickers but they felt uncomfortable and so she took them out.

My approach to the habit changed. I was still alert to the times she did it but I reacted in a much calmer way. I put aside my own judgement of the behaviour and I treated it as just another habit that needed to be understood. I still asked her to wash her hands, for her own safety, but I didn't chastise her or get angry. It was a huge learning curve for me and it helped me to replace feelings of disgust or anger with understanding and patience.

This kind of revelation made me think even more carefully about how I would introduce mum to outsiders who would inevitably witness some of these behaviours. I wanted them to treat mum in a kind and empathetic way, whatever she did and however they regarded it.

I spent days compiling a comprehensive folder of everything I wanted strangers to know about mum. This included all of her routines. I took photos of the meals that she enjoyed, the snacks that she ate throughout the day. A page of 'triggers' alerted carers to things that upset and unsettled mum, with suggestions for how each situation may be resolved. I wrote down favourite places to take mum, ideas for activities, notes about her character and her life before dementia. I photographed her outfits and her nighttime needs. Everything was simply documented, well presented, and visually clear.

And then the process of sourcing care began. It took me into the world of Social Services and multidisciplinary agencies. It gave me mountains of information to grasp, endless phone calls and messaging. It introduced me to practices and policies which made great, and little, sense. It meant home visits by assessors and interviews with potential carers. All these tested my resilience, my interpersonal skills, my understanding of systems and the financial implications. It was not a comfortable ride.

As this new world unfolded, I learned that there was a clear distinction to be made between finding a 'carer' for mum and finding a 'companion'. It struck me that 'care' focused primarily on physical things: food preparation; medication; cleaning; washing; toileting; making sure the person was comfortable. Whilst I did need that for mum, my overriding goal was to find her a companion: a carer who wanted to spend time with her, chatting, sharing a meal, looking at photos and books, taking a walk, a drive, a trip to a park or a shop. Normal, everyday things that mum and I did regularly together. There needed to be mutuality: positive, engaging interaction, attachment and emotional support.

I set up cameras in the house and showed them to potential carers. I did a trial weekend away . . . and it was a disaster. The carer that stayed with mum did not want to engage with her. She locked the doors to stop mum wandering rather than 'wander' with her. To me that was not sharing time, being a companion. Mum grew very aggressive over the two days. I had never seen her like that. She hit the carer and screamed at her. Things went rapidly downhill. I was shocked at how quickly a situation could accelerate out of control. The absence of any emotional connection, on the part of the carer, led to very challenging behaviour from my mum.

From then on, the absolute need for close, one-to-one contact drove all my decision-making. It meant that I only chose carers who would respect mum, who saw their role as a friend and significant other to mum. I needed them to have a genuine desire to be there, not just a job to be done. I paid what needed to be paid for quality care because I believed that valuing those carers, financially, was equally important as valuing them personally.

I also appreciated that outside help would mean addressing this financial implication, a topic about which I knew very little. As a family we had never engaged Social Services and, unfortunately, I had heard negative comments about people's experiences with them. This meant that I was very anxious about how things would unfold.

Thankfully, for me, the contact that I had with the service was far more positive than negative. I found everyone to be very supportive and understanding and I gratefully accepted any financial help that was offered.

However, there was one policy which impacted negatively on my ability to choose carers. This revolved around who was eligible to claim money from the Social Services account: the 'pot' of money to which my mum also had to make a weekly contribution.

It was explained that family members and friends could not claim. Neither could any carer who was not self-employed. I found myself unable to use any of the money for certain carers whom I had already chosen and liked. This meant that mum would have to pay privately to keep those carers and could only use a small percentage of Social Services funds each month.

In addition, the assessment that calculated her monthly contribution did not take into account any financial support that she gave me to pay my own costs of living. This came from her Attendance Allowance and pension. It was a nominal amount but hugely significant to me, having given up paid work to care for her.

And that brings me to the point in my story that I am at right now. My journey with mum is ongoing, the future is still unknown. I pray each night that she will be released from her torment and I pray each day that we will get through it together. My resolve to continue caring for her at home is stronger than ever. My love for her and my connection to her are greater. When she smiles, my heart is lifted, and when I see contentment in her face, I cherish it.

I don't want to feel bitterness or resentment towards my family but I do not understand them. Whether it is selfishness, feeling vulnerable, incapable, or whatever, there are times in life when we can rise to challenges and really make a difference. It all revolves around what really matters to us and, more importantly, who really matters to us.

For me my life is different now, not 'put on hold' as others have suggested. It is a privilege to be here for mum, to spend my time with her. My workplace has become my homeplace and the rewards are far more than financial ones. I have a newfound respect for those services that put the care of others, like my mum, at the centre of what they do. It is a complex, challenging role which deserves far more recognition and reward.

My daily routines will continue. I will wrestle with feelings of loneliness, frustration, and despair. I will experience disappointment and sadness. I will question the actions of others and their motives. I will fight resentment. But so too will I wake up thinking about the positive things that may happen in my day, not the negative things. I will seize moments of joy and happiness, of recognition and togetherness. I will know deep inside that I returned the love and kindness that mum gave me throughout my life. The relationship may have turned: I am the giver and she is the receiver, I am the adult and she is the child. Her mind is troubled and confused, but her soul is unchanged.

My parting thought is this:

I do not know who I am to my mum anymore. But does it really matter? I know who she is to me.

Postscript

Three months and six days after writing my story, mum passed away. It followed a very bad attack of shingles and a possible stroke.

I managed to take her to the final post, to keep her in her beloved home, to be there to nurse her at the very end. My sister, who lived 300 miles away, left her young children with her husband and joined me with her teenage daughter for two weeks.

During that time, every agency under the sun came on board as mum's condition worsened. From the doctor to the district nurses, from the hospice staff to NHS-funded carers, the doorbell rang frequently and strangers came into our lives.

I was grateful for their help, but I was equally relieved that I had not taken that path any sooner. It was a bewildering mix of agencies and well-meaning support workers, over which I felt little control, and consequently found overwhelming.

I requested no visitors on the day that I knew would be mum's last.

Mum died peacefully in her own bed; the last hours being surrounded by just the family that she loved so dearly.

My young niece looked at the calmness in the face of the grandmother that she had known for just thirteen years and said, amid her tears . . .

"Nanny doesn't have dementia anymore."

The power of her statement will live me with me for always.

Death was a kind release.

In my grief I could not attend mum's funeral. Rightly or wrongly, I could not face the number of people who would be there, for I knew there would be many.

I wrote a 'letter', in the form of a poem, to mum instead. I requested it to be read aloud at her funeral, so that those who were there might understand why I was absent. I have included it at the end of this story.

I was told that the church was full to overflowing and the garden gathering that followed included friends of many years and family from afar. Mum would have been smiling from ear to ear!

She would not want me to feel bitterness or resentment. Mum always looked for a reason behind behaviours, to see different points of view and to find a way to move forward.

The negative aspects of my story must not haunt me.

I will focus on the mum who gave me the strength to demonstrate my love for her when it mattered most, and to continue living my life with the compassion and care that she so frequently showed to others.

This is my tribute to her.

* * *

Dear Mum,

I'm not here with everyone else right now.
I hope you understand.
I have to be alone with my thoughts today – my last memory to be that of your sleeping face.
We trod a long road together and each turn was unknown.
I watched you struggle with the confusion of your mind and the tricks it played.
When you cried for your dad, I tried to comfort you.
When you called out for your sister, I held your hand.
Like a mum, I combed your hair and washed your face,
I chose your clothes, and helped you dress.
Yet I still saw, in you, a burning flame.
A strength of character and a fighting spirit.
That mischief in your eyes and that sunshine smile.
That look of delight when ice cream appeared!
Your happiness became my life.
I lived to give you joy and laughter,
To find moments of sense and gladness.
To give you peace of mind against the odds.
We hung in there, mum.
My love for you deepened and my resolve grew stronger.
I prayed that I could make it to the final post with you.
To keep you in the home that you loved, to sit in the garden,
To cook your favourite meals (all with gravy!)
To tuck you into your own bed each night.
When you didn't know who I was, it didn't matter.
I knew who you were to me.
And, when I sensed that you were finally leaving this world,
I stroked your hair for one last time and said goodnight.
I saw the peace that graced your face, as all your burdens fell.
Then, in your ear, I whispered three simple words . . .
"We did it."

Reflective Questions

1. How do you feel about caring for someone with dementia?
2. What are the human rights issues in this story?
3. What role does empathy play when caring for someone with dementia?
4. What are the issues for you when one sibling wants their elderly mother to have homecare and the other to send her to a care home?
5. What issues of service co-ordination arise from the story?
6. What are the safeguarding issues in this story?

Photo: Hilde Mjøs

CHAPTER 11

"Kurdistan Is My Country"
Understanding the Importance of Positioning in Stories

Rita Sørly and Vår Mathisen

In this book chapter, we examine the identity-making story of Sera, a young Syrian-Kurdish woman living in the rural Arctic. Identity-making stories are closely linked to positionality. How we position ourselves in storytelling and how we understand the positioning of others in storytelling is of great importance in social science research and practice. It is closely linked to how we understand and perceive each other as human beings, which in turn affects how we act and interact. The study takes a narrative approach and aims to explore positioning in storytelling as a source of empowerment. Through a positioning analysis, we find that Sera actively positions herself as one of the story's characters, in the interactive setting and in the wider context. Her story is interpreted as empowerment on three levels: she fights for her family, for education, and for a free Kurdistan. Based on our findings, we understand her storytelling as health-promoting strategies and enabling integration, relevant for social work research and practice.

Introduction

In 2021, 82.4 million people were fleeing war and conflict. This is the highest number ever recorded (Flyktningregnskapet, 2022). Half of these refugees were children and young people under the age of eighteen, and we know that every five seconds, a new child is forced to flee (UNHCR, 2019). Thirteen million people have been displaced from Syria since the conflict broke out in 2011 (Flyktningregnskapet, 2022). Many of the children and young people fled under very dramatic circumstances. They experienced losing everything they owned and seeing close family members and friends killed or injured in acts of war. They were exposed to traumatic stress (Richter, Lye, & Proulx, 2018). Many had long absences from school, due to their flight and what that entailed. Besides the loss of school skills, and lost contact with friends, important socialization is missed

(Yoshikawa, Wuermli & Aber, 2019). Unsafe living conditions cause these young children to experience stress and anxiety (Bauman, Soerens, & Smeir, 2016). In line with Suárez-Orozco and colleagues (2018), we understand this as an extremely complex situation to live in. The transition from fleeing to arriving in Norway is enormous.

According to research, the well-being of former refugee youth is strongly influenced by their sense of belonging and their experience of inclusion in or exclusion from the local community (Chen & Schweitzer, 2019; Correa-Velez, Gifford, & Barnett, 2010; Mathisen & Cele, 2020). Children and young people can adapt to a new place/culture more easily than adults do (Roche et al., 2015), and psychological resilience and cultural adaptation can strengthen the mental health of young refugees (Dubus, 2018; Hormozi, Miller, & Banford, 2018). The young people must find out who they are, in relation to their new context, and develop a new identity in the new country. Strong family ties are important as emotional support (Calzada et al., 2020). To the extent that research has been undertaken, it has mainly focused on arriving as a refugee in cities and/or multicultural neighbourhoods. It is therefore important to conduct more research focused on arriving in a rural area as a refugee (Pérez et al., 2021). Søholt, Stenbacka, & Nørgaard (2018) and Mathisen & Cele (2020) have conducted research on refugee adolescents living in rural areas of Norway. They emphasize the value of conducting research in rural areas, as this is important for small local communities that design social structures enabling integration and belonging for those who arrive as refugees (Mathisen & Cele, 2020).

The approach to integrating former refugees and their families in Norwegian municipalities varies from municipality to municipality. The focus is often on the formal, standardized welfare programmes initiated by the state and the counties, while less attention is paid to the family as a resource for the local community. The lives of young people in the former refugee families take place within a highly institutionalized context when they arrive in the rural Arctic, where they are expected to spend most of their time on school and leisure activities, and less time with their families (Mathisen & Cele, 2020). Research shows that the well-being of former refugee youth is strongly influenced by their experience of being included in or excluded from the local community (Chen & Schweitzer, 2019; Correa-Velez, Gifford, & Barnett, 2010; Mathisen & Cele, 2020). As noted by Mathisen and Cele (2020), for these young people, educational arenas and sport and leisure arenas are key elements for participation in society.

The municipalities included in our study are three rural areas along the Arctic coastline. During winter it is dark and cold, with no sunlight for three months. Refugees are often placed outside the centre of the municipality, and their children and young people must often travel a long way to get to school or leisure activities. While the adults are in contact with the refugee services and community health services when needed, the young people in these families are mainly in the hands of school employees. These local adults are very often the young people's first contact with Norwegian society, and they play a key role in contributing to the young people's integration into the local community. Against this background, we explore positioning in storytelling.

We have chosen a narrative approach with focus on positioning in storytelling as a tool for *doing* empowerment. By empowerment, we agree with Jacobs and colleagues (2017, p. 51), who define the concept as a process whereby "people become subjects of their own experience and action as an essential part of full humanness. It is a relational and collective process that both promotes individual and group critical awareness, self-esteem, and skills, as well as bringing about social and political change."

Furthermore, we present research on Syrian Kurds in Europe, and a narrative framework for the study. Then we introduce the study context, before presenting the data and methods used. We write a section on ethics, before we say something about the participants. We present Sera's story and offer a narrative positioning analysis. We describe, in depth, the positioning of story characters, the positioning in the interactive setting, and the positioning in the broader context. We then turn to the discussion and the implications for social work research and practice. Finally, we offer some concluding remarks.

Syrian Kurds in Europe

The Kurds are a stateless people, belonging to areas of the Middle East: south and east Turkey, and parts of Syria, Armenia, Iraq, and Iran. Kurds are the fourth largest population in the Middle East, described as indigenous people of Mesopotamia (Sørly, 2024). There are no official statistics for the number of Kurds in the world, but this is estimated at between 25 and 35 million (Ameen, 2019). In modern history, the Kurds have fought for independence and autonomy in the four states of Iran, Turkey, Iraq, and Syria. Turkey has been considered to be the most democratic among these states, yet thousands of Kurds are imprisoned in the country. Their language is banned, their identity is denied, and villages and cities have been destroyed (Ameen, 2019). Statelessness is an overlooked and often invisible feature of the migration context in Europe (McGee, 2019).

Stateless people have often experienced restrictions in terms of public services, and limited rights of ownership and inheritance. Kurdish children born in exile are at risk of statelessness, due to the application of the national law in the countries in which they live, and this is also related to problems with documenting their nationality. According to Eurostat data, Syria has been the main country of citizenship of asylum seekers in the EU member states since 2013 (McGee, 2019, p. 11; Sørly, 2024). Norway has also experienced an increase in the number of Syrian refugees since 2015 (Tønnessen Drahus, & Dzamarija, 2020). A large percentage of these asylum seekers are stateless Kurds. Statelessness is poorly understood within a European context; there is insufficient knowledge and capacity to identify statelessness and tailor assistance to this group (McGee, 2019). Stateless Kurds who arrive in Europe share an ethnic identity and the dream of a historical homeland, but have different nationalities, which has turned their identity and belonging into a contest between the refugees and the host countries (Bahram, 2018). A study by Bahram (2018) of Syrian Kurds in Sweden showed that home as a place was plural and was connected to Syria and Kurdistan to varying degrees. Their identity as Kurds was contested when their Syrianness was evoked, with boundaries limiting their recognition as both Syrian and Kurdish. Similarly, their belonging was challenged by their social position as refugees and their legal belonging to Syria. This involved them in a continuum of politics of identity and belonging ranging between the situational demonstration of their Syrian identity, and their attachment to Kurdishness (Bahram, 2018; Sørly, 2024).

A Narrative Framework

Narratives are meaning-making, local, and symbolic parameters for appropriate behaviour in given situations and show directions for what appropriate reactions to events can be. Narratives can also be understood as markers of identity; through storytelling you say something about who you are. Storytelling is a very important and profound human activity. We understand our environment, context, and belonging from the stories that surround us. People often organize their stories according to culturally available narratives and plots (Sørly, Mathisen, & Kvernmo, 2021). The relationship between culture and identity is complex, and the work on identification is an ongoing process throughout life (Blix, Hamran, & Normann, 2013). According to Eastmond (2007), narratives can help us explore discontinuities in the lives of displaced people, as well as making sense of disruptive change. The experience of being a refugee, and the uncertainty this entails, also engages people to use their narrative repertoire to negotiate what happened, what it means, and how to go forward. Stories can organize experiences, and give them unity and meaning, and they can form part of purposeful and meaningful action to influence the outcome (Eastmond, 2007). We agree with Eastmond on the importance of grasping the predicaments of refugees, and that narratives are part of a more holistic approach that includes access to social interaction. By listening and taking an active part in stories told by former refugee youth, we can understand more of the context and depth of their experiences.

So why do we use the term "storytelling"? In this project, we agree with Senehi (2000) that storytelling can be a significant aspect of community-building and of importance to social work. Stories are accessible and inclusive; no special equipment or training is required to take part in a storytelling act, and stories can be understood by persons of all ages and educational levels (Senehi, 2000). Furthermore, storytelling builds cultural spaces where people come together; they define their community, give voices to their experiences, heal from past conflicts or traumas, and shape the future together (Senehi, 2000).

Stories are always a matter of interpretation, and not windows on an objective reality. To understand youths' stories, we must relate their narratives to the social and political context they are shaped and surrounded by.

In this chapter, we look at a single case study, namely Sera's story. She has experienced a disrupted life course at an early age, and we want to emphasize how her narrative can be interpreted as an empowering activity and health-promoting strategy of importance to social work research and practice. How we position ourselves and others, matters in social work.

The Study Context

The study from which this interview emerged included twelve in-depth interviews with former refugee youth in Northern Norwegian rural areas. These youth belong to families in which one or both parents have health problems and have participated in the Norwegian national introduction programme (IP). The youth study is part of a larger study, HealthIntro, that focuses on the participation of refugees with health problems in IP (Sørly, 2024). The Norwegian IP has the goal to provide individual basic skills in language and fundamental insights into Norwegian social conditions, and to prepare refugees to work or take education programmes in their local communities. Participation in IP is mandatory. IP starts within three months of arrival in the country, and very often in a period when the family is trying to get to know their new home and neighbourhood, new customs, and a new language. The children are starting to go to kindergarten or school, and there are a lot of new things to understand and comprehend (Sørly, 2024). Each municipality is responsible for arranging an IP for the refugees arriving in the country. Norwegian municipalities are obliged to provide adult refugees with IP, but no active measures are taken by the government to help children and youth to become participating members of their local communities (Mathisen & Cele, 2020). It is the municipalities who independently decide how to arrange activities or language training for each child or young person in the community (ibid.). The responsibility is very often handled by schools. The Norwegian settlement plan for refugees has been described as centred around adults (Archambault 2011; Mathisen & Cele, 2020; Sørly, 2024).

Data and Methods

The youth study was approved by the Norwegian Centre for Research Data in 2021. The young people we interviewed all received information about the study and gave written consent to participation. They were able to withdraw from the study at any time, without having to give a reason. One of the young people had an interpreter, while the others preferred to speak Norwegian. In one interview, we had to use English in parts of the dialogue. The study aimed to contribute to our knowledge of what can give former refugee youth a good start on arriving in a Norwegian municipality. What do they need? What is important for their health and well-being? How can they become active residents of a small municipality in the north of Norway? (Sørly, 2024).

The participants were recruited by the IP coordinators in each municipality, who either knew the young people themselves, or their parents. Information letters were distributed, and individuals who were interested in participating signed letters of consent. A thematic interview guide was used, and most of the interviews were around thirty minutes to one hour long. Interviews were digitally recorded, and the sound files were transcribed verbatim (Sørly, 2024).

Ethics

Narrative research is interwoven with a concern for social change and empowerment, and narrative researchers often emphasize the process of storytelling as promoting social justice (De Haene, Grietens, & Verschueren, 2010; Sørly, 2024). In line with De Haene, Grietens, and Verschueren (2010), we agree concerning the importance of seeing the act of storytelling as an opportunity for personal growth among the participants in a study. It is also important to be aware of potential risks and benefits in narrative health research, in our case among former refugee youth. Undertaking narrative health studies among former refugee youth can be understood as being in dialogue with a particularly vulnerable group of people (Sørly, 2024). Our aim has been to promote well-being and self-reliance among our participants, and to encourage empowerment and empathy within host societies. To do this, it is necessary to fully involve the complexities of narrative, suffering, and healing within the storytelling process (Sørly, 2024). There must be an open dialogue on potential harmful aspects that may emerge (De Haene, Grietens, & Verschueren, 2010).

The participants in our study could bring along a companion if they so wished, but all of the participants chose to come alone. During our interviews, we repeated that the participants only had to answer the questions they wished to answer. They did not have to explain if there was something they did not wish to talk about. It is also of great importance to understand storytelling as being shared within the specific participant and research community that the researchers wish to reach (Sørly, 2024). As underlined by De Haene, Grietens, and Verschueren (2010), narrative researchers working with people with traumatic experiences must be willing to hold harm. Holding harm means being willing to share pain, to remain present, balancing between suffering and recovery, and to accept some of the responsibility of the host society, represented by the research context. As researchers, we were prepared to listen ethically, "not only to the experience of trauma within participants' lives, but equally to the experience of trauma within the research relationship itself" (De Haene, Grietens, & Verschueren, 2010, p.1673).

The Participants

We interviewed twelve former refugee youth. There were four boys and eight girls aged between sixteen and twenty. They came from countries in the Middle East and Africa. Some of them had arrived with their families several years before, while others had only been in Norway for a year. Some had been in transit for years; others had come directly to the municipality from their home country. We conducted all the interviews as physical meetings. Ten interviews took place at the local refugee office (which also includes the IP classrooms). An interview with two young people (siblings) took place at their home in the countryside. It was important for us to meet all the young people face to face, in their local environment (Sørly, 2024).

We will now take a closer look at the interview with Sera, a young Syrian girl who identified as Syrian Kurdish.

Sera's Story

In the following, we present an excerpt from Sera's story. We have chosen to emphasize the part where Sera talks about her everyday life at school and her relation to Norwegian schoolmates. Thereafter, we analyse the story, using a narrative positioning analysis. Sometimes the borders between the positioning levels are clear, and sometimes the levels are interwoven with each other.

Sera, a nineteen-year-old girl, lives in a rural area of Northern Norway. She turned fourteen in the summer she arrived in Norway. She fled the war in Syria with her parents and three siblings. They lived in Turkey for three years, waiting for a destination. She had to stay at home during these years, to take care of her siblings. She could not go to school, and she seldom went outside the flat. She had never heard about Norway before she came. It was a new society for her. A new way of living (Sørly, 2024).

INTERVIEWER: Can you say something about the experiences you have had, or do you find it difficult? You can refrain from saying some things; you decide.

SERA: Yes, yes, I know. From war to everything we have experienced. I do not like to mention what happened, like . . . But difficult things, when you go through difficult things, you know what the most important things are, really. What is the most important thing, for example when I sit with Norwegian pupils, or . . . I do not mean to be unfair! But they are actually young aren't they, they're living their lives now, it's their time! But I am not interested in the same things that they are interested in now at that age. It makes a difference.

INTERVIEWER: Yes. And you might have other perspectives on what really matters?

SERA: Yes. I struggle to make friends. But it is on my side, it is not wrong, but it's me who can't, not them, there's nothing wrong with them.

INTERVIEWER: Do you think it would have been different if they knew more about what you have experienced, or . . .

SERA: I know that they know that there is a war and that we fled and all that. But if the person themselves does not have the same experience, then they cannot really care. Some people can care, adults can care because they have experiences from their lives, but I do not think that young people can really . . .

Sera has had difficult school experiences since she lived in Syria. When the interviewer asked her about the beginning, the first few days in Norway, she said:

Me and my father, we went to the shop and [we] did not know how to shop with Norwegian money. So, we just went in and bought a lot, it was a long invoice, we didn't know it costs so and so . . . we mustn't spend so much money. But we just did, because we did not know, we just used lots. The first time I went to school I met my class and all that. But I could not communicate with them because I do not know English, I have not learned it because I didn't go to school. From fourth to fifth grade, or . . . I do not know, I don't remember much, but I didn't go to school. Even though I went to school in Syria, it was not a good school, because there was a war, and nobody cared about the school in it. So, my chance to learn was wasted.

INTERVIEWER: So maybe there was not that much school in Turkey either?

SERA: I did not go to school, I was at home because mom and dad had to work, so I had to take care of my siblings for three years.

INTERVIEWER: Yes, and then you were very young yourself.

SERA: Yes, I was eleven. Ten to eleven [. . .] Yes, I had to do everything, wash and take care of them [the siblings]. I could not make friends then, because in Turkey most people were racist towards us.

INTERVIEWER: Yes. Since you are Kurds, yes.

SERA: Plus, we are Syrian people, they didn't like us.

INTERVIEWER: Yes, then you had to grow up very early.

SERA: I had to be alone all the time.

Later in the interview, Sera talked about her siblings being bullied at school, and how she had to defend them against the bullies. She had to be strong and stand up for them. Sera said it was important for her that her siblings were becoming strong grown-ups. Sera talked about a lack of understanding from the people in their surroundings. They did not understand what Sera and her family had gone through. The interviewer asked her:

If you should have said something about how to really care. What should you do to show that you really care?

SERA: One thing, I don't want, I don't ask them to care about us. I just want to say: If you don't know how we feel and what we've been through, don't bother us. Because, really, when a person comes and bothers you, and you're having a really hard time, in the future you're going to . . . I just want to say don't feel sorry for us, don't care. But don't touch us, don't do anything. [. . .] That's just what I wanted to say.

[*There is a pause in the conversation.*]

INTERVIEWER: I'm looking at the jewellery you have around your neck.

SERA: Yes, it is from Kurdistan. It's my country.

Narrative Positioning Analysis

We understand the story told as a performative act of identity construction. The story is performed in social interaction with the authors in the interview context, and we focus on the storytelling act in our analysis. As narrators, we construct our and others' identities *here and now*. Integrating and differentiating a sense of who we are, in relation to others, takes place in moment-by-moment navigations, and stories about ourselves are understood as navigating our identity (Bamberg, 2020; Sørly, 2024). This is also transferable to social work practice.

How we position ourselves to others, and how we understand their positioning, helps us work towards an understanding of positionality as an ongoing identity-making-within-storytelling practice. To take a closer look at how the narrator constructs other people's identities through stories, we will use a three-level positioning analysis as an approach to the study of practitioners' understanding of working with youth with refugee experiences, inspired by Bamberg (1997, 2006, 2020) and Bamberg and Georgakoupolou (2008). Positioning level 1 highlights the question *What is the story about?* and focuses on how the story characters are positioned in story time and place. How are the story characters constructed in terms of their relation to one another within the specific sequence of narrated events? (Bamberg, 2020). Positioning level 2 addresses *Why is the story told in this way, at this particular time?* The interactive setting between the interviewers and the interviewee in the interview situation is analysed, as well as how the narrator positions herself towards an audience. Positioning level 3 investigates the narrator's positioning of herself in relation to the broader context of the Syrian Kurds' fight for independence (Sørly, 2024). The narrator constructs a local answer to the question *Who am I?* (Bamberg, 2020). We seek to understand how the story is situated in relation to the broader social and cultural processes beyond the immediate telling situation (in line with De Fina & Georgakopoulou, 2008; Blix, Hamran, & Normann, 2015).

Positioning of Story Characters

At positioning level 1, Sera positions herself and her experiences as something different from what young Norwegians have experienced. She has memories from war and an ongoing fight for her stateless nation, being a Kurdish Syrian. Sera says she has a hard time finding friends of her own age, and she thinks older people can understand her better than her peers. At the same time, she says it has to do with herself: "I struggle to make friends. But it is on my side, it is not wrong, but it's me who can't, not them, there's nothing wrong with them." Because they do not have the same experiences as her, they cannot understand what she has been through. She expresses loneliness in her storytelling. Later in the interview, Sera talks about the time when she and her family lived in Turkey. She did not go to school but had to stay at home and take care of her siblings while her parents were working. She missed the opportunity for education while in transition in Turkey. Her emotional loneliness was ongoing. When the interviewer comments on her story and says that Sera had to grow up very early, she responds "I had to be alone all the time."

Sera positions herself as a strong, independent child and now, a young woman. She has been struggling for her entire life, and she does not depend on anybody except herself. She has had caregiving duties since she was a very young girl. School in Syria was affected by the war, and in Turkey she could not prioritize school because she had to take care of her siblings. She was alone, she did not have friends. And when she came to Norway, and started school, it was still hard to find friends. At positioning level 1, Sera's story places her as a fighter, and she has managed herself throughout traumas, loneliness, and escape. Her family has been stable, and she still takes care of her siblings, and she has had to teach them to be strong and independent. The war has had enormous ripple effects for Sera (Sørly, 2024).

Positioning in the Interactive Setting

At positioning level 2, we look at why this story is told at this particular time, and how the narrator positions herself vis-à-vis her audience. Sera is still in school at the time of the interview, and she is planning her future education. A central aspect of Sera's story is related to her education, or lack of education. An excerpt from her story, where she talks about how she and her father went to a Norwegian shop for the first time, underlines how she lacked practical knowledge in the new context she was living in:

> Me and my father, we went to the shop and [we] did not know how to shop with Norwegian money. So, we just went in and bought a lot, it was a long invoice, we didn't know it costs so and so . . . we mustn't spend so much money. But we just did, because we did not know, we just used lots. The first time I went to school I met my class and all that. But I could not communicate with them because I do not know English, I have not learned it because I didn't go to school. From fourth to fifth grade, or . . . I do not know, I don't remember much, but I didn't go to school. Even though I went to school in Syria, it was not a good school, because there was a war, and nobody cared about the school in it. So, my chance to learn was wasted.

War does not permit children to get an education. If Sera and her family could have lived in peace, she would have gone to school from an early age. Now, she was robbed of that opportunity.

Another focus at positioning level 2 is to ask to whom the stories are told. According to Blix, Hamran, and Normann (2015) and Randall, Prior, and Skarborn (2006), listeners' stories, including their background, professions, gender, and interests, shape the stories tellers choose to tell. When Sera emphasizes her missed opportunities to go to school at an early age, we must look at who she is telling her story to. She is being interviewed by two female researchers, from the university, who are interested in refugee adolescents' experiences on first coming to Norway. In the Norwegian welfare state, education is of extreme importance for children and young people. By telling her story about difficulties and loneliness in relation to her schooling, Sera points to the importance of being able to get an education and to have friends. This is perhaps somewhat taken for granted among Norwegian adolescents, and Sera underlines that this is extremely different to her own experience. She is finally living in peace, and this enables her to go to school. She is at a place in life where she can plan her further education. In her story, when she defines Norwegian adolescents as different from her, this might also include that they take their right to education for granted.

As narrators we direct our stories to both the present and a ghostly audience (Pasupathi & Wainryb, 2019). The ghostly audience can be a representation of real other people's perspectives and views in the narrative, or it can be an imagined audience. If it is the former, it might be relatives or family who are not present during the conversation. If it is the latter, it might be a wider audience; it might be, as in this case, Norwegian youth, the educational system, or the political government. If the narrator combines these types of audience when telling her story, this can reveal something about how narrative aspects of personality bridge these audiences. According to Pasupathi and Wainryb (2019), the telling of the story can reveal evocative and individually distinctive elements of interactions. In Sera's story, her experience from fleeing and arriving in a new country, she underlines how she and her father were not prepared when they first visited a Norwegian shop. They did not understand what to do, or how much money to spend. Can this be a story positioned to the local community? Sometimes people need help and guidance with everyday tasks. When Sera describes the trip to the shop, she relates the lack of practical knowledge to education. Is this a question of getting help in the community? Both in the everyday, practical things that need to be done, but also in becoming integrated among peers at school? (Sørly, 2024).

Positioning to the Broader Context

At the third positioning level, it is posited that by constructing content and audience, the narrator appeals to master narratives. Sera's story must be analysed in a broader context, taking the Syrian Kurds' independence struggle into consideration. In Syria, millions of people have experienced war and trauma, and many of these are stateless Kurds. When Deane (2016) emphasizes that Syria has a lost generation, this is related to the loss of education and welfare needs. According to Deane, an appropriate education policy response to the refugee crisis can reduce the risk of stigma, isolation, intra-community tensions, marginalization, and even radicalization (2016, p.35). This includes young adolescents from war zones. Education is a question of social security. When children have to flee from war and conflict, social cohesion and child protection concerns cannot be taken into consideration. When identifying as Kurdish, Sera relates her own story to an oppressed people. The importance of ethnic identification is a central aspect of the Kurdish resistance. By identifying herself, she relates to a specific set of characteristics to emphasize who she is, and to distinguish herself from others (in line with Story & Walker, 2016; Gourlay, 2018). Identity construction is a result of political and societal conditions, and Sera has spent many years in Syria and Turkey, where the Kurdish people have experienced harsh oppression. According to Gourlay (2018, p.132), Kurdish identity has been contested and shaped by historical and political events at individual and collective levels. Seen this way, identities are constructed in a "continual and never complete process. The identity as Kurdish must be restored, again and again" (Sørly, 2024).

Discussion

In this paper, we have studied Sera's experiences in relation to moving to an Arctic rural area and neighbourhood, through her storytelling. We have looked at how we can analyse positioning in stories. How do we position ourselves when we narrate? What is of importance for the listener to understand? How did Sera position herself in the storytelling act? As researchers we believe that the stories told by our participants carry knowledge of value to researchers and practitioners who meet these young people in local communities. By conducting a positioning analysis of Sera's story, we interpret her story as an act of empowerment and a health-promoting strategy. Her story can be related to a three-positioned struggle, at micro, meso, and macro levels. According to social psychology theories, a person's individual relationship with the social world must bridge micro, mesom and macro processes. While the micro level constitutes the smallest, individual unit of analysis, the meso level focuses on the various social group memberships of the individual. The macro level may include societal ideologies and social representations (Jaspal, Carriere, & Moghaddam, 2016; Sørly, 2024).

At the first position level, Sera is struggling for her family and her everyday life. This is her micro-level struggle. At the second position level, Sera is fighting for her right to education and to belong to the local community. This is her meso-level struggle. At the third level, Sera is fighting for the rights of Kurds, on a macro level. While telling her story to us, she presents herself as a fighter at three levels, and we understand her positioning as an empowering act of renarration and as promoting well-being and health strategies. According to Stokke (2019), language skills, employment, and political participation are often used as measurements of integration. If we look at Sera's story in relation to this understanding, she is presenting her integration narrative. She has fought to learn the host language, and for her education, and she is politically engaged in the Kurds' freedom struggle. She is showing us her belonging to the community, and to the new everyday life, within her narrative positioning. Within this context, this is the narrative of a highly engaged young woman, who is finding her own way in a new society.

By telling stories, we become empowered. By telling and retelling stories, our positionings can change, and new narratives can come alive. We consider narratives to contain empowerment and health-promoting strategies, as shown in our positioning analysis of Sera's story (Sørly, 2024).

Implications for Social Work Research and Practice

This research can have implications for social work research and practice. As both researchers and practitioners, we can benefit from listening and actively engaging with stories about everyday lives, as this will help to better understand how storytelling can act as empowerment. Positioning is a central part of storytelling, and when we engage in a storytelling practice, we need to understand why people tell the stories that they do. Why the story is important, why it is told in the manner that it is, and who the characters are in this story. Telling a story is very often connected to reaching out a hand to the other: "Do you see me? Do you understand my story?" Through empowerment, we think that both former refugee youth and researchers and practitioners can learn from telling and listening, and actively engaging with stories. There are elements of tension and ambivalence in Sera's resettlement story: balancing between family obligations and independence, finding friends as part of an exerting process towards establishing social connections, and coping with belonging and planning a future (see Eide et al., 2020). These tensions need to be narrated and renarrated within a storytelling framework.

Concluding Remarks

Stories and storytelling are important pillars for how to meet people in their local communities. Stories can give a higher degree of not only empowerment, but also *mutual* empowerment. In terms of mutual empowerment, we see a need to create levels of trust that allow us all to tell stories, ask questions, and share experiences. For these stories to become mutual empowerment and health-promoting strategies, there is also a need to recognize positioning as a storytelling strategy, common for everybody. Fostering mutual empowerment requires an effort to understand positioning as a tool to sustain or improve a sense of belonging in the community.

Reflective Questions

1. How can positioning in stories tell us something about the challenges of the storyteller?
2. What are the human rights issues in this story?
3. What role does recognition in stories play, in a relationship between the service user and the social worker?
4. What issues of participation and involvement arise from the story of Sera?

Acknowledgements

This chapter is based on previously published work in a Norwegian book on narrative methods, and for some Norwegian readers there will be an overlap and recognition from this work (Sørly, 2024).

REFERENCES

Ameen, R. F. H. (2019, 24 January). Kurds and their quest to establish an independent Kurdistan. *History Repeats Itself – Stories of 20th Century Partition*, https://partitionhistory.wordpress.com/2019/01/24/no-way-2 (accessed 11 October 2019).

Archambault, J. (2011). *Refugee Children, Citizenship and 'the Best Interests' of the Child: Experiencing Settlement as New Citizens in Norway*. Trondheim: Norwegian Centre for Child Research, NTNU.

Bahram, H. (2018). Kurdish guests or Syrian Refugees? Negotiating displacement, identity and belonging in the Kurdistan region. Masters thesis, Linköping University.

Bamberg, M. G. (1997). Positioning between structure and performance. *Journal of Narrative and Life History*, *7*(1–4), 335–42.

(2006). Stories: Big or small: Why do we care? *Narrative Inquiry*, *16*(1), 139–47.

(2020). Narrative analysis: An integrative approach. In M. Järvinen & N. Mik-Meyer (eds.), *Qualitative Analysis: Eight Approaches for the Social Sciences*, pp.243–64. Los Angeles: Sage.

Bamberg, M. G., & Georgakopoulou, A. (2008). Small stories as a new perspective in narrative and identity analysis. *Text & Talk*, *28*(3), 377–96.

Bauman, S., Soerens, M., & Smeir, I. (2016). *Seeking Refuge: On the Shores of the Global Refugee Crisis*. Chicago, IL: Moody Publishers.

Blix, B. H., Hamran, T., & Normann, H. K. (2013). Struggles of being and becoming: A dialogical narrative analysis of the life stories of Sami elderly. *Journal of Aging Studies*, *27*(3), 264–75.

(2015). Roads not taken: A narrative positioning analysis of older adults' stories about missed opportunities. *Journal of Aging Studies*, *35*, 169–77.

Calzada, E. J., Roche, K. M., White, R., Partovi, R., & Little, T. D. (2020). Family strengths and Latinx youth externalizing behavior: Modifying impacts of an adverse immigration environment. *Journal of Latinx Psychology*, *8*(4), 332–48.

Chen, S., & Schweitzer, R. D. (2019). The experience of belonging in youth from refugee backgrounds: A narrative perspective. *Journal of Child and Family Studies*, *28*(7), 1977–90.

Correa-Velez, I., Gifford, S. M., & Barnett, A. G. (2010). Longing to belong: Social inclusion and wellbeing among youth with refugee backgrounds in the first three years in Melbourne, Australia. *Social Science & Medicine*, *71*(8), 1399–408.

Deane, S. (2016). Syria's lost generation: Refugee education provision and societal security in an ongoing conflict emergency. *IDS Bulletin*, *47*(3), https://bulletin.ids.ac.uk/index.php/idsbo/article/view/2729/HTML (accessed 11 October 2022).

De Fina, A., & Georgakopoulou, A. (2008). Introduction: Narrative analysis in the shift from texts to practices. *Text & Talk*, *28*(3), 275– 81.

De Haene, L., Grietens, H., & Verschueren, K. (2010). Holding harm: Narrative methods in mental health research on refugee trauma. *Qualitative Health Research*, *20*(12), 1664–76.

Dubus, N. (2018). Integration or building resilience: What should the goal be in refugee resettlement? *Journal of Immigrant & Refugee Studies*, *16*(4), 413–29.

Eastmond, M. (2007). Stories as lived experience: Narratives in forced migration research. *Journal of Refugee Studies*, *20*(2), 248–64.

Eide, K., Lidén, H., Haugland, B., Fladstad, T., & Hauge, H. A. (2020). Trajectories of ambivalence and trust: Experiences of unaccompanied refugee minors resettling in Norway. *European Journal of Social Work*, *23*(4), 554–65.

Flyktningregnskapet. (2022). www.flyktninghjelpen.no/flyktningregnskapet (accessed 4 February 2024).

Gourlay, W. (2018). Oppression, solidarity, resistance: The forging of Kurdish identity in Turkey. *Ethnopolitics*, *17*(2), 130–46.

Hormozi, T., Miller, M. M., & Banford, A. (2018). First-generation Iranian refugees' acculturation in the United States: A focus on resilience. *Contemporary Family Therapy*, *40*(3), 276–83

Jacobs, G., van Lieshout, F., Borg, M., & Ness, O. (2017). Being a person-centred researcher: Principles and methods for doing research in a person-centred way. In B. McCormack, S. van Dulmen, H. Eide, T. Eide, & K.-I. Skovdahl (eds.), *Person-Centred Healthcare Research*, pp.51–60. Chichester: Wiley-Blackwell.

Jaspal, R., Carriere, K. R., & Moghaddam, F. M. (2016). Bridging micro, meso, and macro processes in social psychology. In J. Valsiner, G. Marsico, N. Chaudhary, T. Sato, & V. Dazzani (eds.), *Psychology as the Science of Human Being: The Yokohama Manifesto*, pp.265–76. Cham: Springer.

Mathisen, T., & Cele, S. (2020). "Doing belonging": Young former refugees and their active engagement with Norwegian local communities. *Fennia*, *198*(1–2), 39–56.

McGee, T. (2019). *From Syria to Europe: Experiences of Stateless Kurds and Palestinian Refugees from Syria Seeking Protection in Europe*. Institute on Statelessness and Inclusion (ISI); European Statelessness Network (ENS); & ASKV Refugee Support.

Pasupathi, M., & Wainryb, C. (2019). Ghosts in the story: The role of audiences in stability and change in twice-told life stories. *Qualitative Psychology*, *6*(2), 178–93.

Pérez, I. E., Wu, R., Murray, C. B., & Bravo, D. (2021). An interdisciplinary framework examining culture and adaptation in migrant children and adolescents. *New Directions for Child and Adolescent Development, 2021*(176), 13–39.

Randall, W. L., Prior, S. M., & Skarborn, M. (2006). How listeners shape what tellers tell: Patterns of interaction in lifestory interviews and their impact on reminiscence by elderly interviewees. *Journal of Aging Studies*, *20*(4), 381–96.

Richter, L. M., Lye, S. J., & Proulx, K. (2018). Nurturing care for young children under conditions of fragility and conflict. *New Directions for Child and Adolescent Development, 2018*(159), 13–26.

Roche, K. M., Lambert, S. F., Ghazarian, S. R., & Little, T. D. (2015). Adolescent language brokering in diverse contexts: Associations with parenting and parent-youth relationships in a new immigrant destination area. *Journal of Youth and Adolescence*, *44*(1), 77–89.

Senehi, J. J. (2000). Constructive storytelling: Building community, building peace. PhD thesis, Syracuse University in Florence.

Søholt, S., Stenbacka, S., & Nørgaard, H. (2018). Conditioned receptiveness: Nordic rural elite perceptions of immigrant contributions to local resilience. *Journal of Rural Studies*, 64, 220–9.

Sørly, R. (2024) Fortellinger som posisjonering. In Sørly, *Narrativ metode*, pp.131–47. Oslo: Cappelen Damm Akademisk Forlag.

Sørly, R., Mathisen, V., & Kvernmo, S. (2021). "We belong to nature": Communicating mental health in an indigenous context. *Qualitative Social Work*, *20*(5), 1280–96.

Stokke, C. (2019). Do antiracist efforts and diversity programs make a difference? Assessing the case of Norway. In P. Hervik (ed.) *Racialization, Racism, and Anti-Racism in the Nordic Countries*, pp.205–28. Basingstoke: Palgrave Macmillan.

Story, J., & Walker, I. (2016). The impact of diasporas: Markers of identity. *Ethnic and Racial Studies*, *39*(2), 135–41.

Suárez-Orozco, C., Motti-Stefanidi, F., Marks, A., & Katsiaficas, D. (2018). An integrative risk and resilience model for understanding the adaptation of immigrant-origin children and youth. *American Psychologist*, *73*(6), 781–96.

Tønnessen, M., Drahus, K. M., & Dzamarija, M. T. (2020). Demographic profile of Syrians in Norway. In E. D. Carlson & N. E. Williams (eds.), *Comparative Demography of the Syrian Diaspora: European and Middle Eastern Destinations*, pp.281–301. Cham: Springer.

UNHCR. (2019). Global trends: Forced displacement in 2019. www.unhcr.org/flagship-reports/globaltrends/globaltrends2019 (accessed 4 February 2024).

Yoshikawa, H., Wuermli, A. J., & Aber, J. L. (2019). Mitigating the impact of forced displacement and refugee and unauthorized status on youth: Integrating developmental processes with intervention research. In M. Suarez Orozco (ed.), *Humanitarianism and Mass Migration: Confronting the World Crisis*, pp.186–206. Oakland: University of California Press.

Photo: Hilde Mjøs

CHAPTER 12

Living in a Pause
Experiences from Conflict Resolution in a Mexican Migrant Shelter

Mónica Ayala-Mira

> Bridges are thresholds to other realities, archetypal, primal symbols of shifting consciousness.
> They are passageways, conduits, and connectors that connote transitioning, crossing borders, and changing perspectives.
> Bridges span liminal (threshold) spaces between worlds, spaces I call nepantla, a Nahuatl[1] word meaning tierra entre medio.[2]
> Transformations occur in this in-between space, an unstable, unpredictable, precarious, always-in-transition space lacking clear boundaries.
> Nepantla es tierra desconocida,[3] and living in this liminal zone means being in a constant state of displacement – an uncomfortable, even alarming feeling.
>
> Most of us dwell in nepantla so much of the time it's become a sort of "home". (Anzaldúa, 1999)

The Migrant Shelter

That day, my heart was beating so hard *pum pum pum, tolón, tolón, tolón* . . . like a Mexican drum.

It was my first time supporting in conflict resolution at a migrant shelter. I was there to assist Doña Martha, the manager, with a huge problem among the women. Chore responsibilities were ignored. Name calling, slapping, and hair pulling were involved.

As I was walking through the patio, there were little girls and boys laughing, trying to look through the windows of the big hall.

The children were curious about the disturbance:

GIRL: Oh my god, Gina said to Lola *Vete a la chingada!!!!*[4]

[1] Nahuatl (Aztec) is a language of the Uto-Aztecan language family, spoken by an estimated 1.5 million Nahua people, mostly living in Central Mexico.
[2] A land in between. [3] Nepantla is an unfamiliar land.
[4] It is a phrase widely used in Mexico; it is colloquial, and it is an insult.

All of the children were laughing.

BOY: They are yelling at eachother!!!
GIRL: Doña Martha is very upset . . . they´re both going to be in trouble.

All of the children were laughing.

Inside the hall:

LOLA: Stop being so mean. You slapped my face . . . yelled at my son . . . you are not perfect, not a good mom . . . you don´t really help out with the chores . . .

GINA: Hey I do them, everyday . . . you are *cochina*[5] and lazy. Also, your kids . . . they always spill water and crumbs everywhere, you are such an hypocrite . . . I hope you and your kids get kicked out, you guys are a problem . . . everybody knows it.

LOLA: Hey I am not insulting you, so stop it . . . And that´s not true, you are a liar, you also eat all day long and don´t help out with cooking or dishes.

GINA: That´s because you said that my cooking was awful . . . too salty . . . last dinner you didn´t eat my chicken broth . . . one spoonful was enough and even then you spat it out.

DOÑA MARTHA: Ladies!! Stop, you are in the same boat. You should stop fighting . . . you need each other.

GINA: Yes, we should, but Lola is just complaining all day long, constantly crying . . . I can´t stand being near her!

OTHER GIRLS: Yes that's true, she is a problem . . .

That's where I asked them: Is Lola the real problem down here?

(*Silence.*)

The Context

Gina and Lola are part of a group of twenty-five Mexican and Central American women displaced due to criminal and gender-based violence. They have been waiting for several months in a women´s shelter with their children in Mexicali, Baja California, Mexico's northernmost city. A city of light and shadow, a desert and a fertile place formed by immigrants who came from China, and since then has grown thanks to migration of people nationwide from Sinaloa, Sonora, Veracruz, Puebla, Chiapas, and Michoacán.

Waiting, due to the changes in US immigration policies after the COVID-19 pandemic. Title 42,[6] revived by Trump in 2020, trapped a

[5] Dirty [6] For furher information about Title 42, see Ulrich and Crosby (2021).

large population in involuntary displacement within Mexican borders because of the stagnant application process for asylum seekers. At the end of last year, the US opened asylum applications and people left in large groups. But at the beginning of 2023, the US changed the form of application process from written to digital, the CBP One app.

However, the app is ineffective, and many people are in forced encampments along the Mexican border or in continuous displacement throughout the border ports of entry. Their worst scenario: cross without asylum or residence with a *coyote o pollero*,[7] or go back to their communities. This is part of the policy "Stay in Mexico, do not cross or you will be deported."

Internal and cross-border displacement is a constant throughout human history, in diverse historical and geopolitical locations. Currently, displacement from the Global South to the North is recognized as forced displacement for economic reasons, organized crime, authoritarian and military regimes, natural disasters, and gender-based violence, which have increased significantly in recent years (Kelley, 2022).

In the Global South, the *Abya Yala*,[8] in forced internal displacement, the number of women and their children seeking to cross into the US is very notable. Mexico is experiencing forced internal displacement due to organized crime. The war against drug trafficking, which began during the six-year term of Felipe Calderón,[9] promoted a series of reconfigurations and diversifications of the organized crime groups. This resulted in extreme violence against the civilian population in the form of extortion, kidnapping, human trafficking for the purpose of sexual and labour exploitation, and the annihilation of their ways of life and their lives. There is no government-level census or care and integration programme for the various destination places in Mexico.

Waiting in Nepantla

The first time I met Gina, Lola, and the other women in this shelter, they were obsessively typing on their cell phones, click click click click . . . refreshing the CBP One app over and over, as if in a trance. Their faces revealed all the tension, anguish, worry, and guilt over the wait. That's why they fought, not over the shelter's chores. That was what the silence was made of. They

[7] A person who helps someone to cross the border illegally for a high payment, mainly in dollars.

[8] Synonym, in the Cuna language, for America, which means mature land, living land, land that flourishes.

[9] Former President of Mexico (2006–12).

were going through the uncertainty described in *Nepantla.*[10] A space of possibilities for great transformations, but also for a fall down to the bottom.

The gender-based violence articulated with the brutality of the Mexican criminal class, *la maña* (the cartel), the violence of the *endriagos,*[11] expelled them from their communities. They had to flee at night with their children, wearing only the clothes they had on and with a few pennies in their bag.

The Story of Lola, the Story of Many

Lola's village[12] in Michoacán is indigenous (Purépecha), and she used to be a textile artisan there, embroidering the traditional clothes of her community. There, the law is that of men in the cartels and of customs and traditions. The state does not interfere there. She never received support. The violence she experienced almost cost her life, and she had to leave. Her husband, her family, the men and women of the community, all repudiated her. They spat on her in the street, shouted at her, and planned to stone her to death in the street just because she decided to leave her husband. Her husband was part of *la maña*, one of the most powerful leaders of that community.

She fled to Morelia, the capital city, to a shelter for battered women. There, she received individual and family therapy. Her cell phone was taken away and kept in custody for a month. After this time, she managed to contact a family member in California with the idea of them sponsoring her to achieve asylum. With that hope, she arrived in Mexicali, as did the other twenty-five women, and the waiting began.

During this time, very few have managed to get an appointment with migration, and even fewer have achieved asylum. Desperation takes the form of insomnia, anxiety, irritability, hormonal imbalances, sadness, and guilt. These are emotions and feelings that people share but cannot express openly because doing so only brings back their own sorrows and pains, both physical and emotional. It is more beneficial to remain silent and suppress these feelings.

10 Anzaldúa (1999) reclaims the náhuatl word that means *the land in between*, a liminal space.

11 They are monsters, part dragon and part hydra. Martínez (2013) named men who use violence as a means of survival *endriagos*.

12 These indigenous villages in Michoacán are called *tenencias*, regulated by ancient traditions, mostly conservative and misogynistic.

That's why Lola is a problem, she talks about her sorrow, their sorrow.

Did I have to come all the way here?
What will I do if I don't make it?
What will happen to my children?
Will I be able to find a job, a home?
Will my husband find me?
What will happen if my husband finds me?

The Uncertainty

There are people who are considered privileged because they have a routine that gives them a sense of control and security. They know what their day will look like and have plans for the future. As a result, they feel relatively calm and safe in their environment. However, this is not the case for everyone. Those who don't have a routine may feel uncertain and vulnerable, not knowing what the future holds. This can make it difficult for them to feel at ease in their surroundings.

Consider the scenario where we have to leave a place where we were subjected to various forms of abuse and violence and arrive in a new place that is unfamiliar and unsafe with different customs. The fear of being found by those we escaped from always looms over us, making us constantly anxious and on edge. And if we add to this that we don't know where we are going, we may have possibilities, but without any clarity . . .

That stops us, hinders us, pauses our life, and keeps us in a constant state of waiting like Lola, Gina, and the other twenty-five women.

How can they inhabit these spaces and moments of waiting? How can they survive? How can they maintain hope? How can they survive and resist all that can't be changed? All the institutional violences, necropolitical policies, colonial discourses and practices.

Currently they can just wait and keep trying to get the CBP One app working. Living in Nepantla, in a state of pause.

Reflective Questions

1. How can conflict be solved when the participants' stories are coloured by turbulence and uncertainty?
2. Can a researcher contribute to change ongoing stories? If yes, in what way?

3. At the end of this story, we do not see any solutions for the participants in the study. How can we deal with situations like this – as researchers or practitioners of social work?

REFERENCES

Anzaldúa, G. (1999). *Borderlands/La Frontera: The New Mestiza*, 2nd edn, intro. S. Saldívar-Hull. San Francisco, CA: Aunt Lute.

Kelley, N. (2022). *People Forced to Flee: History, Change and Challenge*. Oxford University Press.

Martínez, M. Á. (2013). Capitalismo gore. (Sayak Valencia). *Kamchatka: Revista de análisis cultural*, *1*, 244–9.

Ulrich, M. R., & Crosby, S. S. (2021). Title 42, asylum, and politicising public health. *Lancet Regional Health – Americas*, *18*(7), 100124.

Photo: Hilde Mjøs

CHAPTER 13

Promissory Notes and Other Forms of Consent

Tracie Rogers

Social Work Research as an Active, Engaged Practice

This story unfolded on a cool breezy day, in a seaside rural village in South Trinidad, where a social work researcher set out to conduct an in-depth interview with an eighty-six-year-old woman. The interview was part of data collection efforts for a larger qualitative study commissioned to assess the potential cultural impact of building an aluminium smelter. When the interviewer arrived, she was quickly dismissed with a waved hand and mutterings about the work to be done that day. What was conceived of as a ninety-minute interview stretched over eight hours, and challenged the core of what we are conventionally taught about epistemology, ethics, and engagement in research. This story interrogates notions of reciprocity as the researcher picked breadfruit, dug up yams and sweet potatoes, opened coconuts from the garden, husked fresh corn, and shelled pigeon peas at the kitchen table. Stories of oppression, the historicity of black people's connection to the land, and Caribbean black womanhood are layered between grief, food, memory, and defiance. These stories are interwoven with the researcher's story of questioning the Western cultural lens through which we are taught to judge credible, valid, ethically sound social research. The researcher utilized arts-based inquiry as a frame to craft this story, and ultimately presents an intergenerational dialogue between two Caribbean women. The reader is invited to consider social work research as an active, engaged practice.

Promissory Notes and Other Forms of Consent

More than fifteen years ago, in a rural fishing village along the southwest peninsula of a beautiful Caribbean island, a graceful woman in her late eighties, whom I will call Ms J, afforded me one of the most memorable experiences I have ever had as a social work researcher. On a quiet clear morning, I mounted the staircase at the front porch of Ms J's wooden home – a young researcher fluent in the mechanics of data extraction. When the sun descended later that day, my body was riddled with data, my understanding of knowledge generation, historicity, and ancestral connection forever altered.

The researcher I aspired to be the morning that I made my way to Ms J's home, and the researcher I am today, work from irreconcilable mindsets. Instead of using literature reviews as an entry point to creating a research story of any kind – be it a proposal, journal article, or book chapter – I first engage in some form of artmaking. I create art to clear a path for the work to unfold, to unearth somatic knowledge and tap into collective consciousness. My entry point to telling this story is a blank canvas measuring sixteen inches in width and thirty inches in length, acrylic paints, scraps of cloth, and collage paper.

I never anticipate what will be produced when I utilize arts-based inquiry. This immersive, transformative process disrupts dominant colonial discourses around knowledge creation, and as such, the process is the product. Centring my marginalized identities, I position myself in dialogue with the subject matter. I start the research journey as an embodied knower, rather than one who must justify and rationalise their way to the mantle of expert. When I started the painting in Figure 7, my deepest desire was to commune with Ms J again. I wanted to explore the data she offered me through a lens I was too naïve to craft in my twenties.

In this chapter I tell two parallel stories. One story is about a young woman in her late twenties who sets off to the countryside to collect data about the sociocultural and psychosocial experiences of people who lived in a small village. The painting titled *Unmasked* tells another story. *Unmasked* is the story of a black Trinidadian woman, social work educator, and researcher, who returned to a seminal experience accrued nearly sixteen years prior, to unveil and reintegrate its lessons into *self*. Both are stories of gratitude; they are the blossoming of seeds planted by a wise woman.

* * *

The journey from the town of San Juan, about twenty minutes outside of the bustling capital city Port of Spain, to the idyllic fishing village of Chatham takes about three hours by car. However, if you attend to the sights and sounds along the way, in those three hours, you can travel through decades of the country's diverse cultural, historical, and socioeconomic landscape.

Figure 7 *Unmasked* (mixed media and acrylics on canvas). (Photo: Tracie Rogers)

Trinidad is the southernmost island in an archipelago stretching between the North and South American continents, flagged by the Caribbean Sea to its west, and the Atlantic Ocean to the east. Trinidad, and its sister isle Tobago, form a single republic state previously colonized by several European countries, the last of which was Britain. Branded by colonialization and European voracity, our country, like many of its Caribbean neighbours, bears a multitude of scars. These include the near genocide of its First People and hundreds of years of European conquest. This country was forged by the exploitation of African people extracted to provide free labour that built northern empires. It was fashioned by the ruthlessness of indentured servitude endured by South East Asians imported to work sugar plantations after the abolition of slavery. Many cultures and struggles have moulded this land, from Chinese and Syrian immigration in the early and mid 1900s to the discovery of oil and gas and an entirely new era of exploitation.

As I exited my parents' driveway, I welcomed dawn with the calming melody of the *Adhan*, calling Muslims to prepare for the *Fajr* morning prayer. Driving in solitude across highways and crooked dilapidated country roads, my thoughts meandered along our cultural terrain. I relished the sights of the country yawning, as wholesale vendors queued to enter complexes for Saturday Markets, and a host of food trucks set up to sell local street food. Along the highway, which connects North and South Trinidad, and through the forested winding roads, I passed oil refineries, the play of bareback boys spilling onto sidewalks, and women and men of every hue about Saturday business. With equal amounts of joy and deep reverence, I tasted the salt of the Gulf of Paria and welcomed the stench of the fish markets. I soaked it up with an open heart and revelled in the cross-section of beauty that is our multiverse.

The diversity of sights and sounds contained in such a small country, along a mere 95 kilometres, is incredible. At one point, I crawled slowly for a few kilometres behind a Hindu funeral procession. Fifteen minutes after that, I was driving at the edge of an expansive cane field with the smell of molasses heavy in the air. Another fifteen minutes later, I drove past international food chains, and a monstrous shopping mall. A mere twenty minutes after those sights, I gazed out at the pitch lake, one of the eight wonders of the world, with the burgeoning smell of asphalt saturating the air. From one village to the next, I absorbed all the sights and sounds, while replaying the carefully worded questions and prompts for the in-depth research interview I was about to conduct. I entered the final leg of my journey on the southwestern peninsula, ready to skilfully and smoothly conduct a ninety-minute interview chock full of data. I smiled gleefully as I absorbed the pristine, placid village of Chatham all around me.

Ms J's house sat atop a small hill off the narrow, asphalt main road – the only way to enter and exit the village. This road runs along the coast, all the way to Icacos Point. Icacos is at the very tip of the peninsula. On a clear day you can stand at its point and see the Venezuelan coast on the South American continent.

I switched off the car engine and stuck my head out of the open window as a gentle breeze brushed against my cheek. Through the chain-linked fence I saw the outline of a woman, standing arms akimbo, in a pale-coloured house dress. The figure wore a broad-brimmed straw hat and stood among narrow pigeon pea trees. The small evergreens stretched to about five feet, almost as tall as the woman. I waved my right arm as I hung out of the car window, calling out "Good morning." The figure seemed to look right at me for a few seconds, then with a swift dismissive wave returned to her pigeon pea trees. This was the first of many waves of uncertainty to come over me during that day.

Two weeks prior, I visited with a team of researchers contracted to complete an assessment of the impact of building an aluminium smelter on the villagers of Chatham and the neighbouring village of Cap de Ville. Beyond the possible health and environmental risks, there was concern about the possible social impact on the community. I was tasked to conduct a cultural impact assessment. This study aimed to identify potential constructive and adverse effects on cultural values and social relationships. The Village Council identified a diverse group of community gatekeepers to participate in in-depth interviews to inform the assessment. It was during that visit I was introduced to Ms J. With a suspicious smile planted on her face, she bluntly asked:

"They send you to talk to me because I am old?" Caught off guard, I muttered my protest and was about to respond until her voice silenced me.

"I speak the truth you know." She nodded her head, gave me her telephone number, and briskly walked away.

The interaction was brief and potent. Ms J wore a full crown of grey and a comfort in her bones that I had rarely seen. In her presence, my back straightened, shoulders became alert and my chest rose. I left with the distinct feeling that I should not waste her time.

I sat in my car entertaining doubts. Shifting my eyes to the bag on the front seat, I recalled the hours of preparation for this interview and wondered if I would indeed waste her time. I took a deep breath, threw my bag across my shoulder, exited the car, and approached the front gate. I hollered, "Good morning Ms J."

* * *

Ms J's light blue wooden house sat atop several concrete stilts about twelve feet off the dirt ground. After a few minutes of calling at her gate, Ms J invited me to wait on her veranda. With a berating tone, she informed me that she had expected me to arrive earlier: "Town people always expect us to move on *their* time," she exclaimed, motioning towards the staircase as she walked away. Ms J continued to mumble something about not liking to be disturbed when she started working in her garden. I doubted she heard my apology since she had already returned to her pigeon pea trees.

As I walked up the stairs, I wondered about her "town people" scolding. My parents are from rural communities, and I grew up with a keen awareness of the tension between urban and rural residents. My aunts and uncles on my mother's side of the family, who had migrated from their rural communities, would tease, and at times be condescending to those who still lived there. There were two wooden rocking chairs on the veranda, both facing the sea. I absentmindedly chose one and sat with thoughts swirling in my head. *Town people! This was surely a bad start to our interview.*

Gently rocking back and forth in the chair, I begun to imagine how things would have been different had I left home at five o'clock in the morning. From the perch of Ms J's veranda, I looked out to the endless sea. It was absolutely mesmerizing. The salt of the sea filled Ms J's home, and the small waves one after the other, tumbling up the shoreline and gently swinging back to the sea, provided a soothing, constant melody. I was looking at the sea when Ms J interrupted my thoughts. She was at the top of the staircase carrying a large sack of pigeon peas.

"Have you had breakfast yet?" she asked. "Come for some tea."

I would learn that most of Ms J's questions were rhetorical. Furthermore, she almost always provided the answer for any question that was not rhetorical. When I turned towards her voice, she had already disappeared into the house. I followed the creaking sounds of her feet walking across the wooden floorboards into the house.

As I pushed past the curtain dancing with the sea breeze at the entrance to her living room, the smell of cedarwood and cocoa was all around me.

The room was filled with wooden furniture – a love seat, two single chairs, a rocking chair, a medium-sized chest of drawers, and two cabinets. One cabinet had wooden doors, while the second one had glass panes through which I could see a variety of drinking glasses, stacks of plates, and numerous ceramic and glass trinkets. There were black and white vintage-looking photographs on the walls of elegantly dressed black people in suits and fancy church dresses. None of the faces were smiling; they all wore stern looks, their poised bodies in starched crisp linens with carefully positioned legs and arms. There was wood all around me, from the exterior and interior walls to the floors beneath my feet and the ceiling above me. Along the right side of the living room, there were two doors that led to adjacent rooms.

"Are you all right ma'am?" Her words interrupted my veneration. Her home was soothing and made me feel at ease.

"I am, Ms J," I responded quickly while I impulsively ran my fingers along the wooden walls. I walked from the living room into the large kitchen where she stood facing a huge sink.

"My father and grandfather made everything you see in this house," she said with pride.

In the middle of the kitchen there was a beautiful wooden table surrounded by six chairs. I walked to the table and placed my hands on the back of one of the chairs. My fingers wrapped around the curve of the chair. At the same time, a gust of wind blew through the house. The breeze danced through the living room and out of the windows and opened front door.

"You can sit," she gently commanded as she invited me to her kitchen table.

"Thank you." I pulled a chair out and sat facing her, my back to the living room door. Draping my bag on the chair back, I made a mental notation about the kitchen and the countenance of the woman to whom it belonged. I smiled, remembering my grandmother's sink hanging out of her kitchen window in the village of La Lune, Moruga on the southern coast of the island. I had only seen kitchen windows like this in rural Trinidad; as a child I was fascinated when my grandmother closed the kitchen window at night. It was as though the sink disappeared at night and it was no longer part of the house.

The sound of dishes jolted me out of my thoughts and brought me back to Ms J busily placing dried dishes in cabinetry, before walking towards the whistling kettle on the stove. As she turned the stove off, she looked towards me and asked if I wanted fever grass tea or cocoa tea with my breakfast.

"Thanks Ms J, but it's okay. I do not . . ." My voice trailed off as our eyes locked. Her disapproval was evident.

"What time did you leave home this morning?" Before I could respond, she rejoined, "Before the sun came up, I am sure." Her tone grew threatening, "You eat anything for the morning?"

"No, I haven't but . . ."

"Good. Fever grass tea or cocoa tea?"

"Fever grass please."

* * *

We sat across from each other with a large circular flat roasted coconut bake, about twenty inches in diameter, between us. There was also a medium-sized bowl with salt fish seasoned with tomatoes, chives, and cilantro, her cup of cocoa tea, and my cup of fever grass tea. Amid the flavours of the food, the warmth and fragrance of the tea, the crisp freshness of the air, I could easily forget why I was there. I took a deep breath and decided this was a good time to start the work I came to undertake.

"Thanks so much for your hospitality Ms J," I exhaled with a gentle smile. I became very aware of the cadence and rhythm of my speech. "Thanks for the breakfast and thank you for agreeing to participate in this interview. The interview . . ."

"Tell me about your people," Ms J interrupted.

I was caught off guard by her question; however I quickly reasoned that this would be a great way to build rapport before starting the interview. I responded to Ms J's inquiry between sips of tea and bites of bake. I told her about where I lived, the schools I attended and what I studied at university. Her elbows on the table, body leaned towards me, she listened to me attentively while sipping her cocoa. When I was finished, she leaned back in her chair, placed her hands on her hips, and said,

"Now. Tell me about your people." Her eyes were fixed, lips pouted towards the left of her face, her head tilted to the right.

The interview would not proceed until I shared the personal information requested. Ms J needed to know about my genealogy. I identified where my maternal and paternal grandparents were born. My paternal grandfather's mother was from Barbados and my maternal grandfather was from Carriacou, a tiny island off the coast of Grenada. I explained that my maternal family's home was located in rural South Trinidad, while my paternal grandparents settled in North East Trinidad. I described our extended family, pointing out that my grandparents had many children – on my father's side there are fourteen aunts and uncles while on my mother's side there are twelve. Ms J's eyes opened with delight when I mentioned that my father's brother was married to my mother's sister, which made our families a little more tangled than most. I briefly spoke about where my aunts, uncles, and cousins lived in Trinidad and Tobago and overseas. She listened intently and nodded her head as though she was drawing a genogram in her head. I gave factual information, avoiding sharing anything that was provocative. Moreover, my cocky twenty-something-year-old self was quite impressed with her judicious self-disclosure. By the time I was finished, so was my breakfast.

"You have people!" Ms J laughed and nodded. "You come from hard-working people too." She seemed pleased with my account and I felt satisfied that we could now begin the interview. I reached into my bag and pulled out a few sheets of paper, among them informed consent forms, an agency referral list, and an information sheet about the study.

"I know that you agreed to participate in an interview." I spoke with confidence, satisfied that I had built sufficient rapport and we were ready to get to the reason I barely slept the night before. "Before we begin I would like to go over what this interview is about." I lightly patted the forms lying before me. "We now have an opportunity to talk about any questions you have. That way you can be certain that you want to speak with me."

There was a long pause.

"Hmmm," she exhaled, looking at the sheets of paper on the table between us. Her affect was flat, and I did not know how to interpret her nonverbal communication. She did not look as though she was going to object, but she also did not look as though she was willing to agree. I reached into my bag again, and this time I withdrew a writing pad, a pen, and a small auto recorder. I placed them on the table next to the consent forms and continued speaking,

"I will review the consent forms with you," I continued, "and if you agree and are comfortable, we can start right away." Determined, I pushed forward despite my uncertainty about whether she would agree to participate in the interview. "I would like to record our conversation to help me ensure I correctly capture all the information you share with me. But if you are uncomfortable with the recording, we can proceed without it."

There was a longer pause than the one before.

"Hm," she exhaled again. This time her response sounded like a song.

"We do not have to record our conversation," I swiftly assured her. "Let me know how you would like to proceed."

This was the longest pause.

The air between us felt thick and I was already rehearsing my "Thank you for being willing to participate."

"I don't know about all of that," her words broke a tension that felt endless, "but I know I have plenty work to do this morning." She rose from the table, wrapped the remaining bake in a kitchen towel, reached for an empty old Danish cookies tin on the counter, in which she placed the bake. "You know what happened on Saturday mornings?" she asked, turning towards me.

I nodded my head, knowing that this was a rhetorical question.

"Yes sir! Saturdays are important days in this home, as it was in my parents' home and their parents' homes. It is a day of preparation."

Ms J started to hum a church hymn. It was a slow melodic hum of a spiritual refrain, heavy with sorrow yet soothing, hummed the way I have only heard older Caribbean women drag a tune. The hum faded as Ms J disappeared into a door off the living room. It rose again when she returned with a straw hat. She looked at my hands on the consent forms, handed me the straw hat, and motioned for me to follow her out to the garden.

"I am making cow heel soup today. There is yam and sweet potatoes to dig." She motioned over to a bed of ground provisions as we exited the kitchen through the back door. "We can't have good soup without dumpling," she exclaimed. Suddenly her body became still; I was standing next to her, our shoulders almost touching. She turned her head to me, pursed her lips, and asked, "Can you knead flour, right?"

* * *

My mother's family hails from a village called La Lune, in an area known as Moruga. The village runs along a body of water called the Columbus Channel. The adjacent town Grand Chemin is known as the location where Spanish conquerors first came ashore in the late 1400s. While La Lune is a fishing village, it is also home to a dense forest, diverse plant and animal life, rich soil populated with cedar and mahogany trees, and old cocoa plantations.

My father's family on the other hand hailed from an area called La Baja, in North East Trinidad. La Baja is only a few kilometres from St Joseph, the first capital of the country, and about an hour away from Port of Spain, the current capital. The main difference between La Lune and La Baja to my child eyes was their closeness to the sea. On my visits to La Baja, once my grandmother served breakfast, my cousins and I disappeared into acres of trees. We resurfaced for lunch and then disappeared amongst the trees again for several hours. There was always a fruit in season for us to gorge on, from nearly a dozen type of mangoes to cashews and sapodillas, tippi-tambo to tonka bean, orange and guava to sour cherries and chenet. Those memories of climbing trees, digging our fingers into dirt, discovering ravines and chasing chickens seemed so distant. While digging up provisions from the ground in Ms J's yard, I was struck by how strange, yet familiar, it all felt.

"Yes, that's enough," she told me as she lifted a large piece of yam and placed it into a crocus bag beside her. I rested the last sweet potato I dug up into the basket as well. When we returned to the kitchen, Ms J poured me a glass of coconut water and instructed me to catch my breath. I nodded in agreement as I removed the straw hat from my head. I felt as grateful for the shelter of the hat, as I was for the many stories Ms J told me as we worked in the garden. While digging ground provisions, she dished out stories of her parents and grandparents and the stories they told her. On one occasion, I asked if she would mind if I went to the kitchen to get my interview guide. She assured me that she would "definitely mind" and instructed me to stay. I began to reconcile with the reality that I would be unable to use any of this information in my research report.

I was not allowed to rest for too long. The cow heel, pumpkin, and split peas had been cooking in a pot all morning, and it was time to get the ground provisions into the soup. We diced and sliced sweet potatoes, yams, dasheen, and green bananas, as Ms J explained how our ancestors came to create meals around animal parts discarded by the self-proclaimed slave masters. I learned this information in high school; however, the way in which Ms J told it felt more like family business than it did facts thrown at me during social studies classes.

"One day our ancestors were told that they were free." Ms J told this story as routinely as she threw vegetables in her soup. "They were emancipated. The next day they woke up the same condition they were in the day before. What to do?" She continued telling the story as her grandfather told her when she was a little girl. As she disclosed the tale, I imagined the tall elegant man with broad shoulders in his wood shed on Sunday mornings after church. Staying faithful to Ms J's descriptors, I visualized the way he alternated between wiping his brow in rest periods, and pushing his weight on the wood saw.

"They walked back to the plantation and asked massa for work," Ms J stated dryly. "He paid them three pennies and charged them four pennies for the food and shelter he provided. Do you know how these ancestors were paid?"

She waited for me to answer. This question was not rhetorical. I tried to recall what I could from history and social studies classes in high school. I had no idea how the formerly enslaved were paid for their labour.

"No. I do not know."

"The same way many white planters would pay for enslaved people," she told me. "With promissory notes!"

There was a pregnant pause.

"Our ancestors would dip their thumbs in ink and make their marks. They did not know how to read or write."

The air between us grew heavier.

"After all this time, they are still asking us to make our mark on promissory notes as they talk about aluminium smelters."

The storytelling paused for the next hour or two. We worked in silence. Ms J let the flour dumpling slide off her fingers and into the cow heel soup. I cleaned the kitchen table with a cloth, washed the dishes, dried them, and returned them to their cabinets. We also started parcelling the provisions, fruits and vegetables we gathered from the garden. She informed me that before I left her, we would place these packages in my car and deliver food baskets to families in the neighbourhood.

* * *

"A man can be stupid, but a stupid woman must die." Ms J let the words roll off her lips with a piercing tone.

My body jolted, the chair I was sitting on shifted a little, and the wooden floor beneath me made a small creaking sound. It was about three o'clock in the afternoon when Ms J emptied a sack of pigeon peas on the kitchen table. I had forgotten about the pigeon peas she was picking when I arrived that morning, as well as the sack she dragged into the veranda. We began the work of pulling the shells open and prying the peas out into a large bowl.

I slowly looked up from the pigeon peas I was shelling. There was wisdom folded into the small sachets beneath her eyes and the slant of the lines etched on her face. Something about her gaze made me uncertain about whether her meaning was metaphorical or literal. My discomfort must have been evident, because she reached over, gently touched my hand, holding my gaze as she whispered:

"We cannot afford stupidity, Tracie."

Like a master theorist, Ms J wove meaning through a tapestry of stories about the formerly enslaved women and men who returned to the sugar-cane and cocoa plantations after the emancipation proclamation. These stories depicted them making sense of this new terror – a time when slavery was illegal, but the chattels of slave labour were institutionalized in a new way. The tales unfolded, and mended fractured understandings about our contemporary relationships with our intimate partners, families, and communities. Ms J's wisdom resonates with Collins's writing about black feminist thought: "As members of a subordinate group, Black women cannot afford to be fools of any type, for our objectification as the Other, denies us the protections that White skin, maleness, and wealth confer" (Collins, 2000, p.257). Collins makes a distinction between knowledge and wisdom; the latter built on the lived experiences of Black women which are indispensable to our survival. With this appreciation of the intersectionality of vulnerabilities, Collins forwards that "knowledge without wisdom is adequate for the powerful, but wisdom is essential to the survival of the subordinate" (p.257).

* * *

The cool breeze tickling our faces, five o'clock in the evening found Ms J and myself gently moving back and forth in the wooden rocking chairs made by her father. We had not too long returned from delivering packages to women and elderly persons, all of whom lived within ten minutes of her home. I had made fresh lime juice a few hours before, and now we sipped the cold drinks. She hummed a sweet song that danced with the sound of the waves crashing against the seashore. I imagined the heroines of all the tales she shared of women nurtured in multiple communities across time and space. These were stories of survival, defiance, of holding silences and screaming truths. I had more data than I knew what to do with.

"You got what you needed?" she asked quietly.

"Much more than I knew I needed." I did not hesitate to respond to her; this was not a rhetorical question.

"What are you going to do with it?"

"I am going to keep it close and share it generously."

"Hm," she sighed. "Bring your forms for me."

Reflective Questions

1. In this story, the researcher deals with expectations and preconceptions about what will be happening during her data-gathering. How can preconceptions stop us from really listening to stories?
2. Storytelling is not only about the stories being told. How can 'doing things together' be a form of conversation or storytelling?
3. In what way would you say the storyteller has changed her expectations towards storytelling, after her meeting with Ms. J.?

REFERENCE

Collins, P. H. (2000). *Black Feminist Thought: Knowledge, Consciousness, and the Politics of Empowerment*, 2nd edn. New York: Routledge.

Photo: Hilde Mjøs

CHAPTER 14

For Some People You Make a Difference, You Carry Their Hope

A Social Worker's Story

Sheila Zimic

Social services in Sweden today are exposed to many challenges. An international disinformation campaign was spreading fear and growing mistrust among citizens towards Swedish authorities. Some employees in social services are being threatened and harassed. Social workers testify to an increasingly pressured work situation, more cases with difficult problems, and at the same time, too few resources to use. Often, in media, we are presented with a dark picture of social services. Another image, which is not given much attention, is that social services are the ultimate safety net for all individuals who need society's help, for example to get out of their addiction, domestic violence, financial difficulty, criminal or destructive behaviour. Behind every individual who managed to turn their life around, with the help of social services, there are proud social workers. In this text we will meet Helen (not her real name), who took her social work degree in 1983. Since then, she has worked mostly in social services, with various tasks, including case work, family therapy, management, and service development. This is her story.

Helen

You don't always reflect about why you have chosen your profession. Why your life has turned out in a certain way. In my case, my family had quite a lot of political engagement. We have always discussed at home that the collective is more important than the individual. That it is important to help each other. Solidarity. I was also politically engaged before I started at the college for social work. At the time, I thought it was very much a coincidence that I applied for social work. Later I realized that it wasn't just the political engagement that got me in to this choice. I had experienced a trauma in my teens, which I have repressed, but most certainly it had an impact on my interest and my engagement with people. I didn't know that at that time.

When I was working as head of department and as I had dialogues with my employees, I learned that many social workers carried their own traumas. I think that is a decisive factor in choosing a profession like this. There are many who have been hurt. And if you don't work on your trauma, it can affect you in your profession. But if you do work with your own trauma, it can be an asset. I'm happy I made the choice to become a social worker, because it has made me a better person. And my life experiences have made me a better social worker.

So, in 1983 I took my degree and ever since I have been in the social work profession. We had internships during the education. As early as 1981, I had practised in social services and was then allowed to work during summer periods. I was then twenty years old. It was kind of fascinating and I remember how different it was. It was sort of better in some ways and worse in others.

The best thing about being a social worker is that you can contribute to development and change on many different levels – from individual level to changing organizations, and even sometimes on a national level, through, for example, national reference groups. The best thing, without doubt, is that I have been able to participate in and contribute to different types of development and that I have met so many fantastic people! Of course I have experienced very sad things too, and the work is a huge responsibility. But it also contains an incredible amount of freedom within the given legal frames.

Together with the people you meet, you can actually do almost anything. Things that benefit them. As long as you stay within the legislation, you can do a great deal and make a difference for other people. Even though there are situations when you can't do much. That's the hard part, that you can't make a difference. The fact is that you have to learn over time to be able to continue working. That it doesn't only depend on you, it also depends on the other person. It depends on where they are in their life. What opportunities they have and how they cope at the moment. Right then and there, you have to be able to accept it. And it's not that simple. But even if there is no change right now, you may still have contributed to the fact that the next time someone else meets this person, things will go better.

I remember a woman. She was in her forties when we started to have meetings. We worked with her addiction. She was using pills and alcohol, not so much other drugs. She lived with a man who was abusing her, who was severely alcoholic. She had no job and no home of her own. She lived with this man, and she had three children who had been placed in foster homes a long time ago and with whom she had no contact. She had a very hard time getting out of the relationship due to the normalization process that comes with violence.

We met often and for a long time. I don't remember how many years we had been meeting before there was a change. She had very little hope in her own capacity for change.

In any case, I managed to persuade her, "Of course you can manage without this man. Social services will help you if you decide to get a life of your own." And so, we did! She applied for and got a place of her own. She broke up with this man, which meant things got worse for a while before they got better. We had a lot of contact at times and later she got another place to live and started to study. She had lived with her addiction for probably twenty years, so she hadn't worked that many years in her life. Anyway, she trained as an assistant nurse, got a permanent job and a more dignified life, if you ask me. We then kept in touch for a long time afterwards, although she didn't have to keep in touch with me anymore, just occasionally, and I've always been curious to know what made the difference.

One day I asked her – what was it that time that made the breakthrough? I mean, she had tried everything. She had been in treatment homes several times. She had been in outpatient care plenty of times. She had really tried. And then she said: "Even when I didn't believe in myself, you still believed in me. You never gave up on me." (At this point Helen could not suppress the tears. With a shaky voice, she continued.) That's what made her not give up either.

Then, when she became sober and free from drugs, she regained contact with her children and grandchildren. The sad thing is that she got sick. It was something with her heart. She couldn't continue working and she got retired early. It was a pity. She liked her work. Another thing is that she was so hurt that she lost all faith in men and romantic relationships. But she did get a better life in that she connected with her children and grandchildren, and she moved closer to them, to a region where she had previously lived. She became sober.

Then I have met people who have had addiction problems and who have died. It's so sad. They are really fantastic people too. Sometimes it seems it's just chance that determines what happens to people. The difficult thing about being a social worker is that it is so complex. Situations cannot be predicted in advance. What is it that leads to one thing or the other? There are no causal relationships. A does not always lead to B. There is no way to know in advance whether what I do today will be of any use or not, and that means you have to put up with living in uncertainty.

Still, it's the best. Despite all the tears I've shed throughout the years, it's still worth it. The joy is much larger. I must say, it's very fun, interesting work! It is something that allows you to still feel proud of things you have done. That you know that for some people you make a difference.

* * *

In Helens story it is possible to recognize some key elements significant for the social work profession. First, a *freedom to take action for change*, a change which of course should be in accordance with legal frames and the client's expressed wishes to make a change. Social work practice can be defined as aiming at change in socially vulnerable life situations (see for example Blom, 2009). Believing that change is possible is a central aspect of social work. However, change can never be forced upon people. According to Blom (2009), social work aims at changes that are not normative, meaning that desirable conditions cannot be defined beforehand, but must be created in concert with the socially vulnerable person, whenever possible (see also Morén, 1994).

Helen mentions that not everything is dependent on the social worker. For a change to happen, the person who is receiving help must be motivated to take a leap into something unknown, something possibly scary and something that takes an effort, but which can lead to a better situation in the person's life. The situation for the woman in Helen's story got worse before it got better. A positive change does not happen instantly, thus a second element identified in Helen's story is *persistence*. This type of persistence in creating hope, in motivating individuals, is tightly coupled to seeing the uniqueness of every individual and creating a relationship. It is in a close and tenacious relationship between the client and the social worker that change takes place. Only in a trusting relationship can spaces of mutual understanding and openings towards new possibilities to act occur (Blom, 2009; Morén, 1994; Nygren & Soydan, 1997). According to Bornemark (2018), these horizons of new possibilities occur when we are in connection to our capacity to relate to not-knowing. It means that all human relations are conditioned by not-knowing or *un-knowing* (Blom, 2009) aspects. Working to assist individuals to make a change means accepting that you cannot know how the individual is encountering herself. Thus, as a social worker you must be open to the unpredictable and accept that results (of an intervention) cannot be planned entirely

(Blom, 2009; Morén, 1994). Helen says, "You have to put up with living in uncertainty," which is interpreted as a third element – the *un-knowing* aspects as a central part of social work.

Lastly, Helen expresses her joy and the reward of being a social worker. She says, "Despite all the tears . . . it's still worth it." The fourth element could be *human value through self-reflection.* It is difficult, perhaps impossible, to remain unchanged or unaffected while closely participating in other peoples' change. The relation-bound knowledge which emerges will affect you, and in some cases it will cause distress, maybe anger and frustration. However, making a difference for some people is not a small matter. It is something to be truly proud of.

Reflective Questions

1. In what way can personal stories from practitioners in social work bring in something new in education?
2. What issues connected to the joy of practising social work can be transferred to social work education?
3. How can stories from practitioners be told to service users, to become relational bridges that connect people?

REFERENCES

Blom, B. (2009). Knowing or un-knowing? That is the question: In the era of evidence-based social work practice. *Journal of Social Work, 9*(2), 158–77.

Bornemark, J. (2018). The limits of ratio: An analysis of NPM in Sweden using Nicholas of Cusa's understanding of reason. In B. Ajana (ed.), *Metric Culture: Ontologies of Self-Tracking Practices*, pp.235–53. Bingley: Emerald Publishing.

Morén, S. (1994). Social work is beautiful: On the characteristics of social work. *Scandinavian Journal of Social Welfare, 3*(3), 158–66.

Nygren, L., & Soydan, H. (1997). Social work research and its dependence on practice. *Scandinavian Journal of Social Welfare, 6*(3), 217–24.

Photo: Hilde Mjøs

CHAPTER 15

Partner in Decolonization

A Tale of Two Strangers United by a Common Interest

Pratiksha Ghimire and Raj Yadav

Prologue: We Are Not Storytellers, but We Have Something Important to Tell

Pratiksha and Raj were extremely excited when the editors invited them to contribute a story for this book. Their excitement however did not last for long as they soon realized that they were not storytellers; for neither of them was story-writing their strength. They had written a few academic books, articles, and chapters, but they had never produced such a work before. Things got worse when they had to decide on the topic and theme for the story that they wanted to tell through this chapter. Out of several topics and themes that Pratiksha and Raj brainstormed, they eventually decided to tell their own story through this chapter.

Again, both Pratiksha and Raj faced doubt and dilemma. On one hand, as Yadav (2023) has explained, Pratiksha and Raj wondered whether their story would result in a "narcissistic-expression-of-themselves" and would suffer from "them/their syndrome." On the other hand, they also asked themselves: Why should their own story be a part of a book like this? Why should audiences read a story which is about the storytellers themselves? And, will audiences learn anything from their story? Caught by such doubt and dilemma, Pratiksha and Raj then thought to drop the idea to contribute to this book. But before doing this, Pratiksha and Raj had second thoughts and critically and systematically probed their own life experiences, their encounter with social work education, their expectations of and disappointments from social work, and the coincidence that had brought them together for a purpose. Once they reflected this way, they found themselves holding extraordinary life experiences that may inspire those who have gone through similar struggles. Eventually, they decided to tell their story.

Pratiksha and Raj present this story mainly in a conversational style. By doing so, they intend to demonstrate that the story that they have presented here in this book is a real one. In addition to this, they want the audience not only to gain information but also to an extent to create images of events that have been presented in this story. Materials used in this story have been mainly derived from Pratiksha's and Raj's personal memories and their past conversations, and when there was need, they discussed some of the materials used.

The story that follows contains three parts. Part I describes an encounter between Pratiksha and Raj and how they set forth their partnership in decolonization. In Part II, Pratiksha and Raj discuss their own life story and struggles and how these led them to social work. In this part they also discuss why they were disappointed with social work. And finally, Part III presents their world view about decolonizing social work in Nepal.

Before readers delve into this story, Pratiksha and Raj believe that it is important that they know about Nepali social work. The excerpt below from Yadav (2019, p.xxi) provides basic information about Nepali social work and its colonial and imperial roots.

> Missionaries introduced social work into Nepal as a modern, scientific project based mainly in psychological models. The education program they introduced targeted young peoples, mainly in the capital city of Kathmandu, and linked them physically through social work institutes, ideologically through Western concepts, and technologically through universal skills and techniques. The landscape of this new idea allowed previously disconnected Nepali youth to think and act homogeneously by introducing them to Western texts, concepts, and, above all, the idea of cultural production. Its English language lent common terminologies of doing service that had no equivalents in Nepali languages. Despite all these, it failed overall to encourage a critical engagement with Nepal's multilinguistic, multicultural, and multiethnic populations. One of the dubious contributions of the Western missionaries, or colonisers in general, to Nepal was that they introduced colonial concepts, the English language, and rational models. They also aided international aid agencies that shaped non-government services in Nepal. An elite group of social work educators readily adopted the Western social work approach and embraced its fundamental tenets . . . the driving question is, 'Are Nepali social workers happy with this?'

To this end, Pratiksha and Raj not only thank the editors for an opportunity to tell their story through this book; but also, meantime, they believe the audiences who are going to read it may get something out of this and apply it in their own lives.

Part I. Present: Encounter for a Purpose

Raj had recently joined the University of the Sunshine Coast, Australia, as a lecturer in social work. It was a warm day of November; extreme humidity had upset everyone's mood. Being of Nepali origin, and having lived in Nepal for most of his life beneath the Himalayas, this extreme warm weather was beyond his tolerance. And therefore, he was rushing to his air-conditioned office. Just a few metres away from his office building he saw a lady sitting on a bench and smiling at him. For a moment, he wondered why a stranger was smiling at him. Nevertheless, as a courtesy, he returned a smile to her, too. He was surprised when someone whom he thought was stranger addressed him by his name.

PRATIKSHA: Namaste! Raj sir.[1]

RAJ: Namaste! Do you know me? How? Where are you from?

PRATIKSHA: Yes sir, I know you very well. I am from Nepal. I was your student. You taught me few years ago back at one of the colleges in Nepal.

RAJ: Yes, I taught there. Now I remember you, but I am sorry I do not remember your name. What is your name?

PRATIKSHA: Pratiksha.

RAJ: What are you doing here at this university? Are you a student or an employee?

PRATIKSHA: I am a student. I am in the second year of Master of Social Work (Qualifying).

RAJ: I am glad to know that you have continued your social work journey. *Before Pratiksha could say anything further, Raj said, but this time with both excitement and hope:* You must join a PhD programme in social work after you complete this degree. I would recommend you further my work on decolonizing social work in Nepal.

PRATIKSHA: I do not want to study anymore once I complete this degree. This will be my last qualification at the university. Saying this she outright rejected Raj's recommendation.

While both Pratiksha and Raj were happy to meet each other after a long time, this encounter was disappointing for them, too. Pratiksha then thought she should not have defied Raj's suggestion. At least for the sake of respect to him,[2] she should have shown interest in a PhD. Raj regretted offering unwanted advice.

Time flew like anything. Almost a year had passed since they had encountered each other. During this time, they met each other in

[1] Nepali students call their teachers sir or madam.

[2] Culturally a student does not say 'no' to his/her teacher in Nepal, especially when a teacher offers career advice.

classrooms, at the university's cafes, and, occasionally, at the festivals that Nepali diaspora celebrated there. Whenever they met, they discussed nothing but social work – social work in Nepal in particular. Often, if not always, they interrogated Nepali social work's imported and colonial roots; and, in doing so, were also concerned with the way Nepali social work did not suit Nepali society. Both had concluded, as others have argued elsewhere (Yadav, 2019), that the 'social' was missing in 'Nepali social work'.

Pratiksha had already come to an end of her master's degree. And, on one surprising day, she called by phone about meeting Raj to discuss her PhD. Raj set the meeting for the following day.

PRATIKSHA: My circumstances have changed and I want to join the PhD programme. As you suggested almost a year ago, I would like to explore decolonisation, social work, and Nepal.

Her interest in undertaking a PhD, in particular in the area of decolonization and social work, made Raj extremely happy. Before he could say anything, Pratiksha further said:

> But my idea of decolonization has been shaped by different standpoints. Your work on decolonization and Nepali social work is praiseworthy; nevertheless, you have emphasized the promotion of culture in your work (Yadav, 2019), which is problematic when it comes to Nepali women. In many circumstances culture is violent for Nepali women.
>
> Culture itself is discriminatory. Not to mention, culture, when it comes to women in Nepali society, creates an androcentric space that further perpetuates exploitations, humiliations, and oppressions. An uncritical promotion of culture within decolonizing social work needs to be questioned.

Pratiksha had a lot to say that day. It felt like she was angry and had been suppressing her years of feelings about herself, and about social work and Nepali women, too. Thus, she continued:

> I strongly associate myself with feminist perspectives not because I am a woman but for the reason that women's true liberation and likewise their genuine emancipation in Nepali society are yet to be materialized in daily practice. The works of Simone de Beauvoir and bell hooks, who question the identity of women under various themes such as gender discrimination, objectification, oppression, patriarchy, stereotyping, history, and aesthetics (see Beauvoir, 1949; hooks, 2000) have highly influenced my world view. Also, critical theorists such as Antonio Gramsci and Jürgen Habermas, who focus on society and culture to explore, understand, reveal, critique, and challenge power structures (see Fraser, 1985; Gramsci, 1971), have shaped my thoughts. Whenever I view Nepali women through such lenses, I see

> they are merely an 'object' in Nepali society. A profession like social work whose foundations are based on rights, justice, liberation, and emancipation ought to respond to such objectification. However, an uncritical importation of Western social work in Nepal has been unable to do so. If Nepali social work genuinely wants to respond to Nepali women's issues, then it should embrace feminist and critical ontologies; and, in doing so, it should engage with relevant epistemologies that will furthermore allow Nepali social workers to produce knowledge from a woman's perspectives. What I believe is that a robust knowledge about Nepali women and social work will only prevail by acknowledging their personal experiences and stories that they face in their daily lives. Neither imported knowledge nor experiences can solidify Nepali women's struggles and emancipation. And hence, I would like to commence a PhD on decolonizing work with Nepali women.

Raj, who had similar views on Nepali social work, but more related to ethnicities and their marginalization and development, appreciated Pratiksha's critical and feminist social work standpoints. With his support, Pratiksha soon got admission to a PhD in social work programme at the University of the Sunshine Coast, Australia.

In order to further understand what informs Pratiksha's and Raj's world view on decolonizing social work in Nepal, and why they believe what they believe on decolonization of social work, it is crucial to look back to their past.

Part II. Past: Two Strangers Born Just a Few Miles Apart

Mithila – the holy land of Goddess Sita – is now a part of modern-day Nepal. Situated in the southern part of the country bordering on the neighbouring nation of India, it boasts rich culture, language, and religious diversities, as well as being the place of the famous Mithila art. Hundreds of castes and ethnics groups of Nepalis call it home today. Once known for its glorious, glamorous, and golden history with rich literary, artistic, and folk traditions, Mithila, like any other part of the country, is gradually shifting towards imported modernism and Westernism. In other words, in more recent years, it is caught in the contradiction between an imported modern, Westernized lifestyle and ancient cultural practices. Worthy of note, this place and its people have been historically ignored, and politically ill-represented in the country. Pratiksha and Raj were born just a few miles apart in this place about four decades ago. Both were strangers until the first time they encountered each other at one of the private social work colleges in the capital city Kathmandu in 2010. Then Pratiksha attended one of Raj's classes; and as she recently shared about this, she was quite impressed with the radical viewpoints that Raj held then about Nepali social work and society:

> It was during the second year of my Bachelor of social work degree that I had an opportunity to meet you. That was a turning point for me in my social work journey when I found you talking about Nepali society, its social and cultural traditions, Indigenous values, norms, and customs and how these tied Nepali societies together, historical and political structures and the ways these contributed to Nepali social issues; and, while doing so, you advocated that Nepali social work required a homegrown perspective.

I clearly remember in one of your lectures you said "Mahila ko chhura ko aawaj le uni kata ke gardai chhinn bhanera sanket dinchh" (that loosely translates as "A woman's bangles that she wears in her daily life let others know her whereabouts or what she is doing"). It was really fascinating and insightful to me and I was forced to think about how such things had become socially accepted and normalized cultural behaviours in Nepali society. Much later when I encountered works of feminist writers such as Gayatri Spivak, Simone de Beauvoir, Judith Butler, to name only a few here, I then realized you spoke of this from a feminist perspective.

I was in the second year of my degree programme. Till then, nobody had provided such critical insights about Nepali society and social work. On top of that, they were drawing on Western psychologized, individualistic, skewed social work paradigms and perspectives. When you made me realize about all these, I was angry that Nepali social work has not made any effort to divorce itself from Western ideals.Despite sharing a common birth region and growing up in similar social and cultural environments, Pratiksha's and Raj's life experiences greatly differed due to their respective intersectionality. Pratiksha, a first female child to her parents, was born as a Bahuni[3] in a relatively well-educated family. The Muluki Ain – Nepal's first legal code – of 1854 had vertically categorized Nepal's caste and ethnic groups, and according to this, her affiliation with the Bahun caste put her at the top of the caste hierarchy. Also, in general, in the part of the country where Pratiksha and Raj were born, Bahun is socially and culturally considered to be a higher caste than others. Nepali, which was until then the only official language of the country, is her mother tongue. All this not only socially and culturally privileged her but also helped her to complete

[3] An adjective used for female Bahun.

secondary school in a society where sending girls to school was not preferred.

And yet, Pratiksha, if viewed through the lenses of gender and religion, was a mere object in the society where she grew up. Like any other Nepali female who grew up in a strict religious Hindu family, she faced restrictions. Worthy of note in this regard, such restrictions are ancient, written and advocated long ago by the infamous Manusmriti:

> बाल्ये पितुर्वशे तिष्ठेत् पाणिग्राहस्य यौवने ।
> पुत्राणां भर्तरि प्रेते न भजेत् स्त्री स्वतन्त्रताम् ॥ १४६ ॥
>
> In childhood she should remain under the control of her father, in youth under that of her husband, and on the husband's death under that of her sons; the woman should never have recourse to independence.

As Pratiksha recalls at the time of writing this chapter, restrictions were based on high caste versus low caste, touchability versus untouchability, purity versus impurity, and freedom versus control (Ong, Mellor, & Chettri, 2022). Given her affiliation to a high caste, she was discouraged from interacting with those who were considered to be so-called low caste in the society of that time. Although caste-based discrimination was outlawed on 24 May 2011, social and cultural practices to an extent remain the same in the country (Johnson, 2011). The majority of Nepali people still prefer not to marry those who are lower than their own caste. The so-called lower-caste people were considered untouchable and therefore higher-caste people should not touch them. If one does so, even by mistake, then one has to be purified following proper religious rituals. However, such practices are eroding gradually in Nepal.

Purity and impurity were, and to an extent still remain, highly important amongst members of the caste of which Pratiksha is a part. Women were considered impure when they menstruated, and hence, they were not allowed to take part in any household activities. They were not only barred from entering the kitchen, but also at the time of menstruating they were not allowed to worship. It was worse for an adolescent girl when she menstruated for the first time. During her first menstruation, she had to strictly follow rituals, according to which she must live in isolation for fifteen days and must not see any male caste members (Gurung, 2023; Pariyar, 2020).

As Gupta, Madabushi, and Gupta (2023) noted, women and young girls are restricted from speaking freely since it is considered rude and unwomanly to provide one's opinion as a woman. If not always, quite often women are accompanied by males if they are going outside of their home, no matter even if that is to school.

PRATIKSHA: [*Recalling her past*] My life experience has not been different from those mentioned above. I was restricted in many ways and that happened just because I was born as a woman. I, too, was dehumanized. The feelings, when I recall them now, are not only sickening but also maddening.

Unlike Pratiksha, Raj was born to a family of relatively low sociocultural status. His affiliation with the Yadav caste, which is not an untouchable caste group but still inferior to Bahun and Chhetri in the caste hierarchy, gave him a lower sociocultural status in the society he belonged to. Moreover, the geography where he was born, and the local dialect called Theti that he spoke as a mother tongue, made him *Madheshi* or *Madhishe*. Especially in the hill region of the country, the term *Madheshi* or *Madhishe* is used in stereotypical manner to denote those seasonal labourers who migrate from the neighbouring states of India – Bihar and Uttar Pradesh – and work in informal job sectors. In political terms, the term *Madheshi* or *Madhishe* has been also used to refer to 'less-nationalist'. Quite often Raj has been a victim of such a stereotype, which in many ways manifests suppressions and oppressions of his kind by so-called mainstream groups in the country.

In the 1990s, there were 1.9 billion people, almost 36 per cent of the world, living below USD 1.90 per day, the extreme poverty line; 28 per cent of them lived in South Asia (Kharas & Dooley, 2022). Raj grew up during this era in a family which was in a dire economic condition. His father, who was the sole breadwinner in the family, earned around USD 50 per month as his salary, less than what was defined as the extreme poverty line at the time. This, of course, was not sufficient for a family of six to live a decent quality of life. And thus, Raj was one of the 36 per cent and 28 per cent of the world and of South Asia respectively.

What did poverty mean to Raj? As has been explained by Ridge (2009), it was damaging and corrosive. Not only did it lead to exclusion but also on several occasions he was stigmatized just because he was poor:

> As I remember my childhood, I lived with extreme poverty. It was the most traumatic stage of my life. All of us, my two elder brothers, an elder sister, and myself, used the same piece of cloth for everything – for school, for sports, and for home. In winter, my mother used straw and rice sacks to weave beds and blankets for us. I remember once I was thrown out of a private tuition because my father could not pay the Rs 100 (USD 0.75 as per today's conversion rate) tuition fee on time. The tutor said, "Get lost from here and never come back. No money, no tuition." All the kids there were laughing. I felt humiliated and powerless. Years have passed, but I can't forget this moment in my life. I still get angry when I remember this now.

Pratiksha and Raj were unfamiliar to social work education given they grew up outside the capital city Kathmandu. Until then, social work education was a capital-city-centric education and taught by just a few private social work institutes in the capital city Kathmandu. It was accessible to, and popular amongst, those young people who either went to capital-based schools or were the children of parents who maintained higher positions at the government and non-government agencies in the country. There were, however, exceptions, and both Pratiksha and Raj were such exceptions.

Social work's promotion of human rights and social justice, and likewise its advocacy for liberation, had attracted them to become social workers. And hence, both Pratiksha and Raj joined social work education believing that it would liberate them from the suppressions and oppressions that they had experienced in their own lives. In addition to that, they also believed that, once they had graduated with their social work degrees, they would ally themselves with those people in the country who had experienced similar struggles.

While telling stories, like the one in this chapter, storytellers must be honest, trustworthy, transparent, and in being so, must present the full account of their story. It is not only ethical for a storyteller to do so but also it is about being honest with the audiences who expect to learn something from such a story. And hence, Pratiksha and Raj as the storytellers here are compelled to disclose their vested interests, too. As Raj has mentioned elsewhere about himself (see Yadav, 2023), Pratiksha's attraction to social work education, too, was not only limited to becoming an agent of liberation but also there were inherent vested interests. She was drawn to social work education expecting that she would be offered an attractive position and handsome salary by the international development agencies and the United Nations Organizations once she graduated with a social work degree.

In the beginning, although Pratiksha and Raj found social work useful, they soon realized it was problematic for Nepali society, given was built on a foundation of Western ideologies and Christian Protestant, modernistic, and individualist viewpoints that did not synergize with Nepali socio-cultural-political structures and social issues. As Raj wrote much later in 2023 (see Yadav, 2023), when they dug deeper and scrutinized social work and its history, they agreed that the imported and colonial social work model did not fit the Nepali context for several reasons. These related to: (i) "Western social work's unwarranted prestige in Nepal," (ii) "its forceful existence that ignored Nepali society's positionality and pluralistic epistemologies," (iii) "its inconsideration of Nepali changing time and space," (iv) "its inability to integrate a hermeneutic understanding of social work," and (v) "its colonial and imperial connections and neoliberal insti tutionalisation of Nepali social work" (Yadav, 2023, p.1190).

All this, Pratiksha's and Raj's own life experiences and struggles, their aspiration to liberate themselves and others with similar experiences and struggles, and likewise their disappointments with social work in Nepal, led them towards the critical issues of decolonizing social work.

Part III. Back to Present: Partner in Decolonization

Two strangers, Pratiksha and Raj, who were born just a few miles apart in Nepal, have now coincidentally come together far from their birthland in Australia and are currently partners in decolonization. While in general they explore decolonizing social work in Nepal, Pratiksha in particular explores decolonizing social work with Nepali women and Raj's works encompass broad topics under decolonizing social work and social development in Nepal. Despite their independent standpoints on decolonization and social work, as Tusasiirwe (2023, p. 7) suggested elsewhere, Pratiksha and Raj now continuously engage in decolonizing process through "remembering, questioning, reflecting, re-thinking, and re-imagining" social work in Nepal; and, in doing so, ask what should be considered as legitimate, valid social work in Nepal.

Decolonial scholars within and outside of social work inspire and influence the world views of Pratiksha and Raj. Within social work, seminal works *Professional Imperialism: Social Work in the Third World* authored by James Midgley (1981) and *Decolonising Social Work* jointly edited by Mel Gray, John Coates, Michael Yellow Bird, and Tiani Hetherington (2013) have greatly influenced Pratiksha's and Raj's decolonial world views. Alongside these, Pratiksha and Raj follow various scholars on decolonizing social work from Australia (Briskman, 2016; Dittfeld, 2020), North America (Sinclair, 2004), Africa (Nhapi, 2021; Tusasiirwe, 2023), and Asia (Das et al., 2023; Yellow Bird & Gray, 2016), and, to an extent, they draw on their perspectives while thinking about decolonizing social work in Nepal. Outside of social work, postcolonial scholars such as Frantz Fanon (1967), Gayatri Spivak (1988), Arturo Escobar, Edward Said (1993), and Walter Mignolo (2011), to name only a few, inform Pratiksha's and Raj's positionalities and works on decolonization.

Pratiksha and Raj give due credit to those above-mentioned scholars and acknowledge their insights on decolonizing and social work. As emerging scholars in this area, Pratiksha and Raj also stand in solidarity along with them and promote a global movement of decolonization and social work. With them we imagine a decolonialized world in which it is possible for the victims and survivors of colonization to reorganize themselves and reorder their lives in their own way. And, in doing all this, Pratiksha and Raj, like Gayatri Spivak, ask: Can Nepali social workers speak? They also ask: Should they reorganize themselves and reorder Nepali social work? While they agree that Nepali social workers can and should, they find that there has not been action in relation to this.

PRATIKSHA: Can Nepali social workers speak?

RAJ: Yes, they can, but the problem is that they are not doing so.

PRATIKSHA: Why do you think Nepali social workers are not speaking about decolonizing social work?

RAJ: The case of Nepal is a unique one. In several other contexts, for instance if you take as an example our neighbouring country, India, which was a British colony for a long time, the importation of social work from the West was easily felt as a colonial discipline and practice. But our case is different. Nepal was never colonized. This has been touted in our daily lives such that we are not only proud of it but also, we boast about it. Unfortunately, what we have failed to understand is that colonization is not always by force. It may occur, as Osterhammel (1997, pp.21–2) has argued, through "quasi-colonial control," "informal rule," and "non-colonial influences." If we view Nepal through this lens, Nepal has been colonized in several ways. When you critically read Shrestha (2002, p.xiv), it is quite clear that, as they write, "Nepal, which had managed to maintain its relative independence, was independent no more. Nepal was kept as a semi-colony subjected to every savagery and trickery of colonialism that the world has known since its dawn – basically the same fate that Caliban was forced to suffer in Shakespeare's play . . . still reeling from the lingering spectre of British colonialism." Nepali social workers are oblivious to these critical perspectives, and therefore, they are yet to see social work as a colonial product in the country. And hence, they cannot speak.

PRATIKSHA: It may sound blaming to other Nepali social workers, but I do agree with you on this. Nepali social work has about three decades of colonial and imperial history. And yet, there have been few efforts to decolonize social work in Nepal. There is only a handful of scholars like us who are involved in this effort. While our effort continues in this area, what do you suggest should be done to further strengthen decolonizing social work in Nepal?

RAJ: As pioneers in this area in Nepal, we have two roles to play. First, we will have to help Nepali social workers to be critically aware about the colonial and imperial roots of Nepali social work. In so doing, we will have to also demonstrate that existing social work does not match Nepali social, cultural, historical, and political dynamics. Once this happens, then, second, we will have to organize those interested in participating in decolonizing social work in Nepal.

PRATIKSHA: Are there any particular frameworks, strategies, or ideas that you think would be suitable for the Nepali context?

RAJ: In more recent times, decolonizing social work has become a hip-hop. A plethora of ideas that might play a role in the decolonizing of social work. While plenty of these are good ideas, meantime we should be mindful of the politics of decolonization. Today everyone wants to write about decolonization and associate themselves with this since it is considered to be contemporary. Every now and then the major social work journals publish articles on decolonizing social work. With a few exceptions, the majority of these ideas originate from former colonizer nations. It seems even the idea of decolonization has been colonized by the colonizers; and thus, the idea is flowing from Global North to Global South, which was supposed to be otherwise. Hence, personally, I am not in favour of adopting already existing ideas on decolonizing social work in Nepal. Rather it should an original – a home-grown Nepali perspective – if we genuinely seek to decolonize social work in Nepal.

PRATIKSHA: In that case, I believe the rejectionist positionality best suits us in our context in Nepal. Like you, I too believe that our standpoints on decolonizing social work in Nepal should be informed by an insider perspective (see Gray and Hetherington, 2013).

RAJ: As I have explained elsewhere (see Yadav, 2019), critical junctures in the formation of the Nepali state, various sociocultural groups of Nepal, and the cleavage, conflict, and new politics that these produce, give rise to the quest for rights, justice, and inclusion in the backdrop of recently ended Maoist insurgency, and distinct Nepali cultural narratives makes Nepal a unique nation. Nepali issues, including structural discriminations, suppressions, and oppressions that we have faced in our own lives and discussed above, are rooted in these critical historical junctures, sociocultural relationships amongst various caste and ethnic groups, and cultural practices. A solution to these problems will not come from outside. It should be rather an insider perspective through which we not only critically understand the structural issues but also propose constructive solutions to those problems. Neither the imported social work nor the imported ideas of decolonization can do justice to the Nepali context. Hence, we should aim to develop our own ways of giving social work in Nepal its own identity.

PRATIKSHA: The idea of decolonizing social work is all about self-determination, in other words.

RAJ: Let us put it this way. Decolonization is a political project for us. Within this political project, first, the aim is to reject (after careful analysis) any imported ideas, including decolonial ideas and perspectives. And, second, it is about politically positioning social work such that it contributes to the emancipation and liberation of all those Nepali who have been historically oppressed and suppressed.

PRATIKSHA: Overall, we are seeking to revolutionize social work through a decolonial perspective. A revolution that will not only allow us to reorganize ourselves to reject colonial and imperial social work in Nepal; but also, in the meantime, will allow those who are committed to this to try to reorder our social work in our own ways.

RAJ: That is true.

Epilogue: Where from Here?

The decolonizing path ahead is full of challenges and ethical dilemmas for Pratiksha and Raj. Still-lacking consciousness amongst Nepali social work actors and agencies of de/colonial social work poses great challenges for them. In addition to this, there is not only lack of social work leadership but also social workers are unorganized in the country. There needs to be greater allyship and positive mobilization. As pioneers in the field of decolonization in the country, the task for both Pratiksha and Raj (and likeminded others) is to enable more social workers to become critically aware of the nation's social work histories.

Pratiksha and Raj face an ethical dilemma too, while engaging themselves in decolonizing social work in Nepal. Born in Nepal, now they make Australia their temporary homes from where they research, explore, and write about decolonizing social work in Nepal. Often, they ask questions of themselves, namely whether it is ethical to write about and advocate for decolonization of social work in Nepal from overseas. Although few might consider this unethical, both Pratiksha and Raj have probed this question ethically and honestly. They find when they write or advocate about decolonizing social work in Nepal, they write being Nepali. They also find themselves writing from their hearts, which are genuinely concerned to decolonize social work in Nepal for the benefit of Nepali people and especially women.

Despite such challenges and dilemmas, Pratiksha and Raj have promised to continue their decolonial journey. In the future, no matter what comes ahead, we wish to write and rewrite, think and rethink, and advocate and re-advocate about decolonizing social work in Nepal.

Reflective Questions

1. What characterizes decolonial social work?
2. How can cultural practices and sociocultural relationships among different caste and ethnic groups be valued through acts of storytelling?

3. Social work's promotion of human rights and social justice can be challenging in everyday practice in Nepal. How can you as a social worker, living somewhere else, contribute to support colleagues living in these areas?

REFERENCES

Arturo, E. (1992). Imagining a post-development era? Critical thought, development and social movements. *Social Text, 31*(32), 20–56.

Beauvoir, S. de (1949). *The Second Sex*, trans. H. M. Parshley. Harmondsworth: Penguin.

Briskman, L. (2016). Decolonizing social work in Australia: Prospect or illusion. In M. Gray, J. Coates, & M. Yellow Bird (eds.), *Indigenous Social Work Around the World: Towards Culturally Relevant Education and Practice*, pp.83–93. London: Routledge.

Burke, S. (2018). Supporting Indigenous social workers in front-line practice. *Canadian Social Work Review, 35*(1), 5–25.

Butler, J. (2011). *Gender Trouble: Feminism and the Subversion of Identity*. New York: Routledge.

Das, T. K., Mehta, B., Nikku, B. R., Omer, S., & Granich, S. (2023). Decolonizing South Asian social work: An analysis. *Social Work Education, 42*(5), 601–19.

Dittfeld, T. (2020). Seeing white: Turning the postcolonial lens on social work in Australia. *Social Work & Policy Studies: Social Justice, Practice and Theory, 3*(1), 1–21.

Fanon, F. (1967). *Black Skin, White Masks*. New York: Grove Press.

Fraser, N. (1985). What's critical about critical theory? The case of Habermas and gender. *New German Critique, 35*, 97–131.

Gramsci, A. (1971). *Selections from the Prison Notebooks of Antonio Gramsci*. New York: International Publishers.

Gray, M., & Hetherington, T. (2013). Indigenization, Indigenous social work and decolonization: Mapping the theoretical terrain. In M. Gray, J. Coates, M. Yellow Bird, & T. Hetherington (eds.), *Decolonizing Social Work*, pp. 25–41. Aldershot: Ashgate.

Gupta, M., Madabushi, J. S., & Gupta, N. (2023). Critical overview of patriarchy, its interferences with psychological development, and risks for mental health. *Cureus, 15*(6), 1–11.

Gurung, I. (2023). Menstruation stigma: A qualitative exploratory study of the lived experiences of Nepali women. PhD thesis, University of Louisville.

hooks, b. (2000). *Feminist Theory: From Margin to Center*. London: Pluto Press.

Johnson, C. (2011). Nepal: Law on discrimination based on caste. Library of Congress, www.loc.gov/item/global-legal-monitor/2011-05-26/nepal-law-on-discrimination-based-on-caste (accessed 27 January 2024).

Kharas, H., & Dooley, M. (2022). The evolution of global poverty, 1990–2030. Brookings Global Working Paper 166. www.brookings.edu/wp-content/

uploads/2022/02/Evolution-of-global-poverty.pdf (accessed 27 January 2024).

Mignolo, W. D. (2011). Geopolitics of sensing and knowing: On (de) coloniality, border thinking and epistemic disobedience. *Postcolonial Studies, 14*(3), 273–83.

Nhapi, T. (2021). Social work decolonisation – forays into Zimbabwe experiences, challenges and prospects. *Social Work & Policy Studies: Social Justice, Practice and Theory, 3*(2), 1–15.

Ong, T., Mellor, D., & Chettri, S. (2022). Females are always dominated and disregarded by males, just because they are female: The continuation of patriarchal norms for young trafficked women in Nepal. *Culture, Health and Sexuality, 24*(10), 1350–65.

Osterhammel, J. (1997). *Colonialism: A Theoretical Overview*, trans. S. L. Frisch. Princeton, NJ: Markus Wiener.

Pariyar, S. (2020). A touchable woman's untouchable daughter: Interplay of caste and gender in Nepal. *CASTE: A Global Journal on Social Exclusion, 1*(2), 187–92.

Ridge, T. (2009). Living with poverty: A review of the literature on children's and families' experiences of poverty. Department for Work and Pensions (UK), Research Report 594. www.bristol.ac.uk/poverty/downloads/keyofficialdocuments/Child%20Poverty%20lit%20review%20DWP.pdf (accessed 27 January 2024).

Said, E. W. (1993). *Culture and Imperialism*. London: Vintage.

Shrestha, N. R. (2002). *Nepal and Bangladesh: A Global Studies Handbook*. Santa Barbara, CA: ABC-CLIO.

Sinclair, R. (2004). Aboriginal social work education in Canada: Decolonizing pedagogy for the seventh generation. *First Peoples Child Family Review, 1*(1), 49–61.

Smith, R. M., Parrott, D. J., Swartout, K. M., & Tharp, A. T. (2015). Deconstructing hegemonic masculinity: The roles of antifemininity, subordination to women, and sexual dominance in men's perpetration of sexual aggression. *Psychology of Men and Masculinity, 16*(2), 160–9.

Spivak, G. C. (1988). Can the subaltern speak? Reflections on the history of an idea. In C. Nelson and L. Grossberg (eds.), *Marxism and the Interpretation of Culture*, pp.271–316). Urbana: University of Illinois Press.

Tusasiirwe, S. (2023). Disrupting colonisation in the social work classroom: Using the Obuntu/Ubuntu framework to decolonise the curriculum. *Social Work Education, 43*(8), 2170–84.

Yadav, R. (2019). *Decolonised and Developmental Social Work: A Model from Nepal*. London: Routledge.

(2023). The doctor, development and (un)sociable monkey: An autoethnography of a social worker. *International Social Work, 66*(4), 1183–96.

Yellow Bird, M., & Gray, M. (2016). Indigenous people and the language of social work. In M. Gray, J. Coates, & M. Yellow Bird (eds.), *Indigenous Social Work around the World: Towards Culturally Relevant Education and Practice*, pp.59–69. London: Routledge.

Photo: Hilde Mjøs

CHAPTER 16

Human Rights Approaches of Pashtun Tahafuz Movement

A Case of De Facto Social Work?

Farhat Taj

Introduction

This story shows how a de facto social work promotes social work, in line with a global definition of social work.[1] De facto social work means a social work conducted in the absence of a legal framework and without formal social work education.

The chapter presents a social movement in Pakistan, called the Pashtun Tahafuz (Protection) Movement, PTM, as a case of de facto social work (Aslam & Neads, 2021; Jafri, 2021). It discusses how PTM promoted human rights, in a conflict-ridden civilian space where de jure social work was not possible due to security challenges and legal shortcomings.

The PTM adopted human-rights-based approaches to deal with state impunity in the context of the post 9/11 US-led war on terror. The PTM activists who initiated and carried out the de facto social work suffered state oppression but eventually made the same state, Pakistan, lose some of its impunity in terms of extrajudicial killings, forced disappearances, and undignified treatment of public at military check posts, and provide some relief to victims of landmines. Not only that, the PTM generated enough public pressure to compel the state to replace the over a century old British colonial law, called Frontier Crimes Regulations (FCR). The FCR was contrary to human rights norms (Khan Zubair, & Hussan, 2016). After having achieved some impressive human rights successes, the PTM compromised its human rights stance in the face of ethical and political challenges emanating from the geopolitics of the region.

[1] "Social work is a practice-based profession and an academic discipline that promotes social change and development, social cohesion, and the empowerment and liberation of people. Principles of social justice, human rights, collective responsibility and respect for diversities are central to social work. Underpinned by theories of social work, social sciences, humanities and indigenous knowledge, social work engages people and structures to address life challenges and enhance well-being. The above definition may be amplified at national and/or regional levels" (IFSW, n.d.).

PTM as a Case of De Facto Social Work

PTM is a grassroots social movement without a formal legal framework, organizational structure, or professional training. It is driven by collective action and mobilization of community members, especially young people, through social media, rather than adhering to the conventional structure of professional social work (Jafri, 2021). The PTM is not a professional social work intervention or exercise. Nevertheless, the way PTM protected and promoted one of the key principles of social work, i.e. human rights, in an intense conflict situation, makes it an insightful case for professional social workers. I consider the PTM's rights-based approaches as a case of de facto social work.

The term 'de facto social work' is not a widely recognized concept within the field of social work. The reason is that modern, professional social work is de jure practice. It must be conducted under a formal legal framework consisting of policies, regulations, educational requirements, and ethical standards set by legal institutions and professional social work bodies. Further, it must be carried out by formally trained individuals, called social workers.

De facto social work is undertaken without a legal framework or in a legal 'gray area' and carried out by individuals or groups who are not formally educated as social workers. I consider PTM as a case of de facto social work because it was undertaken in a legal gray area and conducted by young men who grew up in the war-on-terror years, and who never had formal social work education.

At the time of the war on terror, Pakistan's border tribal area, where the PTM emerged, was administered under the British colonial legislated FCR. The administration under the FCR excluded the area from the normal framework of Pakistan, including the country's human rights laws and its regulations concerning professional social work.

Pakistan is a signatory to the Geneva Conventions and party to key UN conventions on human rights, such as the Covenant on Economic, Social and Cultural Rights (CESCR) and the Covenant on Civil and Political Rights (CCPR). This implies that international humanitarian law (IHL) and international human rights law (IHRL) apply to the war on terror in Pakistan. Both IHL and IHRL protect civilians in armed conflicts. Both Pakistan's armed forces and the Taliban non-state armed groups have violated IHL and IHRL during the war (Shah, 2010).

PTM adopted human-rights-based approaches to generate public awareness about the massive rights violations and to provide rights-based assistance to victims of the war on terror, especially social and political rights. PTM's narratives successfully articulated the grievances of the war victims in the human rights language enshrined in the UN conventions to generate collective actions and public support against rights violations in the war on terror. PTM's de facto social work, therefore, does not confirm Hopgood's theory about "endtimes of human rights," which claims that international human rights instruments and regimes do not work in non-Western contexts (Hopgood, 2018). Social media engagement with international human rights regimes, such as international human rights organizations, in international human rights language, is a central strategy in PTM's struggle against the massive rights violations in the war on terror. The strategy successfully brought both national and international media and academic attention to PTM's work for human rights, which contributed to pressure on the army that reduced its impunity (Borthakur, 2021; Hameed, Jan, & Hussain, 2023; Jafri, 2021; Yousaf, 2019).

In the context of this chapter, human rights mean the rights enshrined in the UN Covenant on Economic, Social and Cultural Rights (CESCR) and the UN Covenant on Civil and Political Rights (CCPR). The rights of special relevance to this chapter are social rights as defined in Articles 11 and 12 of CESCR concerning, i.e., rights to adequate food, clothing, housing, right to health, and right to education; and political rights refers to the rights as defined in CCPR's Articles 6, 9, 19, and 26 concerning the right to life, right to liberty and security of person, right to equality before law, and protection of law and freedom of expression. Pakistan is party to both UN covenants.

Placing Myself in the Context

The chapter draws on my years of research (Taj, 2011a, 2011b, 2017, 2021, 2022; Taj & Rothing, 2011, 2013). The research also includes several meetings and data gathering, both face-to-face and digital, with prominent PTM activists, including its charismatic young leader, Manzoor Pashteen. I have also had discussions with some security personnel of Pakistan who fought the Taliban and Al-Qaeda militants on the frontlines.

As an ethnic Pashtun[2] who was born, grew up, and has spent most of his lifetime in the Pashtun area of Pakistan, where part of my family lives, my research interests and personal pursuits have focused on understanding the

[2] Pashtuns are a nomadic, pastoral, Eastern Iranic ethnic group primarily residing in northwestern Pakistan and southern and eastern Afghanistan.

troubled dynamics of Pakistan–Afghanistan relations. The war on terror profoundly affected the Pashtun area of Pakistan, including my own hometown, Kohat, which suffered multiple deadly terror attacks, killing and wounding tens of people, including people whom I personally knew. My own student from Kohat University, where I taught (2013–15), disappeared for over a year. The disappearance was caused by Pakistani intelligence agents. No one dared question his disappearance. The disappearance destroyed his academic career and negatively affected his health, in addition to making his family suffer in agony when he was disappeared.

At that time, I was one of few people who asserted the need for resistance against the impunity of state agents in Pakistan and the Taliban atrocities in the war on terror. Another person was Dr Mohammad Taqi, a Pakistani Pashtun physician based in the US, who like me, wrote in newspapers and on social media against the massive rights violations in the war on terror. Dr Taqi and I could openly speak because we both sat at a safe distance abroad, away from the war on terror in Pakistan. Media in Pakistan could not independently report about the war on terror (Sultan, 2010). People in mainland Pakistan thus remained unaware about the war on terror's atrocities. The area was closed to non-locals due to security reasons. People in the war on terror area could not openly speak due to fear of the Taliban and the intelligence agencies of Pakistan.

I was happy when PTM came into being in 2018. I saw it as a ray of hope for the war victims, a hope that would impede the rights violations by state agents and Taliban militants.

I disagreed, however, when PTM began to associate itself with the anti-Pakistan Afghan diaspora, which openly advocates the disintegration of the Pakistani state. This association, in my view, is detrimental to PTM's rights claims on the state of Pakistan, because it makes PTM look like a movement with secessionist tendencies, which the state will not tolerate. Consequently, the state will deal with PTM as a security concern, which will take the state's focus away from the human rights claims and make it less likely for the wider public in Pakistan to support the movement's goals.

In my mind, the PTM should keep its struggle within constitution of Pakistan and disengage from the geopolitics calling for destruction of the state of Pakistan. Due to the disagreement, I often receive social media hate, even threats from some of those who disagree with me, especially people in the Afghan diaspora. Nevertheless, while acknowledging my personal biases and difference of opinion, I strongly believe that PTM is a powerful voice for protection and promotion of human rights that deserves to be studied as a case of de facto social work. This is the reason

I write this chapter to initiate a scholarly discourse about de facto social work with PTM as a point of departure.

The Larger Sociopolitical Context

This story of de facto social work begins in Waziristan, one of Pakistan's tribal districts along its border with Afghanistan, and arguably the district most affected by the US-led war on terror. The then Taliban-led government of Afghanistan fell in the post 9/11 US invasion of Afghanistan, and resultantly thousands of Taliban and Al-Qaida militants crossed the porous border and took refuge in the border districts of Pakistan, especially Waziristan. Local Taliban groups emerged in support of the incoming militants. The local Taliban groups formed an umbrella organization, called TTP (*Tehrek-e-Taliban Pakistan*, Pakistan Taliban Movement), which was fighting against the security forces of Pakistan, a US ally in the war on terror (Nawaz & De Borchgrave, 2009).

Pakistan had yet to recognize that there was an armed conflict in the tribal districts despite deployment of over 145,000 troops in the area (Taj & Rothing, 2013). Meanwhile, Pakistan entered into several agreements with the Taliban, all of which violently collapsed, causing mass rights abuses in the area (Tajik, 2011). When the Taliban could not be won over to agreements, the army started operations against them, over a thousand small and large military operations, which also included indiscriminate aerial and long-range artillery bombardments (Express Tribune, 2012). During the war, the area was gripped by fear of both the Taliban and the intelligence agencies of Pakistan. The area was not accessible for independent news reporting due to widespread Taliban violence and clashes between the Taliban groups and Pakistan (IMS, 2009; Ricchiardi, 2012). The society suffered massive human rights violations committed by the Taliban and the armed forces of Pakistan, such as targeted killings, forced disappearances, mass-scale internal displacement, among others (Amnesty International, 2010a, 2012; Crawford, 2019). Amnesty International termed the area a "human rights free zone" where millions of people suffered (Amnesty International, 2010b).

PTM: Emergence and De facto Social Work Successes and Setbacks

PTM as a movement emerged from the Mahsud Tahafuz Movement (MTM) in Waziristan. Mahsud is a tribe in Waziristan. In 2015, about seventeen young men from Waziristan formed the MTM to give a voice to victims of the war on terror.[3] They used social media to create public awareness about the sufferings of the war victims, document the victims' experiences, and mobilize wider public support (Jafri, 2021). They also conducted voluntary work to support internally displaced people, in terms of shelter and access to food and healthcare. They interchangeably called themselves 'social workers' and social activists.

All the seventeen young men suffered from state oppression. Manzoor Pashteen, who led the MTM (later PTM), was jailed several times. Another member, Alamzeb Mahsud, authored a whole book narrating how he was arrested and tortured in jail for running awareness campaigns about disappeared persons and victims of landmines (Mahsud, 2020). The booked is banned in Pakistan.[4] Hayat Preghal, a pharmacist working in the United Arab Emirates and running the social media campaigns from there, was arrested during a family visit to Waziristan, put in jail for months without conviction, later released but not allowed to travel outside Pakistan for four years, during which he faced court trails. He lost his job in UAE. Akhtar Khan, a political science lecturer in a Pakistani university who provided insights from academic literature about how to deal with state oppression, was arrested by the intelligence agencies of Pakistan and tortured. Similarly, other de facto social workers and their families faced state oppression – threats, intimidation, and arrest on fabricated charges. However, in 2018 an incident in Pakistan's port city, Karachi, proved a game changer.

Naqeeb Mahsud – a Karachi-based, internally displaced emerging fashion model from Waziristan – was extrajudicially killed by the police in Karachi. In response, the de facto social workers of MTM led a protest march from Waziristan to Pakistan's capital city, Islamabad. On the way, war victims from other border districts joined. Wider public opinion in Pakistan had already been sensitized by the social workers though their social media campaigns about the massive rights violations. The killing of Naqeeb Mahsud became an occasion of public sympathy for the movement. The movement was no longer limited to the war victims from the Mahsud area of Waziristan. By reaching Islamabad, the movement had become a collective voice of all ethnic Pashtuns in Pakistan who had

[3] The young men included Manzoor Ahmad Pashteen (who is now the charismatic leader of PTM), Idris Mahsud, Alla-u-din, Waqar Mahsud, Amir Hamza, Abid Mahsud, Alamzeb Mahsud, Rizwan Mahsud, Mustafa Pashteen, Zainullah, Amin Shah, Sherullah, Bilall Mahsud, Abdul Waheed Mahsud, Manzoor Mahsud, Akhtar Khan, and Hayat Preghal.

[4] An electronic copy of the book is available in certain Facebook and WhatsApp groups.

suffered in the war on terror. The movement now enjoyed massive public goodwill and support, especially in the ethnic Pashtun area of Pakistan. As a result, the MTM was renamed as the PTM by its leaders.

Civilian government in Pakistan has little control over the military-dominated security policy of Pakistan. Therefore, the movement put forward its five demands directly to the Pakistani army: end extrajudicial killings, end forced disappearances plus presentation of disappeared persons to a court of law, dignified treatment of the public at military check posts, the removal of landmines and IEDs in Waziristan, and justice for Naqeeb Mahsud's family.

Pashtun are one of the largest ethnic groups in Pakistan. They are also integrated in the state structure of Pakistan, namely, the armed forces and bureaucracy (Fair & Nawaz, 2011). A movement that enjoys wider public support among Pashtun, as the PTM did, is difficult for the powerful Pakistani army to ignore. The initial reaction of the generals was careful, to an extent positive, and included some 'guarded sympathy'. Some of the demands put forward by the PTM begin moving towards resolution.

Manzoor Pashteen, leader of PTM, has confirmed that since the emergence of the movement hundreds of disappeared persons have come back to their homes, and the intelligence agencies' practice of disappearing people has greatly slowed down. Killings of Pashtun have been reduced. The army security forces' behaviour to people has improved. Victims of landmines are now treated in military hospitals in Pakistan, and the Pakistani army sent teams to clear Waziristan of the landmines. For the very first time in Pakistan's history, the country has a peaceful rights movement led by young people from poor families, that can look straight into the eyes of the country's powerful generals and compel them to address the army's wrongdoing.

Any social or political movement may be vulnerable to manipulation or co-option by vested interest. PTM is not an exception. Pashtun nationalists in Afghanistan and among Afghan diaspora in the West and some Pashtun nationalist elements from Pakistan are seeing an opportunity in PTM to review the old politics of irritant Pashtun nationalism, i.e. Pashtun areas of Pakistan belong to Afghanistan and must be returned to it, by force if necessary (Qassem & Durand, 2008).[5] The movement that

[5] A section of the population in Afghanistan holds Pakistan wholly responsible for the destruction of Afghanistan since the days of the Soviet invasion of Afghanistan. Others have never accepted Pakistan as a state and would like to eliminate it as soon as possible. They have claims on Pashtun areas of Pakistan and have declared them a "Pakistan occupied part of Afghanistan" or "occupied Pakhtunkhwa."

emerged from real-life, mass-scale suffering of people and stands for their right claims is being hijacked by vested interests, or at least stands divided on the issues of Afghan claims on Pashtun areas of Pakistan: some in the movement support the claims and some do not.[6] This has also weakened the Pakistani Pashtun public support of PTM. The Pashtun public supports PTM for its rights claims on the Pakistani state but most disagree with the idea to disintegrate Pakistan to incorporate the Pashtun areas in Afghanistan, as per my understanding.

Moreover, seemingly inspired by the Afghan narrative, some young, emotional PTM supporters have been seen misbehaving with the army soldiers on duty in public places. Some PTM members run social media campaigns against the Pakistani army based on unsubstantiated information. PTM's initial demands – disappeared people, extrajudicial killings, army soldiers' behavior with public on check posts, the Waziristan landmines, and justice for Naqeeb Mahsud – have not yet been fully met by the army, but still PTM keeps expanding the circle of its demands. Now it also challenges the army's control over the natural resources of Pashtun areas and has even questioned the parliamentary democracy of Pakistan, which in its view does not fully protect the rights of the ethnic minorities of Pakistan. There is basically nothing wrong in questioning any shortcoming in the resource distribution and the constitution of Pakistan. Nevertheless, when seen in combination with the Afghan diaspora's activism in the name of PTM, the expanding circle of the PTM demands looks as if the PTM is out there for more than meet the eyes. Prominent PTM figures, including its leader, Manzoor Pashtun, digitally participate in anti-Pakistan demonstrations of Afghans based in the Western countries, including in front of Pakistani embassies in the West. The Afghans openly call for destruction of the Pakistani state and its armed forces.

All this is too much for the Pakistani army to tolerate. Resultantly, the powerful Pakistani army generals, who were careful in dealing with PTM after the 2018 killing of Naqeeb Mehsud, are now more confident to oppress PTM, and there is no public backlash, which would, probably,

[6] The Afghan diaspora have created platforms abroad in the name of PTM where they routinely use abusive language against the Pakistani army, and entice the Pashtun of Pakistan to revolt against the army and break the state of Pakistan as soon as possible. The situation becomes more suspicious when the PTM leaders in Pakistan begin addressing such overseas PTM gatherings via Skype or telephone. Some of the PTM leaders also use some of the same Afghan narrative conspicuous for its hatred of the Pakistani state. Sometimes it seems that some of the PTM narrative, despite its main thrust on the rights claims within the constitution of Pakistan, is resonating more with the anti-Pakistan narratives of the Afghan diaspora.

have been the case, if the PTM did not appear to be supporting the anti-Pakistan Afghan narratives. Today, Pakistani media report nothing about PTM. PTM workers are routinely arrested, and some have their families intimidated. Some PTM workers are killed, and their violent deaths almost never get investigated.[7] Even the top PTM leader, Manzoor Pashteen, has been arrested multiple times under badly substantiated charges and later released. Anyone who sympathizes with PTM is potentially exposed to threats and intimidation by the intelligence agents of Pakistan.

More dangerously (from human rights perspectives), Pakistan has imposed the Actions in Aid of Civil Power Ordinance (2019) on the entire Khyber-Pakhtunkhwa province, the Pashtun-dominated federating unit of Pakistan. Under the law the security forces have sweeping powers to suspend human rights for indefinite periods (Shah, 2019). It authorizes the use of force against anyone and the detention of anyone without charge for an undefined duration while denying him/her any judicial remedy. For example, the army can put people in army-run internment centres, which are basically state-run torture cells in which the forcibly disappeared people end up. This implies that the British legislated FCR law, which was terminated under PTM pressure, has now been re-enacted in a more draconian form. Although the Pakistani army is careful not to treat Pashtun citizens in the war-on-terror-affected areas indiscriminately and with impunity, as it did prior to the emergence of the PTM, the Actions Ordinance is a constant threat under which anyone in the Pashtun area can be deprived of human rights at the behest of the army. This is a setback to human rights, especially the political-rights-based de facto social work approaches of PTM. The ordinance is now being challenged in the Supreme Court of Pakistan by prominent political activists of Pakistan (Ahmad, 2019).

Fight for Social Rights

Due to fear of violence, the young men who united in 2015 under MTM started very cautiously. They focused on violations of social rights caused by large-scale internal displacement: about 3 million people from the area were displaced due to the clashes between the army and the Taliban. They ran campaigns to address shelter and social protection needs of the displaced population, including access to food, water, sanitation, and healthcare.

[7] Such as Arman Loni and Arif Wazir.

A large number of people had no access to humanitarian assistance due to various bureaucratic or communication hurdles or lack of identification documents (IDMC, 2015). Two thirds of the millions of internally displaced persons (IDPs) had no adequate access to food, housing, and basic services, and lived below the poverty line (Taj & Rothing, 2013).

In general, the intelligence agencies of Pakistan showed no opposition to the social-rights-related humanitarian work. Similarly, the Taliban also showed no blanket objections to provision of social-rights-related assistance to the IDPs (Khan, 2010).

It was thus 'safe' for the de facto social workers to highlight the humanitarian needs of the displaced population through social media campaigns. The social workers also collected donations to support the IDPs who had no access to UN humanitarian assistance. They contacted the authorities and NGOs to facilitate the access to humanitarian aid of those in need. They lobbied rich businessmen from the tribal area based in other parts of Pakistan to employ the IDPs in their businesses to support their struggle for survival.

Their focus on social rights violations was also a strategy to sensitize national and international audiences about the sufferings of the people trapped in the war. The focus was important because at that time both Pakistani media and international authors were portraying the entire population in the tribal districts as "Taliban and Al-Qaida sympathizers" (Fair & Chalk, 2006; Gul, 2009). This portrayal could dampen humanitarian sympathy for the displaced war victims. Some people in other parts of Pakistan were protesting against the arrival of the IDPs in their area on the ground that Taliban militants might be hiding among them. PTM's communication via social media went a long way in countering the stereotypical imagery of the IDPs and helped sustain humanitarian sympathy and solidarity with the IDPs among the wider population of Pakistan.

Fight for Cultural Rights

Since the British colonial period, Waziristan has been stereotyped as an 'unconquerable' culture peopled by 'furiously autonomous' tribesmen. The British left the area following the end of the British Indian Empire in 1947 but the stereotypical imagery of the entire tribal area carried on, such as the imagery frozen in Rudyard Kipling's poetry about the area.[8]

[8] See for example Kipling's poems "Arithmetic of the Frontier" and "The Ballad of the King's Jest."

Sadly, Pakistan, did nothing to confront the stereotypes with a reality check to establish a more realistic, more humane view of Waziristan by separating myths from verifiable facts. Consequently, the myth that Waziristan has a strong culture of resistance to state armies was perpetuated in public imagination, both national and international.

During the war on terror, the old British-era stereotypes about Waziristan were projected onto the Pakistani army through media headlines when the army clashed with the Taliban (IECAH, 2009). Responding to the stereotypes, a spokesman of the Pakistani army declared that "the myth has been broken that this (Waziristan) was a graveyard for empires and it would be a graveyard for the [Pakistani] army" too (Al Jazeera, 2009). This declaration, coupled with massive rights violations and the inaccessibility of the area for independent news reporting, was interpreted by educated people of Waziristan, such as the young men who made MTM (later PTM), as a 'deliberate' attempt to 'aggrandize' the Pakistani army by belittling the history, culture, and people of Waziristan (i.e. by telling the world that the Pakistani army achieved what the British colonial army could not: subjugation of the tribes).

The de facto social workers highlighted all kinds of rights violations – cultural, social, and political – in the area due to the war on terror, and attracted national and international attention to human sufferings in the area. The PTM successfully engaged the war victims in its de facto social work (peaceful demonstration, protests, and social media campaigns), especially women. At PTM events, ordinary women, men, children, and youth participate. They seek information about missing relatives, and demand compensation for war damage (Yousaf, 2019). In a conservative society where women's participation in the public sphere is limited, PTM's success in mobilizing a large number of women is remarkable. It underscores the local public ownership of the de facto social work and by extension pushes the traditional gender boundaries of the tribal society.

PTM's struggle has inspired local poets and musicians, who have composed poetry and music in the Pashto language to attract public support for the war victims; famous Pashto-language singer Shaukat Aziz sang several popular songs in support of PTM.[9] The poets and musicians played an effective role in popularizing the PTM narratives.

[9] For example, see his song "Ghadar Yama" (I am a 'traitor'), www.youtube.com/watch?v=uVXzZpT3s-Y.

Fight for Political Rights

All human rights are interconnected and indivisible. This is especially so in conflict situations, like the war on terror. For example, the massive violations of social rights (homelessness as a result of large-scale internal displacement; lack of access to food, healthcare, and education) emerged from the widespread violations of political rights in the war on terror (right to life, right to equality before the law). It was thus not possible for the de facto social workers to ignore the violations of political rights even in the face of immense fear of the Taliban and the intelligence agencies of Pakistan. They took up some of the most pressing political rights violations on social media, such as the plight of victims of landmines in the area.

In December 2009 the Pakistani army started a large military operation, Operation *Rah-e-Nijat* (Path to Salvation) in South Waziristan against the Taliban. The population was asked to vacate the area. The area was not open for the population to return until 2012, when most IDPs wanted to voluntarily return to their homes and the government also favoured swift return. However, persistent insecurity, damaged houses and public infrastructure, and inconsistent damage compensation by the government ensured that those who had the means to continue living in displacement, continued to do so, and only the poorest people returned to Waziristan. They erected tents on the ruins of their homes. They had expected the destruction of their homes but what they did not expect were landmines planted in several parts of the area. People, most of them children, wounded in the landmine blasts were in a pathetic condition. The army did not provide any help and hindered the transportation of the wounded to the nearby hospitals outside the tribal area. Pakistan did not want the world to know about the landmines on its soil. Landmines killing people in an area that is claimed to have been cleared by the army and declared safe for the displaced people's return will show the army in a bad light.

Deaths and injuries were growing and so the de facto social workers decided to start a public protest campaign about it, led by Manzoor Ahmad, who later became leader of the PTM. At the time Manzoor was a first-year student. He launched the social media campaign with this post (16 December 2016) on his Facebook page, which is now one of the most popular social media pages in Pakistan:

> This is the 20th incident of Pakistan army implanted IED explosion in Mahsud area of South Waziristan. In Khaisora (South Waziristan) 10 years old Shakirullah (son of Saeedullah Jan) seriously injured. He is transported in serious condition to district hospital in Dera (nearby city outside the

Table 1

De facto social workers with real names and face	Unknown accounts, apparently operated by people linked with the intelligence agencies of Pakistan
The Pakistani army has planted Waziristan with landmines that are killing people, mostly children and animals.	This is propaganda against the army. There are no landmines in Waziristan.
Photos of the injured children and animals are circulated on social media.	These landmines were planted by the Soviet Russian soldiers during the Afghan Jihad days (1979–89).
The Russians never crossed the border into Pakistan. They were in Afghanistan only. But even if they did, how come the Russian landmines remained silent for decades and now suddenly have started exploding after the Pakistani army retook the area from the Taliban in the war on terror?	There are Taliban sympathizers among the IDP returnees who plant IEDs and landmines to kill Pakistani army soldiers and sometimes the devices explode in their hands while implanting them.
Are you telling us that children as young as five to ten years old (who got killed or injured in the blasts) were planting landmines on behalf of the Taliban?	The landmines were planted by the Taliban when they controlled the area (2003–9).
Suppose this is correct, but still whose responsibility is it to clear up the area? Only the Pakistani army has the expertise and resources to clean the area of the landmines. Why are they not clearing up the area, when it has been declared safe for return of the IDPs?	The usual charges that the 'social workers' are promoting an anti-Pakistan agenda.

tribal districts). A few weeks ago, the movement (MTM) decided to start public protests against such (landmine and IED) explosions. Everyone is requested to join us to halt the brutality. Our struggle will continue. So far only young people are coming forward, although we have requested everyone to join us.

Manzoor's dedication inspired the other de facto social workers to intensify the social media campaign. In response, unidentified social media accounts appeared – apparently linked with the security agencies of Pakistan – to counter the campaign. A summary of their social media arguments and counter-arguments appears in Table 1.

Concluding Comments

In the post Second World War period, there were, for a long time, no big wars but many small wars or conflicts around the world. The brutality of the small wars has escalated and is still increasing with the arrival of more and more lethal weapons in the hands of state armies and non-state armed groups. Civilians trapped in the small wars are in urgent need of basic rights protection and social work services. In some conflict situations, as the PTM case shows, de jure social work may not be possible. In such situations de facto social work may be the only way to address social issues and rights violations.

Around the world, there are countless social-work-like activities that are undertaken by individuals or groups who may not have formal education in social work, or may have to operate in legal gray areas, or both. The activities are undertaken by volunteers, community activists, concerned individuals, or informal networks providing human-rights-based support and services in conflict situations. The diverse nature of these informal helpers and the varying levels of knowledge, skills, and resources they possess make it challenging to establish a standardized definition or recognition for de facto social work. Nevertheless, their work deserves scholarly attention to draw lessons for the benefit of professional social work.

As the PTM case shows, to be in line with the key social work principles (such as human rights and collective responsibility), the goal of the social work, whether de jure or de facto, has to be 'legal' and 'moral'. The PTM's struggle for political, social, and cultural rights was legal and moral. The PTM managed to generate massive public support for its legal and moral goals. The support could not be ignored by the powerful Pakistani army, which thus responded by moderating some of its impunity and addressing some of the rights violations. When the PTM 'drifted' a little from its legal and moral path by engaging with geopolitics (anti-Pakistan voices from Afghanistan), the army reasserted its impunity by bringing the entire Khyber-Pakhtunkhwa province under a draconian law (the Actions in Aid of Civil Power Ordinance).

Certainly, publicly misbehaving with army soldiers performing their duties on check posts, videotaping it, and posting it on social media; calling them names or obstructing them from performing their duty; or running social media campaigns against the authorities based on unsubstantiated information is neither legal nor could be seen as moral. Moreover, mixing of PTM's rights-based narratives with discourses from abroad that ask for destruction of the state and its armed forces, could hardly be seen as 'legal' by the state and has compromised the potential of the de facto social work. Nevertheless, useful social work insights can be obtained from PTM's non-violent struggle against state impunity that led to some remarkable human rights successes. PTM as a case of de facto social work is also a reminder that a social work intervention that engages established structural inequalities and is surrounded by intensely competing geopolitics, can be easily derailed from its key social work goal – protection and promotion of human rights.

Reflective Questions

1. How can de facto social work be supported in the fight for human rights?
2. As the author writes in this story, working in conflict areas might be dangerous. Think of how social workers can help to secure people in situations where they are threatened because of their engagement or political opinions. How do you think social workers can become a part of changing the everyday life of people in these situations?
3. In what way can de facto social work lead to collaborative support from a community in danger?

REFERENCES

Ahmad, Z. (2019). 'Action in aid of civil power' ordinance challenged in SC. *Business Recorder*, www.brecorder.com/news/532130/action-in-aid-of-civil-power-ordinance-challenged-in-sc.

Al Jazeera. (2009, 17 November). Pakistan 'clears Taliban towns'. www.aljazeera.com/news/2009/11/17/pakistan-clears-taliban-towns

Amnesty International. (2010a). *'As If Hell Fell On Me': The Human Rights Crisis in Northwest Pakistan*. London: Amnesty International Publications. www.amnesty.org/en/documents/asa33/004/2010/en

(2010b). Millions suffer in 'human rights free zone' in Northwest Pakistan. www.amnesty.org/en/latest/press-release/2010/06/millions-suffer-human-rights-free-zonein-northwest-pakistan

(2012). *'The Hands of Cruelty': Abuses by Armed Forces and Taliban in Pakistan's Tribal Areas*. London: Amnesty International Publications. www.amnesty.org/en/documents/asa33/019/2012/en/

Aslam, W., & Neads, A. (2021). Renegotiating societal-military relations in Pakistan: The case of the Pashtun Tahafuz Movement. *Democratization*, *28*(2), 265–84.

Borthakur, A. (2021). The Pashtun trajectory: From the colonially constructed notion on 'violent' Pashtun Tribe to 'non violent' Pashtun Tahafuz movement. *Asian Journal of Middle Eastern and Islamic Studies*, *15*(3), 360–78.

Crawford, N., & Lutz, C. (2019, 13 November). Human cost of post-9/11 wars. Watson Institute Costs of War Research Series. https://watson.brown.edu/costsofwar/files/cow/imce/papers/2019/Direct%20War%20Deaths%20COW%20Estimate%20November%2013%202019%20FINAL.pdf

Express Tribune. (2012, 18 April). Tribal militancy: '1,000-plus operations conducted in 2009–10'. https://tribune.com.pk/story/366216/tribal-militancy-%E2%80%981000-plus-operations-conducted-in-2009-10%E2%80%99

Fair, C. C., & Chalk, P. (2006). *Fortifying Pakistan: The Role of US Internal Security Assistance*. Washington, DC: US Institute of Peace Press.

Fair, C. C., & Nawaz, S. (2011). The changing Pakistan army officer corps. *Journal of Strategic Studies, 34*(1), 63–94.

Gul, I. (2009). *The Al-Qaeda Connection*. London: Penguin.

Hameed, Z., Jan, G., & Hussain, W. (2023). Pashtun Tahafuz movement: An analysis of Twitter usage during a protest movement. *Global Social Sciences Review*, 8(1), 396–409.

Hopgood, S. (2018). *The Endtimes of Human Rights*. Ithaca, NY: Cornell University Press.

IDMC. (2015, 24 August). Solutions to displacement elusive for both new and protracted IDPs. Internal Displacement Monitoring Centre. www.internal-displacement.org/sites/default/files/publications/documents/201508-ap-pakistan-overview-en.pdf

IECAH. (2009, 4 November). A risky gambit: The Pakistani army campaign in South Waziristan. Instituto de Estudios sobre Conflictos y Acción Humanitaria. https://iecah.org/en/a-risky-gambitthe-pakistani-army-campaign-in-south-waziristan.

IFSW (International Federation of Social workers). (n.d.). Global definition of social work. www.ifsw.org/what-is-social-work/global-definition-of-social-work.

IMS. (2009). Between radicalization and democratization in an unfolding conflict: Media in Pakistan. International Media Support. www.mediasupport.org/wp-content/uploads/2012/11/ims-media-pakistan-radicalisation-2009.pdf

Jafri, Q. (2021). The Pashtun Protection Movement (PTM) in Pakistan. International Center on Nonviolent Conflict, Special Report Series 8. www.nonviolent-conflict.org/wp-content/uploads/2021/09/The-Pashtun-Protection-Movement-PTM-in-Pakistan.pdf

Khan, A. (2010, 25 December). Pakistan aid-center bomber a woman. *Seattle Times*, www.seattletimes.com/nation-world/pakistan-aid-center-bomber-a-woman.

Khan, N. H., Zubair, M., & Hussan, S. (2016). Frontier Crimes Regulations (FCR), status of fundamental human rights in FATA and Pakistan's international obligations. *Global Social Sciences Review, 1*(2), 74–97.

Mahsud, A. (2020). *I am Plaintiff, Not Criminal*. Peshawar: Kitab Kor.

Nawaz, S., & De Borchgrave, A. (2009). *FATA – A Most Dangerous Place*. Washington, DC: Center for Strategic and International Studies.

Qassem, A. S., & Durand, H. (2008). Pak-Afghan relations: The Durand Line issue. *Policy Perspectives, 5*(2), 87–102.

Ricchiardi, S. (2012). *Challenges for Independent News Media in Pakistan*. Washington, DC: Center for International Media Assistance. www.cima

.ned.org/wp-content/uploads/2015/01/Challenges-for-Independent-News-Media-in-Pakistan_Ricchiardi-updated.pdf

Shah, N. A. (2010). War crimes in the armed conflict in Pakistan. *Studies in Conflict & Terrorism*, *33*(4), 283–306.

Shah, W. A. (2019, 18 September). Ordinance extends actions in aid of civil power to entire KP. *Dawn*, www.dawn.com/news/1505809.

Sultan, K. (2010). Covering the "War on Terror" challenges for journalists – the case of FATA. *Journal of Media Studies*, *25*(1), 21–32.

Taj, F. (2011a). A critical perspective on a recent survey of opinion in Pakistan's tribal zone. *Small Wars & Insurgencies*, *22*(2), 402–13.

(2011b). *Taliban and Anti-Taliban*. Newcastle-upon-Tyne: Cambridge Scholars.

(2017). *The Real Pashtun Question: How to Control Religious Extremism, Misogyny and Pedophilia?* New Delhi: Kautilya Books.

(2021). Stable regime, historiography and truth commissions: A case study of Pashtun Tahafuz movement of Pakistan. *Review of Human Rights*, *7*(1), 67–88. https://doi.org/10.35994/rhr.v7i1.192

(2022). Clash of identities: Ontological (in)securities of Afghanistan and Pakistan, and the repercussions. *Policy Perspectives*, 19(2), 1–20.

Taj, F., & Rothing, J. (2011). Can Shi'a and Sunni overcome the sectarian divide? Displacement and negotiations in Kurram, 2007–2011. Internal Displacement Monitoring Center briefing paper. https://farhattaj.org/wp-content/uploads/2016/07/briefing-paper-kurram.pdf

(2013). Northwest Pakistan: Massive new displacement and falling returns require rights-based response. Internal Displacement Monitoring Center. https://api.internal-displacement.org/sites/default/files/publications/documents/201306-ap-pakistan-overview-en.pdf.

Tajik, S. H. (2011). Analysis of peace agreements with militants and lessons for future. Pakistan Institute for Peace Studies. www.pakpips.com/article/1469

Yousaf, F. (2019). Pakistan's "tribal" Pashtuns, their "violent" representation, and the Pashtun Tahafuz movement. *Sage Open*, *9*(1), 2158244019829546.

Photo: Hilde Mjøs

CHAPTER 17

Empathy from Origin
A Colombian Social Worker's Life Story

Maria Deldén and Gull Törnegren

"I can understand my story through the metaphor of the coffee tree; from the connection between the coffee seed planted in Colombian soil, through the cultivation in a process of authentic social work and empathy, to a cup of coffee enjoyed by a Swede sending a thought to the youngsters of Colombia, in process of rebirth."

This metaphor entails the life story of Liam Girmarland who came to Sweden in 2005 as a political refugee. He came out of violence, prison, and ashes from the civil war in Colombia. His story tells the struggle and the joy of meeting Swedish society, but also the way back to a socially engaged work in Colombia.

> In Sweden I learned and began to develop new thoughts on what resocialization could mean, as an art of authentic change. In 2017, the peace process in Colombia opened an opportunity for me to return, with the aim to work for a shift in young persons' minds and hearts. My outer and inner journey to Sweden had prepared me with tools to recreate an association that I had started before my exile – AJOVEC (Association for Young People in Change).

Liam and Maria Deldén are talking on the phone; he is in Colombia, and Maria is in Sweden. We have known each other since he came to Sweden, and we have shared many experiences. Now we are going to do an interview about his life experiences in the social work field, as part of writing this chapter. But before we start the interview, Liam says:

> I would like to give this chapter the title *Empatía del origen*. The expression 'empathy from origin' is an expression that has come to me lately and I think it captures many of the aspects of the social work I have been organizing and performing during the last twenty-five years. It highlights the importance of empathy in the resocializing processes that I have experienced myself and that I have seen other persons experience.

The story we will meet in this chapter is an interpretation from interviews, informal discussions, and exchanges of ideas that have taken place between Liam and Maria during the last six years. Maria has been doing research on the association AJOVEC that Liam runs in Colombia. AJOVEC works for change and transformation in young persons' lives, what Liam describes as resocialization. Members of AJOVEC on site in Colombia have also been interviewed as part of the research project, and some of that material is used in this chapter. All conversation between Liam and Maria has been in Spanish or in Swedish, and the chapter is written in English. Gull Törnegren was invited to co-write the chapter, and together Maria and Gull have formed the text. Liam has given ongoing input throughout the process.

The places of importance to Liam's story are Sweden and Colombia, two countries tied together by migration and exile perspectives. By sharing his inner and outer journey Liam invites us to reflect upon education and identity formation in a broader sense; how education outside the formal educational system, along with empathy and the recognition of reflection upon one's own lived experiences, can become powerful tools for the change of direction in a person's life.

Made in the Conflict

Liam was born in the 1970s in a town located in the coffee district of Colombia. As the eldest of four siblings, he was raised by his mother, who was a single parent. Despite that, he maintained good contact with his father, whom he respected. Liam's father had multiple marriages and had children with other women, leading Liam to spend time with his half-siblings in their households. This was not easy, and he often felt like he was a problem that was moved here and there. From an early age, Liam was labelled as troublesome and often reacted violently to the abusive treatment he received from adults. His conflict-filled upbringing sometimes led him to stay in the streets intermittently. Living in the streets was hard, but according to Liam it also gave him invaluable experiences, in meeting persons who shared their life stories with him.

Liam's background is also impregnated by the violent conflict that has been the history of Colombia since 1948, when the liberal leader Jorge Eliecer Gaitán was murdered in Bogotá. The years that followed the assassination have been called *La Violencia* – the violence – because of the brutal and violent conflict between liberals and conservatives that took place. During this violent decade armed groups both to the left, *guerillas*, and to the right, *paramilitares*, were formed. After an agreement between the liberals and the conservatives to end the conflict and to block the left parties from having any power, the civil war received new fuel from the conflicts that arose between the guerilla and the paramilitary groups. These violent and armed conflicts got worse when the narcotraffic and the cartels grew strong in the 1970s and onwards. The armed conflict in Colombia was a reality when Liam was born, and you could say that everyone born in Colombia in the last seventy years was 'made in the conflict'.

Like many other young men, Liam was recruited to the army, and in his twenties, after having ended his military service, he worked for the armed forces of Colombia. One day he received an order to locate a group of young men in an area where he was stationed. He found the group in a school building, and when he entered the room where they were, something unexpected happened, and he can see in the rearview mirror that what took place marks a turning point in his life – a first step towards the area of social work, and a contact with a new way of understanding the word resocialization. Liam tells me about his first meeting with a young woman called Victoria and how the association AJOVEC was born:

> I had the order to fulfil, I was working for the military intelligence. We came to this place, a school, in a municipality, where seven persons from a list that we had were gathered. We were dressed as civilians, and we entered the room with focus on completing our mission. As I start to look around, I suddenly see among the persons who were there, a young relative in my close family. It moved me but I could not show it. Together with the group in the room there was also a young woman, we can call her Victoria, who I think sensed that something was going to happen. It was something about the way she looked at us, with curiosity and suspicion at the same time. I wanted to know if I was right, and I therefore took her aside to talk to her. She told us her story, about the social work she was doing with the group, and she invited us to join them. She acted as if we were another group of young men, like the group already there. She started to talk about opportunities to study, to get involved in transformational activities to change one's life and to inspire others, in a non-violent form. She reached and touched something in us, and we decided to join the group. We then went back on several occasions, and this is how the first group of AJOVEC was formed.

Liam tells us how this moment changed something in him, not immediately, but more like a change in the life course, like when you set a compass direction. If you change your direction by just one degree from the original direction, you won't notice much of a difference in how you are walking at first. But gradually, the difference between the new direction and the original direction becomes greater. Eventually, you will end up in a completely different place even though the starting point remains the same.

The Foundation of AJOVEC and the Importance of Others

AJOVEC stands for *Asociación de jóvenes en cambio* (Association for Young People in Change). It was founded in 1996 from the experiences of realizing that there were other ways to confront problems than violent ones. Victoria and Liam started to work together, and meeting with her marks a transformation for Liam. He started to question for himself the violent communication that had formed him up till then. He says:

> The idea with AJOVEC was to offer opportunities for young people to make changes in their lives, to choose non-violent forms of action. We organized sport events and other kinds of activities to activate young people and to raise consciousness about personal responsibility. The following years we worked with various groups and eventually in 2001 we got help to register the association legally.

During this time Liam came to understand resocialization as something more than the process which describes a person leaving a criminal way of life to live inside the frames of the law. Resocialization has to do with personal growth and the recognition of one's own responsibility for the choices one makes. Without thinking of it at that time, Liam laid the ground for the non-formal education that during the next twenty years came to be his academy. Liam is an example of how the area of non-formal education, that is, collectively organized education outside the formal education system, or popular education, can make a difference for persons. Liam describes himself as a person who is self-taught and has educated himself in different subjects or disciplines without formal instruction or guidance from a teacher or institution. He has taken upon himself to acquire knowledge, skills, and expertise through his own efforts, often by reading books, attending lectures or workshops, or practising and experimenting on his own. In the case of Liam, the non-formal environment of AJOVEC was of great importance. Liam understands personal growth as something that is in interaction with, and depends on, the lifeworld you embrace. In this interaction the dialogue is crucial, and as Freire explains, you need others to "read the world," to understand how meaning-making is contextually related. One example of this is the interaction between Liam and Victoria, where the dialogue between them helped Liam to "read the world" in a new way (Freire, 1998, 2017).

Liam explains that during the second half of the 1990s AJOVEC managed to engage a lot of young people in the urban area where they were active. When they got their legal registration as a non-governmental organization in 2001, they also began to cooperate with the municipality in different projects, and they successfully contributed to a decrease in homicide and criminal activity in the area. But around that time the situation in Colombia got tenser and even more dangerous due to the internal conflicts. Many young persons were recruited to groups outside the law. Liam explains what implications this had for the association, and for him personally:

> The police started to work with associations that were engaging young people, among them AJOVEC. We were told we would get information and training from the police, but the actual objective for the police was to infiltrate the association. Shortly after the police started to 'collaborate' with us, four of the social leaders disappeared, and I was arrested, accused of being the leader of a group outside the law. I was victim of being a false positive, *falso positivo*. The police confiscated all our possessions, and they burnt our office. Shortly after this my close relative, who was very active in the association, was murdered.

Being accused of being a *falso positivo*,[1] Liam was sentenced to prison, where he had to spend almost three years before it was proved that he was innocent. About his time in prison, he shares: "I started a process of empirical studies to inform myself of my rights and how to educate myself, even without formal academic training." Following his release in 2004, Liam was the victim of an attempted murder and sought refuge at the Costa Rican embassy during his recovery. He was granted a visa and eventually settled in Costa Rica in Central America, a democratic country without internal armed conflicts. However, due to the presence of many Colombians who had fled the conflict in their home country, Costa Rica was not entirely safe for someone with

[1] The phenomenon of false positives in Colombia refers to a type of human rights violation in which members of the Colombian army or the police, sometimes with the complicity of state agents, have killed or arrested innocent civilians and then presented them as guerilla fighters or members of the paramilitary, in order to show results in the fight against illegal armed groups. This phenomenon has occurred in the context of the internal armed conflict that has affected the country for decades and has left thousands of victims among the civilian population. The pressure to show results in the fight against illegal armed groups, combined with the lack of adequate supervision and control over military operations, has led some members of the army and the police to commit this type of human rights violation. False positives are a very serious phenomenon and have been condemned by the international community, human rights organizations, and a large part of Colombian society. The Colombian state has taken some measures to investigate and punish those responsible for these violations, but much remains to be done to ensure that they do not happen again in the future and to guarantee truth, justice, and reparation for the victims.

Liam's background. Seeking assistance, Liam turned to UNHCR (United Nations High Commissioner for Refugees) to be accepted as a quota refugee.[2] At their office he met with representatives from Canada, Switzerland, and Sweden. Liam recalls that the Swedish representative Emelie spoke so highly about Sweden that he ultimately chose to settle there as a refugee. The only thing Emelie failed to mention was the cold and the darkness of Swedish winters.

The Exile to Sweden and the Meeting with Popular Education

It was snowing heavily when Liam arrived in a small municipality in the north of Sweden in December 2005. It was dark outside, as it always is in wintertime in the north, where the nights are long and the days short. "What is this place?" went through his mind, but immediately he recaptured the last three years of his life, and a sensation of relief and gratitude wound through his mind and body. He felt like the phoenix bird. He had lost all his feathers, had lost everything when he was sent to prison. As in the myth of the phoenix, he had died, bursting into flames, and burnt into ashes, only to be reborn. Coming to this snowy place was his path to rebirth, to rise again strong and renewed. Metaphorical stories are powerful companions, and Liam learns through his own experiences how to accompany himself with stories that support him in his actions and in his personal growth. This knowledge and understanding have become significant parts of AJOVEC's work today, and we will return to that in the last section of the chapter.

Liam describes with warmth in his voice his meeting with the Swedish educational system:

> When I came to Sweden, I started to study Swedish, first at a study centre organized by the municipality, but I soon entered an education programme in a *folkhögskola*, folk high school, where my studies in Swedish were combined with art courses. This kind of education was new to me, and I experienced the richness in forms of education for all persons. I also got in

[2] A quota refugee is a person who is selected for resettlement in another country, typically from a refugee camp or situation of displacement. The selection process is usually based on certain criteria and the number of refugees accepted by the receiving country is predetermined or limited by a quota system; a country may agree to accept a certain number of quota refugees each year, as part of its commitment to humanitarian and international protection. These refugees may be selected by the UNHCR (or other organizations whom they cooperate with) and referred to the receiving country for resettlement. Quota refugees differ from asylum seekers, who seek protection in a country after arriving there and applying for asylum. Asylum seekers are subject to the legal and administrative procedures of the country in which they apply for protection, while quota refugees are pre-screened and accepted for resettlement in another country.

> contact with popular education in the form of study circles, which are common in Sweden, and which I did not know before. The various study associations such as the Workers' Educational Association and *Folkuniversitetet* offered me training in study circle leadership and social entrepreneurship, which was new to me. I liked the idea of popular education combined with social work and entrepreneurship, to create change more than profit. Due to this I entered a process of acquiring knowledge in the area of social work. I started groups for young persons, I started my own organization, and I also kept in contact with remaining persons in AJOVEC, with the idea of one day being able to return and to continue my work in Colombia.

What Liam met was Sweden's long history of popular education (*Folkbildning*, or *educación popular*).[3] Even if the popular education of Sweden to a large extent was new to Liam, he could easily relate his new experiences to the experiences from Colombia, and he could reflect the different contexts in each other.

But not everything he met in Sweden was that fruitful. In his meeting with different people in Sweden, he became aware of how the prejudicial image of Colombia put obstacles in the way of communication:

> Living in Sweden I became aware of the image of Colombia as synonymous with drugs and violence, and I felt it was so frustrating because Colombia is

[3] The history of popular education in Sweden goes back to the creation of the popular movements at the end of the nineteenth century. Parallel to the creation of the popular movements was the creation of educational movements. The first folk high schools were created by the peasants' movement as early as 1868, to give education to the young men in the countryside, followed soon after by the folk high schools funded by the workers' movement and the temperance movement that was at that time closely related to the workers' movement to give possibilities for education for their own members. Other forms of popular education practised by these movements from the early twentieth century were so-called lecturers' associations and 'study circles' (educational circles). Sweden also has a long tradition of free folk libraries, of which one of the first was started as early as 1799 by a minister in a small parish in the county of Södermanland. During the years to come, popular education grew into a major actor that could not have been foreseen in Swedish society. Today the organized popular education movement consists of ten national study associations with local branches all over the country, and 150 folk high schools with participants from all over the country. *Folkbildningsrådet* (Swedish National Council of Adult Education) is a non-profit association with certain authoritative tasks delegated by the government and the Swedish Parliament to distribute government grants to study associations and folk high schools. The different study associations and folk high schools have different profiles, ideological backgrounds, and content of programmes. But according to *Folkbildningsrådet* (2013) they all share some common basic ideas that render popular education distinct in the educational society that it is at the same time a part of:

1. Learning is related to the person's entire life situation.
2. Knowledge and education have intrinsic value.
3. Public education is free and voluntary.
4. The participant is an active co-creator.
5. Community involvement is stimulated and channelled through the anchoring of public education in popular movements and associational life.

> so much more than this. One among many examples of how this prejudice could reveal itself was a situation with my eldest son, who had come to Sweden with the rest of my family to join me. We were at soccer practice when the headmaster from the school came to talk with us. He was friendly and just wanted to chat. He soon asked about the drug situation in Colombia and when I tried to explain the complexity of the situation in my broken Swedish, he held out his hand to me and my son, and asked "How much?" (meaning how much to pay for drugs). Situations such as this made me both sad and angry, and a driving force for me in my work in Sweden was to change that image. I wanted to change it for many reasons. First, Colombia is far more than drugs and violence. Second, the drugs and violence in Colombia are directly linked to the consumer market in Europe. We are in this together. And third, I had put so much effort into fighting the narcotraffic in Colombia that it almost cost me my life. Being forced into exile means you lose your identity, and you have to rebuild it again. And if the image that you meet of your country is built on stereotypes and prejudices, the reformation of your identity becomes even more difficult. For me it was a very hard process that has left its marks on me.

In 2011, a peace process began in Colombia, which had an impact on Liam's life. In 2016 an agreement was reached between the government and the guerilla group FARC (Fuerzas Armadas Revolucionarias de Colombia), which resulted in a possibility for Colombians in exile to return home. The program *Reparación de víctimas* aimed at reparation and reconciliation for many of the victims of the conflict. These efforts opened the possibility for Liam to return to Colombia, which he did in 2017. But due to his history in the social work field, and the reasons for his exile, returning has had its challenges associated with security. In Colombia social leaders are confronting threats and murder; in 2022 alone, 215 social leaders were assassinated (Reynoso, 2023). Because of this, Liam did not resume collaboration with any authorities in the area where AJOVEC is active. Independence is crucial for the security and the integrity of the association.

Resocialization is an Art: Returning to Colombia

After returning from Sweden, a new phase of social work in Liam's life took place. The formation in social work he had experienced in the popular education field inspired him to further develop the work of AJOVEC.

> When I came back to Colombia, I felt very strongly that I wanted to contribute to a change in young peoples' lives, people from vulnerable

> socioeconomic backgrounds, people that society did not care about, people I could identify with. It was mostly young men, but even a few women. Many of them came from difficult home situations where the lack of economic possibilities and educational support made them vulnerable to drug micro trafficking, prostitution, and other criminal activities. But they were not only these things; they were also competent and creative human beings. Because of my own experiences during my childhood and from the first phase of AJOVEC, I knew I could support these persons to make a change. I was fulfilled by a feeling and a will to support them in the process. I wanted to leave a mark, and also live my life in a way that would dignify the persons that no longer were with us.

Liam started to rebuild the foundation on the idea of study circles, and he was strengthened in his struggle for non-violent communication. "Choose a book, not a weapon" was his motto when he went back to Colombia. He felt like a living example that this change in choice is possible.

The word resocialization is, as we have seen, a key concept for Liam and for AJOVEC since the first meeting with Victoria back in the 1990s. When he started to connect with her group, he understood that victims and perpetrators could be seen as interrelated. He reflects on his first meeting with Victoria's group:

> I was a young person as they were, we had a lot in common, but we had ended up in a situation where I was in the role of the perpetrator, and they were the victims. I could identify with them, also because I found my close relative in the group. And I started to think that there must be ways less orthodox and less aggressive to deal with the situation. To contribute to a more positive solution we started the process of resocialization. It has a lot to do with listening to each other's stories and the desire to change the directions of one's own life, and the lives of others. In the deepest sense it is about saving lives. I started to find solutions instead of creating more violence. I realized it was about transformation as we got to know the stories and that what seems to be the problem entails the solution.

The word resocialization has its history for Liam, and it entails several meanings for AJOVEC nowadays. The concept has developed during his time in Sweden due to his experiences there. In Spanish the concept is written in reflexive form, *resocializarse*, which highlights the active role of the subject in the resocialization process, according to Liam. He explains how it is an action that binds subject and action together. Resocialization in this interpretation requires the agency of those who for various reasons are to be returned to society; agency as active participants both in their own lives and in the community. Resocialization is also described by Liam as an art (*resocializarse es un arte*). This shows both the complex processes that resocialization involves, but also that AJOVEC use different means of expression in their work, expressions that promote creativity, creativeness, and growth. In the written material from AJOVEC explaining their work for resocialization, four words are central to their pedagogy: to be (*ser*), to do (*hacer*), to know (*conocer*), to coexist (*convivir*). These verbs tell something about two important aspects of education in the association: non-violent communication according to Rosenberg (2006), but also sustainability.

So, how has the work of AJOVEC developed since Liam returned to Colombia? One aspect, the aspect of sustainable development, had struck Liam during his time in Europe: the consciousness of the need for sustainable development through Agenda 2030 (United Nations, 2019). Liam talks about the necessity to understand development among the population he engages with as not only socioeconomic, but also environmental. These aspects are interrelated, as described in Agenda 2030. It is notable how activities begin with both non-violent communication and sustainability; how the participants are recognized in their own right and how their life experiences count as valuable, and as assets for change. Liam, when talking to one of the participants now active in AJOVEC, said:

> It is within yourself that the most important change takes place, and it is you as a person who is important. Who do you want to be? What kind of person do you want to be? AJOVEC can support you but cannot make the change for you.

Another important change was to re-establish the work without ties to the authorities. But most important of all was the inspiration from popular education in Sweden and from social entrepreneurship. Also, the awareness of thinking in terms of sustainability made AJOVEC move towards activities combining social, economic, and environmental dimensions. AJOVEC started to work with cultivation, first in a very small scale together with private homes, schools, and other institutions in socioeconomically vulnerable areas. Successively, the association started to lease land to cultivate with the purpose of combining education on Agenda 2030 with socioeconomic sustainability. Eventually, and with economic support from Sweden, this effort resulted in a coffee farm that now is the base for AJOVEC's work with sustainability. The cultivation and production of specialty coffee[4] offers an arena for the association to develop ideas of social entrepreneurship.

[4] Specialty coffee refers to high-quality coffee that is produced with exceptional care and attention to detail throughout the entire supply chain, from cultivation to brewing. Specialty coffee is typically

To change, to transform, to resocialize, is recognized primarily as a personal responsibility in the association. But to manage this personal achievement the environment is vital. Liam works with young persons in change, and one of the participants in AJOVEC, Luisa, talks about how she constantly learns from the others in the group, and how she enjoys teaching others from her experiences and knowledge:

> I really, really like working with young people, with children, because well, they learn from you, but you learn from them. And perhaps many times the experience that I have had, I have spoken with many young people, ... I have spoken to them a lot, I have the experience of being in the world of drugs, so I talk to them, and that gives me satisfaction, I feel happy. I really like working, for example when we do groups with mothers, with women, that satisfaction it gives me to see their happiness ... for example, the women who came to do the ceramics course, they are women who are isolated in their environment, always in the house cooking, so they never put their mind to other things, like they forget the world. And then to see them here, all motivated, working, creating, they discovered things that they thought they could not do. To see that joy, that satisfaction. That's why I like working with AJOVEC. (Luisa, 2018).

It is notable how individual growth in the sense of becoming a unique person is interwoven with interaction with others. There is a seamlessness between one's own processes of transformative learning and teaching others.

To cultivate is both a reality and a metaphor for personal growth, as the activities at the coffee farm can show. Jorge is one of the participants in AJOVEC, and he shares his experiences with us:

> I see the coffee process as a life process. I assimilate cultivating and picking coffee as a life process. Maybe one has experienced bad things, the same happens with coffee, it has dry leaves, it has bad beans, the same happens with oneself. When you clear the coffee plantation from weeds you also can do it with yourself. (Jorge, 2021)

Jorge was trying to escape drug abuse when he heard about AJOVEC and their work. He had had some experiences of the healing power of nature, so he was very anxious to get involved in cultivation activities. He moved to the coffee farm and stayed there for several months, working with the

made from Arabica coffee beans, which are known for their nuanced flavour profiles and complexity. It is produced in a sustainable and ethical manner, with a focus on transparency and traceability. Specialty coffee is often sourced from small-scale farmers who are paid fair prices for their beans, and who use environmentally friendly growing practices. The quality of specialty coffee is judged by a combination of factors, including the flavour, aroma, body, acidity, and aftertaste of the coffee.

whole coffee process. He had a dream to study agronomy, but it would be a very long and costly path to reach that dream, because he dropped out of elementary school after year six. So, Liam made an agreement with Jorge. AJOVEC would support him to achieve an economic sustainable outcome if he could get clean. Jorge had the idea of starting a delivery service on motorbike. They agreed that Jorge's salary would be saved, and after he had got clean, the money saved would be spent on a motorbike. This is what happened, and Jorge now has his small business that can support his wife and child.

The farm is a possibility to realize the resocialization process that always has been at the heart of Liam's and AJOVEC's motivation to contribute to transformation and change. Liam reflects about the fact that his life journey has a lot to do with education and social work, without him having an academic diploma. He talks about the importance of non-formal learning opportunities, for him as well as for the other participants in AJOVEC:

> We are working with young people outside the formal learning system. They have no or very little chance of getting any higher education. In Colombia, this reality forms the way people see themselves, as doomed to a life without education. But, as I learned in Sweden, you can always educate yourself. But to do that, you need the support of others. AJOVEC aims at inspiring to a change of self-understanding and at organizing possibilities to study. I see it as especially important to cross boundaries between formal and non-formal education.

As we can see, a continuous thread in Liam's story is non-formal education. As we describe it in this chapter, it is characterized by its position outside the formal education system, but unlike informal learning, which is situated in the family or among friends as a spontaneous, inescapable part of daily life, it is carried out in organizational frameworks. It also differs from formal education that is carried out in schools and other educational institutions. Formal learning is directed towards the intentions of the educators and is to be understood in relation to goals and standards decided by others than the learner (Brennan, 1997; Council of Europe, 2019). Non-formal education can be seen as a form of situated learning in communities where certain practices are essential. The members of the community share a common interest or need to learn, and the learning is based on processes of sharing knowledge, information, and experiences in order to fulfil the needs of the members and the group (Lave & Wenger, 1991; Wenger, 1998). Learning, and teaching, emerge from the initiative of the members themselves and the power over the learning processes lies among the members.

Liam explains how after returning to Colombia he has worked to integrate AJOVEC with professionals from universities and schools in Sweden and Colombia. The idea is to combine experiences from non-formal education with the academic world – not only to exchange experiences and knowledge, but also to develop the quality of formal education, and create possibilities for persons in non-formal education to formalize their knowledge and competencies. However, this vision of crossing boundaries is easier said than done. Even if non-formal learning in organizations such as AJOVEC leads to personal transformation, the step to transformation in a broader societal aspect is far away. The participants increase their learning and their teaching skills but due to the education system they still are excluded from formal studies. They feel better but they do not change their position in the societal context, as Jorge's story tells us.

Empathy from Origin

The title of the chapter is "Empathy from Origin" as Liam wished it to be. It is a concept he has developed from his own experiences during the inner and outer journey we have pictured in this chapter. The expression is particularly important to Liam, as it has evolved from ideas of resocialization into a relevant pedagogical tool. We will try to explain what empathy from origin means by starting with Liam telling a story:

> Recently, the center where AJOVEC has its office was robbed by a former member of the association. Despite being in contact with us and frequently visiting the office, the perpetrator entered at night and was not immediately suspected by neighbours. However, as he began to remove various equipment, including green and roasted coffee, coffee machines, a printer, computers, a clearing saw, and an oven, the neighbours became suspicious and contacted the police. Although the former member had already fled with most of the valuable items by the time the police arrived, we reported the incident to the authorities. While some participants expressed a strong desire to seek revenge through violence, I urged them to co-operate with the police. This was hard to do even for me, because of the disappointment I felt over the former member. It was a person I trusted, and I had invested engagement, hopes, and my time in his resocialization process. Even worse was the fact that he took advantage of a situation where I was sick; during the robbery I was hospitalized, and he knew it. This woke very strong feelings of anger, feelings I knew very well from my past.

After a hard internal struggle, I overcame these feelings and acted in line with the person I wanted to be. Consequently, we reported the robbery to the police, and the case was forwarded to the prosecutor. But from there it did not proceed further. This whole situation created enormous frustration among the members, and also in me.The idea of empathy from origin can be understood in Liam's life story as a continuation of the work with resocialization. For Liam a key understanding of resocialization is that "being part of a problem means you also should be part of the solution." Today Liam connects this understanding to the importance of empathy; to sense how really listening to others' stories can lead to transformation. But it is not just a feeling for or with someone else. Liam continues:

> Maybe the most important part of empathy is to connect to yourself, to empathize with yourself. That is why I call it empathy from origin, because oneself is the origin in one's life. When I was young, I was convinced that the best thing to do in a situation where you were provoked was to give a strong violent response coming from the anger you felt. If you didn't do that you would lose respect. In this way I was part of the macho culture in which I was raised. During these years since I came back to Colombia from Sweden, I have started to question this way of handling my feelings and performing my actions. It is like laying a puzzle where all the pieces from my life come together, and I can see that many situations where my reactions have had fuel from my anger or frustration have resulted in situations not productive either for me or for my environment. I can see that I have not thought about the damage these actions have had on me. So, when I started to empathize with myself, I also started to think of how my behaviour reflects not only empathy with others but also with myself.
>
> How can I better clarify the concept of empathy from origin by relating it to the story of the robbery? In the aftermath of the incident, I empathized with the younger members of the association who were eager for immediate retaliation. Reflecting on my past violent reactions, I realized that I had lacked a deeper sense of empathy with myself and a connection to values that lead to a better life. With this perspective, I spoke to the group, encouraging them to recognize the choices available to them in each moment and to strive towards becoming the person they want to be in the long run of life. I emphasized that the actions of a perpetrator not only harm the victim, but they also have consequences for the perpetrator himself as a human being. In this way, the former participant had not only caused damage to our organization but also to something valuable within himself. I warned that seeking revenge would only perpetuate the cycle of harm and ultimately make us perpetrators to ourselves.

In Liam's story we meet his experiences of positive change and transformation both for himself and others. But it has never been a straight journey. Liam points to numerous disappointments and backlashes that he has faced when participants in AJOVEC have fallen back into drug consumption, criminal activity, violence, and even being killed. On such occasions it is hard to stay and to continue the social work. But at the same time, he asks himself what the options are. To not feel empathy? To not try to create opportunities for young persons to change? He thinks back on his own life, and what would have happened if he had not met people who inspired him to make the choices that he did. Who would he have been today? Would he even have been alive?

Final Words that Are to Be Continued

During our conversations Liam sometimes refers the metaphorical work with coffee in the resocialization processes as "social work poetry." Poetry has the power to get right to you and makes you understand something that you didn't know before without really controlling the whole process of understanding. Poetry talks to you without filter, and you end up connected to yourself, the words, the world. It is somewhat the same thing with growing coffee. You get connected to yourself, to the plants, to the world. Maybe it could be described as resonance, as the sociologist Hartmut Rosa puts it (2019). Social work poetry in its deeper sense aims at visualizing the importance of authentic resocialization. In all social work, inside or outside institutions, we need to consider the importance of connectedness, with ourselves, with others, and with the world.

Liam's story can show us how a person's journey to resocialization is not instrumental, but dynamic, seeking, full of connectedness and empathy. His story is not a linear story with a beginning, middle, and ending. It is rather a process that goes back and forth, and in which the threads of the stories that Liam met in Colombia and in Sweden are interwoven. This entails recurring transformations to enable Liam to grow into the person he wants to be. In the process, his stories are entangled with other persons' stories. In the same way as Victoria's story had the power to change Liam's direction, the stories of Liam can be powerful resources for other young people to change the courses of their lives. And now that we are sharing Liam's story in the context of this book, our hope is that his story can continue its work as a resource for other persons engaged in social work for transformation and resocialization.

Reflective Questions

1. What insights about different ways of becoming a social worker has Liam's life story brought to the fore?

2. What stories have you met in your own social work practice that have affected your way of understanding what ought to be the core of social work?
3. How do you from your own experiences understand the expression "social work poetry"? How could it be an inspiration in your own work?

REFERENCES

Brennan, B. (1997). Reconceptualizing non-formal education. *International Journal of Lifelong Education*, *16*(3), 185–200. https://dx.doi.org/10.1080/0260137970160303

Council of Europe. (2019). Linguistic integration of adult migrants: Formal, non-formal and informal learning. www.coe.int/en/web/lang-migrants/formal-non-formal-and-informal-learning

Folkbildningsrådet. (2013). Folkbildningens vägval och vilja. www.sverigesfolkhogskolor.se/globalassets/dokument_fso/vagval-vilja-folkbildning.pdf

Freire, P. (1998). *Pedagogy of Freedom: Ethics, Democracy, and Civic Courage*. Lanham, MD: Rowman & Littlefield.

(2017). *Pedagogy of the Oppressed*. London: Penguin.

Lave, J., & Wenger, E. (1991). *Situated Learning: Legitimate Peripheral Participation*. Cambridge University Press.

Rosa, H. (2019). *Resonance: A Sociology of Our Relationship to the World*. Cambridge: Polity Press.

Reynoso, L. (2023, 23 January). Colombia registra el asesinato de 215 líderes sociales en 2022. *El País*, https://elpais.com/america-colombia/2023-01-23/colombia-registra-el-asesinato-de-215-lideres-sociales-en-2022.html.

Rosenberg, M. (2006). *Comunicación no violenta: Un lenguaje de vida*. Camarones: Gran Aldea Editores.

United Nations. (2019). The Sustainable Development Agenda. www.un.org/sustainabledevelopment/development-agenda

Wenger, E. (1998). *Communities of Practice: Learning, Meaning, and Identity*. Cambridge University Press.

Photo: Hilde Mjøs

CHAPTER 18

Welfare Transitions in an Agrarian Community
Solidarities, Subsistence, and Struggles of Older Women in Uganda

Venesio Bwambale Bhangyi

Introduction

Under the scorching afternoon sun, she sits at the edge of her compound, only saved from the heat by the shade of the coffee plant. This spot has become her safe sanctuary in the afternoons as the sun's heat has become unforgiving. The choice of this spot could be attributed to her knowledge of weather and climate patterns, and of what to do to mitigate their impacts at the personal level. Her gaze, fixed on a line of women carrying jerry cans of water on their backs trekking a path on the hilly slopes in the distance, reminds her of the cycle of life in this mountainous community. Only the smell of burning food reminds her that her lunch is about to go to waste. She quickly jumps from her deep thoughts and rushes to rescue what remains of her lunch meal. Such a misfortune (burning food) may force her to skip her lunch entirely as replacement food is hard to come by. But things never used to be like this. Something somewhere has gone wrong and even at eighty-six years old, she cannot put her finger on this occurrence. She is not the only older woman in this community struggling to make sense of how life has changed over the years. Many others like her, frail and unable to engage in the energy-sapping activities of agrarian rural life, spend most of their later lives immersed in their solitary thoughts that young folks have no idea about. Aging as a woman in an agricultural rural community, where production and consumption shape everyday life, is known to create perilous conditions in later life (Nagaddya, 2023).

At eighty-six years old, she has lived a long and eventful life. In our conversations, she jokes about not knowing when she married, but she estimates she could have been between fourteen and sixteen years old. Thus, her lived life is an eternity to the extent that even some of her strongest early life memories have long been forgotten. All her siblings are long dead. Brothers, sisters, and cousins. She last visited that side of her family about twenty-five years ago. However, she is the rock and ever-present figure in her marital family, and currently lives mostly in the company of her grandchildren, their children, and their grandchildren. This means that she has lived to see her great-great-grandchildren. It is very common to find up to five generations in her household when her children come visiting. Her failing health, marked by declining hearing ability, weakening physical health, complete loss of teeth, and laboured movements, are indicators of a life nearing the end. She is a fighter who is great at hiding the pains of her life. Having given birth to nine children, only two survived to adulthood, the last to depart robbed from her life during the 1980s war.

Thus, this chapter engages with the life story of three older women, who in their heyday were matriarchs leading their extending families but now live their later lives in reflection, worry, and uncertainty. It begins by presenting the storytelling methodology that informs this chapter. As the African saying goes, *an older person is the village library by holding stories of their times.* I then explain the ways in which the passage of time in their lives is a manifestation of welfare transitions in their agrarian welfare systems. This is followed by the changes in their solidarities and how these have impacted their subsistence over the years. Then, the struggles of their daily living over the years are also illustrated to show the pains of old age. Implications for social work are drawn in the conclusion. This conclusion also includes key questions for critical reflections by the reader.

Methodology: Telling This Story

This chapter uses storytelling as its main methodological approach. An African story is told through a recollection of the author's conversations, interactions, observations, and his general collective memory about the three older women used as the characters informing this discourse. His recollections are further informed by his personal experiences of living with the case studies in the same community. Thus, the collective memory of living with, seeing, listening to, and interacting with some of these older women is instrumental in guiding this story. Names have not been used in this narration and care has been taken to ensure that examples of lived experiences of the cases shared here cannot identify or point to any of the main characters.

During the story narrations, the personal experiences of the cases discussed are infused, where needed, with ideas obtained from reviewed literature. The literature materials have been purposively selected to talk to the story being discussed. In this way, the chapter addresses the growing calls for African social work research to incorporate grassroots knowledge systems that are indigenous, increases African involvement in research, and promotes an African heritage to deeply contribute to meeting the needs in our communities (Chigevenga, 2022).

An Agrarian Community

These three older women have lived the entirety of their lives as peasant farmers. They tilled and still till the hilly lands for food production for their household use. It is a traditional practice in this community that the women and children are responsible for household food production processes. However, there is evidence across Uganda that the impact of global economic and social changes on the elderly has been ignored (Nagaddya, 2023). At their age, most of their children and grandchildren have migrated to other lands to seek livelihoods and start families, or moved to towns in search of opportunities. This has left these older women to till their land on their own, without the traditional support of children and grandchildren. In their villages, the main cash crop is coffee, but this is controlled by men, and in their cases, it is now under the custodianship of their grandsons. This has left them with little to no cash income for sustenance. The economic strategy in the 1990s to promote non-traditional cash crops such as maize, beans, etc. added an extra burden on women in terms of labour and ignored rural gender realities in which men controlled the cash (Whitehead et al., 2000).

While these older women in their younger and stronger days held herds of goats and flocks of chickens for food, the cash was controlled by men when they were exchanged for money. It is my observation that with their weakening health and physical fragility, they can hardly engage in any meaningful agrarian actions. The rigour, energy, and gravitas to engage in agriculture have slowly drained away. This is a far cry from years past when they held a lot of foods crops. She often laments about the declining food productivity of her lands, arguing that there is nothing she can do about the poor soils, pests, and bad planting materials. This misery could be attributed, in part, to the lack of technology use in their farming (Bamwesigye et al., 2020, p.7). Thus, a shift from the times of food security with plenty to a state of persistent lack, hunger, and two uncertain meals a day appears too painful for a person surely walking their last steps on earth to handle.

A Life through Welfare Transitions

When you live this long, you see and experience so many changes. Changes in your welfare provisions thus shape your life's experiences. The family has always been the source of welfare for these older women. Therefore, a tight kinship welfare system is the wish of every family. Bhangyi, Kiconco, & Chu (2023) and the Ministry of Gender, Labor, and Social Development (2020) have illustrated how the family, and the kinship community, are instrumental in care and support services in communities. This evidence is borne out by the fact that in years past, these three older women lived in families that included grandparents, parents, siblings, in-laws, and children. Nowadays, however, they are the grandparents, the oldest persons in their households. Their family structures have changed over time and several times. All their children are also grandparents. All these three old women now live with their grandchildren and great grandchildren. While still living in a kinship family, changing values due to land shortages and a creeping cash economy have made their lives difficult. Their grandchildren have become more individualistic than their children were, thereby changing family care values.

In addition, these women live in times of changed land-based welfare. As discussed in their struggles below, the tradition of land subdivision (Ashaba, 2023) is a great concern to these women. They have lost most of their land to relatives through this culture of subdivision and inheritance. Their current lots do not produce sufficient food to feed them. In the past twenty years, two new land trends started to emerge in this community. One was renting of one's land to another person for cash. However, this meant that land rented had no time for fallowing to regain fertility, and male relatives became greedier to have more lands for renting out. Second, monied people started to purchase lands in the community. This distorted the hereditary land system. Some of their sons/grandsons sold their inherited lots and mostly squandered the cash. Some, though, used the money wisely to buy other lands elsewhere, far beyond walking distance. Those who misused the cash from the land sales then came back to the clan/parents to ask for more customary land entitlements. Eventually, these older women lost more land and were squeezed onto smaller lots. Bare, exhausted, and overused, the small lots cannot produce sufficient food for a decent living.

These transitions are not helped by the mirage of government promises of social services. These older women were in their early years when Uganda regained its independence in 1962 from its colonial master Britain. The promise of building a community of hope, one which cared for the welfare of all Ugandans, was exciting. Such promises were made by the Obote I government in 1962 (Obote, 1962). Over sixty-one years since these promises were made, these older women have nothing to show. The peace and security delivered by the present government have brought sleep, but a hungry body finds it had to sleep. A sickly one cannot sleep either. The nearest hospital (health centre) is about 5 kilometres away, a great health services achievement compared to past years. Yet, when you are hungry, frail, and sick, walking this distance is more of a painful experience than a promise of hope. Most times, this walk is avoided until the illness is critical. The recently launched senior citizens grant of the Ugandan government under the social assistance grant for empowerment (SAGE) has not benefited them despite their advanced age. This service is premised on an advanced age of eighty years as indicated on the claimant's national identity card. But fate is cruel. Born in villages with community birth attendants, birth records were unheard of. They have given up attempting to rectify their birth records on the national identity card to gain access to this service. As such, they miss out on the monthly payment of 25,000 UGX (approximately 7 USD). Thus, achieving the national eligibility age of eighty (Nakirigya, 2023) does not guarantee access for these three older women.

Such a monthly payment would make a lot of sense in the context of a cash economy that is now a dominant force in their community. In days past, they would only need money to buy a few basics such as salt, paraffin, and clothing. Other household items were either produced on their land or acquired through barter exchange. Sometimes, they would carry, on their backs, food stuffs for sale in the local market to get the cash needed for these home items. Then, food production from their lands declined. They began to rely more and more on the market to buy food. Their sons, grandsons, daughters-in-law, and other relatives could help with cash for food occasionally. But modern monetary demands on the families of those relatives have meant that these old women are quite often left to fend for themselves. At their ages, this is a life-defying ask. To survive in the harsh realities of their communities, social solidarities are critical. However, these have also changed over the years, leaving these older women to *eriyiya* (local saying meaning 'scratching their heads to find the means of survival').

Changing Solidarities and Building Resilient Subsistence

These older women have witnessed and lived through a raft of generational changes in their lifetime. Marrying into their present families as teenagers, they held the status of in-laws or wives – a socially prestigious position in the community. Unfortunately, marriage and sexual abuse of girls in the communities is still a great problem despite the passage of time (see Tumwekwase, 2023). They progressed to motherhood, aunthood, and years later to being grandparents, and eventually great-great grandparents. The gift of life has enabled them to live in families with four to five generations. All these bring along different solidarities, alliances, friendships, and networks. Despite weakening family ties, I have seen these helping. As new members come into the neighbourhoods, new alliances are formed, and old ones reconstituted. The new neighbours also become *family* members despite having no blood relations with these old women. However, an outside person may view the responsibilities of these older women for childcare and family provision as burdensome. Yet, they are intricately linked with the care and support that these old women get. For it is this that bonds them together with stronger members of their family and community.

Over the years, the old women have learnt how to build social capital to anchor their subsistence. They talk fondly for example about how they built a lasting sisterhood even though they were all married into this family and community. One of them fondly says that it is the heart that loves, not the head, and not the material things that you have. So, love, compassion, comradeship are the roots for building social capital. In recent times, these old women have interacted with their grandsons with the same old respect they accorded to their husbands (RIP). They use this to build mutual respect, since it is these grandsons who are now the dominant male authorities in these families. Creating friendship in the community is a crafted action, one which builds their social support capital. Many young and old people, relatives, and just recently arrived community members respect, check on, and care for these three older women.

The cornerstone of their subsistence is the family, and they spare no effort to build and maintain a family system. *Eka* (nuclear family, or in this case a small family of six or fewer people) is now the dominant family type they live in. This is a great transition from the *erihika* (large extended families) in which they lived twenty-five or so years back. *Olhughanda* (a super-extended family of members of the same clan, usually with a great grandparent or *sokulhu*) is what constitutes most of the people in their community and villages. Just last year, one of these older women offered four of her goats to a great grandson to meet bride price expenses. In this way, both the incoming bride and great grandson owe a debt of gratitude to her. This debt of gratitude will translate into care and support at one point of need in the old woman's life. These old women possess historical knowledge of their families which helps them to navigate family conflicts and offer support and wisdom to family members. This resourcefulness glues aspects of their families together and these families then meet some or most of their welfare needs. It is only the family resource inadequacies that limit how much these old women receive.

Life's a Journey of Struggles

First, these older women have struggled with the declining land-based welfare system. At first, each of their families owned huge swathes of land as far as the eye could see. During these good old times, the population in the community was very small, with an easily countable number of people. These women only accessed land through their associations with their husbands and, in old age, their children. This was because women then, and even now in these traditional communities, do not adequately enjoy land ownership rights (Ministry of Lands, Housing, and Urban Development, 2018). As their sons got married, quite often with multiple wives, the population exploded. The system of land inheritance, where sons inherit land through subdivision of the original lot, has led to each successive generation owning smaller lots. As such, overuse has exhausted the potential for the land to yield sufficient food for any household. This land subdivision is not an isolated occurrence in this community but is widely spread across Ugandan communities. This has irritated the president of the country who has made persistent calls for this tradition to be abolished so that larger lots can be available to facilitate social economic transformation (Ashaba, 2023).

Secondly, these older women have come to see the dangers of a changing environment. They talk of the disappearance of forests and grasslands that covered their lands. As, their community's population expanded, trees and bushes were cleared to make way for gardens and to secure building materials and firewood. The lack of replacement tree-planting means that the land has become bare. The heat from the sun has also become harsher, and rains have become scarce and unreliable. This is a phenomenon called climate change. In their community, they simply wonder what went wrong, as narrated in the introduction of this story. This climate change has also produced persistent environmental disasters in these communities (Bhangyi, 2023). So, their efforts to spend afternoons hiding from the sun have become a strain, with some using shade from crop plants such as coffee trees. Since water has become scarce, they sit wondering how their younger counterparts will meet the water needs of their households. The line of women carrying jerry cans of water across the hills is a reminder to these old women of what has gone wrong. For in the past, streams, ponds, rivers dotted the hilly villages, and rains were plentiful, thereby supplying the water needs of all in the community with ease.

These thoughts and worries about the harshness of the weather are worsened by the challenges of loneliness that has become more evident as these women age. At first, it was their children leaving them to get married and start families. Then, their husbands died many years ago. These three older women have lived on average for the past thirty years without their husbands. Men in this community tend to die early despite recent improvements in public health. Then, their grandchildren also became adults, got married, and even became grandparents. These younger generations also scatter, some to distant places in a quest for social and economic opportunities. While these older women used to live in the company of many other older women, death has taken most of their peers one by one. The latest succumbed to old age complications in this past year at the ripe age of 105 years old. Although they know each other since they have lived and grown in the same community as a cohort, their poor physical health means that, for months at a time, they can no longer visit each other for social support.

This poor health of the three older women has in recent years become a popular talk of the village. As community members interact, they quite often inquire of the health of their older comrades. The community and relatives are quite resigned, only waiting for death to snatch them. This resignation is in part due to extreme poverty levels in this community. Thus, the medical bills deter the community from constantly seeking professional medical care for these older women, only taking them to health facilities when they are critically ill. All these three older women now stay within the vicinities of their homesteads, and are thus unable to socialize or even engage in many community life activities such as the Sunday prayers and the weekly market activities.

As noted earlier in this story, these women now live on small plots of land rather than the large chunks of land they used to hold. What remained for them as the land was shared by relatives through inheritance is also under threat. For one of my older women, their land has been grabbed by their great grandson, only leaving the lot on which the house is standing. This will surely be grabbed the day she dies 'before she settles in the grave' as the popular saying of the community goes. Due to lack of a strong male character to defend her land rights, she lives in precarity. It is not uncommon in Uganda for relatives to kill or evict their older relatives (parents or grandparents) to grab their lands (Kinene, 2023). I have observed that these women prefer to live their last years in peace rather than compete for and wrangle over land. They have resigned themselving to dying of hunger rather than be killed over land.

Reflections, Implications, and Recommendations for Social Work

In view of the above story of the three older women discussed in this chapter, I distil several unresolved issues. These I present as reflection points and questions to warn social workers in Uganda and beyond. These questions hold significant implications for social work practice, research, policy, and education.

1. How could social workers engage with gender inclusivity in rural, traditional, and agricultural communities? This is because the above story shows that gender justice is a major issue affecting the welfare of older female populations in Ugandan communities.
2. What kind of environmental sustainability and environmental justice actions are required from social workers engaged with agrarian communities? This reflection could be guided by the conclusion from this chapter that marginalized and vulnerable persons in these communities face the direct consequences of climate change and environmental disasters. Older women are at much greater risk due to their traditional care responsibilities.
3. How can social work in the Ugandan context gain entry to and traction in agrarian communities? This question is derived from the significant or even total absence of social workers in the lives of the three older persons, yet their life history indicates an intersectional marginalization and disadvantage. These are the social issues that social workers should deeply interrogate.
4. How can social work engage with public social services, programming, and policy to address the absence of government services in communities where traditional, informal, and self-help approaches dominate welfare provision? In this reflection, how can social workers position themselves to address the gaps and pitfalls in public and community social services for older women?
5. How can social work learn from agrarian, community, and land-based welfare approaches to inform professional social work education, theory, and practice? Could this learning promote local solutions to local problems?

In addition, in this life story of the three older women in this community, I propose the following four interlinked concluding recommendations. First, that social workers in Uganda should work co-operatively with communities and community structures to advance the well-being of older persons. This will require learning from grassroots aspects of older women's care and support knowledge and practices. Second, social workers should actively research older women in community contexts to build local indigenous knowledge and theory to promote their well-being. The participation of older women in such knowledge-building should be the core of research. Third, social workers must rigorously integrate local welfare provision strategies into formal public social services. This will enable social workers to work towards eliminating the injustices embedded in traditional community support systems, and those embedded in public social services, and to align both with the mission of social work. It will also open a window for social workers to address intersectional disadvantage of older women and client populations in community contexts in general. Fourth, social workers must promote social protection programmes at both national and community levels. These will increase provision of social and economic safety nets for all vulnerable persons in Uganda, including older women. Voicing the injustices in current provisions for old women, such as those articulated above with regard to the senior citizens grant, could be part of this promotion.

Conclusion

In this chapter, I have shared the story of the lives, trials, and tribulations of three older women in Uganda. In their story, I have demonstrated that old age in an agrarian community is linked with traditions, social solidarities, family, land, the environment, and transitions in welfare systems. I have further illustrated that in all three cases, the absence or inadequacy of target interventions for older women has led to precarities in their struggles for survival. Thus, in their context, which is devoid of a public welfare system for older women, the declines in land, familial, and environmental resources for their sustenance are painful and exhausting. Their story shows that while they contributed to the progress of their families and community in their early and middle life, old age has pushed them to the periphery and has tested their endurance. As one of them always reasons, in old age, you count each day until your last day. The pleasures, resources, and joys of the community pass you by in your forgotten state.

Social work therefore has a duty, a moral and professional obligation, to serve these populations at the margins. The absence of social work services in this community to glue together the resources that should ensure their well-being is therefore a tragedy in a modern welfare state. The pains, struggles, and sufferings of these and other older women are therefore a strong call to duty for social work. Their story has demonstrated that older women in such contexts face an existential threat, one which collective community systems are gradually but increasingly failing to address. These collective failures could be fixed by a social work that promotes family, community, agrarian, and land-based welfare approaches in its interventions. Bhangyi, Namuwanga, Kilama, Toko, & Balyejjusa (2023) have argued that such approaches are plentiful, trusted, known, and accessible. In addition, their adoption in professional practice is both decolonizing and indigenizing for social work in the Ugandan context.

Reflective Questions

1. What are the necessary issues of engagement in rural, traditional, and agricultural communities to make a change?
2. What kinds of justice actions are required from social workers engaged with agrarian communities?
3. How can social work learn from different community approaches to update professional social work education, theory, and practice? Can this learning promote local solutions to local problems?

Acknowledgements

The author acknowledges the three older women in this community, on whose lives the storyline of this chapter is based. His interactions with them over the years have informed the context and nature of this text. The recollections of these shared experiences were instrumental in the formulation of the chapter.

REFERENCES

Ashaba, A. (2023, 6 March). Museveni warns locals on land fragmentation. *Monitor*, www.monitor.co.ug/uganda/news/national/museveni-warns-locals-on-land-fragmentation-4147916.

Bamwesigye, D., Doli, A., Adamu, J. K., & Mansaray, K. S. (2020). A review of the political economy of agriculture in Uganda: Women, property rights, and other challenges. *Universal Journal of Agricultural Research*, *8*(1), 1–10. https://doi.org/10.13189/ujar.2020.080101

Bhangyi, B. V. (2023). Directions in constructing a body of knowledge in eco-social work education and practice in Uganda: Actions, channels, and implications. *African Journal of Social Work*, 13(2), 70–7. https://dx.doi.org/10.4314/ajsw.v13i2.3

Bhangyi, B. V., Kiconco, M., & Chui, H. W. (2023). The informality paradigm in social work practice in Africa: Philosophy, continuity, and prospects for integration into professional practice. In S. Levy, U. Okoye, P. Tanga, & R. Ingram (eds.), *Routledge Handbook of African Social Work Education*. London: Routledge.

Bhangyi, B. V., Namuwanga, S., Kilama, D., Toko, F., & Balyejjusa, S. M. (2023). A collaborative agenda for health and wellbeing: Social workers working with a community church. In D. Androff & J. Damanik (eds.), *The Routledge International Handbook of Social Development, Social Work, and the Sustainable Development Goals*. New York: Routledge.

Chigevenga, R. (2022). Decolonizing research methodologies in the Global South: Experiences of an African social scientist. *African Journal of Social Work*, *12*(4), 199–206.

Kinene, E. (2023, September 25). Police arrest man in connection to murdering elderly couple over land. *Uganda Radio Network*, https://ugandaradionetwork.net/story/police-arrest-man-in-connection-to-murder-of-elderly-couple-over-land.

Ministry of Gender, Labor, and Social Development. (2020). *National Child Policy 2020*. https://www.unicef.org/uganda/media/8166/file/Final-Uganda-National%20Child%20Policy-October-2020-lores.pdf

Ministry of Lands, Housing and Urban Development. (2018). Land and property ownership: The gender strategy for national land policy implementation. https://mlhud.go.ug/wp-content/uploads/2019/06/Gender-Strategy-on-Land-for-the-NLP-July-2018-reviewed.pdf

Nagaddya, T. (2023). A rural-centric model for understanding women's later life precarity in an agrarian economy in Uganda. *Poverty & Public Policy*, *15*(3), 290–307. https://doi.org/10.1002/pop4.376

Nakirigya, S. (2023, 13 September). Govt rejects use of mobile money to send elderly cash. *Monitor*, www.monitor.co.ug/uganda/news/national/govt-rejects-use-of-mobile-money-to-send-elderly-cash-4367458.

Obote, M. A. (1962, 9 October). Prime minister Obote's speech on eve of Uganda's independence 1962. *The Independent*, www.independent.co.ug/obote-speech-on-eve-of-ugandas-independence-1962.

Tumwekwase, S. (2023, 20 June). 330 Bushenyi teenagers impregnated in 3 months. *Monitor*, www.monitor.co.ug/uganda/news/national/330-bushenyi-teenagers-impregnated-in-3-months–4276330.

Whitehead, A., Vivian, J., Lockwood, M., & Kasente, D. (2000). Gender and the expansion of non-traditional agricultural exports in Uganda. UNRISD Occasional Paper no. 12. www.econstor.eu/bitstream/10419/148818/1/863101526.pdf

Photo: Hilde Mjøs

CHAPTER 19

Former Refugee Youth in Rural Northern Norway

Stories as Knowledge Development for Social Work in Refugee Services

Vår Mathisen and Rita Sørly

This chapter is based on a qualitative study on former refugee youth experiences when entering a new country, and their everyday life in rural areas of Northern Norway. We have interviewed twelve young people with refugee experiences, asking them about family, school, friends, and hobbies. What was challenging when entering their new home place, and do they wish something was different? What do they miss, and what do they appreciate?

We present excerpts from the interviews, that are everyday stories from the life in their new country. Stories from people with former refugee experiences are often dominated by loss, trauma, and grief. These stories are stories of a better and safer everyday life, possibilities for free education, and a future without threats of war and violence. Stories of hope and stories that acknowledge that these young people's narratives and experiences not only have a place in the communities where they live; stories are also important for knowledge development for social work in refugee services. We have so much to learn from these stories.

Introduction

> I was so happy when they said I was coming to Norway. Because every day I just said: ok, I don't want to be here, because it's so difficult here. I can't go to school and must help so much at home and such... But here I am now... I'm so glad they told us we could go to Norway. I knew that I would get the chance to go to school and do things I need to do, so I can achieve my future dreams.

This is an excerpt from Ameena's story. She was, at the time of the interview, seventeen years old. She is from the Congo, and she arrived in Norway after many years in a refugee camp in Uganda.

After several decades of immigration, Norway has become a pluralistic and more multicultural society. There are several reasons why people come to the country. Seeking education and work is the main reason (Ødegård & Andersen, 2021). Another central reason is flight from war and conflict (Hammar & Tamas, 2021). 82.4 million people worldwide fled war and conflict in 2021 (Norwegian Refugee Council, 2022). This is the highest recorded number of people in flight, ever (ibid.). Those who flee dream of creating something new and different in safe surroundings. Among these, many are adolescents.

A characteristic of flight is that it creates rupture. Not least in relationships. Some flee, but often more people stay. While in flight, most are exposed to stress, both before and during the flight. Many refugees have one or both parents, other family, and/or siblings with them (Kumar & Diaz, 2019). We also know that there are more young people who flee alone (Brook & Ottemöller, 2020; Moe & Ytterhus, 2022). Half of the refugees in 2022 were children and young people under the age of eighteen, and we know that many fled under very dramatic circumstances that have caused traumatic stress. They might have experienced family, friends, and/or neighbours being injured and/or killed (Bauman, Soerens & Smeir, 2016; Richter, Lye, & Proulx, 2018). In refugee camps, there is often a lack of clean water and proper food. Also, the school or education possibilities are poor (Yoshikawa, Wuermli, & Aber, 2019). For many, everyday life is characterized by fear of assault and mistreatment (Norwegian Refugee Council, 2022). This is an extremely complex, unpredictable, and often dangerous situation to live in (Norwegian Refugee Council, 2022; Suárez-Orozco et al., 2018). In this life situation, young people tell the Norwegian Refugee Council that "we want the same things as most young people. We want to be with friends and family, go to school, fall in love, and do leisure activities. We want opportunities and education, and to be part of something" (Høvring, 2018, p.1).

Adolescence is characterized by changes and transitions, often between extremes of emotion. Changes and transitions are linked to puberty and associated hormones. Development takes place in many areas, cognitively, physically, emotionally, and socially. Traditionally, adolescence is referred to as a period of exploration: *Who am I? What do I want with my life? Who do I want to become?* Figuring out these great and important questions requires processes of exploration. The exploration often take place in companionship with friends. Many young people recognize friendship as linked to activities that are done together and are experienced as significant. Youth also recognize that what for a period was exciting, motivating, and identity-creating can change quickly. For a while football or the band was exciting, until it was replaced with gaming, girlfriends, or maybe outdoor life? Many young people apply to upper secondary schools specializing in what (currently) suits their future dream of becoming a hairdresser, carpenter, musician, or electrician.

In adolescence, friends are of great importance, and parents and family matter less. At the same time, it is a period when young people need to practise practical skills precisely to eventually separate themselves from their parents. Learning and development of autonomy and independence, forming close relationships with friends and perhaps lovers, washing your own clothes, practising cooking, making good choices, acquiring new roles and routines – these require good conditions in a safe environment that you are familiar with (Vroman, 2020). All young people have these needs, wherever they come from, and wherever they live.

Research shows that young people who flee are both a particularly vulnerable group, and a group with many resources (Svendsen et al., 2018), who often adapt to a new place and new culture more easily than adults (ibid.). Eide et al. (2020) show, for example, that unaccompanied refugee minors have great ambitions for the future.

Increased migration naturally leads us as researchers to examine young people's experiences of coming to Norway, in new social, cultural, and material contexts. Research on refugee youths' experiences in Norway has particularly focused on coming as a refugee to big cities and/or multicultural neighbourhoods, in Oslo and the eastern region (Eide et al., 2020; Engebretsen & Fuglerud, 2007). Much of the Norwegian migration research has dealt with marginalization and crime (Jakobsen et al., 2017; Lid et al., 2022). These research results and statistics have been picked up by the newspapers and other media and have led to negative comments about immigrant/refugee youth.

To a very small extent, research has focused on refugees coming to rural areas and small towns (Pérez et al., 2021), not least to Northern Norway. Mathisen and Cele (2020) highlight how former refugee youth actively work to find belonging in the new place in Northern Norway, and in that respect, place, space, and time play an important role. Søholt, Stenbacka, and Nørgaard (2018) point out that rural areas and small towns can be of importance in relation to resilience, since refugees are considered valuable in small places in relation to the local economy and population growth.

In this study, we have interviewed young former refugees who live in rural areas in Northern Norway. This study aims to contribute knowledge regarding stories from young former refugees about important aspects of their lives. How did they experience coming to Northern Norway, and how is their everyday life today?

The structure of the chapter is as follows: First, we describe the study context. We present the methods used, including participants, recruitment, the interviews, and ethical reflections. We describe the narrative approach, with a focus on storytelling, everyday life, and mattering, inspired by Prilleltensky (2020). Next, we do a thematic analysis (Sørly, Mathisen, & Kvernmo, 2021). The results indicate how mattering is related to meaning-making processes of everyday life in a new community. We present excerpts from the participant stories before discussing the results. In the end, we offer some reflections on social work practice.

The Study Context

The former refugee youth we interviewed live in rural areas in the Arctic part of Northern Norway. The region measures in area one third of Norway and has 9.1 per cent of the population. The area is characterized by long distances and very scattered settlements. The Norwegian settlement plan for refugees has been described as centred around adults (Archambault 2011; Mathisen & Cele, 2020). Municipalities are obliged to provide adult refugees with an obligatory Introduction programme, but it is up to each municipality to decide whether, and how, to arrange activities or language training for each child or youth in the community. The responsibility is very often handled by schools (Mathisen & Cele, 2020).

Arctic referers to the region above the Arctic Circle. It is an area that can be extremely cold and snowy. During the winter there are long periods of darkness, and in summertime there are long periods of light. The seasons and the climatic conditions are full of contrasts. The participants in the study talked about the cold weather, snow, and darkness. When we asked what it was like to arrive in Northern Norway, Bashir (seventeen-year-old boy from Syria) said:

> Oh, I'll never forget that. A few hours before I arrived, I was on Google Maps and searched. Ouch. It was far north. Then suddenly we came to Norway, oh God! It was snowing here! And then OK, I must continue, I can't say I want to go back, no, it won't work. I came to a better life. So OK, it's snowing, it's cold. Sometimes you forget what the sun looks like. But you must try it. After two years, it is completely normal for me not seeing the sun for two months.

Methods

A qualitative research approach makes it possible to be close to what is to be investigated. The proximity makes qualitative research exciting and

Table 2

Municipality 1	Municipality 2	Municipality 3
Sana, 19 years old. From Syria, Kurdistan. Had lived for several years in a refugee camp in Turkey.	Marla, 17 years old. From Eritrea	Sacha, 17 years old. From Syria. Had lived for many years in a refugee camp in Lebanon.
Bashir, 17 years old. From Syria. Had lived for several years in a refugee camp in Lebanon.	Kenji, 17 years old. From the Congo. Had lived for several years in a refugee camp in Uganda.	Selda, 17 years old. From Syria. Had lived for many years in a refugee camp in Lebanon.
Ameena, 17 years old. From the Congo. Had lived for several years in a refugee camp in Uganda.	Kanika, 19 years old. From the Congo. Had lived for many years in a refugee camp in Uganda.	Sibel, 16 years old. From Syria. Had lived for many years in a refugee camp in Turkey.
Leon, 17 years old. From Somalia.	Amne, 18 years old. From Syria, Kurdistan. Had lived for many years in a refugee camp in Lebanon.	Aram, 19 years old. From Syria. Had lived for several years in a refugee camp in Turkey.

intense, and as researchers we must be prepared to adjust and adapt along the way, since there is a complex relationship between topic, method, and data collection.

Participants

We conducted twelve personal interviews with adolescents who have former refugee experience, from three different, small municipalities in the north. At the time of the interviews, all the participants lived with their families in small municipalities in rural Northern Norway. Some had lived longer in Norway (up to six years), others only a year. The participants were between sixteen and nineteen years old, four boys and eight girls. They had fled from the Middle East and Africa. We have created an overview (see Table 2). All the participants have been given fictitious names.

Recruitment

The participants were recruited by social workers[1] from the refugee services in the representative municipalities, who knew their parents and/or

[1] The social workers in the municipalities are educated as social workers, nurses, and teachers. 'Social worker' is a common occupational title in Norwegian refugee services.

the young people. The social workers provided oral and written information about the study. When we met the young people, we went through a consent form for participation. All were informed that they could withdraw from the study whenever they wanted, without having to give any reason for doing so.

The Interviews

We started the interviews by introducing ourselves, talking about our own home place, our families, and hobbies. The participants introduced themselves with the same information. Further, a thematic interview guide was used. The questions were linked to being young and in flight and coming to a small municipality in a new country, in an Arctic area. We asked them about their everyday life, family, school, friends, and leisure activities. What did they miss and what did they appreciate, coming to Norway? What was challenging when entering their new home and what did they wish was different? We also asked questions about what is important for people in the municipalities to be aware of when families and young people arrive? What can make a difference at arrival, during the establishment and the integration process?

All the interviews were conducted as physical meetings, and the young people helped decide the places of the interviews. Ten interviews were conducted in the premises of the refugee service in the municipalities. A pair of siblings wanted to be interviewed at home, with their mother present. An interpreter was present during one interview. Otherwise, all interviews were conducted in Norwegian. In some interviews, all parties used some English terms to ensure that we had a common understanding of questions asked or answers given. Gesticulation and body language, as well as clear and slow speech, were also key tools in the dialogue. The interviews lasted from thirty minutes to an hour. They were recorded digitally, and the audio files were transcribed verbatim.

Ethical Reflections

The youth study was approved by the Norwegian Centre for Research Data in 2021. The young people we interviewed all received information about the study and had given their written consent to participation. Asking young people with a former refugee background to talk about their experiences of being in flight and coming to a new place can be understood as both challenging and risky. We strove to be open, flexible, welcoming, and curious about what for us was a new research field. During the interviews, we acquired a lot of information and impressions. As trained therapists, we have extensive clinical experience of talking to people in crisis. At the same time, we want to project storytelling as an opportunity for personal growth in study participants (De Haene, Grietens, & Verschueren, 2010). During the interviews, we endeavoured to promote security and autonomy among the young people. It was important to support the young people, especially when they talked about issues that were obviously difficult and painful for them. In line with De Haene, Grietens, & Verschueren (2010) we were prepared and willing to share pain, and we sought a balance between emotional support and search for resources in the dialogues. We exercised ethical reflexivity (Guillemin & Heggen, 2009). It was important for us that the young participants should not be subjected to additional burdens by meeting us.

Storytelling, Everyday Life, and Mattering as Theoretical Framework

The study has a narrative approach. As humans, we give meaning to our own lives through storytelling, and in that way our past, present, and future are fitted into a coherent whole. Which stories we choose to tell is related to the social context in which they are told, and which audience is present. We negotiate meanings of stories to adapt and innovate our identity under changing social and historical conditions (Langellier & Peterson, 2004). Understanding how the stories we tell relate to social contexts requires an understanding of what those contexts do with words. The social consequences of stories must be understood in relation to what is at stake in the everyday storytelling context (Gubrium, 2005; Klausen et al., 2017; Sørly, Mathisen, & Kvernmo, 2021). Researchers have often focused on the narrative restoration of meaning as a central mode of post-trauma reparation (De Haene et al., 2018), but there are also other stories that need to be heard (Olguin & Sanders-Smith, 2021).

In this study, the context was framed within a research project focusing on everyday life for former refugee youth. Our theoretical approach draws attention towards understanding, valuing, and emphasizing storytelling and everyday life in a new life situation, in a changing social and historical condition for our participants. Everyday life is where each individual lives. An everyday perspective is based on human interaction, experience, imagination, and tries to understand the social and cultural contexts that form the framework around people's lives (Arntzen & Gramstad, 2017).

We create everyday life in an ongoing process, and everyday life has a vital function when it comes to learning, change, and development (ibid.).

Closely related to the creation of our everyday life, is the concept of mattering. Prilleltensky (2020, p.17) writes that mattering, being of importance, is a psychological need, a result of values, and the subject of political dispute. Mattering consists of *feeling valued and adding value.* It can also be linked to telling. The life that unfolds in the narrative can be experienced and understood as a continuation of a desired and/or determined narrative. For that reason, people strive in everyday life, through daily activities, to continue history in a way that they themselves perceive as significant, satisfying, and achievable. Tensions in history that are expressed in 'plots' are often linked to important questions in people's lives, such as meaning (Mattingly, 1998). Such an existential understanding of meaning is, according to Mattingly (2010), often expressed as hope or longing, and forms motivational forces that link individuals to an overall meaning in life.

Analysis

In our thematic analysis we aimed to focus on *what* was said rather than *how* the words were spoken. We performed an experience-oriented inquiry (Sørly, Mathisen, & Kvernmo, 2021). We started with a single interview at a time, isolating and ordering the episodes into different themes. There were several themes intertwining with the meaning-making process of everyday life in a new community. After completing this process with all interviews, we sharpened our focus and attempted to identify themes related to mattering as (1) feeling valued in the community and (2) adding value to the community. The personal stories of our participants and their experiences provided the basis for determining the themes (ibid.). The themes belonging to feeling valued are connected to *being welcomed by the community* and *being seen by teachers at school.* The other themes, belonging to adding values, are connected to *continuing to be a care provider in the family* and *becoming involved in local relations.*

Table 3

(1) Feeling valued	(2) Adding value
(a) Being welcomed by the community	(a) Continuing to be a care provider in the family
(b) Being seen by teachers at school	(b) Becoming involved in local relations

In the following section, we present some excerpts, followed by interpretations, and our own impression of the storytelling dialogue with our participants.

(1) Feeling Valued

People have a desire to belong to a group, and to feel valued by others, such as friends and family. When we feel valued, we feel respected and recognized (Prilleltensky, 2020). In the following we will present two themes that relate to the youths feeling valued in their new municipality.

(a) Being Welcomed by the Community

All the participants said that they had felt very welcomed when they arrived in their new municipality. We asked was important when they came to Norway.

Sana (nineteen-year-old Kurdish girl from Syria) said: "Someone waited for us and gave us a house we could call home. Imagine, we came to a house. A house of our own! A separate room! A bedroom just for me. I loved it! And people were ready to help us with practical things like requisitions and money, and they showed us where to shop for food."

Marla (seventeen-year-old girl from Eritrea) said: "What I remember best, is that we got toys when we arrived."

Sacha (seventeen-year-old girl from Syria) told us that she and her family were greeted with "Welcome to us. Here is your room, and there is a shop where you can buy food."

Getting practical help is mentioned by the participants as central after arriving in a foreign place. The feeling of having an available refugee service, both practically and emotionally, was considered as very important in all the interviews. The participants talked about having a friendly face to relate to, and a place to go to if needed.

Marla (seventeen-year-old girl from Eritrea) continued her story:

> It was very important that we were allowed to continue with activities while the adults talked together at the refugee services. We were several children and Norwegian adults who, among other things, drew and played board games together. It was the [local] adults who took responsibility for connecting children together, and initiated things we could do. It felt safe and good. For many, this was the start of a lasting relationship.

Both before and after the interviews, we saw the social workers of the refugee services meet the young people and give them a good hug or a friendly pat on the back. They asked how the young people were doing and asked them to send regards to their parents.

The participants also said that it was significant that they had received information about Norway, for example about the Norwegians' folk spirit. As Sana said, "Norwegians can be somewhat reserved, but decent nonetheless."

Ameena (seventeen-year-old from the Congo) said it was useful that the Norwegian Directorate of Immigration (UDI) called and gave information about what Norway is like, what the culture is like, how people in Norway speak and relate to each other. This is what she emphasized:

> they [UDI] said that Norway is a nice country, you get everything you need and go to school and become whatever you want. It's free to go to school, you don't have to pay. Afterwards, when you finish school, you get a job. And then they said that Norwegian people like to help, but they are reserved. So, you must be in a team with Norwegians so that they get to know you. And then you get to know the culture over time.

In summary, the stories from the participations can be understood as stories about the importance of getting practical and emotional help at arrival to a new home place. That made them feel wanted and valued as new members of the community.

(b) Being Seen by Teachers at School

All the participants emphasized school as an important arena when arriving in the new country.

Kanika (nineteen-year-old girl from the Congo) wanted to go straight to school after arriving in Norway. She said: "I was 'super ready' and very motivated, and fortunately after two weeks in Northern Norway I started. And it went well. First, we went and saw what the school looked like. They showed us the class, and we got to greet the others, then we went back after two days, to school."

She experienced school as a great privilege in Norway, and an important stepping-stone for the rest of her life since she was planning to become a nurse. It was her dream. Going to school has changed her as a person:

> Because when I was in Uganda, I had a challenge . . . when teacher asked a question . . . I could have an answer but was afraid that the answer was wrong. So, it was a little bit difficult for me when the teacher asked questions. I just kept silent even if I knew the answer. So, when the person next to me gave the answer, I say "Oh . . . it was correct." So somehow that was my challenge for a long time since childhood. But now I have a teacher who can help me. Whenever they ask questions, I'll be the first to answer, and if they ask if I have a question . . . then I can ask for help.

Aram (nineteen-year-old boy from Syria) talked about the importance of having teachers whom you can grow to like, and trust. He said: "I have good and kind teachers who constantly say that I must ask for help if I need it. And if I don't ask for help, they will get in touch. They don't give up. They keep going until I understand. But it's nice."

Ameena (seventeen-year-old from the Congo) started immediately in a Norwegian class. After some difficulties in the start, things had started to improve. At the time of the interview, she had a dream of becoming a psychologist. When she experienced getting a grade 1 in the subject, she was shocked. "*Not passed!*" Then she went straight to her teacher. She told about what happened next:

> I am very happy with this teacher. He is my favorite teacher. The shock of failing the test freaked me out. Then my teacher said we should do an experiment. We looked at the text I had written, and it was not very creative (I think creative in this case means the use of technical terms) but written in such an everyday language. Then the teacher started asking me about what I had written, then he asked questions from the psychology book. Then he said: "Wow, you can do an incredible amount! Better than the Norwegian students. But you failed because you have challenges expressing yourself in writing."

In summary, the stories from the participants can be understood as stories about experiences of being recognized, included, and respected by those around them, which made them feel valued as members of the community.

(2) Adding Value

A value is a principle that guides us towards desirable and morally justifiable outcomes (Prilleltensky, 2020, p.25). Human beings can add value to self, others, work, and community. In the following we will present two themes that relate to the youths adding value in their everyday life and to their new municipality.

(a) Continuing to Be a Care Provider in the Family

The time from arrival in Norway to the family finding themselves in a completely new life is very short. Often it only takes days or weeks before the whole family must establish new routines. From being a family with different tasks, it is school and learning the language that becomes the new priority. It demands a lot from adolescents.

Sana (nineteen-year-old from Syria) told us:

> So when we got home, everyone was tired. No one had energy. All six of us [in the family] didn't understand what happened at school. It was very difficult.

> [. . .] We were all hungry and just looking at each other. "Who will cook?" I just said, "I have homework." Mom said," I also have homework," and dad said, "I also have homework." So, we just had to eat slices of bread with cheese.

Most part of the participants told us that after dinner they had to help younger siblings with homework, then their parents. After that, they could do their own homework. "The first period was crazy," said Sana. "It was stressful, because we didn't know anyone here. But our neighbours were very kind."

In addition, the participants had many care tasks in the home, to make the home go round. Picking up siblings from daycare, cooking, looking after parents who need help with their health challenges. Several of the participants said they were tired, but after all, they did well.

We asked Ameena (seventeen-year-old girl from the Congo) if she had to help her mother a lot with her younger siblings. She told us: "Yes, we help each other. If any problems happen, I will come and help [her mother]. You know, they are adolescents, so you must talk to them [her younger siblings]. Maybe they don't listen to mum, but if you come and play with them and say things are like this and like that – then 'Yes!'

The care tasks were explained within a cultural frame; the youths' parents expected them to be carried out. Many of the tasks had become a natural part of everyday life after many years in refugee camps where everyone had to help to look after each other and earn money. After arrival in Norway, the young people have been assigned new tasks on top of the original ones since the parents have to spend a lot of time on schoolwork. Helping was explained as adding value to the family.

(b) Becoming Involved in Local Relations

All the participants in our study wanted to meet peers. It wasn't easy when they arrived in a new community.

Aram (nineteen-year-old boy from Syria) told us how he came in contact with Norwegian peers:

> you have to know someone you can talk to. Getting to know people of the same age is easy and difficult at the same time. Norwegian boys, they never come up to me to tell me their name. So, I'm the one who must go up to them and tell them my name, that I'm nineteen years old and so on. And I got to know someone. When I walk down the street and they see me, they smile and say hello. But Norwegians are perhaps a bit shy. . .?

Norwegians are perceived as a bit reserved and shy. The fact that young people, both Norwegian and the participants, do not speak the same language complicates the process of getting to know each other.

Sibel (sixteen-year-old girl from Syria) said: "to be integrated, you must learn the language. And that requires a lot from you, as it involves daring to jump without a parachute." She explains the "jump" as demanding and sometimes scary, "as it involves saying a lot of wrong things, in a new mother tongue, hearing others laugh at you, and at the same time not giving up."

To get to know each other, the young people highlight the benefits of doing activities together. During the interviews, we were told about many activities that the young people do in their spare time, often together with siblings. They play volleyball, PlayStation, watch films, dance, play the violin, shop, watch movies, and not least 'hang out' on Facebook and other social media. Doing an activity makes it less difficult to get to know Norwegian young people, several said.

In summary, the stories from the participants can be understood as stories about doing activities that add value in everyday life. Having friends is important to feeling valued.

Discussion of the Results

Waiting to be told whether you will receive help and a residence permit in a new country can be an exhausting process (Schein et al., 2019; Robleda, 2020; Haj-Younes et al., 2022). The relief of getting a positive decision is explained as enormous. Getting a good start in your new life is important. Mattering, the experience that you are valued and that you can add value, is relatable across geographical and cultural boundaries (Prilleltensky, 2020). The stories of the participants in our study confirm this. In what follows, we discuss what promotes experiences of (1) feeling valued and (2) adding value, with a focus on social work practice. At the end of the chapter, we briefly reflect on issues in relation to the balance between these two.

What Promotes Experiences of Feeling Valued?

Practical things were ready for the refugee families upon arrival in the municipality in the rural Arctic. The receiving municipalities in the study had good routines for welcoming families. The youths in our study highlighted that they received toys as particularly significant. It was also told through their body language and their voices when they described this. It was as if they imagined how the professionals had carefully made up the bed and put the teddy bear by the headboard. What these stories tell us is that this gave children and young people experiences of feeling valued, respected, and included. Being seen as children was a contribution to making them feel valued.

The stories are important reminders that what is often considered trivial can have great significance. 'Here is your room' reflects the imperatives in social work; you are met and seen as a unique person. Sana emphasized the importance of having "A separate room! A bedroom just for me." A private and undisturbed place can give young people more opportunities for the development of autonomy and independence. Having a place where they can receive visitors and talk undisturbed on social media, matters (Vroman, 2020). That somebody saw the youths' needs, after they had been sharing a room with parents and siblings for many years, was clearly appreciated.

Just as belonging is a powerful tonic for well-being, exclusion is toxic for health, says Prilleltensky (2020, p.18). Being prepared for the Norwegian folk mood was explained as essential. Possible explanations for rejections are important when one longs for contact with peers and struggles to make it happen. When it comes to the development of self-efficacy (Banduras, 1997), the participants particularly spoke of the teacher's role. For the participants in our study, the teachers were everyday heroes, supporters, cheerleaders, and enablers with their display of creativity and willingness. Going to school is a key resilience factor for refugees, not least since this is where they meet peers (Lauritzen & Sivertsen, 2012; Mathisen & Cele, 2020).

The gesture of toys, and information that 'It's not you that's the problem, if your peers don't make contact' are important contributions to coping with everyday life. If the families and young people are helped to free their resources, they will be in a better position to deal with their own life situation. This is also the core of social work.

What Promotes Experiences of Adding Value?

All the participants talked about their caring duties in the family. The stories were not answers to specific questions from us about tasks, but a rendering of what they themselves experienced as significant and satisfying in everyday life (Mattingly, 1998). Ameena was one of several who shared stories about cooking and picking up and bringing younger siblings to kindergarten. As a follow-up question, we asked if she had to help her mother a lot, to which she replied: "We help each other." We are sure that helping in the family was felt to be important to her.

Norway is (like many other Western countries) characterized by more individualistic values such as autonomy and self-reliance. In countries with more collectivist-oriented values, it is probably more common to take more responsibility in the family as a child or youth. For young people like Ameena to experience that she adds value to others (and thus herself), social workers must be aware of *their* own values and perspectives, so that they do not stand in the way of the family's practice of their own routines and values (Hammell, 2013).

Another key aspect of adding value was making friends. The participants described getting to know peers as challenging. Everyone highlighted doing things together as important for getting to know each other. According to Wilcock (1999), it is through participation in activities that we create and maintain our belonging to society. Especially people who have experienced crises have a need for meaning, purpose, and choice following life disruptions (Hammell, 2013). By helping refugee youths to form friendships and thus effect social change, the social workers at the refugee services made it possible for liberation, development, social cohesion, and empowerment of the young people to take place.

Reflections on Social Work Practice

In this chapter, we have shared stories from young people's everyday lives. We have talked with twelve former refugee youths who have fled from the Middle East and Africa. Our participants had many care tasks and a lot of homework. At the same time, they are expending energy to get to know their peers. Humans have a limited capacity to handle everything and everyone, Prilleltensky (2020) reminds us. At the same time, it is important to be aware of what is important and right for each young person. This can be situation-dependent and change over time. The need for unity and cooperation is fundamentally important to all of us.

Our participants told us what has contributed to the fact that they experience having a good and safe everyday life today. In addition to feeling valued, being welcomed by the community and being seen by teachers at school are of great importance. The possibility of continuing to be a care provider in the family and becoming involved in local relations are of significance when it comes to adding value. The stories give us knowledge about the connection between being aware and accessible and the release of 'social capital'. The things close to us are more important than we remember in everyday life. The stories are therefore important for knowledge development for social work in the refugee services, and in other arenas.

Reflective Questions

1. In this story the researchers understand mattering as a core value in social work. How can mattering be practised and expressed in social work research?
2. What issues of feeling valued and giving value arise from this story?
3. How could the stories of the participants be presented to social work students in an educational setting?

REFERENCES

Archambault, J. (2011). Refugee children, citizenship and 'the best interests' of the child: Experiencing settlement as new citizens in Norway. PhD thesis, Norwegian University of Science and Technology.

Arntzen, C., & Gramstad, A. (2017). Aktivitet i hverdagsperspektiv. In H. K. Kristensen, A. S. B. Schou, & J. L. Mærsk (eds.), *Nordisk aktivitetsvidenskab*, pp.171–92. Copenhagen: Munksgaard.

Banduras, A. (1997). *Self-Efficacy: The Exercise of Control.* New York: Freeman.

Bauman, S., Soerens, M., & Smeir, I. (2016). *Seeking Refuge: On the Shores of the Global Refugee Crisis.* Chicago, IL: Moody Publishers.

Brook, M. I., & Ottemöller, F. G. (2020). A new life in Norway: The adaptation experiences of unaccompanied refugee minor girls. *Children and Youth Services Review, 117*, 105287.

De Haene, L., Grietens, H., & Verschueren, K. (2010). Holding harm: Narrative methods in mental health research on refugee trauma. *Qualitative Health Research, 20*(12), 1664–76.

De Haene, L., Rousseau, C., Kevers, R., Deruddere, N., & Rober, P. (2018). Stories of trauma in family therapy with refugees: Supporting safe relational spaces of narration and silence. *Clinical Child Psychology and Psychiatry, 23*(2), 258–78.

Eide, K., Lidén, H., Haugland, B., Fladstad, T., & Hauge, H. A. (2020). Trajectories of ambivalence and trust: Experiences of unaccompanied refugee minors resettling in Norway. *European Journal of Social Work, 23*(4), 554–65.

Engebretsen, A., & Fuglerud, Ø. (2007). *Ungdom i flyktningfamilier: Familie og vennskap – trygghet og frihet?* NOVA Rapport 3/2007. https://oda.oslomet.no/oda-xmlui/bitstream/handle/20.500.12199/4943/2558_1.pdf?sequence=1&isAllowed=y

Gubrium, J. F. (2005). Introduction: Narrative environments and social problems. *Social Problems, 52*(4), 525–8.

Guillemin, M., & Heggen, K. (2009). Rapport and respect: Negotiating ethical relations between researcher and participant. *Medicine, Health Care and Philosophy, 12*, 291–9.

Haj-Younes, J., Abildsnes, E., Kumar, B., & Diaz, E. (2022). The road to equitable healthcare: A conceptual model developed from a qualitative study of Syrian refugees in Norway. *Social Science & Medicine*, *292*, 114540.

Hammar, T., & Tamas, K. (2021). Why do people go or stay? In T. Hammar, G. Brochmann, K. Tamas, & T. Faist (eds.), *International Migration, Immobility and Development: Multidisciplinary Perspectives*, pp.1–19. New York and London: Routledge.

Hammell, K. R. W. (2013). Client-centred practice in occupational therapy: Critical reflections. *Scandinavian Journal of Occupational Therapy*, *20*(3), 174–81.

Høvring, R. (2018). 10 ting ungdom på flukt sliter med. Norwegian Refugee Council. www.flyktninghjelpen.no/nyheter/2018/august/10-ting-ungdom-pa-flukt-sliter-med (accessed 2 February 2024).

Jakobsen, M., DeMott, M. A. M., Wentzel-Larsen, T., & Heir, T. (2017). The impact of the asylum process on mental health: A longitudinal study of unaccompanied refugee minors in Norway. *BMJ Open*, *7*(6), e015157.

Klausen, R. K., Karlsson, M., Haugsgjerd S., & Lorem, G. F. (2017) Narrative performances of user involvement among service users in mental health care. *Narrative Inquiry*, *27*(1), 149–68.

Kumar, B. N., & Diaz, E. (2019). Migration and migrants: What we know about worldwide mobility and why it matters. In Kumar & Diaz (eds.), *Migrant Health: A Primary Care Perspective*, 1–14. Boca Raton, FL: CRC Press.

Langellier, K., and Peterson, E. (2004). *Storytelling in Daily Life: Performing Narrative*. Philadelphia, PA: Temple University Press.

Lauritzen, C., & Sivertsen, H. (2012). Children and families seeking asylum in Northern Norway: Living conditions and mental health. *International Migration*, *50*(6), 195–210.

Lid, S., Rosten, M. G., Dullum, J. V., Hyggen, C., & Andersen, P. L. 2022. *Forebyggende tiltak mot Ungdomskriminalitet i Oslo kommune. Følgeforskning og evaluering*. NOVA OsloMet, NOVA Rapport 8/2022.

Mathisen, T., & Cele, S. (2020). "Doing belonging": Young former refugees and their active engagement with Norwegian local communities. *Fennia*, *198*(1–2), 39–56.

Mattingly, C. (1998). In search of the good: Narrative reasoning in clinical practice. *Medical Anthropology Quarterly*, *12*(3), 273–97.

(2010). *The Paradox of Hope: Journeys through a Clinical Borderland*. Berkeley, CA: University of California Press.

Moe, G., & Ytterhus, B. (2022). Health and meaning through "doings": A qualitative study with young unaccompanied refugees in Norway. *Social Science & Medicine*, *315*, 115542.

Norwegian Refugee Council. (2022). 117,3 millioner mennesker er på flukt. https://www.flyktninghjelpen.no/flyktningregnskapet (accessed 2 February 2024).

Ødegård, A. M., & Andersen, R. K. (2021). Arbeids-og levekår for bosatte arbeidsinnvandrere fra Polen og Litauen. *Fafo-rapport*, *14*.

Olguín, A. A., & Sanders-Smith, S. C. (2021). Honoring their stories: Exploring the richness of the refugee experience. *Teachers College Record*, *123*(7), 1–28.

Pérez, I. E., Wu, R., Murray, C. B., & Bravo, D. (2021). An interdisciplinary framework examining culture and adaptation in migrant children and adolescents. *New Directions for Child and Adolescent Development*, *2021*(176), 13–39.

Prilleltensky, I. (2020). Mattering at the intersection of psychology, philosophy, and politics. *American Journal of Community Psychology*, *65*(1–2), 16–34.

Richter, L. M., Lye, S. J., & Proulx, K. (2018). Nurturing care for young children under conditions of fragility and conflict. *New Directions for Child and Adolescent Development*, *2018*(159), 13–26.

Robleda, Z. W. (2020). Re-inventing everyday life in the asylum centre: Everyday tactics among women seeking asylum in Norway. *Nordic Journal of Migration Research*, *10*(2), https://journal-njmr.org/articles/10.33134/njmr.251.

Schein, Y. L., Winje, B. A., Myhre, S. L., Nordstoga, I., & Straiton, M. L. (2019). A qualitative study of health experiences of Ethiopian asylum seekers in Norway. *BMC Health Services Research*, *19*, 1–12.

Søholt, S., Stenbacka, S., & Nørgaard, H. (2018). Conditioned receptiveness: Nordic rural elite perceptions of immigrant contributions to local resilience. *Journal of Rural Studies*, *64*, 220–9.

Sørly, R., Mathisen, V., & Kvernmo, S. (2021). "We belong to nature": Communicating mental health in an indigenous context. *Qualitative Social Work*, *20*(5), 1280–96.

Suárez-Orozco, C., Motti-Stefanidi, F., Marks, A., & Katsiaficas, D. (2018). An integrative risk and resilience model for understanding the adaptation of immigrant-origin children and youth. *American Psychologist*, *73*(6), 781–96.

Svendsen, S., Berg, B., Paulsen, V., Garvik, M., & Valenta, M. (2018). *Kunnskapsoppsummering om enslige mindreårige asylsøkere og flyktninger.* Trondheim: NTNU Samfunnsforskning, Mangfold og Inkludering.

Vroman, K. G. (2020). Adolescent development: Being an adolescent, becoming an adult. In J. W. Solomon & J. C. O'Brien (eds.), *Pediatric Skills for Occupational Therapy Assistants*. Amsterdam: Elsevier.

Wilcock, A. A. (1999). Reflections on doing, being and becoming. *Australian Occupational Therapy Journal*, *46*(1), 1–11.

Yoshikawa, H., Wuermli, A. J., & Aber, J. L. (2019). Mitigating the impact of forced displacement and refugee and unauthorized status on youth: Integrating developmental processes with intervention research. In M. M. Suárez-Orozco (ed.), *Humanitarianism and Mass Migration: Confronting the World Crisis*, pp.186–206. Berkeley, CA: University of California Press.

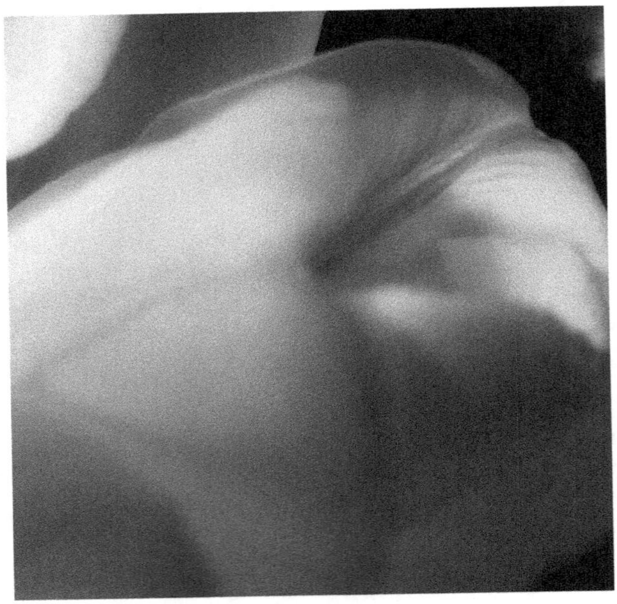

Photo: Hilde Mjøs

CHAPTER 20

Social Work

More than Just a Profession?

Pauline Camilleri

This is my story of becoming and being a social worker in Gozo, a little island outside Malta.

Being a social worker is no joke. I believe that working towards the ethos of this vocation necessitates a high level of commitment, resilience, and passion for this dynamic job. Social work requires deep involvement at all levels of intervention. Presence, self-awareness, acceptance, and flexibility are required for the practice. It enables us to be capable and competent to provide the best possible service to our service users while also managing our own mental health. A social worker can be exposed to people who are experiencing social or emotional distress, and resilience can be helpful in many situations. Resilience does not imply the absence of anxiety, fear, or uncertainty. Resilience allows us to face these and other stressful experiences with greater confidence, allowing us to recover more quickly. This fortitude allows us as practitioners to recover from any additional stressors or trauma we may experience in our working life.

Many professionals are drawn to the social work field because they are driven by a desire and passion to assist others and do meaningful work. But we are also driven by a sense of social justice and a desire to address societal inequalities and injustices.

Mental Health Social Worker

I started off as a welfare officer since at that time this was a new profession in Malta. I was upgraded to a social support worker until finally I got warranted as a social worker. Working in the generic social work field for a full fourteen years has been a meaningful experience. I encountered endless challenges, including stories of domestic violence which at that time was considered a harrowing taboo in Malta. Thereafter I was requested to relocate to mental health services social work which at that time was also non-existent in the hospital. Transitioning from generic to mental health social work was not easy; the change in environment, colleagues, work demands, and case typology was challenging enough. Giving your full support and care to people who are struggling with mental health and enabling them to achieve better outcomes further increased my determination. I went a long way. I wouldn't change it for any other job. Mental health social work became an important part of my life.

Stigma

One of the most difficult challenges that a social worker working on the small island of Gozo faces is the stigma associated with mental illness. Because of the stigma associated with mental illness, many people in Gozo who are diagnosed with mental health issues are hesitant to seek help. It was only twelve years ago, and for this sole reason, that a group of mental health professionals founded the Association for Mental Health, primarily to combat the existing stigma. Since its inception, the Association has never stopped campaigning and advocating for stigma alleviation by raising awareness about mental health issues and educating people on the importance of seeking help. Significant progress has been made over the years, and more people are coming forward to seek help. Can we stop dreaming or be content with achieving our goals? Never. When we stop dreaming, we halt. Dreaming keeps you alive. It keeps you motivated to attain more.

Self-Care

As social workers we have our meltdowns, distresses, and burnouts. Our profession is often so focused on others that we tend to lose sight of ourselves. We tend to get into the mindset that, as social workers, we must give all that it takes to our jobs, to the exclusion of taking care of ourselves, and sometimes with a detrimental effect on our loved ones.

Self-care is regarded as an essential professional practice in the field of social work because it lessens stress. It is important for social workers to maintain a work–life balance for our well-being. This can only be attained if mental, emotional, and physical needs are met. It is indispensable for us social workers to schedule self-care activities that help us cope with our daily stress and burnout. A key factor is to detect from an early stage our stress markers as a red flag so as to seek immediate assistance. When we as practitioners lack or are unable to practise self-care, we ought to seek support from our supervisors, colleagues, as well as qualified mental health professionals. This will serve as a safe space for personal reflection and recollection of self to monitor our emotional responses to the demanding nature of our work to increase self-awareness and avoid burnout. Work–life balance is essential.

Social workers have a sincere deep desire to support and assist others. We are motivated by an aspiration to improve the quality of other people's lives. With empathy, we can put ourselves in another person's situation. Social work goes beyond a normal caring profession. To be an effective social worker, one must have the primary main factors that generate a high-standard professional methodology, and which are fundamental to having a deep-rooted desire to work in the sector: high resilience, determination, empathy, and strong interpersonal and listening skills.

The primary mission in the life of a social worker is to strengthen human well-being and ensure that basic and complex needs are being met, with the specific aim of focusing on those who need help. Nevertheless, despite the challenges of always being on the fast track due to the demands such a profession entails, becoming a social worker has been one of the most gratifying, positive, rewarding choices in my life. Responding to the needs of people in need of help through empathy and compassion is fulfilling enough to keep me going, to keep me inspired and motivated relentlessly towards achieving tiny but significant miracles, which mean the world to the people who cross my path. It is so gratifying when we hear from our service users that they appreciate how we helped them through the process and relieved their distress without passing judgement. This gives us the drive to take on the next service users, who are new referrals, and begin a new chapter in the life of the social worker. Their successes serve as a source of tenacity, bravery, and ongoing inspiration.

Social Workers: Are We Superheroes?

As social workers we tend to forget our personal needs or tend to put ourselves second to being loyal to our profession. Social work is a fast-paced and exciting pitch. The practice keeps us in continuous collaboration with individuals, families, and groups to keep the world moving in a positive direction. To help, we liaise and team up with medical teams, law enforcement, schools, social services, non-governmental entities, and other related bodies. We are the sympathetic ears that empathically attend to those in painful situations or suffering as they share issues and confidential matters with us that others are unwilling or unable to hear. Yes, indeed, to our service users we are their superheroes. We are the discerning eyes that value the worth, self-respect, and beauty of the person underneath the surface appearances or behaviours of those who have been stigmatized. And this is despite challenging situations which we as humans encounter throughout our personal journey. And I am no exception. The sudden death of my only son at the time, followed some years later by the sudden death of my only brother, were difficult times, to say the least. Yet, when one emerges from such distressing circumstances, one becomes more empathic towards others and resilience reaches an all-time high.

We are the powerful advocate who advocates and speaks on their behalf, and the empowering defender who shows service users how to advocate for themselves. We are the caring persons who give out unconditional acceptance, concern, and care to those who have been marginalized and have no voice – who feel as if no one cares. We use our knowledge and skills to strengthen relationships, to break generational cycles of trauma and substance abuse, and promote good mental health, resulting in helping families and communities aiming to restore stability.

The Importance of Humour

Usually, workplace laughter is frowned upon and, in my country, not considered appropriate in our profession. Nowadays, this is more accepted by employers, managers, leads, and human resources. The benefits of workplace humour are various and extensive, especially in stressful workplaces like social work environments. Using humour as a tool against distress has positive impacts with ripple effects. Humour alleviates the daily stressors in our work environment because it is beneficial and uplifts our morale. When it comes to building engaged and effective multidiscipline teams, humour brings the team together, because it alleviates stressful situations while increasing resilience and preventing burnout. Using humour appropriately can immediately benefit our service users because it lowers barriers, boosts engagement, and makes collaboration easier.

Having happy employees results in healthier work outcomes. Since morale is directly connected to motivation and enthusiasm, it is in every leader's best interest to promote high morale. Humour enhances communication between employees and can be an icebreaker.

Meeting Jane

I met Jane, a forty-two-year-old lady, on a bitterly wintry day in January after her partner, who was a farmer, chucked her out of their home in the middle of the night because, according to the information gathered, she was not strong enough to see to the daily farm needs and home chores. Without any place to go, and a lack of financial means, Jane was visibly frightened and emotionally distressed. After the crisis intervention took place, an immediate plan of action was drawn up, to guarantee Jane a safe place for the night, while also ensuring that health-wise she was doing fine. An emotional and heart-breaking moment came when Tim, her nine-year-old son, was forced by his father to remain with him. A harrowing emotional moment I recall was when Jane described that the father would brainwash his son from a tender age and that whatever happens to his mother, Tim is to remain with his father. The husband verbally bullied Jane, saying that he will fight for his right to custody.

Jane was provided with general support, either through individualized psychosocial support or full integration into a supportive social network, where her voice could be heard and valued for the first time in years. Slowly yet surely, Jane started regaining her self-esteem, self-respect, and, most importantly, her independence. Over time, and with the full support of the social work system, she was allocated a place of her own where, for the first time in so many years, she was able to live in peace and serenity, without any form of emotional or physical abuse. Now that she was living a decent life, she was determined not to return to her abusive partner. Despite the fact that her family's support was restricted, Jane chose to live within her limitations, and her freedom was regained.

Her life revolved around the wait for the weekend when her son Tim used to visit at home. These moments were the spark of courage that kept her going. With no family support, as they always opposed her toxic past relationship and were not ready to give her the much-needed support, the world revolved around her son!! Whatever she did or whatever she decided from now on was that her son took priority over her own needs. She wished to give him the best quality of life she could during the limited time she had together with him. He was her focal point, her ray of hope. All his needs took priority over hers and she did whatever it took to compensate for the limited quality of life at home, and was determined to engrain in him strong values of respect and honesty towards others.

In view of her mental illness, limited mobility, and age, she was not able to find a steady job. This surely imposed certain financial limitations. I recall when she used to say that it saddened her immensely because she could not shower her son with treats, especially around Christmas time and on his birthdays. The only pampering that she could afford was cooking decent yet not special treats meals that he could take home with him to serve him for the week ahead.

As a social worker, I used to ceaselessly encourage and motivate her to overflow her dear son with unconditional love always . . . After all, unconditional love does not cost a cent! To me, that was by far more important than any material thing that she could purchase for him. Her relationship with her son steadily strengthened over time. She worked on good quality time while she worked with her son on moral principles, honesty, and respect. The fact that her son remained with her ex-husband did not dishearten her from becoming resilient and persistent, so her son will become anything but a copy of his father.

The strength that she acquired was only possible through genuine supportive and reassuring intervention, besides intensive psychotherapy sessions, where the positive outcomes within her led to a positive leap forward in her life. She was living with dignity and respect.

Life at the farm had remained demanding, with the father stubbornly refusing to get additional assistance on the farm. The son had no choice but to look after the livestock and the fields. This has hindered him from further academic achievements. His life revolved around farming and weekend visits to his mother, with non-existent social networks. His mother was aware of this and she was concerned to say the least – she was distraught, worried, and angry, but managed to self-control her emotions and to fill her son with hope and hide from him her frustrations and anger, whilst hoping for better days. She nurtured hope. That was something that her ex-husband could not take from her.

Years went by and her son never missed his weekend visits. He has now become an adult himself and has a full-time job in cleaning while assisting with farming needs.

One fine morning the son took a huge decision. He went knocking on his mother's door, literally asking her if she could take him in. He had had enough of his long-time abusive father and was now begging his mother to let him live with her. He explained to her that all through these years he had tried endlessly to understand his father's ways, and had hoped that his difficult character would change, but to no avail. He also narrated that throughout these years he was forced to lie and minimize certain happenings, and now that he was an adult who could easily leave his father's home, he understood that his father, unfortunately, has manipulated so many people. There was no way for him to return home. Like his mother, he was yearning for freedom from poor quality of life and hardships. The shackles of life were to end.

This case was one of the last that I worked on in the generic social work field. Since then, about nineteen years ago, I have moved on to a very different area in social work. My journey then started in the mental health social work field. I must admit that it was challenging to adapt at first, as working in a clinical environment, with different case dynamics, can be stressful and time-consuming. However, I overcame this challenge. Was it easy to adapt? Of course not, yet with perseverance, determination, and resilience I managed to overcome the fears of change. Now I was dealing not only with social and emotional poverty but also with people who mostly suffer in silence because of mental health challenges, including stigma, shame, and a lack of resources. Now that I have been working in the mental health field for more than nineteen years, my work in this specialized profession has become my passion. Even though it is extremely intense and demanding, small victories are gratifying every day. My service users have given me a lot in return. I have learned so much from them, and it is crucial that you stay highly motivated in your profession and look forward to going to work every day with a positive attitude. My second family can be found within the confines of my workplace. One of the main reasons I have become addicted to my job is the fantastic and effective multidisciplinary team. I am fortunate to say that I have found another family at work, where my co-workers, who are psychiatrists, occupational therapists, psychology nurses, and carers, all have the same goal: to help our service users without prejudice or judgement.

Meeting Adam

Around the time that I started working within mental health social work, I met Adam, a young adult in his early twenties. His family was passing through a critically devastating moment, and this was related to a sudden tragic death of a family member due to a horrific accident. The family was shaken to the core, trapped in a nightmare, and flooded with despair and numbness. Still in the process of grief and denial, still exasperated and trying to heal from this shattering blow.

Adam became quite withdrawn, depressed, and lost interest in life. He was unable to find meaning in life, whereas before this happened, Adam used to find inspiration in creative kite-making and art, painting beautiful drawings that conveyed positivity. I recall him saying, "My mind has gone too dull to create." Adam became a secluded person behind the walls of the home. Rejecting his family's support and the friendship of his closest friends, he sank deeper into a dark tunnel of depression. His life revolved around his psychiatric appointments and home seclusions.

This is where I met Adam as a psychiatric outpatient service user. His family was very concerned about his sudden change in behaviour, and the more they showed their support and compassion, the more he felt lost, isolated, and hostile towards them. His opposition grew and evolved into a containment challenge for his loved ones, something Adam had never experienced or manifested before. His quality of life had significantly deteriorated by this point. He began to miss his psychiatric treatment, which resulted in paranoia towards his loved ones and, at times, verbal and physical aggression. Adam's family was unable to manage him at home, but shame and stigma prevented them from admitting him to the hospital. They were still holding out hope that this would pass.

I met Adam's family. Adam was referred to the hospital's social work services; however, in such critical situations, a social worker must examine not only Adam's critical moments but also the family dynamics as a whole. Adam needed to be admitted to a psychiatric facility as soon as possible to be monitored and treated. Nonetheless, Adam's parents remained hopeful. It was not until I got a call from Adam's mother, who sounded terrified and distraught, that I realized the gravity of the situation. His mother was shattered, distraught, and engulfed by fear. The parents were feeling sad. He was unreachable, as he had switched off his mobile. In less than no time, the police were called for assistance, and after quite a few intensive searches, Adam was found hidden, in the vicinity of the hospital.

The parents had no option left but to admit Adam for psychiatric care, their hope that Adam could be cured in the community and thus sidestep admission having vanished. Devastated as they were and concerned about the consequences of stigma, both were hopeless and helpless.

Adam responded well to the treatment. His admission had a purpose and was not pointless at all. The parents were proved wrong about the preconceptions and stigma behind their dread, because they could see for themselves how Adam was being treated. Adam's psychiatric care revolved around dignity and respect.

As a social worker, during his recovery period I gathered as much essential information about Adam as I could and focused on how skilled, talented, and artistic Adam was. I could visualize this young lad's full potential taking him much farther. Adam was not just a person with a mental condition. He had so much to offer society.

At the time, an ambitious project for a large mosaic mural was in the works at my workplace, a hospital, by a group of community youth mental health service users who attended the psychiatric occupational therapy department on a regular basis. Attendees of this service were either on leave at home or were discharged in the community. This project, which was an innovative venture for our service users, was a huge challenge in and of itself, but it piqued Adam's interest enough that he demanded to be a part of it. Under the supervision of an expert artist in murals, the project took off, and rapidly Adam started to relate to and trust the other service users. This enabled him to improve his verbal communication, address his trust issues, and build his lost self-esteem. Evidently, Adam was exhibiting enough of his outstanding talent, and after a couple of weeks, he was promoted to leader of this group to coordinate the work in complete collaboration with the artist.

In the meantime, Adam was discharged home, a person with high hopes for a bright future, determined to rebuild his life independently. As a social worker, I knew that there was more to come for Adam. During my long conversations with him, he expressed the wish to find gainful employment. Since his family had always protected him up until this point, this presented a challenge for him and the family.

Important People in My Social Work Journey

I must admit that many influential people encouraged and supported me throughout my social work career. Two people have followed me all the way during my journey. Jeanette – a work colleague – is mental health occupational therapist whom I regard as more than just a special and honest colleague. Her drive is amazing. I consider her as the sister I never had. She is an excellent colleague in whom I can confide my concerns, as well as a work friend who extends beyond her profession. She is family. Prof Anton has been my mentor throughout my journey since the very beginning. He has believed in me and nurtured the love and passion I have for mental health. His expertise, knowledge, and humanity extend beyond his field. I am rightly eternally grateful to him. Because of his unfaltering expert advice, I was able to develop strong moral and ethical principles which I will carry with me with my head held high. It is his constant encouragement and support which have made me the professional I am today. You are both a blessing to me.

Self-Reflection

Thirty-three years in the field of social work. It has not been an easy ride. Throughout these years, I have encountered many situations that require steel nerves. Maintaining a work–life balance is also a difficult task. To juggle an intensive and demanding career and home and family, and also your health and well-being, is, to say the least, hard. After all, we are also humans, and many times switching off after a day's work can be challenging, knowing that others are still in distress.

But . . . if someone were to ask me if I would choose this profession again, I would not hesitate to respond with a resounding YES! When you are passionate about your job, there is no turning back, regardless of the work demands, countless burnouts, sleepless nights out of worry, the dangers you face, and most importantly, the challenges. When you are enthusiastic about your job, you tend to extend positivity throughout while transmitting it and inspiring those around you. You are far more productive and content in general. This profession enables you to discover and put to the test your own strengths and weaknesses. I cannot emphasize enough how noble social work is as a profession if it can be pursued wholeheartedly with purpose and fulfilment. Notwithstanding this, every noble job at first seems challenging and difficult, yet where there is a will, there is a way. Nothing is impossible; sheer determination, perseverance, and passion are the key factors to overcoming this.

In all honesty, I cannot imagine doing anything other than social work, and when the time comes for me to retire, I hope and aspire to continue through volunteer work. To summarize my story, social work is more than just a job; it is a life purpose because, when done properly, it becomes larger than life.

Reflective Questions

1. Reflect on the power of personal stories. How can telling your own story of becoming a social worker help others engage in the profession?
2. In this story, the author writes about burnout and the need for a self-reflective practice. Think about how a self-reflective practice can be carried out.
3. In what way can an active relationship with your own social work story be helpful in your everyday practice?

Photo: Hilde Mjøs

CHAPTER 21

Reflections on Psychiatric Social Work in an African Setting

A Story about Challenges

Wilberforce Kurevakwesu

Introduction

Social work is a vital profession that operates within a variety of agency-based settings. Within these agencies, there are primary and secondary settings. Hospital social work is practised in secondary settings where medical practitioners are the primary professionals. Hospitals are multidisciplinary environments established to promote overall health – the World Health Organization (WHO) emphasizes the importance of physical, mental, and social well-being beyond the absence of disease or frailty. Zimbabwe is one of the few African countries that employs hospital social workers, who face numerous challenges in this unique setting. This chapter draws from the author's personal experiences as a psychiatric social worker for two years at the largest psychiatric institution in Zimbabwe, which is also the second-largest in southern Africa (Kurevakwesu, 2021). To best convey the struggles that hospital social workers face, particularly in Africa and Zimbabwe, the author employs a storytelling approach, using his experiences to highlight these challenges and suggest possible interventions or solutions. By using this approach, the author hopes to provide policy insights and ultimately improve the hospital setting for psychiatric social workers in developing contexts.

Hospital Social Work in Zimbabwe: Experiences and Associated Challenges

The two years that I worked in a hospital setting were the most challenging years of my career. Despite the various challenges that I faced, I learned a lot during this time and this helped me grow professionally. As someone who came from the non-profit sector where social work is respected, being in a secondary setting was indubitably challenging. To make matters worse, the institution was not an ordinary hospital, but a specialist referral hospital for persons with psychiatric disorders. As a psychiatric social worker, I worked with other hospital social workers from all over Zimbabwe. There are medical social workers at every central hospital in Zimbabwe and their role is to provide support to medical staff to ensure the overall health of patients. At the psychiatric hospital, we were three 'social workers' and of these, I was the only one who had fitting social work qualifications (a Bachelor's degree in social work) – the other two were working as social workers, yet they did not have requisite qualifications and they were not registered by either the Allied Health Practitioners Council of Zimbabwe or the Council of Social Workers (see Kurevakwesu, 2021). On top of this, I had jumped into a department that was too political and I had to tread carefully if I was to survive because the two 'social workers' that I found there were always fighting over seniority and control of the department. With this, my predicament became compounded considering that (1) I was in a secondary setting where social work is not valued and (2) Zimbabwe's economy was nose-diving head-down – meaning that salaries were poor and resources were scarce.

I shared an office with one of the 'social workers' and we had two office assistants assigned to the department. Fortunately, the office assistants were passionate about social work and one of them was pursuing a degree in social work at a local university. Contrariwise, the two assistants became my mentors and they taught me how things were done, and we could discuss at length how work ought to be done because they were the most experienced members of the department. When I started, there was no job description – only an orientation session around the hospital. Given this, I had to bank on the two office assistants to appreciate my duties and execute them accordingly. This was necessitated by the fact that these assistants were doing all the 'social' work because the 'social workers' were using an excessively delegative leadership approach. From the assistants, I learnt how to attend to wards, collect data from the wards, interview clients, write monthly reports, prepare for and attend care conferences, and assist walk-in clients – among other lessons and skills. On top of that, it was through the assistants that I got to work with other medical social workers through referrals. For instance, whenever a patient in any one of the wards passed on, we had to notify the family members of the patient, work with the medical social worker from a general hospital to ensure that the body was collected, and if there were no relatives, we would also ensure – together with medical social workers from other hospitals – that the deceased got a decent state-funded burial (pauper burial).

I quickly became good at what I did, but I always felt terrible and anxious because I felt like I was operating in murky waters. I needed to go back to a setting where my work and profession were appreciated. However, because of the lack of opportunities in Zimbabwe, I had no choice but to continue squeezing a living even if I was not comfortable. I also worked with psychiatric nurses in all the wards and these professionals did not have anything positive to say about psychiatric social workers. Because social work is a secondary profession in the health sector, these nurses belittle social workers. From personal observation and interaction with medical professionals, because social workers do not deal with physical conditions and their work with patients is 'latent' – for instance, the provision of counselling services – medical professionals do not see the value of social work. However, in a few instances, they see the need for social workers and regularly summon them to the wards. Many times, primary professionals give social workers several unrelatable or unsuitable tasks, for instance, purchasing groceries on behalf of patients. I remember I used to tell my inner self almost every day that I was not supposed to last three years in this place – and sure I did not. My love for social work and my passion for helping kept me going, together with the fact that I was pursuing a Master's degree in social work at the time, and I outright knew that it was only a matter of time before I left because I had set my sights on academia – something that had always been a childhood dream. This dream might have also been the reason why I did not enjoy working in a hospital setting, because if we were to interview other medical or psychiatric social workers, they might provide positive experiences compared to mine. This is not to say that my experiences were always negative. There were some instances where I would feel like all was going well, for instance, after solving a difficult case, or after successfully helping a client.

Most of the challenges I faced at the psychiatric institution were a clear sign of role ambiguity and role conflict – issues that generated stress and burnout for the social worker. Our supposed role was simple – to ensure that the social needs of patients are appreciated so that their mental health improves. However, the setting is multidisciplinary and at the end of the day, some disciplines would want dominance and this creates confusion and unnecessary stress for the other professionals. Also, as professionals who provided clinical services, we reported to the Clinical Director – a position reserved for medical doctors (psychiatrists). This meant that as far as upward mobility was concerned, we had reached the ceiling. The multidisciplinary hospital setting is also made up of psychologists, occupational therapists, pharmacists, primary care counsellors, and nurse aides, among others. Outside the hospital, as a medical social worker, I used to work with the police, social welfare officers within the Department of Social Development (DSD), and non-governmental organizations (NGOs). Working with all these professionals brought about a wealth of experiences and helped in building social capital.

While I was in this stressful environment, the coronavirus disease (COVID-19) added salt to my wounds. The coming of COVID-19 made the government of Zimbabwe – just like any other government – react in ways that created a 'new normal' that was not normal (Kurevakwesu, 2021; Chineka and Kurevakwesu, 2021). COVID-19 was first documented in Zimbabwe in March 2020, and this precipitated nationwide lockdowns; consequently, all health workers were classified as 'essential services workers' – meaning that they had to continue going to work when other non-essential services staff worked from home. There were COVID-19 cases at the psychiatric hospital and with the loss of lives due to COVID-19, the working environment became frightful. Moreover, as psychiatric social workers who help persons with mental disorders reconnect with their families, we could not visit relatives of patients, and they also could not visit the hospital due to travel restrictions (Kurevakwesu, 2021). In the formative days of the COVID-19 pandemic, there were even transport challenges for health workers and I remember on several occasions I had to walk for nearly 10 kilometres to work because transport operators had been banned. It is always the case that whenever something unprecedented happens, there will be such consequences. With time, however, the government started to provide transport for all government employees who were going to work during the pandemic period.

Of all the things that I enjoyed as a psychiatric social worker, going into the wards was exciting. I would meet new clients and new issues every day and this became a sort of adventure. I would at times roam around the wards supervising my students – social work students on placements – or make rounds whenever I felt like it. At times there would be care conferences in the wards, and they provided a great opportunity to use the various and variegated professionals' eyes as one. This ensured the provision of a holistic assessment of clients and the generation of feasible action plans. During the care conferences, I made various discoveries that centred around the importance of teamwork and this also forced me to appreciate all the various professionals that I worked with because I rose to see their significance in the psychiatric health matrix. This is supported by Epstein (2014) who argues that multidisciplinary teams in health settings maximize patient safety and satisfaction, reduce the length of stay of patients in hospital, improve the performance of health care workers, reduce hospital costs and complications, and increase job satisfaction. Epstein (2014) sees multidisciplinary teams as "well-oiled machines" that are necessary for a productive health care environment for both the patient and health care workers. Another aspect of this relational coordination is that knowledge and experiences from each discipline are brought to the table and help in coming up with a comprehensive treatment plan (Taberna et al., 2020). It also becomes easy to know from care conferences how every professional present is supposed to work towards the treatment of the patient, and in the end, it becomes easy to manage the treatment of the client and also evaluate efforts and make follow-ups later on.

On another note, the lack of recognition of indigenous knowledge systems can be cited as a challenge. I remember one of the days I was summoned to a ward to talk to a client who had episodes of delirium, and after the episodes she could not remember what happened. During the episodes, she would moan. Upon talking to her, she said that she sees two of her male relatives coming towards her and the moment that they grab her she loses herself and only wakes up to surprised faces. There was also a case where a client's relatives claimed that the client developed a psychiatric disorder after he had been suspected of murder. These cases speak to the presence of superstition, and in indigenous knowledge systems such cases are dealt with by *sangomas*. The approach to mental health treatment and care within health institutions is too Western, whereas some conditions require indigenous or traditional knowledge. Because of this, when treating such clients, it seems that the focus is on the symptoms and not the root causes of their problems. As such, embracing cultural and traditional belief systems will be the first step towards holistic mental health care in the African setting – just like the adoption of Ubuntu in social work (Kurevakwesu & Maushe, 2020; Kurevakwesu & Chizasa, 2020). My submission is not that *sangomas* are effective in their work, but they should be given space in mental health treatment as they represent traditional mental health practices that many argue to be effective and acceptable according to African beliefs (Kajawu et al., 2016). Some *sangomas* are still operating in Zimbabwe and Africa in general, and from what I hear, some of them are effective in mental health issues. Such an approach resonates with the need to indigenize and decolonize social work in Africa (Kurevakwesu, 2023; Tusasiirwe, 2022).

Moreover, as argued by Najafi et al. (2022) and Verghese (2008), spiritual health has a bearing on mental health, and it is an ingredient of effective treatment and recovery. In Zimbabwe, at the current moment, there is a total disregard for spirituality in mental health care and treatment. In tandem with the need for indigenous knowledge in mental health care and treatment, there is also a need for religion to be part of the conversation. This is because some of the causes of mental health disorders – as can be seen from the two examples above – are superstitious and 'spiritual'. A disregard for the spiritual dimensions of mental health – a strong bias towards Western thinking – is a digression from the realities of Africans with psychiatric disorders. This neglect of such realities might help explain why psychiatric institutions have exceeded their carrying capacities in Zimbabwe (Kurevakwesu et al., 2023). This was corroborated by Kajawu et al. (2016) when they conducted a qualitative study in Zimbabwe on mental health and African medicine. They found out that patients preferred the use of African medicine over Western medicine because they believed that mental health disorders were a result of witchcraft. Moreover, the majority of participants in their study reported high levels of confidence in African medicine compared to Western medicine.

Whilst working at the mental health institution, the other challenge that I faced was secondary traumatic stress (vicarious trauma). Mental health professionals are not robots, they are humans, and in their empathetic engagement with patients, they may also be affected (Kim et al., 2021). Now, this was happening in an environment that was not supportive and where remuneration was poor. Even though I was passionate about my work, the situations around me did not help create a conducive working environment – they made everything worse. There were no mechanisms in place to detect and assist mental health professionals with vicarious trauma, and I felt a need for such support. The COVID-19 pandemic made the situation worse and most of the interventions for COVID-19 were centred around the manifest effects of the pandemic and not the latent and psychological effects. With the lack of adequate funding for mental health in Zimbabwe, this aspect of mental health is neglected, yet it requires attention. This is because for mental health professionals to be effective in improving the mental health of their patients, their own mental health has to be sound.

In terms of professional social work regulation, there was a tug-of-war between the Council of Social Workers (CSW) and the Allied Health Professions Council of Zimbabwe (AHPCZ). The AHPCZ registers all health professionals in Zimbabwe, and the CSW registers all social workers in Zimbabwe (Kurevakwesu et al., 2023). Social workers working in the health sector are at the boundary of this divide. When I was a psychiatric social worker, I was on the CSW register and my colleagues used to advise me that I needed to be on the AHPCZ register. Even the 'social workers' that I worked with argued that it is the AHPCZ that should register us and this was because they were not social workers and they did not understand social work regulation issues. This is something that needs to be resolved and I think the two regulators need to come to terms and find an amicable way to settle this argument. Considering that social work is trying to gain face in professional settings in Zimbabwe – particularly in the health sector – regulatory issues have to be clear and this will help establish social work as a credible and recognized profession in such settings (Kurevakwesu, Chikwaiwa, & Mundau, 2022). With a strong sense of recognition comes a sense of professional identity and a strong commitment to the ethical principles of the profession. Moreover, this will help cull the profession of non-social workers who masquerade as social workers within the health sector. These individuals are not social workers and they can easily taint the image and reputation of the profession considering that they do not subscribe to the ethical foundations of the profession (Kurevakwesu, Chikwaiwa, & Mundau, 2022).

Hospital social work in Zimbabwe has tended to be remedial – something that has also contributed to its lack of relevance and recognition (Chitereka, 2010; Kurevakwesu, 2017; Kurevakwesu, Dzoma, Mundau, et al., 2022). Social workers in the health sector are reactive and only act to solve the problems presented by patients. It is rare to see hospital social workers working in a preventive role. As someone who was once a hospital social worker, I always questioned this, and I came to realize that the lack of resources and flexibility are major detriments to development-oriented hospital social work. For instance, at the psychiatric hospital where I worked, we realized that most of the prevailing disorders were substance-induced, but there was no thrust to find preventive approaches. With the hospital breaching its carrying capacity, no effort was made to ensure that admissions were reduced through preventive measures. Some of the preventive measures that could be taken to reduce psychiatric admissions or the onset of psychiatric disorders could have been awareness campaigns on drug and substance use, promotion of family and community care, strategies to reduce relapse among community-reintegrated persons, and educational campaigns on mental health in local communities, among others.

I was at the mental health institution for close to two years and I saw a lot of challenges that affect mental health workers and patients. These challenges need to be reduced through various channels, but in line with development-oriented social work, I think social workers have a key role to play in the amelioration of most of the challenges. Social workers are better placed to advocate, research, and challenge prevailing policy directions by governments. I think the key role that they can play is to be the fulcrum between mental health professionals and policymakers. In this way, they can document all the challenges and suggestions for a better work environment, and then advocate on behalf of all other health professionals. If successful, this can cement their position as key professionals in the mental health sphere, or generally, the health matrix. This can be a way forward, together with the following suggestions and recommendations.

The Ways Forward

From the above section, it is clear that being a psychiatric social worker in Zimbabwe is humdrum due to the presence of a plethora of challenges. Some of the challenges that were cited include role ambiguity and role conflict, poor remuneration, lack of resources, poor regulation, vicarious trauma, and heavy reliance on Western thinking and approaches. In light of this, I propose the following strategies towards improving the mental health terrain for social workers.

1. It is crucial to establish adequate mental health support services for mental health workers, including social workers. Unfortunately, many psychiatric institutions and health care facilities lack the necessary structures to provide support for these professionals. As a result, this can have a negative impact on the mental well-being of workers, ultimately affecting the quality of care they can provide to their patients. Offering mental health services can help mitigate issues such as vicarious trauma, stress, and burnout among psychiatric workers.
2. The regulation of professional social work in the health sector needs to be improved if the profession is to be given the recognition that it deserves. This will ensure that social workers become a relevant aspect of the multidisciplinary mental health team, and as such, improve job satisfaction. On top of that, there is also a need to remove non-social-workers from working as 'psychiatric social workers' because they are a threat to the growth of the profession in health settings. These individuals cannot stand up and defend the profession in such settings because they have no requisite social work ethical foundations.

3. Social work practice in mental health, and in the health sector in general, needs to be decolonized. The use of traditional and culture-specific approaches needs to be respected and appreciated in mental health treatment. This will ensure that mental health treatment resonates with existing belief systems and cultures. Western approaches to mental health treatment neglect several key issues that need attention, and the incorporation of these issues in treatment will provide comprehensive services and treatment that address the physical, psychological, social, and also spiritual aspects of mental health.
4. Remuneration needs to be improved among mental health workers as this will reignite their enthusiasm for work and correspondingly improve their mental health. On another note, there is a massive exodus of mental health professionals from Zimbabwe to developed countries and this brain drain has affected service delivery and ravaged Zimbabwe's health care system. On top of this, there is a lack of resources within the health sector, and this affects health outcomes for patients and can breed work stress for mental health workers. Adequate funding needs to be provided and all the necessary resources have to be provided if mental health is to be improved, and this in turn will also improve the working environment for mental health workers, including social workers.

Conclusion

The story above offers a glimpse into the difficulties faced by social workers operating in secondary African settings. These challenges include insufficient resources, a lack of recognition, vicarious trauma, and an over-reliance on Western approaches, among others. The author, who spent nearly two years working as a psychiatric social worker in Zimbabwe, shares his first-hand experiences and provides suggestions for improving the hospital environment. While these ideas are tailored to Zimbabwe, they may also be applicable in other developing contexts facing similar challenges. Even if not directly transferable, they offer valuable insights into hospital settings and how to address prevailing issues. To gain respect and recognition for the social work profession in health care settings, social workers must carve out niche areas and develop the profession from there. Research and advocacy – as the author suggests – are some of the areas where this can be done.

Reflective Questions

1. Reflect upon how the conditions for social workers engaged in mental health work can improve in a Zimbabwean context. What do you think must be the first step?
2. What are the benefits of multidisciplinary work within a mental health environment?
3. How can traditional approaches function together with Western approaches to mental health care treatment in Zimbabwe?
4. How can stories be a way of improving mental health challenges among people suffering from mental distress?

REFERENCES

Chineka, T. S. & Kurevakwesu, W. (2021). Challenges for child welfare and development during the COVID-19 pandemic in Zimbabwe. *African Journal of Social Work*, *11*(4), 209–15.

Chitereka, C. (2010). Hospital social work practice in Zimbabwe. *Social Work in Health Care*, *49*(9), 769–82.

Epstein, N. E. (2014). Multidisciplinary in-hospital teams improve patient outcomes: A review. *Surgical Neurology International*, *2014*(5), 295–303. https://doi.org/10.4103%2F2152-7806.139612

Kajawu, L., Chingarande, S. D., Jack, H., Ward, C., & Taylor, T. (2016). Why do people use traditional healers in mental health care in Zimbabwe? *International Journal of Psychiatry*, *1*(1), 1–6.

Kim, J., Chesworth, B., Franchino-Olsen, H., & Macy, R. J. (2021). A scoping review of vicarious trauma interventions for service providers working with people who have experienced traumatic events. *Trauma, Violence and Abuse*, *23*(5), 1437–60. https://doi.org/10.1177/15248380211991310

Kurevakwesu, W. (2017). The social work profession in Zimbabwe: A critical approach on the position of social work on Zimbabwe's development. *Afro-Asian Journal of Social Sciences*, *8*(1), 1–12.

(2021). COVID-19 and mental health services delivery at Ingutsheni Central Hospital in Zimbabwe: Lessons for psychiatric social work practice. *International Social Work*, *64*(5), 702–15. https://doi.org/10.1177/00208728211031973

(2023). United we stand, and divided we fall: A call to action for the decolonisation of social work in Africa. *International Social Work*, 0(00), 1-4. https://doi.org/10.1177/00208728231196364

Kurevakwesu, W., Chikwaiwa, B. K., & Mundau, M. (2022). The struggle for social work professional identity in contemporary Zimbabwe: A study on abuse of the social work title. *Qualitative Social Work*, *22*(2), 200–16. https://doi.org/10.1177/14733250211061827

Kurevakwesu, W., & Chizasa, S. (2020). Ubuntu and child welfare policy in Zimbabwe: A critical analysis of the national orphan care policy's six-tier system. *African Journal of Social Work, 10*(1), 89–94.

Kurevakwesu, W., Dzoma, F., Mundau, M., Magocha, J. C., Chizasa, S., & Takangovada, M. (2022). Towards the creation of a developmental welfare state in Zimbabwe: An inside perspective on the Department of Social Development. *Social Work/Maatskaplike Werk, 58*(2), 115–30. http://doi.org/10.15270/58-2-1037

Kurevakwesu, W., Masona, G., Mabeza, T. T., Zengeni, F., & Chiweshe, C. C. (2023). Factors responsible for substance use among youths in urban settings and social work-related interventions. *Journal of Social Work Practice in the Addictions, 24*(4), 367–84. https://doi.org/10.1080/1533256X.2023.2212475

Kurevakwesu, W., & Maushe, F. (2020). Towards Afrocentric social work: Plotting a new path for social work theory and practice in Africa through Ubuntu. *African Journal of Social Work, 10*(1), 30–5.

Najafi, K., Khoshab, H., Rahimi, N., & Jahanara, A. (2022). Relationship between spiritual health with stress, anxiety and depression in patients with chronic diseases. *International Journal of Africa Nursing Sciences, 17*,100463. https://doi.org/10.1016/j.ijans.2022.100463

Taberna, M., Gil, M. F., Jané-Salas, E., Antonio, M., Arribas, L., Vilajosana, E., Peralvez, T. E. & Mesía, R. (2020). The multidisciplinary team (MDT) approach and quality of care. *Frontiers in Oncology, 10*(85). https://doi.org/10.3389/fonc.2020.00085

Tusasiirwe, S. (2022). Is it indigenisation or decolonisation of social work in Africa? A focus on Uganda. *African Journal of Social Work, 12*(1), 1–11.

Verghese, A. (2008). Spirituality and mental health. *Indian Journal of Psychiatry, 50*(4), 233–7. https://doi.org/10.4103/0019-5545.44742

PART II

Lenses and Lessons
Towards More Global Perspectives

We suggest that in a disrupted and post-Covid world, it is imperative that our conceptions of social work, embodied in educational curricula and reflected in its relationship-based practices, are relevant, responsible, challenge colonial historiographies, and critically examine alternative epistemologies and long-held preferences for what counts as knowledge worth knowing. This requires embracing the notion of 'perspectivism' (Alcoff, 2019).

In this part of the book we explicity acknowledge the interdependence of the local with the global and that social work is a profession which is shaped by and in turn shapes these contexts. It is a context of multiple global crises. "A once-in-a-century pandemic, widespread economic turmoil, a reckoning on race, democratic backsliding, mass migration, the crisis of social media and rising inequality alongside diminishing trust in public institutions" (Brodin & Tomasdottir, 2022).

Arguably it is a perfect time for the social work profession to (re) consider how it generates, and scales appropriately, knowledge that it claims to be worth knowing and that can be positively impactful in the contexts where it is being practised. The phrase 'thinking outside the box' used to be popular, as it seemed to encourage different ways of looking at a social phenomenon. Then, in a twenty-first-century VUCCAA world (see p. 31) there suddenly was no box any more! So now we may have to take social work to a new place, and in this part of the book we have the opportunity to learn from other places about some micro through to macro issues, ways of thinking, their interactions, and the legacies they leave.

An ongoing challenge for social work is to not lose sight of, or be fearful of, the values and systems that have created and perpetuated current social welfare problems, inequities, structures, and systems that are an ever-present danger and therefore threaten and diminish current well-being. Maybe it is time to take the baton from Kanter (2022) and "think outside the building." By this she means think outside silos and sectors. This, we feel, requires different actions and sensibilities. A critical question, we suggest, arises, namely: *How can we (re)organize social work for positive impact?* Perspectivism can help.

Tony Ghaye and Rita Sørly

REFERENCES

Alcoff, L., (2019) Philosophy and philospohical practice: Eurocentricism as an epistemology of ignorance. In I. Kidd, J. Medina, & G. Pohlhaus Jnr (eds.), *The Routledge Handbook of Epistemic Injustice*, pp. 397–408. London: Routledge.

Brodin, J., & Tomasdottir, H. (2022). Foreword. In D. Cooperrider & A. Selian (eds.), *The Business of Building a Better World: The Leadership Revolution that is Changing Everything*. Oakland, CA: Berrett-Koehler.

Kanter, R. (2022). Taking leadership to a new place. In D. Cooperrider & A. Selian (eds.), *The Business of Building a Better World: The Leadership Revolution that is Changing Everything*. Oakland, CA: Berrett-Koehler.

CHAPTER 22

From Punitive Measures to Comprehensive Services
A Reflection on the Evolution of Social Work Practices in Tanzania

Thomas Ndaluka

Introduction

This chapter offers a perspective on Tanzanian practical experiences and social work as a growing profession in the country. In Tanzania, Kiswahili[1] expressions *ustawi wa jamii* and *afisa ustawi wa jamii*, meaning social work and social welfare officer as practitioner, respectively, give this profession identity in this East African nation. In this chapter, however, we refer to social workers as graduates who utilize their profession, knowledge, and skills to provide social welfare services to individuals, families, groups, communities, organizations or societies (MHSW, 2012).

The International Federation of Social Workers defines social work as "a practice-based profession and an academic discipline that promotes social change and development, social cohesion, and the empowerment and liberation of people" (IFSW, n.d.). Moreover, the principles of social justice, human rights, collective responsibility, and respect for diversities (ibid.) ensure social work practice is conducted in an ethical manner (Ng'ondi, 2021). The definition of social work is broad enough to cover what constitutes the profession and its noble role in the community; however, as its principles attest, social work in practice has far-reaching implications. In fact, based on notions from the humanities, social sciences, social work, and indigenous knowledge, social work is preoccupied with individuals, communities, and organizations to improve wellness and deal with life's obstacles.

In the context of Tanzania, social work practices extend beyond the realm of the conventional field of social work to include other aspects akin to social welfare services. The term 'social work' was uncommon in Tanzania until the beginning of the twentieth century, when the British colonial administration decided to enact several legal documents and

[1] Kiswahili is both an official and national language accessible universally in this East African nation.

policies (Ng'ondi, 2021), and to establish a department of social welfare in 1947 (Mabeyo, 2014). In other words, the term social work, as a profession, in Tanzania was imported from Europe during the British colonial administration. As a result, this term 'social work' and its related concept of 'social welfare' are conspicuous for their absence in any of more than 130 ethnic languages found in the country.

However, lacking the terminology in the local languages does not necessarily mean that prior to colonialism, Tanzanians did not have mechanisms in place for promoting social cohesion, change, development, stability, and the empowerment of individuals and their communities. After all, communities in Tanzania organized social work needs and services through a lineage/kinship, tribal, and chiefdom system. The chapter will further explore this aspect in the following section.

Moreover, the chapter aims to contemplate the path social work has taken and how, via that experience, we may comprehend the part social work has played in advancing social development and improving the health of individuals and communities. The chapter begins with an account of social welfare service before colonialism, then comes the experience during colonialism, and, subsequently, the post-independence period, before providing a conclusion. Moreover, the chapter looks at the future prospects of social work in Tanzania. In this regard, historians teach us that knowledge of the past is useful in understanding the present and making predictions about the future.

Social Welfare Services before Colonialism

Before the advent of colonialism, social work, and/or social welfare services, family members catered for the needs of and provided services to the poor and the disadvantaged, including children, the elderly, and the infirm and incapable members of society (Mabeyo, 2014). In these pre-colonial societies, able members ensured the ready availability of food, shelter, and protection against hazards for all members of the family. However, because societal norms and values approved these acts and, accordingly, governed them, this generosity did not function in a vacuum (Mabeyo, 2014). These traditional societies believed that a family member(s) abandoning, neglecting, or failing to cater for the needs of the other family members would attract a curse. As such, each able member had an obligation to support and help his/her family member(s). Of course, family members who provided services to others also envisaged a future reward. Implicitly, whatever they provided at the moment could be recoverable in future reciprocity, particularly during times of sickness, death, widowhood, or old age (Eckert, 2004). Strong traditional ties also maintained this kind of social protection, in which family resources were shared evenly and passionately (Omari, 2021).

During this period, there were no children without parents or foster parents, widows without families to look after them, or elderly living alone without the support of relatives or their children (Omari, 2021). Marriage was then a family affair, not an individual one, and the society as a whole provided care for the children (ibid.). In addition, issues like street children (now common in the urban lingo), children-headed households, neglected elderly citizens, and homelessness were uncommon and alien in these precolonial societies. During that time, traditional families were able to give their members affection, care, stability, empathy, and freedom. People were subsequently spared, and their anguish lessened as a result.

Furthermore, when families were unable to meet the demands and offer the services that their members required, ethnic groups and chiefs stepped in. Frequently, such interventions occurred in the event of unanticipated natural disasters, such as home fires, earthquakes, flooding, and starvation resulting from protracted droughts. When these disasters occurred, people belonging to that ethnic group compensated the affected family for the losses occasioned by the incident or tragedy. For example, they would provide food, help in building a shelter when the family home was damaged, and help with gardening by offering labour and seeds. Social protection of this kind prevails today in communities that have preserved their ethnic customs and traditions. However, many communities have undergone transformations after coming into contact with external groups and forces through colonialism, urbanization, and migration.

Social Work during Colonialism

Social work, as we conceptualize it today, is a product of colonialism's and capitalism's expansion to Africa generally and Tanzania particularly. As a practice-based profession, social work is an importation from Europe to cater for the problems that colonialism and capitalism had created in the country. Colonialism established administration centres, plantations, factories, and transportation infrastructures at various places. These establishments and infrastructure displaced many individuals from their original arable land to urban and production centres that required labour-intensive engagements in concentrated areas where many locals found themselves landless. In this colonial set-up, individuals were uprooted from their traditional land, where they had worked for generations, to work on the plantations and in factories that the settlers had established. Particularly, the sisal plantations which were first established in Pangani, Tanga in 1893 (Sabea, 2008) received workers from as far as Kigoma, the Democratic Republic of the Congo (DRC), and Zambia; moreover, the central railway construction from Dar es Salaam to Mwanza and Kigoma, which was completed in 1928 (Nkya, 2015), used to ferry people from different locations, including the Sukuma and Nyamwezi from Mwanza and Tabora respectively, to places of labour concentration.

The cotton plantations in southern Tanzania also created several social problems and upheavals, including the Majimaji war of 1905–7. The cotton plantations, which symbolized colonialism and brutality, became a flash point that pitted the Yao, Matumbi, Zaramo, and Ngoni ethnicities against the better-armed German soldiers (De Juan, 2016). The brutal tactics that the German soldiers applied included gutting farm fields and houses, rape, and killing. Despite some Eurocentric researchers celebrating such mayhem, it unleashed social problems on the local populations (Moyd, 2010). The consequences were dire and devastating to the local communities, whose need and distress could have benefited from the professional help of social workers, who did not exist then in the country. Gender inequality and violence began when these communities were left disrupted, uprooted, and impoverished (Sunseri, 1997). Many suffered from ailments and mental disorders brought on by the collapse of the traditional medical system, starvation, migration, and – for the first time – the abandonment of women and children (Rushohora, 2019).

Then came the First World War, with the British and the Germans partly fighting on the territory of then German East Africa, which covered Tanganyika, Burundi, and Rwanda. With Germany losing Tanganyika (before its union with Zanzibar in 1964), Britain took over the country as its protectorate, a colonial reign that subsequently sowed the seeds of social work as we know it now in the country. Moreover, during the Second World War Britain also recruited Africans including Tanganyikans, into their battalions (Westcott, 1986), with soldiers travelling to Europe and other parts of the world to fight. This Second World War experience further compounded the social problems that were emerging as a result of colonialism and the capitalist economy (Eckert, 2004). The difference between the First World War and the Second World War was that the latter was exported to the indigenous populations (Westcott, 1986; Moyd, 2010). The localized war not only caused death to many Africans but also displaced innumerable people and left many others maimed, orphaned, and distressed. In fact, many young and able-bodied individuals who participated in the war could no longer provide support to their families, another cause of distress and unmet wants. Poverty also increased because families failed to engage in farming and production, especially the workers in industries and plantations (Moyd, 2010). Subsequently, homelessness started rearing its ugly head as most of the settlers abandoned their plantations and could not pay the labourers. For the first time, the problem of unemployment became a social issue that the country could not ignore.

After the Second World War, the British colonial administration changed its orientation on social welfare services in the colonies. Of course, this did not happen overnight, let alone willingly – there were pressures from the labour movement, humanitarians, and industrialists in Britain, on the one hand; and the nationalists and returning soldiers in the country who demanded the colonial administrator be more responsible for the well-being of the people, on the other hand. In this regard, Westcott (1986) contends that during the Second World War Tanganyikan (Tanzanian) soldiers were assured that they were fighting for their freedom against colonialism. After the war these soldiers demanded the British colonial administration be more responsible in honouring the promise made during the war.

In the 1940s, the British government enacted several laws and policies, which guided the establishment of social welfare in the colony. For instance, the British Parliament passed a Colonial Development and Welfare Act in 1940 aimed to offer state protection against socioeconomic distress among the people who had been affected by the two world wars. Other laws included the Children and Young Persons Act, Cap. 13, of 1937, the Affiliation Ordinance of 1949, Probation of Offenders, Cap. 247 of 1947, and the Foster Care and Adoption Ordinance of 1955 (Ng'ondi, 2021). These legal instruments – to a certain extent – smoothed economic operations in the colony, and not necessarily for the well-being of the general population, the majority of whom were Africans.

Consequently, to help about 68,000 African soldiers who were discharged after the Second World War to integrate peacefully and easily into the community, the British colonial administration in 1945 established a government Social Welfare Department. This department was established mostly on an ad hoc basis. A social welfare organizer oversaw the Social Welfare Department to make sure of implementation (Mabeyo, 2014) and to ensure order and stability. Additionally, the colonial administration built welfare centres in the forty-two district headquarters. At the time, the British colonialists were uneasy about the returning soldiers after the Second World War. These Tanganyikans had fought shoulder to shoulder with British and other nationals against the German soldiers, implying their consciousness was no longer the same. They were assured throughout the war that they would regain their independence upon returning home (Westcott, 1986), which included being able to work and take on official duties (Eckert, 2004). The British colonial administration was concerned with finding a way to guarantee stability in the colony and to seamlessly integrate the troops into their society upon their return.

Initially, social welfare and social work strategies were not implemented for the common populace by the British colonial administration. The belief was that voluntary and charity institutions would address such social issues as the public countenanced. Nevertheless, most of these charity organizations were situated in remote areas and specialized in specific social welfare services. The majority of individuals in urban areas experienced hardship and maiming poverty as a result of the absence of social welfare services.

In 1950, the colonial establishment restructured the Social Welfare Department and renamed it the Department of Social Development. The objective of the newly reconstituted department was to raise the standard of living for rural and urban populations. The department was under two ministries, the ministries of Local Government and of Social Services. The structure during this period was minimal since it mainly targeted the poor/bankrupt settlers and a select social group, mostly of Asian origin. Evidence from historical studies show that the colonial social provision services did not reach most of the population – the Africans – because the "British were not concerned about the development of Africans" (Pratt, 1969, p.58). Indubitably, the social welfare the British colonial administration introduced was remedial, institutional, and repatriative in nature (Pratt, 1969). Consequently, even the structure of the social welfare services during this period was rather undeveloped with a blurred scope, covering those working in the colonial administration and dealing with those who were in conflict with the law or who were suspected of stirring social disorder (Mabeyo, 2014).

Social Work after Independence

The early post-independence years (1961–7) witnessed Tanzania inheriting the colonial social welfare framework with a mixed feelings in some quarters. To begin with, it was acknowledged that social provision served as a means of promoting social cohesion and economic growth. This type of statement acknowledged that the pressures of modernity and urbanization, particularly in metropolitan and town centres, had undermined the traditional welfare structures and practices, which centred on family and kinship (Pratt, 1969). Therefore, the creation of social welfare served as a safety net for the impoverished whom family systems are unable to assist. On the other hand, many nationalist political leaders were not in favour of social welfare because it allegedly diverted resources from so-called development projects, hence social welfare expenditure was seen to be expensive (Pratt, 1969). To them, establishment of social welfare needed economic development for it to prosper and not the other way round. Another dilemma that the government faced was lack of professional social workers (MHSW, 2012) who could deal with various social problems the country contended with during that time (Omari, 2021). Consequently, there was a delay in establishing and supporting a comprehensive social welfare provision.

In 1967, the Tanzanian government instituted a radical political change by adopting *Ujamaa* or egalitarian economies, an African or rather Tanzanian brand of socialism following the Arusha Declaration (Nyerere, 1968). The principles of social welfare coincided well with the new *Ujamaa* ideology. The government considered social welfare to be an integral part of the development agenda (Pratt, 1969). The government decided to assume full responsibility for the provision of social welfare services. Accordingly, the country envisioned welfare provision to cover the whole country – both urban and rural areas – in a bid to reach all individuals irrespective of their race, religion, creed, ethnicity, age, or gender. In this regard, Pratt (1969, p.65) noted:

> The policy statement was formulated (a) to advocate the extension of welfare services to all main urban areas of Tanzania, (b) to encourage voluntary welfare agencies to take a more active role in the organisation of welfare services by giving them subventions.

In accordance with the *Ujamaa* philosophy, the administration worked to achieve an equitable distribution of social welfare services and resources. Succinctly, the government envisioned a welfare state while also enticing non-profits, primarily religious ones, to help provide services, particularly for children living in vulnerable circumstances, such as juvenile offenders, abandoned children, and the impoverished. The Department of Social Development was first reorganized and given a new name – the Probation and Welfare Department – by the Arusha Declaration. This reorganization of the department aimed to ensure that it adhered to the *Ujamaa* ideology. According to Pratt (1969, p.65), the Probation and Welfare Department's responsibilities following the Arusha Declaration were to:

i. Help families and voluntary agencies responsible for taking care of orphans and vulnerable children.
ii. Find and/or establish foster homes for street children and those with no guardians/parents.
iii. Establish a ministry which will be responsible for social welfare issues.
iv. Provide rehabilitation services for the physically handicapped, people with disabilities and the aged.
v. Extend the National Council of Social Welfare Services to the various regional headquarters.

Consequently, the *Ujamaa* ideology expedited the formulation of several social provision policies, and established a Ministry for Housing and Education, which hosted the Department of Probation and Welfare. These policies extended the welfare services to cover the whole country when public elementary schools and primary health care services (i.e. dispensaries and health centres) were built, including in rural areas, hence facilitating access for individuals residing in remote places, contrary to the reality during colonial times.

Under this ambitious mission, health care and education services were universal and available free of charge. Moreover, the colonial powers built a mental hospital in Dodoma to deal with mental illness, in addition to establishing a mental health department in all regional and district hospitals. Rehabilitation services for the physically handicapped, people with disabilities, and the aged were introduced in all referral hospitals. The government also encouraged voluntary organizations to establish foster homes for street children and children without guardians/parents. Furthermore, this ambitious aim impacted several private institutions, since the government confiscated their facilities under the guise of guaranteeing equitable access to services. As an instance, all the religious hospitals and schools were nationalized and made into state organisations (only seminary schools escaped this nationalization). Notable examples were the Tabora Boys' and Girls' Secondary Schools established by the Catholic missions in 1921 and 1922 to educate the sons and daughters of African chiefs. The Catholic Church also owned the Bugando Hospital in Mwanza, one of the premier health care facilities in the country, which the post-independence government eventually nationalized.

At the national (ministerial) level, Pratt (1969, p.70) identified programmes that were established: (1) social and economic and security programmes, (2) youth development programmes, (3) programmes for and by women's organizations, (4) community development programmes, and (5) childcare programmes. These programmes have remained unchanged till now and they have evolved into independent units within the government ministries. These programmes, therefore, prompted the Department of Social Welfare to offer social welfare services such as counselling, support for the disabled and juvenile delinquents, foster care for abandoned children and children without the care of a fit person, shelter for the elderly, and assistance with matrimonial problems. Social workers were tasked with determining which social groups needed help and what issues needed to be addressed, as well as creating systems for connecting individuals to various volunteer organizations and offering solutions. Additionally, there were initiatives that aimed to build housing specifically for public employees, such as teachers, doctors, police officers, military, and employees of different government agencies and local government. Every area and district had government quarters for public servants.

To address the issue of housing and homelessness in metropolitan regions, the government nationalized a number of privately held homes, most of which belonged to Asians. The National Housing Corporation (NHC), a government real estate organization, was created by the Act of Parliament No. 45 of 1962, and assumed responsibility for nationalized properties and was tasked with addressing urban housing poverty (NHC, 2024). Yet, this organization has been unable to keep abreast of the increasing number of individuals swarming into cities in quest of work and other possibilities, which caused a number of slums and unplanned residential areas in Tanzania's metropolitan centres to become emergency situations. Additionally, the Tanzania Housing Bank started operating in 1972 by offering credits to facilitate the building of low-cost housing (Yona, 1979). Currently, several public and private institutions offer credits to the public for buying and building houses in both rural and urban areas. However, the demand for houses remains extremely high, especially in urban and town centres.

Nevertheless, the Tanzanian government admitted that available public resources were limited, hence making it difficult to realize a universal social welfare provision. The 1980 economic crisis and the implementation of structural adjustment programmes (SAPs) led to the government encouraging voluntary welfare agencies, primarily religious organisations situated in remote areas, to play a more active role in providing social welfare, as reported by Mwaipopo (2023). Government capacity was granted to voluntary groups that ventured to initiate such services. In addition, the government financed these groups through subsidies or assigned medical staff to work for them, and supplied necessary medications (Sundqvist, 2017). A handful of these care centres – like the Kilimanjaro Christian Medical Centre and Bunda Designated District Hospital in the Bunda, Mara region – became district and/or regional hospitals.

Social Work in the Twenty-First Century

From 2000 onwards, the recognition of the importance of social work has upped the tempo, due to the soaring social problems and issues that have required the attention of social work professionals. Problems such as drug addiction, refugees, gender-based violence, disasters, rising cases of chronic diseases such as HIV/AIDS, cancer, diabetes, and cardiovascular, and occurrences of new disease outbreaks such as COVID-19, Ebola, and Marburg also called for social workers' intervention to provide support and help to individuals, groups, and communities. Unfortunately, there are other problems arising from climate change, like protracted droughts, excessive, above average, or below average rains, and erratic seasons that lead to starvation and poverty; natural disasters like landslides, floods, and earthquakes; and gender inequality and harassment, abuse, and exploitation of women and children (MCDGWSP, 2023). A case in point is the November 2023 flood and mudslide in Hanang district in the Manyara area, which resulted in over 80 fatalities and over 110 injuries. Other aspects include poverty, unemployment, and an increased number of children living in vulnerable environments, such as orphans, street children, and kids living in families dogged by abject poverty. Shagembe et al.'s (2022) study on the impact of COVID-19 on people's mental health found that signs of mental health disorder increased in the country, hence the need for individualized and/or group social work services. Symptoms of increased mental health illness in the country are also evident and are reported in the form of soaring incidences of child abuse and abandonment, gender-based violence, and intimate partner killings (World Bank, 2022).

For instance, World Bank statistics indicated that in 2022 40 per cent of all women aged fifteen to forty-nine years had experienced physical violence, whereas 17 per cent had experienced sexual violence. Of the women aged fifteen to forty-nine, 44 per cent had experienced either physical or sexual violence by an intimate partner. Spousal violence prevalence is highest in rural areas, averaging 52 per cent, whereas the prevalence in urban areas averages 45 per cent. Almost 30 per cent of girls experience sexual violence before the age of eighteen (World Bank, 2022). The cases of intimate partner killing were widespread and demanded social workers' attention. As a result, the government raised the stakes and employed more social workers in the 2021/2 fiscal year. The government's plan is to employ social workers in all 1,000 wards in the country, which has yet to materialize due to a variety of reasons that have not been made public, including budgetary constraints.

However, the host ministry for the Department of Social Welfare has always been instable. The department shifted from the Ministry of Housing and Education in the 1960s to the Ministry of Health in the 1990s, to the Ministry of Health and Social Welfare in the 2000s, and to the Ministry of Health and Community Development, Gender, Children and Elderly in 2016. Since 2021, issues of social work and social welfare have fallen under the renamed Ministry of Community Development, Gender, Women, and Special Groups. These changes pertaining to the ministry responsible for social work/welfare services have had enormous impact on the continuity of programmes and policy. Currently, social work/welfare services are not situated in one ministry. Several ministries house an aspect of social welfare services, hence making reporting and monitoring of social work practices and social workers in general a challenge. By 2023, social welfare services can be found under several ministries such as the Ministry of Health, Ministry of Education and Vocational Training, Ministry of Home Affairs, President's Office – Regional and Local Government Authority, and the judiciary. More often than not, the co-ordination of social work services and practices across ministries has been wanting.

Apparently, social work, as a profession, is hardly recognized by Tanzania's local governments. As such, the local government authority does not have an independent department for social welfare that could otherwise have enabled social workers to effectively execute their duties at the grassroots, and, consequently, there is no separate budget for social welfare/social work. Instead, social work falls under the district medical office in these local authorities. Inevitably, this neglect has limited the performance of social workers and their contribution to individuals and community welfare. Currently, at the central government, social welfare is a division under the Ministry of Community Development, Gender, Women, and Special Groups. The Commissioner for Social Welfare leads the division of social welfare. The division has two sections: Social and Child Welfare, and Elderly Welfare. However, the President's commission for reviewing Tanzania's criminal justice system (2023) recommended Social Welfare be established as an independent department within the ministry so that the department can manage its duties and responsibilities across different sectors and all levels in the country much more effectively.

Social Work Training

After the country gained its independence in 1961, social work, as a professional discipline, was not introduced at the University of Dar es Salaam, then the only public university. The government favoured law, education, and science and technology subjects. Consequently, the government established an autonomous institute in 1973 called the National Social Welfare Training Institute designated to train people up to the level of an ordinary diploma in social work. In 1977, the National Social Welfare Training Institute introduced an advanced diploma – which was almost an equivalent of a degree – to meet the demands of the social work profession. The institute has undergone several further restructurings and transformations, including changing its name to the Institute of Social Work (ISW). Such restructuring has allowed the institute to offer programmes on social work, labour studies, and information and communication technology from certificate to postgraduate levels (at least to Master's level).

The continuous and emerging social problems amplified the division of social welfare, which has rendered the National Social Welfare Training Institute unable to cope with the growing demand. High demand for trained social workers has compelled other public and private higher learning institutions to introduce social work programmes, including the University of Dar es Salaam, which introduced an undergraduate degree in social work in the 2014/15 academic year. Other institutions that have joined the bandwagon include the Hubert Kairuki Memorial University, Kampala International University, Mwenge Catholic University, the Open University of Tanzania, and the University of Dodoma.

The Future of Social Work in Tanzania

Tanzania's social work has a bright future because of numerous intersecting societal challenges that demand the social work profession's attention. These include vulnerabilities brought on by gender inequity, mental health issues, poverty, the social marginalization of those with impairments, and the consequences of climate change. Food insecurity, unemployment, addictions, discrimination, disease, social insecurity, mental illness, fatal diseases (communicable and non-communicable), the most vulnerable children, drug abuse, and various forms of social dysfunction are additional issues that people and communities must deal with. These issues threaten not only social development and people's well-being, but also economic development. The National Five Years Development Strategy 2021/2 to 2025/6 is the vehicle through which the National Vision 2025 carries out its goal of developing skills (MFP, 2021). As a result, it is the responsibility of social workers to ensure that vices are avoided, and to protect and strengthen individuals, groups, and communities while assisting them to achieve their desired developmental objectives by applying better coping mechanisms.

Social workers may operate in a variety of social contexts. The three levels of social work intervention in society – the micro, meso, and macro levels – can facilitate the evaluation of the future of social work in Tanzania.

Micro

Social workers have been providing one-on-one services to individuals, families, and groups affected by drugs, accidents, marital problems, abandonment, gender-based violence, mental illness, as well as the effects of climate change expressed in terms of the persistence of poverty, hunger, flooding, and diseases. All these aspects demand a one-on-one intervention of social workers to understand these crises at the level of individuals, families, social groups, and communities. Social workers' services include home-based services and client-based (requested) services. At this micro level, social workers' approaches are case management and clinical social work. Case management is the most preferred and applied in Tanzania. For instance, social workers positioned at medical facilities, mostly referral, regional, and district hospitals, assist clients on a one-on-one basis by giving them access to health care and referral services. They also collaborate with clients who cannot afford to pay the medical fee out of pocket.

In Tanzania, social workers help clients to set up payment plans because most people, especially those from low-income households, do not have health insurance. On 1 November 2023 the Parliament of the United Republic of Tanzania enacted the Universal Health Insurance Bill. This gives clients the ability to get referrals and linkages, as well as appropriate services. In addition, social workers do clinical social work, concentrating on problems including substance misuse, mental health, and gender-based violence. These services are now only available at social worker offices at district and regional headquarters, which leaves many people at risk for mental illness, abuse, and neglect. This entails that many people are not reached by social welfare services, making them vulnerable and susceptible to abuse, neglect, and mental illness.

Meso

Social workers also have a duty to be aware of social concerns and problems that exist at the institutional and community levels. Social workers have been fostering relationships inside the community in order to cultivate transformation at this level. Social workers, for instance, have made a significant contribution to society by managing programmes that attempt to alter unwanted behaviour, such as drug addiction, prostitution, street begging, children working and living on the street, and homeless individuals. Social workers have developed community activities at the district level that raise awareness of social issues and mobilize resources for organizations and individuals tackling these issues. In fact, notable advances are discernible. One example is the creation of a one-stop court where problems pertaining to gender-based violence and child abuse are resolved under one roof (MCDGWSP, 2023). The Social Welfare Division is in charge of registering children's homes and day care centres, an area where the government hopes to collaborate with non-profit and commercial organizations to provide social protection to children. However, social workers have often responded in a reactive manner in instances at this level. Social workers arrive at this stage in order to address a specific issue that has arisen.

For instance, on Saturday 10 August 2019 a tanker carrying petroleum products from the Dar es Salaam port to one of the neighbouring countries exploded in the Morogoro region. The explosion happened in a *bodaboda* (motorcycle-for-hire) parking bay. The explosion claimed the lives of sixty people, with more than seventy people badly injured (*Guardian*, 2019). The majority of the victims were *bodaboda* riders, passengers, and passers-by. After this incident, social workers started working in the community, establishing support groups to assist the community to deal with the grief. The majority of these programmes ceased soon after the event because social workers then moved to other locations or went back to their regular duties.

All in all at this meso level, social workers work to build positive connections between the citizens, local authorities, and institutions. Yet, there is a concentration of NGOs in specific services, particularly services that provide homes and shelters for the elderly and children. Very few of them concentrate on the provision of psychosocial support for individuals and groups inside or outside of institutions and in the community. As a result, the number of mental disorders in the nation has increased and social development has not been realized for the majority in the communities.

Macro

Tanzania had not passed any legislation pertaining to social work or social work practices by 2023. This has been a serious flaw that has impacted social work's standing as a professional practice and a means of promoting social and economic advancement in the nation. Social workers voiced worry about the absence of legislative instruments that acknowledge social work activities during a conference for social workers hosted by the Ministry of Community Development, Gender, Women, and Special Groups in Dodoma from 6–7 September 2023. Even though social workers and social work activities in the nation have yet to be governed by any recognized national legislation, various legal instruments have been formed, including the National Ageing Policy (2003), the Disability Policy (2004), the Child Development Policy (1996), the Child Act Chapter 13 revised in 2019, and the Marriage Act Chapter 29 revised in 2019. These instruments guide the implementation and practice of social work in the country.

Besides the policies and legal instruments that guide social workers in the country, the Tanzania Association of Social Workers was established in 1982 with a mandate to:

i. Make the social work profession demonstrate its impact on enhancing the well-being of people and promoting social justice at local and global levels.
ii. Bring together professional social workers of different professional subcultures from governmental and non-governmental agencies.
iii. Promote social workers' unity in addressing social work challenges facing the country.
iv. Act as a liaison body with national, regional, and international associations involved in furthering social work professional interests.
v. Set standards, policy, and guidelines for social work practice in Tanzania.

vi. Encourage and support the participation of social workers in socioeconomic and cultural planning and implementation.
vii. Ensure effective social justice and welfare for vulnerable groups in society.

For numerous reasons, including the economic crises of the 1980s, the small number of social workers in public offices, and lack of managerial skills of its initial leaders, the association was sluggish and inconspicuous. It was not until 2010 that a rejuvenated association restarted and managed to convene its annual general meeting. By 2023, about 780 social workers registered as members in the organization, out of whom 320 are active members who participate in meetings and pay their annual dues. This suggests that not all social workers have been able to meet and become members of the association. Furthermore, one of the reasons for low registration is the absence of legal authority requiring all social work professionals to be members of the group. This demonstrates that the association has not used its influence to pass laws or establish regulations that govern the practice of social work, among other legislative tools.

Conclusion

This chapter has offered an evolving picture of social work, moving away from remedial and reactive measures and towards a more all-encompassing strategy. It has shown that increased government funding for social welfare programmes, assistance for social workers, and the development of training facilities all account for this surge. Yet, social work is not currently doing enough to address every problem in the nation. The ever-changing nature of society poses new obstacles for people, groups, and communities, resulting in stress, sadness, and mental diseases. Even though both institutional and home-based strategies have progressed in satisfying people's needs, there are still issues that need resolving. In this regard, social workers need to produce strategies capable of addressing various needs of people in a diversity of social contexts. Overall, social work practices in Tanzania are growing, but many intractable institutional and structural obstacles remain. These obstacles include the absence of social work policies and laws, which restricts the social work field's ability to provide services and hinders its expansion and recognition in Tanzania. Furthermore, placing more emphasis on institutional support at the expense of psychosocial support can exacerbate poverty in communities and cause problems such as gender-based violence, desertion, and insecurity. Social workers must interact with people more and offer essential psychosocial assistance as the field of social work develops.

Reflective Questions

1. How can the social work profession in Tanzania continue to improve the well-being of people and promote social justice?
2. There is a need to encourage and support social workers on several levels in Tanzania. What issues of human rights are related to this task?
3. How can social workers living outside Tanzania support colleagues working in the region?

REFERENCES

De Juan, A. (2016). Extraction and violent resistance in the early phases of state building: Quantitative evidence from the "Maji Maji" Rebellion, 1905–1907. *Comparative Political Studies, 49*(3), 291–323. https://doi.org/10.1177/0010414015617962

Eckert, A. (2004). Regulating the social: Social security, social welfare and the state in late colonial Tanzania. *Journal of African History, 45*(3), 467–89. www.jstor.org/stable/4100755

Guardian. (2019, 10 August). Fuel tanker explosion kills scores in Tanzania. www.theguardian.com/world/2019/aug/10/fuel-tanker-explosion-kills-scores-in-tanzania

IFSW (International Federation of Social workers). (n.d.). Global definition of social work. www.ifsw.org/what-is-social-work/global-definition-of-social-work.

Mabeyo, Z. (2014). The development of social work education and practice in Tanzania. In H. Spitzer, J. M. Twikirize, & G. G. Wairire (eds.), *Professional Social Work in East Africa: Towards Social Development, Poverty Reduction and Gender Equality*, pp.121–35. Kampala: Fountain.

MCDGWSP. (2023). *Mwongozo wa Taifa wa uendeshaji, usimamizi na uratibu wa mabaraza ya usuluhishi wa migogoro ya ndoa.* Dodoma: Ministry of Community Development, Gender, Women, and Special Groups.

MFP. (2021). *National Five Years Development Strategy 2021/2022–2025/2026.* Dodoma: Ministry of Finance and Planning.

MHSW. (2012). *Assessment of the Social Welfare Workforce in Tanzania.* Dar es Salaam: Ministry of Health and Social Welfare, Department of Social Welfare.

Moyd, M. (2010). "All people were barbarians to the Askari": Askari identity and honor in the Maji Maji War, 1905–1907. In J. Giblin & J. Monson (eds.), *Maji Maji: Lifting the Fog of War*, pp.149–79. Leiden: Brill.

Mwaipopo, R. (2023). Social policy landscape in mainland Tanzania. In J. Omona (ed.), *Gender-Equitable and Transformative Social Policies for Post COVID-19 Africa: Mapping the Social Policy Landscape in Uganda, Kenya, Tanzania and Rwanda*, pp.157–210. Cambridge: Ethics International Press.

Ng'ondi, N. (2021). Social work ethical principles in Tanzania: A broad historical review. *International Journal of Liberal Arts and Social Science, 9*(7), 17–19.

NHC. (2024). *Strategic Plan 2015/16–2024/25*. Dar es Salaam: National Housing Corporation.

Nkya, E. (2015). The role of Tanzania Central Railway Line in promoting cargo transportation. Master's thesis, Open University of Tanzania.

Nyerere, J. (1968). *Freedom and Socialism: A Selection from Writings and Speeches 1965–1967*. Dar es Salaam and New York: Oxford University Press.

Omari, L. (2021). Evolution of social welfare and social work in Tanzania. In N. Noyoo (ed.), *Social Welfare and Social Work in Southern Africa*, pp.237–53. Stellenbosch: African Sun Media.

Pratt, M. (1969). A study of the development of social welfare in a selected group of African countries: Ghana, Sierra Leone, Kenya and Tanzania. PhD thesis, University of Pittsburgh.

Rushohora, N. (2019). Facts and fictions of the Majimaji War graves in Southern Tanzania. *African Archaeological Review, 36*(1), 145–59. www.jstor.org/stable/45219121

Sabea, H. (2008). Mastering the landscape? Sisal plantations, land, and labor in Tanga region, 1893–1980s. *International Journal of African Historical Studies, 41*(3), 411–32. www.jstor.org/stable/40282526

Shagembe, M. K. (2022). The impact of COVID-19 pandemic on mental health among individuals in Dar es Salaam, Tanzania. *Tanzania Journal of Sociology, 8*(1), 132–53. https://doi.org/10.56279/tajoso.v8i1.80

Sundqvist, J. (2017). *Beyond an Instrumental Approach to Religion and Development: Challenges for Church-Based Healthcare in Tanzania*. Uppsala: Acta Universitatis Upsaliensis.

Sunseri, T. (1997). Famine and wild pigs: Gender struggles and the outbreak of the Majimaji War in Uzaramo (Tanzania). *Journal of African History, 38*(2), 235–59. https://doi.org/10.1017/S0021853796006937

Westcott, N. (1986). The impact of the Second World War on Tanganyika, 1939–49. In D. Killingray & R. J. A. R. Rathbone (eds.), *Africa and the Second World War*, pp.143–59. Basingstoke: Macmillan. https://doi.org/10.1007/978-1-349-18264-0_5

World Bank. (2022, 5 April). Tanzania can do more to protect women and girls by urgently addressing gaps in efforts to combat gender-based violence. www.worldbank.org/en/country/tanzania/publication/tanzania-can-do-more-to-protect-women-and-girls-by-urgently-addressing-gaps-in-efforts-to-combat-gender-based-violence

Yona, D. A. N. (1979). Savings and credit for low cost housing: The experience of the Tanzania Housing Bank. *Savings and Development, 3*(1), 60–74. http://www.jstor.org/stable/25829687

CHAPTER 23

Learning from a Pasifika Perspective
Navigating Social Work across Oceania

Jioji Ravulo

I always knew that I wanted to work in and across the Pacific. Despite being born, raised, and living in Sydney, Australia, on unceded Aboriginal land, I was always drawn to such possibilities. This passion grew as I became older, spurred on by my burgeoning knowledge of Pacific indigenous ways of knowing and doing, being and becoming. At the same time, I was challenged by trying to reconcile my Western and white identity, and how this could possibly support a more nuanced approach to services with Pacific peoples. It's through this struggle that this story of my own personal journey into and across social work is being told and located in the hope that we can all be genuinely part of a shared profession that strives to be collegial, collaborative, and collective. I am greatly motivated to create *safe spaces* for everyone – where people feel valued and visible and able to bring their authentic selves to the places they are located. That despite being different, such attributes can be seen as a source of strength and can be meaningfully utilized when creating solutions towards social mobility and inclusion.

Growing Up Different

Being a child of an iTaukei (indigenous) Fijian father and Anglo (white) Australian mother in the early and mid 1980s within a predominantly middle-class and white neighbourhood made me different. Despite the wealth and high rates of private home ownership around us, my parents, alongside my three siblings, including my twin sister, rented and lived in a small fibro cottage in south Sydney. In our first week of kindergarten, the first formal year of education in Australia, my twin sister and I were placed in the special "English as a Second Language" (ESL) class with a couple of other "Non English Speaking Background" children. It was presumed, due to our ethnic names and appearance, that we needed support with our language and socialization skills. A few days later, my mother furiously attended the front office to inform the principal that her children didn't need ESL support. That this enforced level of intervention was in contradiction to her expectations. Why? My mother was an ESL teacher in her own right, at another local primary school. Her engagement with her own children, as both a mother and an educator, already enabled us to have the prerequisite skills and knowledge to speak and use English. And in essence, the school presuming our need for such support was based on a lack of understanding, appreciation, and consultation with our parents.

But it was the done thing. To presume, based on appearance and names, that such support and intervention was required to make us better. To better support our outcomes. Our needs. Our ability to contribute and be better people.

A couple of years later in 1988, we moved to a public housing complex in southwestern Sydney. Previously known as Herne Bay, it was home to US barracks during World War II, and subsequently changed its name to Riverwood due to the stigma associated with its wayward history and poverty (Cook, 2007). However, such a reputation remained, as public housing properties were established from the 1950s, including the new housing complex we moved into when I was eight. I remember fondly making new friends in the street, which contained a mix of privately and publicly owned properties, but also felt a level of difference living in this complex of townhouses reserved for the perceived needy. As I grew older, I came to realize that my immediate neighbours had high and complex social and welfare needs, which made me further question the role of society in supporting such people and their circumstances.

As I continued my journey in primary school up until the age of twelve, I also realized that I was highly motivated to be a support for those who were perceived to be the 'smelly kid'. The kid that no one wanted to play with, hang out with, or be perceived as associated with. I naturally gravitated to provide such peers with an opportunity to be involved and included in my wider group of mates, rather than allow such kids to be left alone and isolated. This also greatly informed my developing leadership skills and attributes, which led to me taking on the Boy's School Captain role in Year 6. Despite being challenged by my understanding that I was from a public housing suburb, was from an ethnically diverse background, and was starting to feel different in my own sexuality, I knew that creating a safe space for everyone within the classroom and wider school community was important.

My sense of being different continued into high school – if anything, it made me question my own sense of inclusion. Arriving one evening to a school event in Year 9 at the age of fourteen, I hopped out of the car my mother and I travelled in. One of my new peers at this school asked me, "Where's your mother?" "She's here," I replied, pointing to her. "No, where is your mother?" he repeated. "Here" – again pointing. "No – she's not your mother – she's white!" And it was in this moment of time that I realized that my mother was white, and that my father was coloured, and I was biracial. Prior to this, I did appreciate that I was different in my appearance – but I didn't realize that people would perceive me differently because of the way my mother or I looked, in contrast to the perceived norm.

Such indifferent perspectives on my appearance continued to occur at this age, as I started to venture into shopping malls independently of my parents. I started to notice that security guards would purposefully follow me around. At times it was overt, other times it was less obvious until they would walk directly up to me and ask me what I was up to. I started to realize that their intentions, across different stores and different security officers, was to ensure that I wasn't up to no good. That I wasn't going to cause any trouble in such spaces.

This made me further question the way I was understood beyond my appearance. I was starting to develop an insecurity for being psychically different. But it didn't stop me from pursuing my dreams and desires to be in the performing arts. To be an actor, or musician, or both, and to use these developing skills as part of my future goals and aspirations.

This led to me landing a dream casual job in the local cinemas at the age of fifteen. To be surrounded by all the lights and action that movies brought to the world – what a wonderful place to be in! I fondly remember undertaking my first shift, and greatly enjoying the ability to check tickets and to ensure people were ushered in before the session started. I even enjoyed cleaning up before and after each session. I was just elated to be there. I also remember that, during this first shift, the owner of this local cinema complex came to visit. I smiled warmly as they walked by. I left that day feeling grateful for the opportunity to be in this role and job.

My second shift was to occur a couple of days later on Thursday afternoon. On Wednesday morning, the manager called, and requested to speak with my mother. I put her on the phone. I could hear the manager speak with my mother, as I stood close by wondering what this was about. "We are not needing your son to come into his next shift with us," she stated. "Ask her why," I quickly retorted. "The owner came by during his first shift. We believe he is not the right image for our cinema." I was in complete shock. Even as I write this now, I feel a sense of rage and anger that this could occur. But it was the done thing. It was the norm. It was perceived to be in the best interest of the workplace. I had no recourse to do anything about it.

What this incident did though, apart from robbing me of my dream teenager job, was to reinforce a level of stigma and shame I was continuing to develop for being physically different based on my ethnic appearance. It made me question my sense of self-worth, self-value, self-esteem, and self-love.

Developing My Appreciation for Being Different

At the end of this same year, I went on my first ever trip to Fiji to visit and stay with family during the entire six-week summer break. I had just finished Year 10 and was going to start at a performing arts high school in 1997 to complete my last two years of secondary school. Apart from the weather being overwhelmingly hot and humid, I met for the first time most of my Fijian family. My numerous aunties and uncles, cousins, and wider community. I stayed in the western part of the main island near Lautoka, and then spent the other half of the time in the capital city. We spent a weekend visiting my father's village in the region of Ra, a three hour drive north of Suva. As I come from a chiefly family, and carry the chiefly title of *Ratu*, a huge welcoming ceremony took place. Speeches were given to highlight the importance of the visit, and the role such leaders play in serving and supporting the community in which they are located. As I sat centrally in the village meeting hall, surrounded by 200 loving and caring kin, I came to a realization that I did have a role to play. And that my role was embedded within a bigger picture and purpose.

Key concepts that underpin this mentality and broader way of life were starting to make sense by virtue of seeing it play out across the village. As I would come to learn later in life, I was seeing the indigenous practice of *veiqaravi* – serving others. This was further supported by the broader practice of *solesolevaki* – reciprocal living. Where my sense of connection and community comes from the idea that we are all in it together. That everyone has a role to play. It was through the notion of *veirokovi*, respect for self and others, that such loving, caring, and reciprocal relationships with self and others were enacted (Ravulo, 2016b).

This sense of belonging helped shape my growing interest to be involved in a profession that would promote such areas of inclusion, and to create scope for inequalities to be called out and held accountable. To be involved in a job that would provide scope to assist individuals, families, and communities to be inclusive, and to create safe spaces and places for everyone, irrespective of their differences; as we all play a part and have a purpose.

Studying Social Work

With this renewed sense of belonging, I spent the last two years of secondary schooling at Newtown High School of the Performing Arts. The suburb in which this school is located is renowned for being eclectic. It was a home for the creative arts, and people with alternative views and values and progressive lifestyles that generally challenged the quiet and conservative suburban streets lived here. It was also a melting pot of socioeconomic situations, where you had those living in post federation and art deco dwellings, and those who slept and begged for money on the streets. As the suburb is located next to Redfern, the birthplace of an urbanized and contemporary indigenous identity in Australia, Aboriginal people were evident across the neighbourhood. They were visible in various ways too, including those sleeping rough in the streets.

Spending time in this suburb was both a celebration of my growing sense of being and belonging, whilst being a challenging confrontation with human need. I was inspired by the resilience of Aboriginal people, who despite their circumstances, continued their quest to be counted within a country that has differing views on their presence. It was through my interaction with this local community that my passion grew for social work.

What consolidated my need to be part of a progressive profession came from a report published by the Judicial Commission of New South Wales. Titled *Sentencing Disparity and the Ethnicity of Juvenile Offenders* (Gallagher & Poletti, 1998) the report found that "Pacific Islander offenders received twice as many control orders as their Anglo-Australian matches" despite having the same offences and offending history. Once again – shock. Complete shock at a legal system that is said to be designed to help protect its citizens against harm. This blatant example of structural racism that perpetuated violence against Pacific young people, including me at this age, drove my growing passion to be part of a process of change.

I went straight from high school into my Bachelor of Social Work at Western Sydney University (previously known as University of Western Sydney) with a keen interest to better understand why societies create systems and structures that are not inclusive. As part of our journey to becoming social workers, we undertook three field education placements totalling 1,000 hours. I spent my first placement at a Youth Justice Centre (correctional facility) for young offenders. This broadened my understanding of the significant social and welfare needs of such young people and their families. My second placement was at Centrelink, the national social security agency responsible for providing welfare and employment benefits. This provided a deeper insight into the structures and responses put into practice by the federal government, whilst revealing the siloing of human needs across government departments and entities that don't interact effectively or efficiently. My third and final placement was at Long Bay Correctional Facility for adult offenders. I worked within a pre-release alcohol and other drugs counselling unit, where I further refined my clinical skills and perspectives. I also came to appreciate the need to enact early intervention and prevention strategies with adolescents to deter such young people from becoming recidivist and entrenched adult offenders. It was through this final placement that my desire to make a difference with young people was confirmed. I wanted to be involved in supporting safe spaces for young people to be included in their own communities, so that they didn't feel isolated and alone. So that they weren't treated punitively for their differences, especially based on their ethnicity and socioeconomic status. Something I could personally relate to.

Being a Social Worker

My first full-time job upon completing my social work degree in 2003 was as a Post Release Support Program (PRSP) case worker. The PRSP model was created in the mid 1990s in response to Children's Courts sentencing practice where some young people weren't given subsequent parole periods after being incarcerated. Funded by the NSW government and outsourced to non-government agencies across metropolitan and rural regions, my role involved working within the local government areas (LGAs) of Campbelltown and Liverpool. Both LGAs are part of the greater western Sydney region, known for its working-class population and its many public housing communities where the majority of my client base resided. Another common feature of these two localities was their high proportion of Pacific Islander and Aboriginal communities. My case load reflected this demographic, with up to 90 per cent identifying as such.

After receiving the initial referral from Youth Justice NSW (previously known as the New South Wales Department of Juvenile Justice), my role involved meeting the young person in custody six week prior to their release date. During this phase, we would develop the case plan with the young person, creating possible goals and aspirations generally around educational engagement or employment. We would also map out various health and welfare needs. On release, which would generally involve myself picking them up on discharge from the custodial centre, I would work with the young person and their family for up to twelve weeks. Our focus was to implement the case plan developed prior to their release, with a view to empowering the young person to be self-determined and autonomous, leading to the cessation of antisocial behaviour and criminal activities. But this is was where the problem lay: the expectation that (a) the individual would reform and refrain from perceived problematic behaviours and activities within twelve weeks, (b) the responsibility rested on the individual to change, and (c) the significant social and welfare issues that they had prior to their incarceration would not negatively impact on the trajectory. It was almost expected that the complexities and trauma that came from their circumstances would be resolved within this three-month case management period.

I undertook the case management relationship with each young person, and their family, with much optimism, hoping that my support as a freshly minted social worker would make a difference. However, I soon realized that a large part of my role was to help them navigate and connect with community-based resources and supports that would assist with their significant social and welfare needs. This included, to a large extent, creating my own unique and place-based case management tools and resources. For example, I put together group work activities on improving health literacies around problematic substance use, as a large proportion of the young people I was working with had patterns of underage alcohol consumption and marijuana use. Anger management and interpersonal communication skills workshops were also developed and implemented, to further assist. Rather than rely on waiting for other existing youth services to provide such resources and support, I took the initiative to use my role to fill a gap in service provision and delivery. As I continued my role in the community, I realized that the mainstream legal, educational, health, and welfare services, structures, and systems were also not adequately catering for the sociocultural nuances associated with Pacific and Aboriginal young people.

For example, connection to community, space, and place is a big component of well-being for First Nations young people. The case work that was being developed to reduce recidivist offending needed to be grounded in a connection to culture. This requires an intention to ensure that the case work approach intentionally includes the wider Aboriginal community in supporting a thriving individual identity that is also grounded in community context. Within Western models of case work, we fail to privilege such indigenous perspectives and practices, problematizing individual characteristics as being the cause of crime, rather than a lack of connection to community, culture, folklore, and family.

Learning through Social Work and Education

It was through such deficits in responding to the specific and different needs of Pacific and Aboriginal young people that my desire to learn more thrived. In my second year of being a social worker and undertaking post release case work, I enrolled in a Master's of Education course with Western Sydney University. Specializing in educational leadership, middle years learning, and critical pedagogies, I developed my motivation to mobilize the notion and essence of education as a form of social change.

I also refined my ability to create learning environments, through my social work lens, that would strive to meet some of the significant social and welfare needs of young offenders. Many of my clients aged fifteen to seventeen were struggling with their numeracy and literacy skills, which deterred them from learning in mainstream schools or completing vocational courses towards sustainable employment. The Developing Reading and Writing (DRAW) programme was created in partnership with Macquarie Fields TAFE NSW (Technical and Further Education New South Wales). In this programme, my aim was to facilitate lessons on basic numeracy and literacy skills related to vocational needs. An enrolment in the course also provided my clients with an opportunity to be registered as students to receive social security benefits, which supported their access to money, while also developing pathways to workforce participation. All young people who came through the DRAW programme were known to have been previously expelled from special education programmes and mainstream schools. This was generally due to poor engagement and behaviour management issues alongside feelings of not being included in their own learning. In the three years that the programme operated, no significant behavioural issues occurred. Each young person was made to feel included in their own learning environment. The knowledge I was learning from my Master's in Education, especially around educational leadership, middle year schooling, and critical pedagogies, was being applied through this programme. The DRAW program was also helping to create educational responses that understood the sociocultural and welfare needs of our

Pacific and Aboriginal students, by utilizing learning approaches that were focused on supporting diverse learning styles and needs. It was striving to make a difference through understanding the diverse learning needs of young people, whilst helping them to be and feel included.

Specific Pacific

From my ability to intentionally learn to develop an understanding of the sociocultural and welfare needs of Pacific people, a new service, Pasifika Support Services, was established. Such a specific Pacific model was built upon my previous three years of working with Pacific families in the PRSP role. It was now an opportunity to further explore and embed a specific Pacific lens on case management.

In 2004, the New South Wales government created the NSW Youth Partnership with Pacific Communities. This was developed in response to concerns arising across the state at seeing Pacific communities overrepresented in various educational, legal, health, and welfare settings. The government ambitiously created an implementation committee that was tasked to resolve some of the growing issues. The committee comprised director generals of various government departments, alongside key representatives from Pacific communities. One of the key initiatives that came from this group was to provide funding for a specific Pacific early intervention case management service to work in partnership with NSW police. It was tendered out to the community, and various organizations submitted their bids to provide such support. I was involved in developing the bid for the non-government agency Mission Australia that I had been working for in my Post Release Support Program role. In 2005, we were the successful agency bidder, and I was quickly employed to be the team leader of this new initiative, titled Pasifika Support Services. The twelve-week case management model strove to support Pacific young people known to the police, with a view to assisting them in addressing significant social and welfare needs (Ravulo, 2016a).

A major point in my evolving appreciation for promoting a service that was nuanced with respect to cultural differences was the embedded nature of family: that for Pacific people, our families were integral to our individual success. To achieve prosocial and sustainable case work outcomes, we needed to work alongside the wider family, and to take a more holistic approach to our service delivery model and provision. Failure to include family, and the wider community in which they are located, would prevent successful outcomes.

Rather than pathologize the individual for their individual needs, we needed to take a whole-of-family, whole-of-community approach to supporting the young person's success. And this required a specific Pacific appreciation of cultural norms and values, which are inherently and implicitly different from the white and Western views imposed on such ethnically diverse communities. We needed to create a collaborative approach to cultural diversity, rather than a deficit approach and perspective (Mission Australia & Ravulo, 2009).

One question continued to perplex. Despite all our good intentions to create nuanced and culturally safe spaces for Pacific young people involved in the youth justice system, we didn't have research, evidence, data on why such an overrepresentation was occurring. In the second year of implementing the Pasifika Support Services model, I started my doctorate of cultural research to further explore why this phenomenon was occurring. I wanted to know whether it was our cultural differences creating these tensions with the health, legal, education, and welfare systems and structures. I reviewed 100 case files made up of 50 Pacific and 50 non-Pacific offenders to see the differences in their interactions with the police, the Children's Court, and NSW Juvenile Justice. At the same time, I reviewed their interactions with education and health services and access to community support (Ravulo, 2016c).

In summarizing my hundred-thousand-word-plus portfolio submitted for my professional doctorate in 2009, I was tasked with providing a simple summary statement to capture the key message from my research. *You're not different until someone treats you that way* (Ravulo, 2009). In essence, this statement captured the shame and stigma associated with being culturally different in white and Western settings. That failure to fit in was judged as incongruent and inconsistent with societal norms and values. Conversely, this statement was a challenge to create change, to shift such societal structures and systems to be better. To be inclusive of cultural diversity as a source of strength and solutions in creating responses that were inclusive.

Becoming an Academic and Creating Specific Pacific Initiatives

In 2011, I accepted my first full-time role as an accidental academic in social work (I never planned or anticipated going into academia after my many years of study) at Western Sydney University. During my first six months, I was challenged by the lack of Pacific people involved in our space, despite the western Sydney region being home to one of the largest diasporas of Pacific peoples. I created an initiative called Pasifika Achievement To Higher Education (PATHE) that aims to promote vocational and career aspirations in Pacific communities (Ravulo, 2019a). Based again on critical pedagogies on engaging diversity, the PATHE model first worked in supporting existing Pacific university students to be valued for their diversity. For their Pasifika-ness. To show that it was possible to be ethnically diverse in the white and Western settings found within tertiary institutions. And that such settings also needed to be better at responding to and catering for diversity.

In my desire to add value to the ways in which specific Pacific perspectives could influence Western and white spaces, I undertook a trip across the Pacific region, visiting various islands in the second half of 2012 in my academic role. From this trip I continued to learn about the need to help inform educational settings and services, along with social work education, about Pacific perspectives, principles, views, and values. The Pacific Islands Field Education initiative was born at the beginning of 2013, in partnership with the University of the South Pacific. Our three shared goals were to help provide students from Western Sydney University with an international social work field education opportunity, to help support the development of the social work curriculum across both institutions, and to further support the development of social work as a profession across the region (Ravulo, 2019b).

Pacific Social Work

As the Pacific Islands Field Education initiative was being implemented across the region, which included sending our fourth-year social work students to undertake their final placements over four months in either Fiji, Tonga, Vanuatu, or Samoa, I was continuously challenged by the white and Western views still permeating our profession. The need to create visibility around reshifting and refocusing such social work practices was becoming more and more evident, especially as Pacific indigenous people in the islands, and across the diaspora, were continuously being challenged for their diversity. In 2014, a meeting was convened with my very dear colleagues, Professor Tracie Mafile'o, a Tongan academic from Massey University New Zealand, and Dr Bruce Donald Yeates, who helped introduce and lead social work as a discipline at the University of the South Pacific. We proposed to create an edited collection to be published by Routledge, called *Pacific Social Work* (Ravulo, Mafile'o, & Yeates, 2019). Over the next two years, we collaborated with over thirty contributors to co-create and co-author twenty chapters on how Pacific perspectives, practices, views, and values can be meaningfully included in social work education, practice, policy, and research with and alongside Pacific peoples. And that Pacific ways of knowing and doing, being and becoming could be privileged in white and Western systems and structures still evident in post-colonial Pacific islands, and across the white and Western world in which the Pacific diaspora was located.

And it's through this shared commitment to privileging diversity, and its many differences, that I, as a proud iTaukei Fijian, Anglo Australia, queer, person of colour who grew up in public housing in western Sydney, am still located today. It is through my journey of trying to fit in, of trying to make sense of deficits, of trying to promote sustainable solutions, that I have learnt, and will continue to learn, the importance of inclusion. That to be an inclusive society, we need to celebrate diversity and its differences. To be an inclusive social work profession, we need to be intentional about understanding why people are left in the margins. To call out and critique social structures and systems that perpetuate divisions due to their lack of appreciation for knowledges beyond the white and Western gaze.

Instead of being shy, and shunning my differences as something undesirable, I'm now embracing, rejoicing in, and celebrating my multiple and intersecting identities, and am committed to an ongoing collegial, collaborative, and collective journey that strives to make a difference, through our differences. And it's through the meaningful inclusion and mobility of our many areas of diversity that safe spaces can be created for everyone to be valued and visible, and made to feel like they are part of something that in turn gives them a sense of belonging and purpose. This has been learnt from my journey that I've shared with you all across this chapter. It is an important concept that I continue to cherish from my Pacific indigenous perspectives that I am striving to bring into my social work practice, contributions to helpful policy, and applied research approaches in various spaces and places.

Reflective Questions

1. Does social work in the Pacific differ from social work elsewhere? If yes, what is the difference? If no, what are the similarities?
2. What issues of human rights are discussed in this story?
3. What role does indigenous knowledge play in this story?

REFERENCES

Cook, T. (2007). Remembering Riverwood. https://trevorcook.typepad.com/weblog/2007/03/remembering_riv.html

Gallagher, P., & Poletti, P. (1998). *Sentencing Disparity and the Ethnicity of Juvenile Offenders.* Sydney: Judicial Commission of New South Wales.

Mission Australia & Ravulo, J. (2009). *Developing and Implementing a Case Management Model for Young People with Complex Needs.* Western Sydney University. http://nla.gov.au/nla.obj-254917404/view

Ravulo, J. (2009). The development of anti-social behaviour in Pacific youth. PhD thesis, University of Western Sydney.

Ravulo, J. (2016a). An integrated case management model to assist Pacific youth offenders and their families in Australia. *Care Management Journals*, *17*(4), 170–9. https://doi.org/10.1891/1521-0987.17.4.170

Ravulo, J. (2016b). Pacific epistemologies in professional social work practice, policy and research. *Asia Pacific Journal of Social Work and Development*, *26*(4), 191–202. https://doi.org/10.1080/02185385.2016.1234970

Ravulo, J. (2016c). Pacific youth offending within an Australian context. *Youth Justice*, *16*(1), 34–48. https://doi.org/10.1177/1473225415584983

Ravulo, J. (2019a). Raising retention rates towards achieving vocational and career aspirations in Pacific communities. *International Journal of Lifelong Education*, *38*(2), 214–31. https://doi.org/10.1080/02601370.2019.1585393

Ravulo, J. (2019b). Social work as a recognised profession in the Pacific region. *International Social Work*, *62*(2), 712–25. https://doi.org/10.1177/0020872817747027

Ravulo, J., Mafile'o, T., & Yeates, D. B. (eds.). (2019). *Pacific Social Work: Navigating Practice, Policy and Research.* London: Routledge. https://doi.org/10.4324/9781315144252

CHAPTER 24

"I Was So Tired of All the Words"
The Challenge of Epistemic Injustice for Social Workers

Tony Ghaye

What follows are my reflections on conversations-that-matter, over time, with a social worker, ten years post-qualification.

The social worker (Beverly) recalls:

It's 8 am. My first home visit of the day. My sixth visit to this lady.

"OK, deep breath. Be patient. Listen carefully. Be compassionate. You're here to listen and to help . . .where you can."

I keep repeating these words in my head as Rose, an eighty eight year old widow, opens the door to her home.

Rose, whom I have been 'looking after', is dressed in a floral dress that could do with some soap and hot water. Her cataract operation nine months ago, on both eyes, scared her. She says she didn't understand the procedure properly, but she says she can see better now. She is very hard of hearing but refuses to wear hearing aids. She lives in a small, two-bedroom home. She has lived there for forty-four years; forty-one of those years were with her beloved husband who has now passed away. The house is full of memories.

Her eldest son lives far away and rarely visits or phones her. And when he does come, maybe twice a year, but never at special times like Easter or Christmas, he tries to "take over" (as Rose describes it), getting her to do things which make her uncomfortable. For example, taking long car rides into the countryside until every bone in her body aches after sitting in a car for three hours. During this time her son asks her to look here and then to look there! "He frightens me," she told me. "He just doesn't listen. He always thinks what he is doing is right and helpful, but he never listens to what I say."

Her youngest son also lives far away but does phone twice a week and visits her whenever he can. But he is self-employed and has his own responsibilities. Despite finding as much time as possible to spend with Rose, he is still acutely aware that she spends many days each month on her own. I was with Rose one day and met him. He told me how Rose had lost her voice on more than one occasion because she "simply did not use it enough." Whether this was because she saw so few people, or whether she felt there was little point in speaking to those who did come, it was an issue which deeply concerned him.

And now Rose looks at me, the cup of tea in her hand that I have just made, and says, aggressively, "Do you know what's wrong with me?" This tone is unlike Rose. I need to handle the question sensitively – I don't wish to put words in Rose's mouth, although I'm sure so much of what she is experiencing stems from the loss of her husband, Albert. As a social worker I know a bit about how people try to deal with their 'pain' and the way it can often be tied to loss. But I've also learned that change and loss can go together and this can be uncomfortable.

I say nothing for now, allowing her to go on. Rose tries to wipe away her running mascara. "Why did Albert leave me? Why? What is left for me now? I can't believe it. I just can't believe how I've ended up like this. I'm so lonely. Apart from you and my youngest son, I hardly speak to anyone. The 'others' that come here just talk at me, not to me. I don't hear them clearly. I can't follow them. They keep telling me what they think I need. But it's different from what I want! I just want everything to go away. Just look at me! This is not what I wanted: to be living like this. Will I die lonely? Can anyone ever die happy?"

Right here, right now it's so hard to separate my personal struggles with my own elderly and lonely mum's feelings, from those of Rose. Perhaps social work is not for me? Perhaps I should try another line of work? My own eyes start to fill up with tears as I ponder, in-the-moment, where this story might go. I am reminded of a time, when doing my degree in social work, that my professor talked about humility. He said that to be a good social worker we need humility. He explained it as an awareness that there's a lot we don't know, and that a lot we think we know is partial, maybe distorted and even wrong. It seems an acceptance of this is absolutely OK, right now. But what I do know, for sure, is that Rose is very unhappy, eating poorly, and almost always in some kind of physical pain.

I can sense that Rose has some very deep, unanswered questions, but feels that no one truly listens to her when she speaks. She is questioning her purpose and life now, without the husband who loved and respected her for so many decades. Even in her own home, she clearly feels vulnerable. I can imagine Rose, as a younger woman; hardworking, loyal, and with a true sense of pride. Her house tells me that she has taken a lot of care in making it a warm and friendly home. She would have been listened to back then for sure. Her stamp is clearly on the home (and garden) that she has made here:

the choice of décor, the photos, the furnishings, pictures on the wall. There is nothing 'old' about Rose's home; she has moved with the times and chosen carefully all that is inside these four walls.

As Rose quietly sobs, a thousand things race through my mind. I tell myself, "Hey you're a social worker. Remind yourself why you are here. Tell yourself again that your work does not occur in a vacuum. Rose and I, who we are, how we live, how we feel, matters. It REALLY matters. It's so important to feel you matter. I'm not just here with Rose to fill a space. Not just because she feels so lonely. Rose is desperate, confused, lost. She only has her television and radio and her magazines for company."

"I always listen to you, Rose," I hear myself saying.

But, do I? Do I really listen as she talks about things which I have heard over and over again? Or does my mind wander off, without me realizing, until I tune back in again much further down the line? I know that I've answered her sometimes and she has looked at me in a strange way. Perhaps I've missed something critical that she has said, something that was different to the last time we spoke? Rose doesn't have dementia; she is fully aware of conversations that we have had previously and so she would know if I was really listening to her.

Then the next visit . . . all that has gone before has made me determined to tune in more and to find out what Rose has been saying, to me and to others. To discover those things which she feels are either not taken seriously or, worse still, being ignored.

I focus on my body language and turn my chair to face her so that she can see me more clearly. I take her hand in mine and ask her to tell me what she would like me to do to help her today. I know this could spark a sharp retort of "There's nothing you can do to help!" but Rose is now deep in thought and quiet. She is looking at me in a kindly way; the aggression that I saw on my last visit has evaporated.

"Can I tell you what I really want?" Rose says. "I want to have my youngest son here with me. He reassures me and he knows what I want. He listens to me and he is kind to me."

This isn't exactly the request that I was expecting. I thought Rose might ask for some more magazines, or a book from the library, or perhaps some scented cream for her hands. Wanting her son to move in and care for her is a very different proposition. I know, from having spoken to her son, that his workload and commitments will not allow him to live with his mother full-time. He visits as often as he can and spends time staying with her, but this clearly makes the absences even harder when he departs. Rose tells me she cries when he goes, on the doorstep, as he drives away.

I decide to answer Rose with a question because I know that she is more than capable of working out the answer for herself. Old and frail she may look, but her mind is sharp and her reasoning fully intact.

"If your son were here, right now, would you ask him to become your full-time carer?" Rose looks at me with surprise in her eyes. "But I would care for *him*!" she exclaims, "like I always have done. I don't need a full-time carer."

This gives me an opportunity to steer the conversation towards Rose's needs. Her perception of what she is capable of doing is admirable, but she has vulnerabilities which she is unable to accept right now. These are especially on show when she is in her kitchen cooking and making tea. She has a gas cooker. The open flames are dangerous. She knows what she wants, and she is desperate to tell others what her wants are, but then she feels ignored when they are dismissed because other people think they know better!

I'm aware, for example, that she misses her shopping trips and taking her time to pick the best vegetables. Because Rose is unsteady on her feet, she depends on home delivery of her food. She is of an age where ordering food online from the supermarket is beyond her. And she rarely goes out – the last time she did, she fell in icy weather. She tried, before her fall, to walk to her closest bus stop, 100 metres away, down an uneven pavement. Sadly, this made her ill as the bus didn't come on time and she stood there in the freezing cold. No neighbours offered her a lift in their car. "Too busy with their own lives," Rose often said. Social services had a bus and she tried that. But it took two hours to get into town after going around all the houses picking everyone up. And another two hours on the way back. Rose found this very tiring. The town was also very busy and she felt very vulnerable there. So, Rose became increasingly house-bound.

We discuss how she feels about the support she gets with her shopping. I talk positively about her youngest son who genuinely wants to care for her and give back some of the goodness that she has given him during his lifetime. I emphasize that this is a privilege, not a burden, and that she deserves it. I reassure her that I will always listen to what she has to say and that I will offer her what she wants, as far as I am able to do that.

We talk through the things that I enjoy doing for her: making her breakfast when I come at 8 am: a small piece of toast and a cup of tea. Sometimes porridge. Then the cleaning and checking the laundry, looking through the TV programmes for that day and choosing some she may like to watch. Or simply sitting and chatting. That's what she enjoys and wants the most. These conversations, especially over some hot Earl Grey tea and a chocolate biscuit, are what I call moments-of-magic, for both of us, even if some of our conversations are not easy ones!

I feel honoured that Rose has gone way beyond hiding her insecurities from me now. There is more openness. She tells me that she worries a lot about all sorts of things which others may find trivial. She worries when the mail hits the carpet by her front door. It's always greeted with, "Oh God what's that?" Brown-coloured envelopes are the worst. They are usually about bills to be paid and always written in a language she doesn't understand! Jargon she calls it. She worries about the man who comes to clean her windows too.

I often think of the conversations that I've had with Rose (and particularly the one that is summarized below) as 'the beginning of knowing' because I can never claim to know it all. I anchor all my social work on this idea now. I find it helpful as it relates to what Megele (2015) calls "relationship-based social work practice." It's where I finally feel I connect, properly listen to and learn, with an open heart and mind. This takes time. Sometimes it never happens. But that's another story! The story that I want to recall below revealed itself over a number of home visits. I pieced it together and checked out some of the 'facts' by getting a copy of a 'file' of notes that each visitor to Rose's home wrote and left there. Rose never bothered to look at it.

On this occasion, it was a late November morning. I arrived as usual and we started to go through those things which were becoming trusted and respectful routines. Rose was sitting in her favourite chair, clutching a box of tissues, which always indicated that Rose wanted to say something important and she wanted me to know. I sat alongside, acutely aware that I was in that space between knowing and not knowing.

There were many people coming to Rose's house now, but she was still intensely lonely. As she sat with her emotions, after the health and welfare 'people' had gone, her vulnerability made her feel even more lonely, pathetic, and even shameful. I have sat with people who are dealing with all kinds of feelings and situations. The loss of a child, the loss of a partner, the loss of a marriage, a pet, a job, the loss of an identity even. I've sat with people who have lost a dream, a body part, and lost their youth. But what followed seemed different.

Rose began, "You know I don't go out much now. Some time ago, I can't remember exactly when, maybe a couple of months, I slipped and bumped my head and sprained my ankle. I don't know if you know, but that man who runs the newspaper shop, saw me fall. He called for an ambulance. I went to one of the city hospitals. I was a bit confused.

So much was happening. So many people I didn't know. So many questions. Oh, so many questions. One was how they could contact my son, the eldest one as they assumed this was best. They sent me home by a taxi. It was dark. I remember that."

I quickly understood that they had sent Rose home so fast that there was nobody at home to meet her. How on earth could that happen? We at social services were not notified. I was very unhappy about that. She hated asking her neighbours for anything. She was embarrassed, and when her husband was alive, he did everything. So she had no need to ask for their help! Rose told me she spent the next couple of days on her own. Fortunately, there was food in her cupboard. Still no one came. Rose's ankle, she remembers, was very painful. I asked if I could check her phone to see if there were any missed calls. There were and most significantly from Homecare Services!

Then, Rose continued, "All of a sudden, one day, so many people came. They came early. Strangers who said they were there to help me with this and that. And you know I don't like strangers."

I checked back, deep into her file. Someone from Homecare Services and a 'handling officer' came. "They were nice but they told me lots and lots of things. What I could expect to happen now. What was free and what wasn't. I couldn't follow everything. I was so tired of all the words. They didn't seem to notice my tiredness. I wanted to ask them about who would look after me, but they were unsure and they had to go soon. I really wanted to have a shower, but I was afraid I'd slip. So, I didn't ask them to help me in the end. They said a nurse would come later, but they weren't sure when. I was very confused."

Later that morning, according to the notes, a physiotherapist and occupational therapist arrived. Rose wasn't expecting them. "I got upset, very upset. They started to move all my furniture around. They talked a lot to each other, but I couldn't hear them. They were very kind, like the others, but I didn't feel in control of what was happening in my own home. And they didn't notice this."

Rose used to know where everything was. It was being moved for her own safety but not with her full understanding and therefore her full consent. "I felt out of control. They said my big bed had to go and some kind of 'hospital' bed installed that went up and down. My bed was the bed Albert and me had for a wedding gift." What I learned from this was that the 'therapists' were concerned with the increasing risk of Rose developing bed sores, while Rose was *only* concerned about the deep attachments she had with her marital bed.

"In the afternoon the doorbell rang. You know how I hate that sound. I was resting but it kept ringing. I opened it and there was a strange man standing there. My heart raced. He said he had come to fit a safety alarm." Rose didn't recognize him and didn't really know what to do. She felt vulnerable but, nevertheless, let him into the house. This was something else that worried me a lot. He started work. I later discovered that Rose's eldest son had asked for the alarm to be fitted but 'forgot' to tell Rose he was coming! The man explained how it worked and left. Rose wasn't really interested.

And then, later that afternoon a nurse arrived. She looked at Rose's head and ankle, told her to stay inside, not to go shopping and that she would arrange for social services to shop for her. Rose was now feeling very depressed.

When it was getting dark, the house was empty again. Surprisingly her eldest son phoned, and asked lots of questions about who had come and their names. Rose couldn't remember everyone. Her son promised to visit her but then said that he would need to ask if he could get time off work and so he might not come at all. Rose described this as a "nothing conversation"!

During my later conversations about this fall and its consequences, it was clear that Rose had received lots of advice and information. Rose repeatedly said that everyone was kind but that she didn't always agree with them. She felt powerless to argue. She often said, "They have more words than me!"

Rose told me that she used to have two other social workers and that they had become her rock. They helped her with her meals, her laundry, and when it would be best to get her groceries. But then they stopped coming.

And now I was in the role of being her rock. I had to ensure that she always felt sure of me, trusted me, and knew that she could rely on me. So, when she worried about her hair, I would reassure her that someone would cut it for her whilst I was there. When she wanted to try to be a little more active, I could reassure her that the nurse wouldn't get angry. When the physiotherapist visited twice a week to cream her legs and help her with exercises, I could reassure her. These thoughts were a serious reminder to me that I had to do what I promised. I couldn't say one thing and do something else!

I promised to keep the house clean and tidy but take guidance from Rose. I'll be very careful not to move anything without Rose giving it her blessing. I will try to think as Rose would think, to stand in her shoes and imagine what it must feel like to have a voice but not be heard. I thought this was *the* way to continue to win Rose's trust and respect. I always wanted to feel that not only have I done my best for her, but fulfilled my goal to be the best social worker that I can be. That is, to be the best version of me.

* * *

My (Tony's) PERSONAL REFLECTIONS on some aspects of Beverly's experiences with Rose.

I know Beverly very well and we have discussed what follows many times. I have been in a mentoring relationship with her for several years and at all times encouraged her to explore what 'being a reflective social work practitioner' might mean to her. Additionally, we have often spoken about the limits of learning alone. So once every month, she brings her reflective diary (Ghaye & Lillyman, 2008) with her, as fuel for our time together, which we call 'our conversations-that-matter'. She chooses what to disclose from her diary and she keeps her diary with her. It's like an aide-memoire for her. What follows are some of the key issues, core concepts, and practices that have emerged from our many conversations about Rose. Together we became rather addicted to Rose because we felt she helped us come to know ourselves and our work so much better. This filled us with gratitude.

In the Introduction to this book, I set out what we believe to be three intelligences (later referred to as 'frames of mind') for creating social work stories-that-matter. I reproduce it here (Figure 8) as a reference point for what follows.

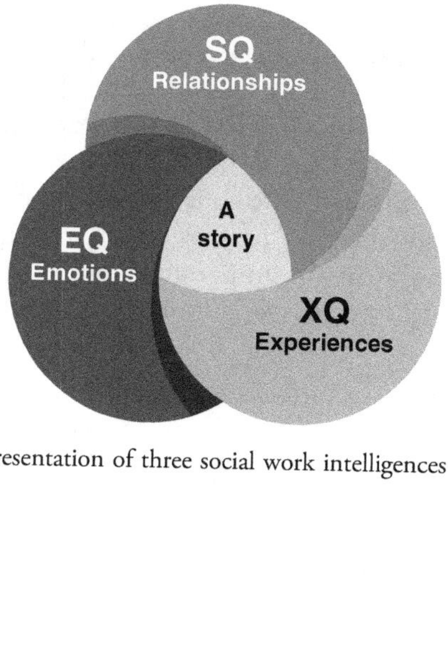

Figure 8 A re-presentation of three social work intelligences (frames of mind)

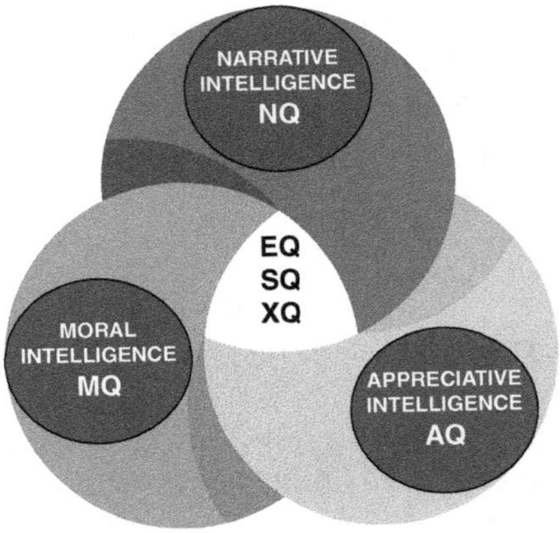

Figure 9 Multiple intelligences (frames of mind) needed for social work

Every day, I (Tony) always ask myself four important reflective questions:

1. What am I learning here?
2. What might I do with what I am learning?
3. What is motivating me to be better?
4. So, what happens next?

In the spirit of this, I now wish to re-present Figure 8 as the more holistic Figure 9. Emotions are intrinsic to social work. Social workers often experience relatively high levels of burnout compared with other health care professionals. The capacity to manage one's own emotional reactions efficiently, frequently in complex care settings, is central to their role (Bunce & King, 2019; Herland, 2022). Social interventions can be very complex and affect social workers' emotional well-being. Hence the importance of EQ in social work (Howe, 2008; Ingram, 2015; Moesby-Jensen & Nielsen, 2015; Ruiz-Fernández et al., 2021).

Social workers also connect with people at points of crisis and need. Therefore, I suggest, the quality of human connection (or relationships) is a fundamental part of social work practices (see SQ). This is elaborated upon in the important work of Pooler, Wolfer, and Freeman (2014). Furthermore, O'Connor helpfully links these two points together thus:

> This relational practice involves emotions in the process of engagement, communication and the building of working relationships. Contextually, such relationships involve diverse emotions, whether social work practice is

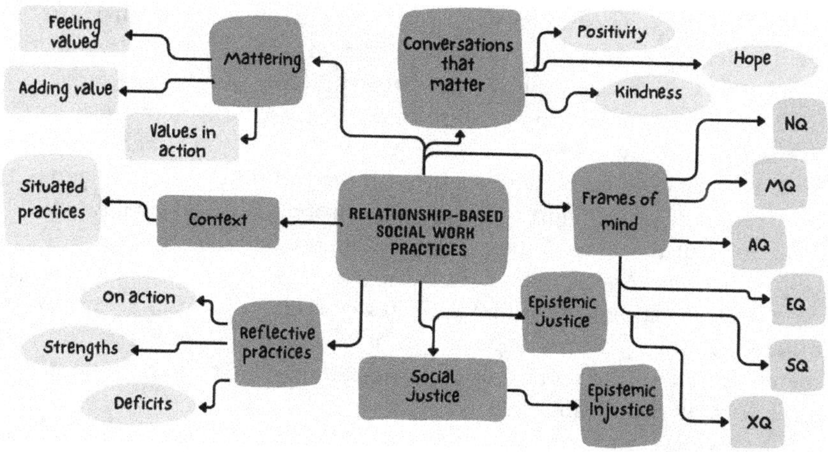

Figure 10 A mind map of social work as relationship-based practice

> occurring in therapeutic, procedural, voluntary or involuntary contexts. It is relevant therefore to ask how social workers themselves understand, relate to and use their emotions in professional practice. (O'Connor, 2020, p.645)

The emotions of both social workers and the people they interact with contribute to the social worker's lived experiences of practice (see XQ). Its essential to remember that practice wisdom is an emergent process.

As I hold this more holistic approach to my work (Figure 9), new and challenging questions always reveal themselves. For example, in relation to Rose and Beverly's experiences, *Is it OK to cry with a client and/or a colleague?* On occasions with Beverly, I felt emotionally overwhelmed. I still justify my tears, not because I felt emotionally out of control, but because I felt an authentic emotional connection with this whole scenario. I am reminded that the social worker's personal and professional identities are interwoven. This affects everything that I have come to know as relationship-based practice. Figure 10 shows this more holistic view of the 'frames of mind' that both Beverly and I claim to make sense of our work. We have co-constructed it.

I explain Figure 10 by referring back to Gardner's theory of multiple intelligences, first mentioned in his 1983 book *Frames of Mind.* The notion of 'frames', I suggest, is extremely helpful for social work education and practices. Frames of mind are an essential broadening of our conception of 'intelligence'. Together they offer us different 'lenses' through which to try to apprehend the world. They give us an added and much needed sense of 'perspectivism'. Social work is much more than simply 'being smart' (i.e. IQ). It's also being smart in complementary ways.

A brief 'walk through' Figure 10 starts with foregrounding narrative as a fundamental organizing process for human experience. Here I use narrative synonymously with story. Narrative intelligence (NQ) helps us make sense of lived experiences across a lifespan (or part of it). Being able to (co) construct a narrative and/or change our personal narratives, helps give life some kind of meaning. When NQ is used competently and wisely it can help social workers explore, with those they care for, how (re)seeing, or even reconstructing (if possible) their stories, seeing them more 'flexibly' or differently, may lead to a greater sense of possibility and 'control' and therefore lead to different kinds of conversations-that-matter. Some stories serve us well, others do not.

The twin notions of *narrative turn* and *emergence* are central to our understanding of NQ. The narrative turn (Polkinghorne, 1991, cited in Goodson & Gill, 2011) is a term used primarily in literary studies and social and human sciences and expresses a shift towards legitimizing people's stories as important sources of empirical knowledge (Hyvärinen, 2010; Bruce et al., 2016). Secondly, the way daily experiences come together to form some kind of account, or personal story, can be regarded as a process of emergence. Stories can take time to emerge and for words or images to be associated with them. Emergence can be a messy, fractured, and often an incomplete process. Sometimes *themes* can emerge from reflections on stories. Themes like hope, attachment, gratitude, pride, growing old, and loss. Three themes in Rose's story are those of loneliness, kindness, and feeling she mattered.

For many people, merely being alone does not necessarily mean feeling lonely. For Rose she was both. Nearly one in four people (25 per cent) worldwide, which translates into more than a billion people, feel 'very' or 'fairly' lonely, according to a recent Meta-Gallup survey of more than 140 countries (Maese, 2023). Social needs are universal and the degree to which they are fulfilled, or not, impacts the health, well-being and resilience of people everywhere (Sagan, 2023). It's also worth noting that some psychologists and social neuroscientists often refer to loneliness as 'painful isolation'. The emphasis on painful is there to make a clear distinction between solitude as the state of being alone, and subjective loneliness, which is the distressing feeling that comes from unmet expectations of the types of interpersonal relationships we wish to have. We can find painful isolation in Rose's story also.

Appreciative intelligence (AQ) also features in Figure 9. I suggest it is another essential frame of mind for social workers. AQ is a way of letting a different (not necessarily a better) future unfold. It emanates from the powerful and impactful field of appreciative inquiry and invites all social workers and educators to contemplate the nature and role of appreciative questions, appreciative voice, and appreciative resilience. I include this 'frame of mind' because it leads us to reflect on something we might call 'appreciative knowing' (Srivastva & Cooperrider, 1999). Due to limitations of space, I use the definition of AQ developed by Thatchenkery and Metzker (2006) as a useful one for social work. They argue that our appreciative intelligence is another type of intelligence within the multiple intelligence field. They propose that there are three components of appreciative intelligence: the ability to appreciate the positive, reframing and see how the future unfolds from aspects of the positive present. For this to happen we need to be persistent, have self-belief, have a tolerance of uncertainty, and have irrepressible resilience. (See also Melander-Wikman, Jansson & Ghaye, 2006, for an elaboration of AQ in the context of home healthcare in Sweden.)

And finally with regard to moral intelligence. MQ influences the nature and strength of one's *moral agency* as well as our ethical decision-making processes. Moral agency, I suggest, can be regarded as a core capability for social workers. Those with low MQ (and of course some with certain kinds of mental illness) sometimes have difficulty knowing right from wrong. More specifically, low MQ in social workers can lead to difficulties in knowing the difference between doing things right and doing the right thing.

MQ is, surprisingly, a relative newcomer on the social work playing field. Lennick and Kiel (2005) suggest there are four "principles" associated with MQ, all of which are relevant to social work. They are:

1. Integrity: Doing what we know is right, acting in line with our principles and beliefs and informed by our duty of care and codes of conduct.
2. Responsibility: This is another key attribute of a social worker with MQ. This can mean taking responsibility for one's actions, (Martin, 2003) and the consequences of those actions.
3. Compassion: This attribute of MQ relates to caring for oneself and others. MQ can help those involved develop a deep respect for others and for themselves.
4. Forgiveness: Without a tolerance for and an ability to learn from our mistakes and failures (as well as from our successes), we are less likely to be flexible and responsive to the needs and wants of those we are

> caring for. Forgiveness is closely supported by compassion. Both (3) and (4) concern how social workers 'see' themselves and how they relate to others. Moral incompetence, moral compass, moral positioning also are all relevant aspects of MQ that, I suggest, social worker education might positively embrace.

Arguably, another appreciation from my reflective conversations with Beverly, is that they have clarified and enriched my understanding of my own practice. It's a reflection of mentoring as a two-way growth process. They have exposed those aspects where I am a living contradiction (not living my values fully in my practice) and also where I can claim to contribute to the well-being of others (a congruence between my espoused values and values-in-action). The essential ideas and processes of what I have come to believe relationship-based social work to be, are shown in Figure 10 as a mind map.

Let me selectively illuminate one major aspect of Figure 10. It's with regard to the challenge of epistemic injustice (EI). I focus on this as an important lens through which we can deepen our understanding of aspects of Rose's story. Epistemic injustices are socially situated, which puts questions of power and social identity centre stage. EI helps us understand the practices of communicating knowledge to others through 'telling'. This, of course, is deceptively complex, if only because what we say is not always what others hear, or are receptive to hearing. Epistemic in/justice is therefore a significant part of what I have come to know as *relationship-based social work practice.*

In Rose's story we see a number of statements referring to what we might generally call 'being listened to' or not! We can also find a disconnect between what Rose wanted and what others felt Rose needed. To understand the critical role that epistemic injustice plays in the practice of social workers, we need to appreciate the various forms of epistemic injustice first elaborated by Fricker (2007) in her groundbreaking book *Epistemic Injustice: Power and Ethics of Knowing.* I suggest this needs to be an essential part of social work education as it encourages us to pay close attention to lived experiences. "Epistemic injustice is concerned with forms of unfair treatment that 'relate to issues of knowledge, understanding and participation in communicative practices' (Kidd, Medina, & Pohlhaus, 2017, p.1) and has been defined as 'any unjust epistemic relation which disadvantages someone in [their] capacity as a knower' (Mitova, 2020, p.708)" (Cummings et al., 2023, p.1967).

Epistemic injustices are linked to larger structures of socioeconomic inequality (Coady, 2017), and may even entrench and amplify them (Kidd et al., 2017).

> "Although this focus on epistemic injustice has great value . . . so far it has largely been divorced from action to address these injustices. Concerted action is needed because, just as 'there is no global social justice without global cognitive justice' (De Sousa Santos, 2016, p.42), there is no global justice without epistemic justice . . . we need to make the optimum use of all knowledges, some of which are obscured and devalued by epistemic injustice, and to make sure that all voices are heard. (Cummings et al., 2023, p.2)

Realigned, this proposition can be transformed into a great question for all social workers, namely, *What knowledges are known, or worth knowing, in order for me to practice well?*

I focus more in this chapter on injustice than justice because EI can be a serious problem. One implication for social work with an eye on social justice, is that it can give an impression that justice is a desirable and achievable norm whereas injustice is the opposite of this. In my personal experience of working internationally, injustice can be 'the norm' and so it's critical to understand how these injustices manifest themselves and, for some, what they might do about them! The challenge is trying to understand both why this is the case and how to work with this kind of normality! It also sets up the idea that to pursue social justice we must eliminate and get rid of injustice. There is a parallel conversation in the strength-based paradigm (Buckingham, 2007; Meyers, 2022; Moore, 2023) where some see 'being strong' as just about the absence of weakness. And in applied positive psychology we find debates about positivity and positive emotions (Collins, 2007; Fredrickson, 2009; Kashdan and Biswas-Diener, 2014) as the opposite to negativity and negative emotions. These polarities are everywhere. For example, wellness is not simply the absence of illness (Searle, Pykett, & Alfaro-Simmonds, 2021). It's much more than this! They all have a part to play in understanding human experience. To clarify, Fricker states that EI is "some kind of 'wrong' done to someone specifically in their capacity as a knower. I call them *testimonial injustice* and *hermeneutical injustice*" (Fricker, 2007, p.1). Due to limitations of space, I am only focusing on testimonial injustice here as it's the most directly relatable to Rose's story. However, the other is just as relevant.

Testimonial injustice is hugely relevant. It's the process whereby someone attributes too little (or too much) credibility to a testimony due to identity prejudice on the hearer's part. For example, it can occur when prejudice causes a hearer (social worker, healthcare worker, others) to give a deflated (or inflated) level of credibility to a speaker's words. For example, what can an eight-year-old tell me that I don't already know? We should listen to them because they are a doctor. And so on.

To elaborate a little. It may be because of the hearer's beliefs and experiences, centred around identity issues like being young/old, qualified, un/professional, an immigrant, black, lover, being a politician, gay, white, inexperienced, disabled, different, orphaned, and so on. This is where we can find identity prejudice. The experiences of some individuals, families, or groups are that they can be subject to being silenced or marginalized, peripheralized or ignored. Simply left out, not noticed, and feeling that they don't matter. 'Silencing' is where the speaker has so little credibility that s/he might as well not have even spoken.

Anderson (2012) makes a distinction between "transactional testimonial injustice," where epistemic injustice is due to the identity prejudice of an identifiable agent, and "structural testimonial injustice," where "institutions are set up to exclude people without anyone having to decide to do so" (p.166). The level of suffering caused by epistemic injustices does not seem to be fully recognized in social work research and practice as yet.

And a final reflection. Last time I met Beverly there was a deep sadness in her eyes. She said, "Last evening at 11 pm, Rose passed away peacefully in her sleep. Her youngest son was with her. He is devastated."

I dedicate this text to Rose's life, the joy she brought to all those she met through 'true presence' and the wisdom she so freely offered. May the girl who was born in a tough mining community, who lost both her parents before she was a teenager, a devoted mother and wife, an inspiration to us all, rest in eternal peace.

Reflective Questions

1. What are your standout social work strengths?
2. In your own work or life, when could a strength also be a weakness?
3. What might you feel was a 'significant encounter' during the last week? Why was it significant for you and others involved?
4. What do you feel are some of the most important things that help, or get in the way of, meaningful relationship-based social work?
5. In what ways have you become aware of epistemic injustice in your work and life?

REFERENCES

Anderson, E. (2012). Epistemic justice as a virtue of social institutions, *Social Epistemology*, *26*(2), 163–73.

Bruce, A., Beuthin, R., Sheilds, L., Molzahn, A., & Schick-Makaroff, K. (2016). Narrative research evolving: Evolving through narrative research, *International Journal of Qualitative Methods*, *15*(1).

Buckingham, M. (2007). *Go Put Your Strengths to Work*. London: Simon & Schuster.

Bunce, L., & King, N. (2019). Emotional intelligence and self-determined behaviour reduce psychological distress: Interactions with resilience in social work students in the UK. *British Journal of Social Work*, *49*(8), 2092–111.

Coady, D. (2017). Epistemic injustice as distributive injustice. In I. Kidd, J. Medina, & G. Pohlhaus (eds.), *The Routledge Handbook of Epistemic Injustice*, London & New York: Routledge.

Collins, S. (2007). Social workers, resilience, positive emotions and optimism. *Practice*, *19*(4), 255–69.

Cummings, S., Dhewa, C., Kemboi, G., & Young, S. (2023). Doing epistemic justice in sustainable development: Applying the philosophical concept of epistemic injustice to the real world. *Sustainable Development*, *31*(3), 1965–77.

De Sousa Santos, B. (2016). *Epistemologies of the South: Justice against Epistemicide*. London: Routledge.

Fredrickson, B. (2009). *Positivity: Groundbreaking Research Reveals How to Embrace the Hidden Strength of Positive Emotions, Overcome Negativity, and Thrive*. New York: Crown Publishing.

Fricker, M., (2007), *Epistemic Injustice: Power and Ethics of Knowing*. Oxford University Press.

Ghaye, T. (2022). Concerned Arctic peoples: Characteristics of conversations-that-matter. In R. Sørly, T. Ghaye, & B. Kårtveit (eds.), *Stories of Change and Sustainability in the Arctic Regions: The Interdependence of Local and Global*, pp.16–40. London: Routledge.

Ghaye, T., & Lillyman, S. (2008). *The Reflective Mentor*, London: Quay Books.

Goodson, I. F., & Gill, S. R. (2011). *Narrative Pedagogy: Life History and Learning*. Pieterlen: Peter Lang.

Herland, M. (2022). Emotional intelligence as a part of critical reflection in social work practice and research. *Qualitative Social Work*, *21*(4), 662–78. https://doi.org/10.1177/14733250211024734

Howe, D. (2008). *The Emotionally Intelligent Social Worker*. Basingstoke: Palgrave Macmillan.

Hyvärinen, M. (2010). Revisiting the narrative turns. *Life Writing*, 7(1), 69–82.

Ingram, R. (2015). *Understanding Emotions in Social Work: Theory, Practice and Reflection*. Maidenhead: Open University Press.

Kashdan, T., & Biswas-Diener, R. (2014). *The Upside of Your Dark Side*, New York: Hudson Street Press.

Kidd, I., Medina, J., & Pohlhaus, G. (eds.). (2017). *The Routledge Handbook of Epistemic Injustice*. London & New York: Routledge.

Lennick, D., and Kiel, F. (2005). *Moral Intelligence: Enhancing Business Performance and Leadership Success*. New Jersey: Wharton School Press.

Maese, E. (2023, 24 October). Almost a quarter of the world feels lonely. *Gallup Blog*. https://news.gallup.com/opinion/gallup/512618/almost-quarter-world-feels-lonely.aspx

Martin, R. (2003). *The Responsibility Virus: Stop Taking Charge or Taking Orders and Start Making Critical Dcisions*. London: Prentice-Hall.

Megele, C. (2015). *Psychosocial and Relationship-Based Practice*. London: Routledge.

Melander-Wikman, A., Jansson, M., & Ghaye, T. (2006). Reflections on an appreciative approach to empowering elderly people, in home healthcare. *Reflective Practice*, 7(4), 423–44.

Meyers, D. (2022). *How Do We Know Ourselves?* New York: Farrar, Straus and Giroux.

Mitova, V. (2020). Explanatory injustice and epistemic agency. *Ethical Theory and Moral Practice: An International Forum*, *23*(5), 707–22.

Moesby-Jensen, C., & Nielsen, H. S. (2015). Emotional labour in social workers' practice. *European Journal of Social Work*, *18*, 690–702.

Moore, T. (2023). Relationships and reciprocity? Strength-based social work in adult social care. In T. Moore (ed.), *Principles of Practice by Principal Social Workers*, St Albans: Critical Publishing.

O'Connor, L. (2020). How social workers understand and use their emotions in practice: A thematic synthesis literature review. *Qualitative Social Work: Research and Practice*, 19(4), 645–62.

Polkinghorne, D. (1991). Narrative and self-concept. *Journal of Narrative and Life History*, *1*, 135–53.

Pooler, D., Wolfer, T., & Freeman, M. (2014). Finding joy in social work. II: Intrapersonal sources. *Social Work*, *59*(3), 213–21.

Ruiz-Fernández, M., et al. (2021). Emotions, feelings, and experiences of social workers while attending to vulnerable groups: A qualitative approach. *Healthcare*, *9*(1).

Sagan, O. (2023). Organised loneliness and its discontents. *Diversity & Inclusion Research*, *1*(1), e12008. https://doi.org/10.1002/dvr2.12008

Searle, B. A., Pykett, J., and Alfaro-Simmonds, M. J. (2021). *A Modern Guide to Wellbeing Research*. Cheltenham: Edward Elgar Publishing.

Srivastva, S., & Cooperrider, D. (1999). *Appreciative Management and Leadership: The Power of Positive Thought and Action in Organization*. Euclid, OH: Williams Custom Publishing.

Storance, K. (2019). Appreciative souls. *AI Practitioner: International Journal of Appreciative Inquiry*, *21*(4).

Thatchenkery, T., & Metzker, C. (2006). *Appreciative Intelligence: Seeing the Mighty Oak in the Acorn*. San Francisco, CA: Berrett-Koehler.

CHAPTER 25

What Next?

Tony Ghaye and Rita Sørly

A number of themes are woven into the fabric of this book. We suggest some of them are:

1. That in our social work we need to constantly hold under review these two questions. *Whose reality counts?* and *Whose knowledge is worth knowing?*
2. That people matter and that social work educational curricula and practices might usefully deepen their understanding of two notions of mattering, namely, (a) feeling valued, (b) adding value to oneself and others' lives. This is at the heart of relationship-based social work practice.
3. That the development and use of 'appreciation' is a fundamental sensitivity for social workers. This means valuing those things of value (however this may be determined) and that enhance human flourishing and well-being.
4. That despite the (still) pervasive deficit-based (problem-solving) social work mindset and pedagogy, social workers might also (re) discover, focus on, and celebrate what works, what's better, and what's possible, right, and just, everyday in their practices.
5. That it's important to create safe and brave places and spaces to have conversations-that-matter and that these are not frivolous or a luxury. Rather, they are an essential way to understand how social workers help each other and the people they care for. Also, they might learn to be creative, get a sense of how they are making a positive difference to the lives of others, and know when working life feels purposeful.
6. That there are many ways to tell, many ways to interpret and potentially learn from stories. Stories of lived experience might provide a welcome antidote to the expansion of social work jargon and borrowed multi-agency slogans. A challenging and contentious

question to take on beyond reading this book might be, *Who's telling the right story?*

7. That we become fully aware of some of the practical dilemmas involved in postmodern critical social work (Fook, 2023), which helps us understand and deal with perspectives that fly in the face of social justice principles. The notions of epistemic justice and injustice need to be more front and centre in social work.
8. That the practices of reflection in, on, and for action (Ghaye, 2005, 2008, 2010; Ghaye & Lillyman, 2014) and the way they generate experiential knowledge (EQ) are a source of learning which can be put to good future use. In turn, how EQ relates to the other five 'frames of mind' articulated in the book.
9. That it's time social work became even more mindful of the dangers of only being consumers of knowledge 'from elsewhere' and especially of knowledge generated from WEIRD interests (western, educated, industralized, rich, and democratic). With its emphasis on stories-that-matter, we are encouraging all social workers to think of themselves as knowledge-creators. The implication of this is to recognize that they are capable of generating valid descriptions and explanations of their own practices and what influences their own learning in their work with others. This opens up the possibility of a socially situated living-theory, as an individual social worker's explanation of their social influences in caring for others (Whitehead, 1993). This avoids the pervasive and limiting duality of practice–theory 'gaps'.
10. And finally, something that was shown in Figure 10 and embedded in many stories, namely the way social work might be construed as practical acts of kindness. These may be seen in at least five ways: (a) as a small act, (b) as a random act, (c) as a planned intervention, (d) as a consideration, (e) as something that makes someone feel good. Kindness is action intended to benefit others. For social work going forward, a challenge is not only about the reason for and the consequences of kindness. It's also about how kindness can be scaled up so that we can begin to build and sustain kind teams, kind organizations, and kind communities through kind leadership.

If social work is to continue to play a vital role in people's well-being, we suggest the following five *work habits* be learned, supported, and sustained. They are;

1. *Reflecting on your values*: These guide everything a social worker does. They are the reason why they do what they do. They can often be tacit

and need to be articulated, discussed, and always open to amendment. This should become a *conscious habit.*

2. *Reflecting on your feelings*: This can be both joyful and painful, uncomfortable and illuminating. It is therefore important to make sure that social workers have some appropriate support to do this. So, this should be a *supported habit.*
3. *Reflecting on your thinking*: This can open up options for future and improved actions. This can be done through conversations-that-matter. There are limits to thinking alone and introspectively. This should be a *collegial habit.*
4. *Reflecting on your actions*: This is essential if we are ever to improve what we do. Much can be gained if this is done collectively, appreciatively, and in spaces and places where kindness circulates. This is a *collaborative habit.*
5. *Reflecting on your context*: Reflecting on each of 1–4 is essential, we would suggest. But reflecting on the context in which your relationship-based practice is embedded is quite another matter. This habit requires more holistic thinking, political astuteness, courage, and an awareness of the interplay between human agency and welfare structures. Social action is context-dependent. These contexts can serve to liberate or constrain us. They can suffocate, disempower, and frustrate us also. This is a *political habit.*

In reading this book, where social work is knitted together with social change, we hope it has helped you become the 'best version of yourself' as a social worker. We hope the stories from the field, together with some wider perspectives, have helped you appreciate different sources of meaning, value, and action in the relational connection between social workers, significant other professionals, and those they work with and care for. Taken together, we also hope the book helps you figure out how you can play a part in creating a world in which we most want to live and work. In editing this book, Rita and I believe that when people create meaning together through stories, they sow the seeds for action. Meaning and social work actions are entwinned. As we generate meaning together we also create the future.

REFERENCES

Fook, J. (2023). *Social Work: A Critical Approach to Practice.* London: Sage

Ghaye, T. (2005). *Developing the Reflective Healthcare Team*, Oxford: Blackwell.

(2008) *Building the Reflective Healthcare Organization.* Oxford: Blackwell.

(2010), *Teaching and Learning through Reflective Practice: A Practical Guide to Positive Action*, London: Routledge.

Ghaye, T., & Lillyman, S. (2014). *Reflection: Principles and Practices for Healthcare Professionals*. London: Quay Books.

Whitehead, J. (1993). *The Growth of Educational Knowledge: Creating Your Own Living Educational Theories*. Bournemouth: Hyde.

Index

For EU product safety concerns, contact us at Calle de José Abascal, 56–1°,
28003 Madrid, Spain or eugpsr@cambridge.org.

www.ingramcontent.com/pod-product-compliance
Lightning Source LLC
LaVergne TN
LVHW052027200926
848481LV00005B/1603
* 9 7 8 1 0 0 9 3 8 6 2 1 0 *